Ethnographica Moralia

Ethnographica Moralia
Experiments in Interpretive Anthropology

Edited by

Neni Panourgiá and George E. Marcus

FORDHAM UNIVERSITY PRESS

New York 2008

Copyright © 2008 Fordham University Press

All rights reserved. No part of this publication may be reproduced, stored in a retrieval system, or transmitted in any form or by any means—electronic, mechanical, photocopy, recording, or any other—except for brief quotations in printed reviews, without the prior permission of the publisher.

Library of Congress Cataloging-in-Publication Data

Ethnographica moralia : experiments in interpretive anthropology / edited by Neni Panourgiá, George E. Marcus.—1st ed.
    p. cm.
Includes bibliographical references and index.
ISBN-13: 978-0-8232-2886-7 (cloth : alk. paper)
ISBN-13: 978-0-8232-2887-4 (pbk. : alk. paper)
1. Anthropology—Philosophy.   2. Anthropology—Political aspects.   3. Art and anthropology.   4. Literature and anthropology.   I. Panourgia, E. Neni K. (Eleni Neni K.), 1958– II. Marcus, George E.
        GN33.E76 2008
        301.01—dc22
        2008005423

Printed in the United States of America
10 09 08   5 4 3 2 1
First edition

CONTENTS

Acknowledgments vii
Introduction 1
    NENI PANOURGIÁ AND GEORGE E. MARCUS
Interview with Clifford Geertz 15
    NENI PANOURGIÁ AND PAVLOS KAVOURAS
Contemporary Fieldwork Aesthetics in Art and Anthropology:
Experiments in Collaboration and Intervention 29
    GEORGE E. MARCUS
Myth, Performance, Poetics—the Gaze from Classics 45
    RICHARD P. MARTIN
The Birth of Anthropology out of a Pause on Pausanias:
Frazer's Travel-Translations Reinterrupted and Resumed 53
    JAMES A. BOON
Anamneses of a Pestilent Infant: The Enigma of Monstrosity,
or Beyond Oedipus 77
    ATHENA ATHANASIOU
Fragments of Oedipus: Anthropology at the Edges of History 97
    NENI PANOURGIÁ
Carnal Hermeneutics: From "Concepts" and "Circles"
to "Dispositions" and "Suspense" 113
    ELENI PAPAGAROUFALI
"Real Anthropology" and Other Nostalgias 126
    KATH WESTON
Canonical and Anticanonical Histories 138
    ANTONIS LIAKOS
Anthropology at the French National Assembly:
The Semiotic Aspects of a Political Institution 157
    MARC ABÉLÈS
"Life Is Dead Here": Sensing the Political in "No Man's Land" 168
    YAEL NAVARO-YASHIN

Text and Transnational Subjectification:
Media's Challenge to Anthropology   188
  LOUISA SCHEIN

Afterword: The Ethnographer's "Gaze": Some Notes on Visuality
and Its Relation to the Reflexive Metalanguage of Anthropology   213
  MARIA KAKAVOULIA

Notes   217

Contributors   271

Index   277

ACKNOWLEDGMENTS

We would like to thank the Center for Neohellenic Research at the National Research Center in Athens and its director (in 1999), Dr. Vassilis Panayiotopoulos, for their generous support of the workshop "Anthropology, Now!" that took place in the context of the center's Hermoupolis seminars. We would also like to thank the participants of the workshop whose work could not be included here. Further support for the workshop was generously provided by the Greek Ministry of Culture and the Hellas 3E Company. We would also like to thank the Department of Anthropology at Rutgers University for its support.

Special thanks are owed to Helen Tartar, our editor at Fordham University Press, who saw the merit of this project, and to the two anonymous readers of the essays, whose substantive comments made the collection a far better one.

The interview with Clifford Geertz was previously published in *Anthropological Theory* 2, no. 4 (2002): 421–431, © 2002 Sage Publications (London, Thousand Oaks, Calif., and New Delhi). Yael Navaro-Yashin's essay "'Life Is Dead Here': Sensing the Political in 'No Man's Land'" was previously published in a slightly different form in *Anthropological Theory* 3, no. 1 (2003), 107–125. Both are reprinted here by permission.

ETHNOGRAPHICA MORALIA

INTRODUCTION

Neni Panourgiá and George E. Marcus

In the spring of 1999, before 9/11—or the possibility of it—entered the public, political, and intellectual discourses, we, Neni Panourgiá and George Marcus, sat talking about what had happened to the critique of anthropology, what critical thought had brought to the project of anthropology and ethnography, and what the theoretically systematic approaches to anthropology had produced in the last twenty years. It seemed to us that what we had come to understand as interpretive anthropology had engendered new, engaged, and sustaining modalities of making the translation process of cultural experience to textual representation possible. With its beginnings in hermeneutics and the continental tradition of inquiry and its commitment to the ethnographic project, interpretive anthropology, by incorporating and participating in the linguistic turn and the crisis of representation, opened up the space for the type of interdisciplinarity that is so characteristic of the field now and made anthropological questions accessible and relevant to neighboring disciplines. Microhistory and classics, psychoanalysis and philosophy, qualitative sociology, literary criticism, and critical legal studies participate in the emergence of this critical space where the aporias about the human condition posited by philosophy are encountered by anthropology and where answers, anchored in experience, are attempted through the ethnographic encounter. In Renato Rosaldo's words, "Culture requires study from a number of perspectives, and . . . these perspectives cannot necessarily be added together into a unified summation,"[1] but they can inform each other's positions that produce fertile positionalities. Those different positions and positionalities, Sherry Ortner has pointed out, can be "located and examined in very different ways" that will, at the end, not only assume (as Ortner suggests) but show with certainty (we would add) that "human social life is . . . meaning-laden, meaning-making, intense, and real."[2]

It seems to us that since the publication of *The Interpretation of Cultures* in 1973, interpretive anthropology has been able to absorb and negotiate the critiques that had originally been articulated about it, from its engagement with the political to the centrality afforded to the notion of culture at large. The project that we undertook in the summer of 1999 was one of translation on a number of different levels that bore within it the felicity of a specific location, Greece. The project sought to enable and facilitate the negotiation of a very specific topos, that of interpretive anthropology, within that very specific ethnographic locus. The resulting seminar that took place under the auspices of the Center for Neohellenic Research, one of the research branches of the National Research Center in Athens, brought together these interdisciplinary perspectives that have been inaugurated by interpretive anthropology, and resulted in these essays. As they appear in this volume, the essays move through this negotiated space of hermeneutics, social theory, and cultural theory, providing critical articulations on the synapses of how actors make themselves understood by the world at large. They are essays that propose new readings of texts that have long been discarded as exhausted, new approaches on political matters that have long seemed all too easily handed over to political science. They problematize the easiness with which the notion of "postcoloniality" has been reproduced as an ideology, and they engage in critical presentations of issues of epistemology that are commonly shared by history, anthropology, law, or classics.

In a reading of Theodor W. Adorno's *Minima Moralia*, Edward Said, in his *Representations of the Intellectual*, picked up the question of displacement and writing that constitutes the backbone of the intellectual praxis, as it for Adorno interrogates the security and comfort of "private life."[3] Said reads Adorno as delineating the experience of writing as the only possible "at home" position of the intellectual, painfully celebrating an "in-betweenness" while warning against its iconization, which can become an ideology as any other.[4]

Anthropology and anthropologists have long accepted this suspended existence of belonging neither here nor there, of leaving "home" as a result of the questioning of its safety and security as a location where subjectivity can be formulated singularly, in order to submit themselves to other peoples' "homes," becoming other peoples' "children," fictive kin, and friends, existing in Victor Turner's "between and betwixt," all the while touching the untouchable, in a way that makes Adorno's understanding of the ethics of being ever so relevant: "For a man who no longer has a homeland, writing becomes a place to live." The anthropologist is asked of "nothing less . . . than that he should be at every moment both within things and outside them—Münchhausen pulling himself out of the bog by his pig-tail"—thus producing "a knowledge which wishes to be more than either verification or speculation," just as Adorno wrote of the thinker in general.[5] Translating thus the experience of being, of "I have been there" and now I am here, the momentary suspension of the comfort of home, or the acknowledgment of the illusion of home, the anthropologist is expected to produce a written product that will provide the means, for the readers, to enter the anthropologist's experience of the (ethnographic) world mediately while creating the impression of immediacy, and all the while retaining the position that the world is real, despite its symbolic mediation (to invoke Ortner's reading of Clifford Geertz's commitment to the reality of the world).[6] It is only in this manner, Adorno concludes, in "abiding so insistently with the particular," that knowledge can "widen horizons . . . [and] its isolation [be] dispelled."[7] It is precisely this relationship between the particular and the universal, the "on the ground" and the "in the world," the here and the there, that the thinker, the critic, the anthropologist, the intellectual, strives to make apparent as much as the person "on the ground," so to speak, each going about it in different manners but all trying to grapple with the same question. This is a question, Michael Jackson proposes in his *Minima Ethnographica*, that exists within the various parameters that bring the project of the trained intellectual (the critic, the anthropologist, the philosopher) to bear on the project of life of the untrained, but no less profound, thinker: "How do local and global worlds intersect, how can ethnographic studies of single societies enable us to say something about the *human* condition, and how is the *lived* experience of individuals connected to the *virtual* realities of tradition, history, culture, and the biology of the species that outrun the life of any one person?"[8] It is to this question that the papers in the present volume try to provide windows into possible answers, frustrating the comfort of secure disciplinary borders, contaminating their respective discourses, becoming guests or cohabitants in each other's intellectual homes.

We tend to make "homes" outside our home in many manners and registers—spatially, ethically, ideologically, in theory. We find ourselves "at home" in our home, in our discipline, in our ideology, in our politics. We are "at home in the world," Michael Jackson offers in his *At Home in the World*,[9] just as Adorno warns us, "today . . . it is part of morality not to be at home in one's home,"[10] not to rest comfortably in our assumptions, in our disciplinary boundaries, in our politics and ethics, but to interrogate their certainty and interrupt their narratives, to be not necessarily homeless but at home in many different homes (to come back to Michael Jackson). Said reads in Adorno that he represents the intellectual as "a permanent exile," as someone who sits uncomfortably on the dialectical edge of the "old and the new . . . dodging both with equal dexterity."[11] Interpretive anthropology set out in 1973, unprogrammatically and, as Geertz himself has admitted, unsystematically and ad hoc, to bring about some "muddles in the models" (to remember David Schneider), to explore the idea (and finally, show) that there was no danger lurking in contaminating the purity of disciplinary explanations and that if there was a danger, we were all the better for having come into contact with it. But it also managed, as Ortner points out, to make "visible the shared ways of thinking between anthropology and the humanities."[12]

George Marcus's article sets the tone for the evaluation of the ways in which interpretive anthropology has produced a new generation of ethnographers, by offering a critical look at the current challenges to the way that the classic scene of fieldwork itself can emerge in the inevitable multi-sited contexts in which interpretive ethnographic research is negotiated today. This assessment, stimulated by an engagement with the ingenious interventions of research-based conceptual art projects, is a valuable means of thinking stochastically about the directions that the post-Geertzian anthropology has taken, a landscape that Marcus and the group of *Writing Culture* have helped map.

Eleni Papagaroufali's essay is the one that draws directly from Geertz's *The Interpretation of Cultures* in her attempt to interrogate the processes of somatization of experience. Papagaroufali uses somatization as an analytical concept to explore the hermeneutical intimacy that informs the relationships of body and organ donors to their lived realities. Positing the presentation of cross-cultural translation or interpretation as a "hermeneutic circle," Papagaroufali problematizes the continuous dialectical tacking between natives' "experience-near" and ethnographers' "experience-distant concepts,"[13] especially when entered from the spatially secure position of considering "experiences" as immediately and really lived, yet internally sensed and unselfconsciously practiced. The former, Papagaroufali argues, are experienced as located closer to one's body, so to speak, whereas the latter are experienced as closer to one's mind. To arrive at this, Papagaroufali imports the concept of a *"carnal* hermeneutics," further complicating the implicit suggestion that the "symbolic means"—words, images, actions—through which both the ethnographer and her interlocutors represent themselves to themselves and to each other are as experiential as experiences supposedly represented. Yet the so-called *immediate* nature of experience is denied here. It is the always already *nonimmediate* character of experience (e.g., that of comprehending or writing about

Other cultural experience) that is responsible for its incompleteness and indeterminacy. Time, rather than space (*near-*, far-experience), determines experience.

This emergent experience constitutes a new somatic intersubjectivity, Papagaroufali points out: instead of "points of *view*" or "*visions* of the world," participant cointerpreters, physically or imaginatively copresent, juxtapose, contest, negotiate, realize, socially informed embodied, and bodying forth, knowledge that traverses the space from *silence* to *gesture* to *language*, thus implicating Bourdieu's *habitus* or *dispositions*. The move away from an ocularcentric analytical framework to a somaticized logocentricity conceptualizes "experience" as a hermeneusis in which mnemonics participates actively.

Shifting from concepts to dispositions implies that ethnographers and interlocutors produce knowledge as sentient agents, that is, through our always already socially informed senses and emotions rather than "minds." And that knowledge becomes constantly embodied and bodying forth through past, present, and future practices sensorily and emotionally shared with persons, objects, and institutions—actual or imagined, seen or unseen or never to be seen.

Marc Abélès confronts the issue of the political in Geertz's work by proposing a Geertzian study of the foundational institution of political modernity, the French National Assembly. He posits a main question, the interpolation of which frames the possibilities of studying the political as part of the ethnographic project. Is it possible to study the semiotic aspects of the state in occidental societies while exposing the ethnocentric conceptualization of politics? Abélès argues in his paper that what Geertz calls the "semiotic aspect" plays a central part in the political process when all the meanings of the "semiotic" are investigated. What emerges, among other things, is the theatricality of power, the strong association between governance, ritual, and symbolism, which folds into it the intricate relationship between orality and writing. Abélès situates politics as taking place in a global universe of *simulacra*, where the mimetics of the simulacrum encounters the mimetics of ritual. Abélès finds in Geertz's *Negara* the inaugural moment for the study of political institutions as cultural performance, whence he examines not simply the institutional ritualization of the Assembly's work but, more importantly, the processual aspects of this institutionalization in what he calls a *ritual struggle*.

Using "no man's land" as a metaphor for an abjected space outside the recognized domains of the international system, here Northern Cyprus, Yael Navaro-Yashin studies subjective experiences under an authoritarian regime. Inviting anthropologists of politics to "sense" the political that underlies contexts that would normalize disruption, the author gathers signs, in the spatial surroundings and subjectivities in Northern Cyprus, of a glossed experiential catastrophe. The study of subjection under a self-declared "state" unrecognized by the international system is matched here with the reflections of subjective experiences in the radically transformed space. "No man's land" as metaphor does not isolate this particular context administered by an "illegal state" as a particular or peculiar space, but invites anthropologists to consider the "no man's land" aspects of other contexts (within the domain of "legal states") that they study. The paper can be read particularly as a critique of anthropologies of globalization and transnationalism that would reify mobility and ignore the immobilities and experiences of confinement that are produced by the very same international practices.

Looking at the myth of Oedipus as a fundamentally political text, Athena Athanasiou posits the question of how a text is reconstituted as political when read through the exigencies produced by feminism and deconstruction. Who is Oedipus? she asks. The skeptic and the hero, the infant and the sovereign, the Hegelian philosopher and the Freudian figure, autonomous and dispossessed—how do the multiple figures of Oedipus enact and inflect the aporias of modern Western biopolitics and biopolitical anthropology? Athanasiou encounters this question by thinking through the cleavages of heteronomy and autonomy, belonging and errancy, sovereignty and liminality, the soma of the masculine leader and the future of the polis. Her reading follows the disorder of Oedipus's body as a topographic map that bespeaks the politics of bodily disorder. She enters into this inquiry at two critical moments that have remained absent within the Freudian appropriation of the myth—namely, Oedipus's encounter with the Sphinx and the eruption of the plague. In discussing the horror of the pestilence and the mystery of the Sphinx, Athanasiou brings to the fore both of them as instantiations of the constitutive force of biopolitical alterity. Athanasiou reads the latter as a binding condition for corporeal affectability that assures the cohesion of the social body while at the same time leaving open the necessary possibility of disruption and dismemberment.

Neni Panourgiá picks up the thread of biopolitics offered by Athanasiou and encounters Oedipus at the location where the articulation of the political and the existential erect a new discourse on ontology, namely, the rehabilitation camp. More specifically, she looks at the concentration or rehabilitation camp(s) for Leftists and Communists established in Greece at the end of the Second World War by the democratically elected government of Greece, in an attempt to redefine the notions of the "human" (*anthropos*) in its contestation between the state and the Leftists, along with the new articulations of the "homeland" (*patrida*) and the "national" (*ethnikon*). In this process of rearticulation and reinscription of political ontologies, Panourgiá finds the stigmata that explode this synallagmatic relationship between the state, the citizen, and life as a social category. The specter that haunts this relationship is that of Oedipus, as he becomes reanimated outside of the colonizing gestures of Freud and psychoanalysis that have taken over the total space of analysis of the psyche. Oedipus becomes paradigmatic in the case of the political as he becomes referenced now by survivors, now by the press, always as the figure that frustrates the certainties of interpretation.

James Boon's essay foregrounds the distinctive combination of James and Lilly Frazer's virtual cottage industry (in league with Macmillan) of publishing in self-conscious formats and translations geared to diverse audiences. He also dwells on coinciding notions of "arcades" in Frazer's work and in Walter Benjamin's—both deriving from Pausanias. Benjamin used Johann Jacob Bachofen's translation of Pausanias, but Frazer relied on his own translation and rigorous on-scene research of archaeological evidence of the warehouse in Piraeus. Boon intensifies questions about Frazerian and Benjaminian notions of "the fragmentary" that open Frazer's lengthy excessiveness to more serious and playful readings. Boon's essay darts among disciplines and across times (from Walter Pater and Alfred Hitchcock to George Stocking and Slavoj Zizek), but in doing so, it ends up in Frazer, particularly as translated into French, and as enacting transgressive readings of seriocomic rites, including those of Bali (Boon's own field area).

Boon produces the paradigmatic text not simply of how interpretive anthropology can be used in reading cultural texts but, far more importantly, of how Boon "does" interpretive anthropology. He does not engage in a dialogue with interpretation, but rather produces a text on Frazer that looks at the Frazerian text as a process of interpretation of Pausanias itself while recognizing Pausanias's project as an interpretive one. Precisely because even textual interpretation, Boon reminds us, can never be confined to a text (or, alternately, a praxis is always as much gestural as textual) Frazer himself actually came out of his armchair to journey to Greece. Frazer was determined to retranslate and retrace Pausanias's travelogue meticulously. In tracing the layers of Frazer's *Pausanias*, Boon goes one turtle deeper by suggesting that today one could conceivably approach

Frazer as (1) a slightly later Bachofen (both retranslated Pausanias, Frazer correcting Bachofen's version) or (2) a considerably earlier Benjamin. Much as Benjamin's imaginative excursions among modernity's "ruins" (via the work of litterateurs) recalled the "ancient labyrinths that Pausanias had entered," so did Frazer's forays among primitivity's "ruins" (via the work of ethnographers). Boon engages the affinities adhering Bachofen, Frazer, and Benjamin to Pausanias (and to each other) to signal endless ironies of transhistorical cross-cultural rereadings.

By reading Pausanias through Frazer, Boon posits a number of disciplinary questions: What might Frazer's disciplinary multiplicity mean, even today, for meaning-in-cultures? Can Frazer, Boon asks, help reinvigorate anthropology's appeal among other fashions of critical consciousness? The method by which Frazer achieved such refraction of matter into sensibility is his style, which has often been misunderstood. Frazer's odd and ample corpus, Boon notes, helps challenge any dogmatic separation of interpretive pursuits: anthropology, history, literature, classics, and so on. Boon suggests that we read Frazer in order to revisit and question some of the existing binarisms in anthropology, such as Frazer (bookish)/Malinowski (fieldworker); Frazer (derivative)/Tylor ("first"); British (empirical)/French (intellectualist); Boasian/Durkheimian.

Richard Martin brings about the painful point of interdisciplinary dialogue. Despite the fact that a lot has been said and written about the desire for fertile intellectual exchanges between the disciplines, Martin argues, in the case of anthropology and the classics, true interdisciplinarity and cross-fertilization remain on the level of desire and discourse. Martin goes to the epistemological hearts of the two disciplines and recognizes that despite the fact that the study of myth is central to both classics and anthropology, any dialogue between the two has been almost completely absent, with a few exceptions that Martin underscores. Sally Humphreys' work on anthropology and the classics and her groundbreaking work on women in antiquity remain largely unknown within anthropology, as does the work by the late John Winkler. Humphreys' work, in particular, remains the best overview of the ways in which scholars of Greek and Roman culture used and abused anthropological ideas, as she takes account of more recent work and renews the call for a more self-aware critique of methodologies in classics, aided by anthropology. Visiting specific epistemological issues, Martin goes further to problematize anthropology's identification with fieldwork and the problems involved, and he suggests that we look at Albert Lord's project on Homeric poetry and fieldwork among Serbo-Croatian singers and at Gregory Nagy's project on fieldwork among the Navaho in reimagining contexts for the lyric poetry of Sappho. The structuralist wave that hit classics in the 1970s and only subsided about 1990 took myth for granted, Martin argues, as a transparent concept and tool, and explored the way traditional tales interacted with Greek social life. Such work, however, should generate a new wave of interest in rereading, anthropologically, ancient dramas—a project that could, in turn, help the classicist toward unpacking a concept that itself has played a formative role in anthropological discussion. A similar genealogy of concepts demands to be written for other terms and concepts inherited by modern social science from ancient Greek sources.

Louisa Schein, through a layered reading of Geertzian culture, suggests a consideration of media's participation in the process of cultural formation. Through E. Valentine Daniel and Jeffrey M. Peck's translation of cultural texts into contextured texts, she raises two main issues: (1) the paradigm agonisms precipitated by the encounter of anthropology with cultural studies and (2) the interconnection between media and transnationalism. Schein argues that media produce a kind of transnational subjectification. Importantly, then, media products are not only about meanings harbored within the actual texts: media's webs of significance are immanent in their social consequences and their relations of production and reception as well. In Schein's analysis, desire, gendered relations, and erotic longings become the substance of transnational imaginings as they structure transnational mobilities. To get at how this works, Schein suggests, we need to turn back to meaning—toward the contents of the media texts that are implicated in a kind of transnational subjectification. By looking at cultural politics and media consumption in post-Mao China, especially among the Miao ethnic group of China's southwest, Schein posits her central questions: How does media as text participate in the formation of a transnational subject? Is text to ethnography as cultural studies is to anthropology?

This sort of translocal subject formation is critical but cannot be bounded, confined to the dyadic articulation between media texts and viewer positionings. Eloquently echoing both Geertz's conceptualization of culture and Lila Abu-Lughod's problematization of this same concept, Schein further problematizes location and textuality as determinants of media analysis. Looking at Miao and Hmong video productions of the homeland (itself a loaded and problematic term) Schein interrogates the desires, the identities and identifications, and the alliances generated by the reception of these images. Looking "thickly" at one of those videos

(*Dr. Tom*), Schein references the distinctly gendered homeland desire of Hmong media in belying and participating in the construction of a complicated erotic subjectification.

Yet even as the Hmong sense of collectivity spans the globe, augmented by media messages, those same media messages may also play a role in refashioning the most intimate of interiorities. Transnational erotics, such as exist in Hmong media, remixes sex and space, revealing that physical distance and proximity are complexly intertwined in the contours of homeland desire.

The papers by Antonis Liakos and Kath Weston engage in a metacritique of their respective disciplines and epistemologies, interrogating the categorical questions that have been posited by history and anthropology, respectively, and the implicit and explicit hierarchizations of these categorical ascriptions. Who can speak for and about history and anthropology? What is a historical fact and what constitutes the object and subject of anthropology and history? What are the limits and delimitations of interiority and exteriority in the process of interminable construction of a discipline?

What do we have in mind when we talk of history and how has this understanding of "History" been formed through interdisciplinary discussions between history and anthropology? asks Liakos. The term *history* is a linguistic and cultural indicator of diverse ways of understanding social temporality. The conception of history and the meaning given to the term depend on the historicity each culture produces—something belied by the fact that in some cultures a corresponding term for history is lacking, since the concept of history and more generally the understanding of chronology belong to entirely different categories of social experience. What in Western tradition we call history exists as the "spring and autumn annals" or the "Tso tradition" in China, as "Rikkokushi" or the "six national Histories" in Japanese culture, as "Itihasa" in Hindu culture, as short histories in Arab and Islamic tradition, as the Bible in Jewish tradition, and as eschatology in Christian tradition. What we call history is strictly woven into each cultural environment, Liakos argues, placed between medicine and rhetoric, at the crossroads of two semiotic systems, investigation and representation. The type of writing that we call history is a product of modernity, a plant of Western culture, transplanted all over the world, obscuring and substituting for other forms of History. In this way, an epistemic rupture took place, which transformed all other histories into the prehistory of History.

Introduction

With a twist on Eric Wolf, Liakos examines the project of writing down the history of peoples without history that was undertaken during colonization by Western missionaries, officials, and scholars. Looking at the interpellations of colonialism and imperialist and capitalist expansion as part of a modernist project, Liakos points at the dialectical relationship between history, modernity, and the nation. With the establishment of national states, local histories were produced as national history, able to be recognized universally. The object of history, namely the nation, became the subject of history, and written history transformed the relationship between the nation and its past. In this way, history did not describe but produced changes. Why do people engage in reconstructing and writing history? Liakos asks. The positing of this question can only be framed by the acknowledgment of the need to treat history making as a field of social and cultural practice, that is, to view historicizing practices as anthropologists view other social and cultural practices.

By looking at the process of writing and experiencing history as an exercise in successive readings, Liakos suggests that the historiographic project becomes a communicative process, which includes the historicizing object, the process of narrativization, and the historicized object. Process and message are subject to and formed by history, and, at the same time, this same concept of history contains the character of a continuous movement in both directions that is impressed as much by the social structures as by the mentality and culture.

This dialectic between *historicizing* present and historicized past Liakos reads as a form of broader cultural communication. Readers of historical texts are authors of their version of history; history writers are readers of sources; archivists evaluate, collect, and organize sources according to their reading of the historical process. Expectations from historical texts arise from experience and practices in which identities, collective and individual, are formed. The fragmentation of universal history into national histories, the institutionalization of history and its employment in legitimizing political decisions, the diffusion of mass education, the display of history in museums and monuments, and the familiarization with history through the mass media provoke a widespread claim of appropriation of the past. The main acquisition of this process is the polyphony of history as well as the limits of value neutrality and historical cognizance. Liakos then approaches history as *cultural semiosis*, where semiosis retains its meaning both as notation and as a mimetic gesture or representation, and where through the notion of culture, the past is incorporated into the present structures of knowledge and the prevailing perceptions of time. In an interesting approach to the problem of "culture" and "history," Liakos enters into the discussion between Lila Abu-Lughod and Geertz on how "culture" is constituted and represented. Culture and history stand as representer and *representment*, as signifier and signified, Liakos argues. The cultural system is the context through which the meaning of history emerges. History and culture form a network of structural relations, a circle *of reciprocal semiosis*.

Kath Weston goes to the heart of the problematic of what constitutes "anthropology" and how interpretive anthropology names anthropological conventions, and she brings to the level of consciousness the discussions about the discipline that have become urgent with the intervention of interpretive anthropology and hermeneutics. Whatever interpretive anthropology's shortcomings, Weston reminds us, anthropology never proposed to be a strictly rhetorical move. Interpretive anthropology has engendered a new respect for modes of presentation and modes of intellectual production, as well as widespread recognition of the inevitability that the ethnographer will have a hand in shaping and selecting data.

If nothing else, Weston suggests, interpretive anthropology has certainly *become* anthropology. These days, the phrase "real anthropology" seeks other targets when it does not dissolve into irony altogether. Are studies of television "real anthropology"? Studies of shopping? Postcolonial fiction? Migration in search of work? There is a certain nostalgia embedded in the phrase "real anthropology," a nostalgia that references an earlier (not just more authentic) time in which anthropologists understood their work and went about it with an almost utopian clarity of purpose. "Real anthropology" is a backward-looking term, floated on beliefs (however vaguely or well substantiated) about the way things used to be for practitioners of the discipline, not only invoking an epistemological timelessness but also making suspect any attempt at naming this nostalgic engagement as such.

Embedded in the contrast between the more innocent time represented by "real anthropology," and the seemingly wider range of studies that now fall within the field's parameters is an element of mourning for the orderliness, the predictability, the constancy, presumed to characterize the discipline in days gone by. "Real anthropology" was, and remains, a disciplinary term, Weston reminds us. Its invocation implies that in contemporary times, when anthropology has stumbled from grace, a policing of the boundaries of the discipline is necessary in order to separate acceptable from unacceptable topics or methods of study. For there is also a political and economic context to the debates about what is to become of anthropology.

Where have the current nostalgias tended to focus? Invoking Geertz's critique of Claude Lévi-Strauss, Weston returns to anthropology's time of scientification. At one time, appeals to the "science" in social science provided institutional leverage, Weston notes: anthropology is real science, hard science, and thus worthy of financial support. In recent decades, the unfortunate association of science with the reductionism of sociobiology has largely relegated interest in the theoretical contributions of math and science to biological anthropology.

In a celebratory gesture that includes both John Comaroff and Simon Robert's formulation within sociocultural anthropology and David Scott's colonial critique, Weston notes the historical reaction against modeling the discipline on "hard" science, which included a move to break away from systemic accounts, replicable generalizations, and rule-bound analyses, as well as the formal mathematical symmetries encoded in structuralist analyses. Weston identifies other "tundra zones" besides science, such as anthropology's colonial history, where lightly equipped nostalgias cannot endure exposure. Further implicating the establishment of an epistemological nostalgia with the actual methodological and theoretical (ultimately political) quandaries that have beset anthropology, Weston drives to the unnamed tension within anthropological praxis, that of "native anthropology."

As the ethnographers that well-meaning colleagues judge to be "natives" studying themselves, "virtual anthropologists" have no chance to become "real anthropologists" in the nostalgic sense of the term. As Panourgiá has also argued elsewhere, the inability or unwillingness of "nostalgic anthropology" to grant "native" anthropologists the status of "real anthropologists" is not only part of an epistemological lacuna but also, and just as importantly, part and parcel of an unfinished colonial critique.

Maria Kakavoulia, in her afterword of this whole project, posits anew the question that launched the critique of representation, namely, the problematic relationship between visuality and knowledge, a question that goes to the heart of the anthropological project. The problematization that was articulated with Geertz's "thick description" and the impossibility of ethnographic truth, echoed in Edgar Morin's problematization of the reliability of the senses—both of which span the length of the anthropological problematic—become the focal point of Kakavoulia's inquiry. Kakavoulia examines the interreliability of the social sciences on the terminology of sciences, which is based heavily on metaphors related to vision, just as knowledge and cognition are metaphorically related to notions of light, "'clear' vision, enlightenment, sight, and insight, and so on." Kakavoulia indicts the collusion of metaphors of visuality, noting that "observation" has become a root metaphor within social and cultural research and that an extensive vocabulary of "visuality" is instrumental for gaining access to and understanding practices of human communities; she turns to Michel Foucault's problematization of the sovereign gaze as indicative of God's omnipotent vision in the formulation of the panopticon.

Turning to interpretive anthropology, Kakavoulia finds a possibility for the dismantling of the weight of visualism for the production of knowledge, since interpretive anthropology, she argues, involves visual practices as both a source domain (seeing) and a target domain (objects to be seen). To what extent is anthropology's self-critique based on forms of self-observation? She posits one further question, namely, To what extent have aspects of vision or visuality such as imagination captured the attention of anthropological study? as she calls for a systematic theory of visuality that would (1) address cultural ocular conventions, (2) explore the visual dimension of anthropological practices, and (3) inform cross-cultural research of power and its representational practices.

Since ethnographic narrativization is already a part of the methodologies used in revelations and explanations of "unseen" or "hidden" discourses, cultures, power relations, and so on, how is vision discursively embedded within anthropological or ethnographic narratives?

We are at a historical juncture where the critique offered by interpretive anthropology, with its insistence on meanings, at a time when in the public sphere and political culture meaning has come to mean mendacity, and where the phenomenology of terms is invoked as a handmaiden to deception—we are at a juncture where this critique needs to be reintroduced.

Interview with Clifford Geertz
Neni Panourgiá and Pavlos Kavouras

Introduction

The interview with Clifford Geertz has a long history. It was originally conceived as part of a profile on Geertz for the Greek independent television program *On the Paths of Thought*, which has hosted such profiles of world-eminent thinkers and artists in various disciplines. To that end, a first interview was given by Geertz to Professors Konstantinos Tsoukalas and Neni Panourgiá in February 1999 at the Institute for Advanced Study in Princeton. A second interview was graciously granted by Geertz to Panourgiá and Professor Pavlos Kavouras during the 1999 seminar in Hermoupolis. (See also the article "Conversations in Hermeneutic Anthropology," *Anthropological Theory* 2, no. 2 (2002): 341–354, which includes interviews with James A. Boon, Michael Fischer, and George E. Marcus.) The finalized profile, as broadcast by Greek National Television, includes portions of both interviews, but the text published here, transcribed by Thomas Abowd, is based on the interview conducted in Hermoupolis.

Neni Panourgiá would like to thank everyone who contributed to these interviews (mentioned above individually) but also would like to thank Stephen Reyna, who invited and scheduled the publication of the interviews, and Richard Wilson, who followed up and made their publication possible.

Neni Panourgiá: Professor Geertz, your name is closely associated with interpretive anthropology. How would you translate this perspective to students in anthropology?

Well, when I am asked, I point to the work that has been done. This is a good question because I came into anthropology without any anthropology. As a graduate student, I had not had any. I went to a college where it was not taught; my own training was in philosophy and literature. When I got to Harvard as a graduate student, I had to find out what anthropology was, and I largely did it the way students should do it now: by reading classic texts and figuring out what it was all about.

Here is one funny story that will probably only make sense to other anthropologists: I went into Widener at Harvard, which is an enormous library with tons of anthropology books, and I pulled off the shelf George Murdock's *Social Structure*, which was about as foreign as anything—I almost quit because it is all statistical tables—but I soon found out that that was not the case with anthropology as a discipline. But I think that it is important to just plunge into it because anthropology does not have a set of theories and practices that you can learn in an abstract way. It is not like surveying, where you can learn how to do it and then go do it. In anthropology, you have to learn to do it and do it at the same time. First you read, and then you do a little bit of it, and you tack back and forth between reading and doing, and that it is how you get it. You can go and get a general characterization—you can do that—but that doesn't help anyone.

Pavlos Kavouras: We have the terms social anthropology, cultural anthropology, *and* ethnology, *all expressing the study of humanity. Is this differentiation in terminology simply a matter of national/historical development, or does it reflect a significant theoretical, epistemological, or practical divergence?*

It is in part simply a difference of different traditions. Social anthropology comes largely out of the British tradition, which concentrates on kinship and social structure. Cultural anthropology comes out of the Boasian American tradition and cultural analysis of Indian groups. Ethnology is the old European term. Ethnology now, even if you hear the word every once in a while, does not really exist anymore, at least not in the United States, and I don't think it exists in general any longer. But there is a distinction between social and cultural anthropology that is more than historical and national. It does have to do with the notion of what it is all about. And you still see polemics on both sides; there is a new book out by Adam Kuper that is a general attack from the British position on the American one. They don't like the idea of culture; they don't like the idea of meaning; they are much more into social structure. Remember the famous statement of [A. R.] Radcliffe-Brown, "Social structure is as real as a seashell"? I mean that's the kind of strict empiricism. Now it does not really sort out that way, because there is a reading of that kind of anthropology in the United States and there are cultural and interpretive anthropologists in Britain and Europe. So there is a difference in view, but it is not a difference in the profession. We are all doing the same thing; we just differ a bit about how to go about it.

PK: How would you describe, thickly or not, the scope and method of interpretive anthropology? Is it a discipline or a perspective? Obviously the key term here is interpretation. Does the notion of interpretation produce a difference between a natural science and an interpretive paradigm in the study of social and cultural phenomena? And does "interpretation" remain monadistic? If we can have not one but many interpretations, does that mean that we can or do have many realities?

Well, it is a perspective, not a discipline—that I would certainly say. Radcliffe-Brown's most famous book is entitled *A Natural Science of Society*, as you remember. And I think that his notion was—it sort of follows on from Bertrand Russell—that you get natural laws, you examine them empirically, and you get social laws of one kind or another. In interpretive anthropology or even anthropology more generally, we don't have much confidence in our capacity to do that, and what concerns us mostly is trying to understand how people themselves regard their lives, what they want to do, and what they are all about. So interpretation in my view is fundamentally about getting some idea of how people conceptualize, understand their world, what they are doing, how they are going about doing it, to get an idea of their world.

Again, an example would be kinship. In the British tradition, you are concerned with kinship and kinship terminology to get a systematic characterization of them. In interpretive anthropology, you are much more concerned with how people thought of their mothers and fathers and brothers—how people saw themselves and how they think the gender issue works out. But I do think it is a perspective—as you say—rather than a discipline. Anthropology has a slight habit of fractioning itself, so you get economic anthropology and political anthropology and so on. The American Anthropological Association now has more than fifty different subgroupings all called something or other. And to me, at least, interpretive anthropology is a perspective and a way of going about it that I have just tried to explicate—not a sort of thing in itself, not a subdiscipline.

I don't want to parody the other side, but I tend to. They think that there is a correct description. They think that you can say that this is the way it is. But interpretive anthropology believes that you can have two interpretations of the same thing. Now that does not mean that all interpretations work; some interpretations are better than others, and we can talk about how you go about one or another, but that is another issue. But you can have multiple interpretations in the field of a particular system and they all have an appeal. Interpretive anthropology draws much more on the literary and philosophical traditions as opposed to the scientific tradition that social anthropology tends to draw on. And so it is used to the notion of there being multiple interpretations of the same "text." Just to give you an example, in *Hamlet* there are two major interpretations that have been in the field, one of which is the Freudian interpretation. This is the story of Hamlet, a man who can't make up his mind, the Oedipal complex. Then there is another political interpretation, the one that Francis Ferguson is most famously identified with, where the key quote is "Something is rotten in the state of Denmark." Both of those readings are possible; you don't have to choose between them; you can't really unify them. You just live with both of them. You can read the play in both ways, and I think that is true of most cultural institutions of major importance. I've done a lot of readings of Bali, but there are others who have done other readings, some of which are not very good, but others are equally okay because there's no final place to stop. You just discuss these things. Sometimes these questions disappear because people get bored with them. Some don't work anymore. But there is no sense that we are all going to finally zero in on one final interpretation on something like "Javanese society" or "Moroccan society." That just isn't going to happen—not in this tradition anyway.

NP: You have often drawn an intellectual genealogy of interpretive anthropology that references the genealogy of hermeneutics. The terms hermeneusis *and* interpretation *produce the same meaning in Greek. Would you like to expand on this genealogical affinity?*

It starts with [Friedrich Ernst Daniel] Schleiermacher and so on, and then it continues on with [Hans-Georg] Gadamer and people of this sort, which rests on biblical criticism but is secularized. And I, at least, have learned a great deal from that tradition, but it's not mine. I mean I do not come out of that tradition. I mean I come out of a different kind of tradition that is Anglo, which is the study of meaning by [Charles S.] Pierce and a philosophical tradition of a different sort. There are some problems in the German tradition that we do not address and we are not concerned with, the truth and reality of these things, to the same extent that biblical criticism was. But the techniques we tend to borrow are not from the philosophical disciplines but from the literary disciplines; there is a whole literary tradition of hermeneutics. So there are lots of different interpretive things. The thing that the Germans did, and they deserve credit for this, was that they did methodologize it a bit—they did reflect on the process of interpretation. And you don't get much of that in the Anglo tradition, and indeed there is something of a resistance to overconceptualization of the tradition, of which Wittgenstein is a good example.

PK: How does interpretive anthropology differ from other interpretive approaches in the social sciences?

I don't quite know the answer to that. I don't know what interpretive sociology is or would be. Anthropology is a great "invader" of other people's turf—we do politics, we do sociology—so it is hard to distinguish anthropology in those terms from other disciplines. The only way you can distinguish it is in the kinds of work that has been done in the past. In some ways, as far as the U.S. is concerned, interpretive sociology is largely parasitic on interpretive anthropology. But [Max] Weber was concerned with the relationship between scientific law on the one hand and moral kinds of issues on the other, and actually interpretive anthropology is very heavily Weberian. So is he an anthropologist or what? The real opposition might be between Weber and [Émile] Durkheim. In the early twentieth century, when these people were practicing, these fields were not crystallized or professionalized the way that they are now; so was Durkheim an anthropologist or sociologist? You could argue either way. He was both. He did studies of Australian totemism, and he did studies of suicide in France. And the same thing is true of Weber, who did studies of economic change and political organization, but he also did studies of religion in China, so that kind of crystallization is posterior, is after the establishment of the interpretive tradition.

I would think that this fragmentation has remained stronger in anthropology than it has in sociology or in political science. But they are all from the same source, and the professional divisions are very recent, post World War II, and somewhat American in some ways. Cambridge did not have a professor of sociology for the longest time, and there was a big struggle over this, and Talcott Parsons went over and spoke, and when they finally got one it was Jack Barnes, who is an anthropologist. Again, in Britain, you don't get that distinction the way you do in the United States. So we who do interpretive work are all descendants of the same ancestors, but now that we have been divided up into professional cliques, you get these different terms.

NP: You mentioned the fact, and it is apparent in the corpus of your work, that you were not originally trained in anthropology but in literature and philosophy. This interdisciplinary training has framed the way in which you have been formulating the theoretical questions that have guided your research. Are there any landmarks in the history of American interpretive anthropology? Who were your theoretical interlocutors?

First, about when it was formed. It started in the 1960s and early 1970s. There was a group of us. Talcott Parsons is not an interpretive anthropologist, but he made it possible to talk about meaning and symbols and structures, and that was extraordinarily important. But there was also a group of people who all emerged at the same time, more or less: in the U.S. and Britain particularly and in France, with [Claude] Lévi-Strauss's students. Mary Douglas and Victor Turner, myself and David Schneider, even [Edmund] Leach in England and a number of other people. I think the first real move toward doing it in the United States was at Chicago in the early 1960s, when I first got there. And we really did try to change the way things were done. Chicago was in the British tradition then, but it was run by a very marvelous man named Fred Eggan, who was very open to anything; he said, okay, you want to create a revolution, create one. And we restructured the curriculum around notions that we brought with us from different places. Victor Turner was there later, not much later. There emerged something called "symbolic anthropology" at that time, and that is what a lot of people still call it. And it sort of crystallized then, and the reaction against it came largely from what are called cultural materialists in the U.S. We drew from [Margaret] Mead, [Edward] Sapir, [Ruth] Benedict, and we were continuing the kinds of concerns that they had and the reaction against it, the empirical traditions, the positivist traditions, and then comes the emergence of sociobiology. Marshall Sahlins went from one side to the other in a famous flip-flop. He wrote a critique of Lévi-Strauss and then went to France and became a structuralist, but an American-style structuralist because he was concerned with interpretive work. So there was a generational effect, and then we produced students. We introduced a curriculum, an introductory graduate curriculum, that was called "Systems"; it started with Weber and then talked about cultural interpretation. We tried also to reconstruct the history of anthropology, not seeing it so much through [Edward] Tylor but through George Stocking, through the neo-Kantians. So that is where it started, and there was a second generation. And then there was a split where the postmodernists felt, and still feel, that some of us did not go far enough and wanted to be much more critical. And so you get the emergence of people like [Michael J.] Fischer and [George E.] Marcus, who want to take it further in ways that some of us are wary about. So you end up with someone like me who is in between two wings. On the right I am told I am not "scientific" enough, and on the other side [I am criticized] for not being "radical" enough. But that's what makes it an active field. There is something intrinsic about interpretive anthropology that makes consensus impossible. I mean if we had consensus we'd be dead.

NP: How do you situate yourself in the historical trajectory of interpretive anthropology? Moreover, how does your main ethnographic work relate with your contributions to the field?

There are some things that are different about my career than most people's. First, I had no anthropology until I came to graduate school, so I came to it very, very late. I also came to it out of an essentially humanistic tradition. But I came to it with philosophical motives, which is rare, I think. Nearly everyone else in the field was trained as an anthropologist from the beginning. The other unique thing about my career is that I spent very little time in wholly, completely anthropological environments. In graduate school I was in what was called Social Relations, which was a new and innovative field and department that was interdisciplinary. So the things around me were not physical anthropology, linguistics, archaeology, but also sociology, clinical psychology, and so on. So I spent one year at the center and then one year at Berkeley, and there I was in an anthropology department proper. Then I went to Chicago, where I taught half in the anthropology program and half in the new nations program, and I spent ten years building the "revolution" that I spoke of earlier, with compatriots. I then went to the Institute for Advanced Studies, which was a general school of social science, where I was the only anthropologist. So unlike Victor Turner or David Schneider or Mary Douglas, I have always kind of been self-marginalized; I have never really been "inside it."

As for my fieldwork, I went first to Java as a graduate student on a collective project. I spent two and a half years in Java, and I came back and began to write. And there was a division of labor: my wife Hilley worked on kinship and family, and I worked on religion. So I came back and wrote a thesis on religion and then began to develop an essay on religion as a cultural system. That came out of a great summit meeting that was held at Cambridge in the mid-1960s. David Schneider was there; I was there and gave the "Religion as a Cultural System" paper; Marshall [Sahlins] was there. There was this moment of self-recognition when we were going to have this "hands across the sea." It was an amicable meeting and was an attempt to get the two traditions together. Then I went back to Java; then I went back to Bali and Sumatra. I looked at religion and rethought what I had written on. Then there was a big upheaval in Indonesia, and I felt I could not go there with young children, so I went to Morocco instead, to understand the other end of the Islamic world. I then worked on Islam in Indonesia and Islam in Morocco and tried to look at the differences and similarities. There is this very stereotypical view of Muslims that they are alike and that they all go around with knives. People know that Spanish Catholics and English Catholics and American Catholics are not the same, but when it comes to Islam, they think that they are all the same. So I spent time writing *Islam Observed* and other things, trying to get that sense of a differentiated notion of Islam. Then I went back to Java, and I've since then been working back and forth and doing something that is not commonly done, which is comparing two cultures not my own. There has been this tendency to compare a "them" and an "us," and in the U.S. that means Americans and others, and I wanted to compare two societies that did not include the U.S., Morocco, and Indonesia; I wanted to take two societies that were *both* different from my own background and compare them. These two societies have some similarities—Islam, for instance—but they are different places. So I'm interested in looking locally but also comparatively looking back and forth.

PK: You have written extensively on the construction of the "self" and the notion of the "persona" (rather than on people as social subjects). What are the theoretical, methodological, and epistemological advantages that you see in this disjuncture? In other words, how does such an analytical focus help make better sense of the interpretive aspects of human expressions?

Again, that is a place where fieldwork really did have an effect. Because the first time I began to think about this was in Bali, where the distinction between the persona and the self, the creatural self, is strongly emphasized. Balis have a highly dramatistic way of presenting themselves, of seeing themselves. I began to think of how Balis understand the notion of time and self, of the way that etiquette took in the persona, a persona that denies the creatural side. It makes people seem like they are all actors in an endless pageant where individuals replace others as personas just go on. You can see this in the Javanese social system, too.

NP: How does your approach to the making of the self (maybe we could call it an interpretive social poetics) account for such interpretive dualities as self and other, sameness and otherness, identity and alterity, or, especially, the dialectics between difference and otherness?

Well, that is a somewhat Western formulization, and that is not the way that the Javanese or Balinese would think of it. Otherness is differently conceptualized in all three of those societies. But the sharp contrast between self and other is much more muted in Java. Etiquette suppresses it; you are not supposed to let your feelings show directly. You try to reduce difference; certain differences are accentuated, but differences of kind are not. In Morocco, gender is a huge marker and there is gender separation—this is a little bit stereotypical. In Java, it is not that there are no differences, but gender is very much minimized. And in Morocco, differences of status are not emphasized. In Java status is more important, but gender is different; the clothes that are worn in Java are very much the same between men and women. Most of the heroes are androgynous; most of the gods are androgynous. So they try to minimize as much as they can gender differences and accentuate as much as they can status differences. It is a different kind of pattern. Everyone creates their own notion of what is other.

PK: Let's think about the concept of the self in interpretive anthropology: text and context, textuality and intertextuality, text as process and product, text as performance. How does the self encounter the text? How does the concept of intersubjectivity modify—if it does—such an interpretive encounter?

Interpretive models are not only textual. Some are textual, but again there is the dramatic model—I use the theater model sometimes. So I don't want to identify textual things with interpretive models. Not to evade the question, but that is first. Secondly, it is an analogy. My own use of it comes from Paul Ricoeur, who uses it as an analogy: the idea that you can read texts. And there I do think, if you go back to the persona notion, that people understand one another in a sense textualizing, in making them into some sort of story, like "X." That's just like "him" to do that, "it's just like us Javenese to be polite," and so on. There is always that kind of story about people as individuals but also individuals as classes, as personae. So, that kind of textualization of others goes on all the time. We create texts with one another. The text is never created by one person—that is the intersubjective part—it is always created in the context of other people. I mean, this little world we are in right now has do to with me, but also with you and the production that we exchange and so on, and that is how I construct the notion of what I am all about. So in that sense it is a textualization thing and it is intersubjective. You can't make yourself alone. There are all sorts of collective representations of selfhood as in "this is what it is proper to be, to act, whatever."

NP: On the poetics of text-as-performance and the poetics of performance-as-text: how is the rhetorical dimension of such discourses researched and accounted for? Is there a "self" outside of performance and is there a "persona" outside of a "self"?

Interpretive anthropology is very practice oriented, so texts are performed. That is why I say what I say about text analogues. I've read the cockfight as a text. Now that's an action, and I textualize it perhaps, but I've tried to look at it as a Balinese text. I have tried to see how the Balinese make sense of this. So behavior is read by the people who are involved in it. The Balinese cockfight means something, or so I argue, "this is what I argue is going on here, that masculinity is at risk, and so on." And after I wrote that, I got messages from all over the world because cockfighting is one of the most widespread sports in the world, and I had not realized that. And it means something different in different parts of the world. And so it is not a written text, and you don't ask literal questions about it as if it were a written text, and the differences between it and written texts are worth keeping in mind before you go overboard.

NP: Interpretive anthropology has been charged with a lack of focus on power, especially political power, a criticism that has drawn heavily from Foucault's formulations on power and discipline and [Antonio] Gramsci's formulations on hegemony, and Marxist understandings of ideology. Would you like to address this issue of power, discipline, and hegemony in terms of interpretive anthropological analyses?

Well, it may be true that it has not dealt with this—I would argue that it has—but that's a fair question. The real question that is really important is, can it handle questions of power and hegemony? and so on. I must say that I don't see why not, and I have tried to do it in various ways. But the dangers that I think people see is aestheticization and yielding to hegemony and hegemonic views. If you look at some of the work that people have done, it seems to be at least somewhat concerned with power. The notion that it aestheticizes everything seems to me not correct. And certainly it isn't intrinsic to it. I don't see why, again, in the same way that the textualization of the self does not destroy the creaturality, the textualization of power does not change the nature of the Balinese state, which is all about power, warfare, and domination. But the thing that has made that charge more cogent and more current is Foucault's theory of creating subjects and creating domination. So there is not a question of dealing with power but how power should be conceived and whether a disciplinary view of power, which is essentially what Foucault has, is really a valid one. And so it is really not a question of whether one deals with power or one doesn't but how one is supposed to deal with power. I don't think that interpretive anthropologists neglect "real power," whatever that is. Real power is power that is effective, and we can talk about that. Whether we deal with it in a Foucauldian idiom or not? No, we don't. By and large we don't. We have a lot to learn from that. But this is where the criticism has come from, people who want to look at power as a disciplinary force.

NP: How can (or should) the anthropological "self" be situated toward its object of study? Is reflexive ethnographic practice a poetic epistemological breakthrough or a rhetorical ploy?

Well, there is a phrase by David Hoffman, the painter, who said that "our big mistake was to describe the world as though we were not in it." And anthropology did that, including me, and I mean we all did it for a while. But I spent two and a half years in Javanese society, and to describe this Javanese town as though I were not there, I mean it is just false. Now the textual problems of doing that are there, they exist—that is, how you construct a text, whether you do it in the first person, whether you do it by reflexive considerations, whether you do it otherwise, there are all kinds of ways of approaching it. But I think by now, everybody of the interpretive tradition, all recognize the need to include themselves in the world they are describing. That's what we do. Maybe sociology can pass out questionnaires and go hide behind the screen, but anthropologists do not do that. Most of my work has been done by talking to people, living with families, going to the market, walking around, and to make you believe that I got all of this from some information-production machine just does not make any sense. What I mean is that this would be a misdescription of what we are doing. And here I would be quite adamant. Now reflexiveness can be overdone. Books are authored, they are signed, and it is not by our subjects—we have done enough harm to them; we should not make them coauthors of our books. *We* write them and *we* should acknowledge that we write them. Here's a story: When I went back to my town in Java after twenty-five years, the last of my books to be translated into Indonesian was a social history of this town that just came out when I was there. I had changed all the names (as you usually do), and one of my old informants had Xeroxed the text, wrote in all of the proper names, and distributed them to the people there, and so when I went around to talk to them I had a lot of discussions about this. It was great fun—they would pull out the pages—it was great fun.

NP: Over the past twenty years, we have experienced an epistemological fragmentation: an ever-growing corpus of work by anthropologists who come from countries that have traditionally been the object of the anthropological project (and have been called anything from "native" anthropologists to "insider," "indigenous," "at home," and so on) but have participated in the international production of anthropological knowledge (through publications, teaching, and so on), and they are gaining a more active intellectual profile. Subjects and objects of study, subjectivities encountering objectivities. Is it possible to do without the classical epistemological dichotomy of subject-object? Is it possible to avoid or manage alternatively the dialectic between making sense and power?

Well, when I came into anthropology it was largely "Western." In a generation, and partly due, I think, to interpretive anthropology, the first American Indian anthropologists began to emerge, and then there was a group of people from Sri Lanka that became quite eminent, so the whole field has been differentiated. And the other thing that came with this reflexive thing is the notion of the "situated observer," that is, the notion that we don't stand on the moon, we stand somewhere. Sometimes we come from our own society, sometimes not, but wherever we are, we are situated. And so the attempt to cast away all personal identity when you are writing about this stuff is problematic, and so that has an effect on those who are writing about their own societies. There is a lot more work by Americans on American society than there used to be, and I think that the whole notion of the situated observer has made this whole thing much more visible. You don't get to sign just your name anymore, you have to sign your identity, and that is here to stay—it is just never going to go away, especially as anthropology itself differentiates and becomes more cosmopolitan. When I first did work in Indonesia, there was maybe one really good anthropologist; there are now fifty or sixty. In Morocco there were even fewer—there were none—and today still there are not very many, but there are some (including one teaching at Princeton as you know). So the whole field has changed that way, so it is less a matter of "native" versus nonnative—that is not how I usually phrase it—but as situated observers versus people who try to claim that they are looking at things from the sky. But where one stands always has to be foregrounded, or signaled in some way, to make the account readable and interpretable for someone who is reading it. So (I always go back to literary models) just as the narrator has changed in fiction writing—you now have personalized narrators, unreliable narrators, and so on—all this has flooded into anthropological work. I think you also begin to include a critique of your own work in how you write it, so that people do not take it more seriously than it is worth taking. So the framing of the question as "native"-"nonnative"—even in quotes!—is not the way that I would frame it. If there is a conflict, it has to do with the fact that interpretive anthropology fully accepts the reflexive, situated narrator and social anthropology does not do that. I mean, everything is supposed to look the same to everybody for them.

I tend to be skeptical in general about terminological solutions to problems of this sort. It is a problem of building texts, of trying to create a text in which the author is visible and identifiable and can be seen. You are writing a book; I mean, it is not being written by god. But I tend to deal with these problems in terms of writing. Another concern that also emerged out of interpretive anthropology is the concern with the actual literary form of modern anthropological work. And I think that—in so far as we have to solve these problems, or at least face them honestly and directly—it's going to be through both borrowing and inventing literary devices. But I myself tend to do it not terminologically but rhetorically. But my works are constructed differently—they are not all the same kind of form—and I think that is true in general of people who write in the interpretive tradition. And again it is more like a literary analogy than a scientific one, where you want to hold the observer constant, unchanged, and unfeeling, and "un" everything else. There you don't have any kind of literary textual problem; you try to suppress any kind of rhetorical dimension to the text. And in interpretive work you try to maximize the visibility of the text.

NP: Finally, let's look at the practice of anthropology from the perspective of technological globalization. Does doing ethnography from a distance indicate a return to "armchair anthropology" or a matter-of-fact reformulation of a century-old prerogative? Interpretation is always already post- and metafactual. How does (can) an empirical reality totally mediated by technological simulation inform the interpretive process?

Well, I don't see any reason you can't do it from a distance. I've never been much interested in doing it at a distance, but there have been miraculous works done this way; I mean, I still think that *The Chrysanthemum and the Sword* is an amazing work for someone who never went to Japan. So you can do it. It is not something that I do. We are much more involved in the technological world—you know the work of Bruno Latour, beginning to try to think about objects as part of interactions with human beings—and we are much more implicated in technological culture, day by day. We are now connected through nonhuman interlocutors. So it is no longer possible to regard technology as simply a background or a framework on which society rests. It is integrated into the interpretive structure of reality and is not just regarded as an instrument or a tool but as an actor in society. Day by day everything is much more implicated in technology. Everything that we do. There was a blackout in New York the other day and it changed everything. So we can't regard technology as just a passive structure. That's a real change. And I think that change has been recognized, but how to describe it or discuss technology as actors, technological instruments as actors, is the question, and we are just beginning to learn how to do this—some of us inside anthropology and some outside. But I think again that interpretive anthropology is much more hospitable to this sort of thing than any other and that you get involved in science wars because the old positivist tradition is stronger in the natural sciences than in the social sciences. So the whole notion that technology is a passive factor is changing entirely—it is an active force. Of course, it has always been an active force but not so much as now. In a tribal society, you can regard technology as a tool so you can build a canoe so that you can sail and fish. But in modern society it is really not possible to regard technology as external to our lives.

Contemporary Fieldwork Aesthetics in Art and Anthropology: Experiments in Collaboration and Intervention

George E. Marcus

In recent years, Douglas Holmes and I have been working toward an articulation, and a refunctioning even, of ethnographic research practices so basic to the identity of anthropology.[1] It is remarkable to reflect on how much research in social and cultural anthropology, especially in the United States, has consisted of variations on a particular aesthetic of practice that can be condensed to a near-mythic scene of encounter—a Malinowskian one, or latterly, a Geertzian one (e.g., the famous opening of Geertz's "Deep Play" essay[2]). Recall, for instance, these oft-quoted lines from the beginning of the *Argonauts of the Western Pacific*, in which fieldwork is evoked and its practices are inculcated: as Malinowski intones, "Imagine yourself, suddenly set down surrounded by all your gear, alone on a tropical beach close to a native village, while the launch or dinghy which has brought you sails away out of sight."[3] However much this reminds one of the set directions for a classic Hollywood B-movie, Malinowski's evocations of fieldwork most of all established a powerful modality of method for anthropology, highly visual, if not cinematic in character, that has served to the present as the medium of regulative ideals in the doing of fieldwork and the production of ethnography. There is an entire genre of fieldwork literature, of memoirs, still vigorous, that supports it. Yet just about everything that defines this scene of encounter has changed dramatically over the past thirty years, and this is amply reflected in what passes for ethnography today. Nonetheless, both the inculcation of method in the professional culture of anthropology, especially in the training of apprentice anthropologists in the making, and the writing of ethnographic texts themselves remain remarkably committed to the mise-en-scène of the lone fieldworker crossing a marked boundary of cultural difference to temporary life in a community of subjects. Even in works that are far afield from the Trobriands or the Amazon, and even in these places as well in their transformed circumstances today with active indigenous movements, the classic version of writing the Malinowskian scene remains nonetheless de rigueur. Doug Holmes and I are compiling a montage of latter-day Malinowskian scenes of encounter from a wide range of contemporary ethnographies, hoping for an effect similar to the last scene of the film *Cinema Paradiso*. Here, as just one example to measure the change that has taken place in such stories, is an excerpt from Kim Fortun's arrival story, in the mythic Malinowskian scene of encounter, from her remarkable ethnography *Advocacy after Bhopal*, published in 2001 and produced as a first work from her dissertation:

> The timing of my work in Bhopal was out of joint in more ways than one. I arrived in Bhopal in February 1990, one year after the out-of-court settlement of the Bhopal case by the Indian Supreme Court. I did not plan to stay. I had come to India to do anthropological research on environmental politics in Madras. I traveled to Bhopal to collect material illustrative of the background from which concern about chemical pollution had emerged. Immediately, it was clear that Bhopal could not be conceived as a "case study," a bounded unit of analysis easily organized for comparative ends. To the contrary, Bhopal showed no evidence of boundaries in time, space, or concept, the historic and the future, continuity and dramatic change. Only later would I begin to understand the deeply normative implications of how Bhopal is encased in writing by management experts in particular. In 1990, newly arrived in Bhopal, I knew only that I was, indeed, at the scene of disaster, where injustice was complicated by grossly inadequate modes of conception and description, where everyday life screamed for rectitude, without prescriptions for anything more than symptomatic relief."[4]

This montage of what the scene of encounter was then and what it is now that Holmes and I are preparing is more than a homage or tribute to the persistence and regulative power of the Malinowskian imaginary; it is intended as a document that provides a means to probe both stability and significant change in the ethnographic project, as well as what constitutes fieldwork particularly, at least since the moment of the *Writing Culture* critique of the 1980s.[5] And it is a stratagem that we are using to articulate a redesign of the entire ethnographic project on its most sacred and enduring grounds, so to speak. Now, in this sense, and in retrospect, what the *Writing Culture* critique did was to revise and recondition the genres of writing ethnography from fieldwork in light of the mounting critiques through the 1960s and 1970s of the research practices and resulting claims to knowledge of modern anthropology, as an exemplar of a discipline that studied culture as ordinary forms of life. The power of this specific critique was that it partook of and exemplified the vibrant body of theoretical work then being produced that was challenging traditional forms and assumptions of representation generally in Western intellectual life. In retrospect, although powerful enough to signal a profound rupture in the modern tradition of anthropological research from which it is still recovering, or rather, from which it continues to benefit in my view, the *Writing Culture* critique, because it was devoted largely to the preexisting traditional literature of ethnography, actually adapted and more powerfully reinstantiated the Malinowskian scene of encounter by making it more theoretically sophisticated, politically sensitive, and ethically accountable. What it did not do was to anticipate the radically changed present circumstances of anthropological fieldwork, the diverse topical and interdisciplinary environments in which ethnographic projects are conceived, and the altered functions of basic ethnographic knowledge from its classic archival ones.

Nor, more importantly, did the *Writing Culture* critique develop what its own implications were for the conduct of fieldwork, deeply embedded in the norms and practices of the informal disciplinary culture of anthropology. In short, it did not undertake its own "ethnography" of how anthropology mundanely, or as a matter of its ordinary professional culture, distinctively produces ethnographic knowledge, and if it had, it might have seen then the intimate and crucial role of the writing of ethnography within the deeper and more ideological consequential professional culture of "doing fieldwork." Indeed, I would argue that this crucial limit of the 1980s critique was responsible for what success the *Writing Culture* critique had within anthropology.

The critique of outmoded aspects of the anthropological production of knowledge, clearly felt and widely understood among anthropologists in light of critical culture theories circulating in the 1980s, and expressed as a near-literary critical examination of the rhetoric and tropes of anthropological authority, was widely received, especially among younger anthropologists, as both needed and therapeutic. Had the relationship between the tropes of ethnographic writing and the conduct and teaching of fieldwork as a method and expectation of professional culture also been examined, there might have been considerably more resistance to this critique in the 1980s as well as a deeper exploration of research practices, focused on the regulative ideals, or rather an aesthetic of what fieldwork is supposed to be, communicated in the powerful, imagistic, even filmic Malinowskian mise-en-scène that the *Writing Culture* critique reconstructed and reinforced through a particular kind for reflexive writing that it encouraged. This mise-en-scène persists in practice and in writing, especially for every apprentice anthropologist, despite the fact that every actual condition on which it was traditionally founded has disintegrated, fragmented, or morphed.

Anthropology can continue to impose its ideal conditions upon reality with certain results that may or may not be useful for certain traditional knowledge projects that continue on the margins of the field. But in my view, the core research program of social and cultural anthropology, given how it has been reconstructed by present circumstances of trying to do fieldwork anywhere, especially on the part of the discipline's apprentices, requires an explicit rearticulation of its aesthetic of method. In this, the way that contemporary ethnographic works, like Fortun's from which I quoted, are wrestling with the very powerful norms and forms of knowledge making that they have been bequeathed since the *Writing Culture* critiques focused on a very powerful set of expectations of what fieldwork should be is diagnostic, symptomatic, and a way into rethinking the design of research practices themselves.

So although it might appear that our interest in the scene of encounter in contemporary published ethnographies returns us to the primarily textual concerns of the 1980s *Writing Culture* critique, this interest instead is a strategic choice to finally address the operative aesthetic of fieldwork as method and practice at the heart of anthropological research design in an era when what fieldwork is, what it can be, what it might produce—still shaped by the expectations of the Malinowskian scene of encounter—is being addressed with often interesting, but uncertain, results in contemporary ethnographic writing. Our warrant for beginning with the scene of encounter as written is based on our insight, itself ethnographic, regarding the way that method has manifested itself in the professional culture of anthropology. This is a disciplinary culture in which there has been a certain indifference or even antipathy to method as formal procedures, something that can really be taught as such. Indeed, fieldwork as method is most powerfully inculcated as a kind of lore—tales, corridor talk, and anecdotal evaluation among peers, in the pressure of expectation between student and teacher—but if there is a formal instrument in the teaching of method in anthropology, I would say that it is in the reading of ethnography itself. Why read ethnographies if not to gain a semblance of models of practice in this otherwise very informal culture by which method is instilled? Whatever ethnographic texts are as reports and the material form of knowledge claims that anthropology offers the library, the archive, and the world, they are foremost the most effective medium of thought experiments by which apprentice anthropologists conceive of fieldwork before they do it. Built around the Malinowskian encounter, the ethnographic text still evokes, and very visually so, scenarios of practice for apprentice ethnographers, who, if they ever do ethnographic research again in their careers, must at least do so canonically at the very beginning. The first books, writings, that come from these projects that are built around rewriting the scene of Malinowskian encounter are key and strategic materials to work with in coming to a new articulation, a reimagination, of fieldwork itself. This, I argue, is a matter of aesthetics, rather than methods, as traditionally conceived.

I should say before proceeding that this exercise in which we are engaged, of reimagining the scene of encounter of fieldwork in anthropology as it is being experienced—especially by apprentice researchers in launching their career-making projects—is one among a whole range of strategies being tried by other heirs to and makers of the 1980s ruptures that have both signaled and carried out what it is to do anthropological research now in the contemporary world. To me and to others, the most interesting and urgent theoretical questions in anthropology today are precisely about its distinctive technology or aesthetics of form-giving to knowledge; its historic culture of distinctive method; and how it shapes, inhibits, and encourages what the nature of anthropological knowledge is for its publics, for its interdisciplinary partners, and perhaps most importantly, for its own disciplinary community, which is perhaps most perplexed about what "the ethnography" as the major knowledge form of anthropology is becoming and how it might still be the grounds for constituting a distinctive collective discourse that reflects anthropology as a vital intellectual project.

There are some—Paul Rabinow, for example—who clearly reflect the intellectual style and concerns of the tradition of ethnographic research, but who see no need to preserve its precise terms, like *fieldwork, participant observation*, or the term *ethnography* itself. Inspired by a range of theoretical resources and pursuing anthropology in new domains such as the arena of biotechnology, Rabinow has offered a bold reconception of the terms of anthropological research in *Anthropos Today: Reflections on Modern Equipment*.[6] Instead of *fieldwork, culture,* and *ethnography*, he deals in terms (culled eclectically from French theory) like *problematization, apparatus,* and *assemblage* with a wry, half-serious title for this project of research—*Wissenarbeitsforschung*. Of course, he presumes that such a term would never catch on, but he means what it says, as a way of defamiliarizing the ethnographic process from its traditional terms. The aesthetic is very much preserved, but without the powerful strictures of the Malinowskian scene of encounter.

On the other side, Marilyn Strathern, for instance, remains implicitly true to the traditional terms of ethnography in anthropology, but without being literal about it. She appeals to that tradition explicitly by using with great agility materials from the classic settings and tasks of anthropological research, such as exchange systems in New Guinea, as comparative probes into novel settings of knowledge formation and doing science in labs, in hospitals, in her own university.[7] But the essential scene of fieldwork in these settings remains the Malinowskian one, although Strathern (and her many students) have been very adept at making these settings of fieldwork within the machineries of bureaucracies seem very exotic indeed.

And in distinction to these approaches, our strategy in this rethinking of the historic research paradigm of anthropology is quite literally to work with its classic expression focused on the scene of encounter and to morph it or reconfigure it from within its own terms. In a sense, this is a task of translation. So, at least for now, we are rethinking fieldwork and ethnography from within their current expression in professional culture and especially as they operate in the production of apprentice ethnographers who come up with expressions in their first works of what the changing intensities of the de rigueur classic Malinowskian scene of encounter, and thus fieldwork, is becoming in new terrains and circumstances of research. Although some may say that this play of traditional constraints and tropes in new work is merely vestigial, and that it is already too late to save fieldwork as we have known it, I disagree and see such play as the means to articulate a reinvention from the tradition within its own terms.[8] In terms of the politics of knowledge, this strategy of reform is also likely to be more effective, just as the *Writing Culture* critique was during the 1980s and 1990s in reworking the tropes of ethnographic description and analysis in the face of mounting critiques, because it in itself is grounded in ethnographic-like observations of anthropology as an institution and takes fully into account the nature of a distinctive practice of research within it as a technology, an aesthetic, and a power-knowledge.

What is it, then, in the Malinowskian scene of encounter revised today in ethnography that most signals a direction of change in fieldwork? To get a sense of this, we can briefly return to Kim Fortun's writing the scene of encounter into her *Advocacy after Bhopal*, which I quoted earlier. She arrives at the scene of Bhopal in 1990 and immediately realizes that her fieldwork is not literally site specific. This reflects the emergence of multi-sited fieldwork about which I have written, but it does not mean the literal multiplication of successive Malinowskian periods of fieldwork at related sites, which many have viewed as impractical as well as diluting the standard of fieldwork. Rather, it entails constructing fieldwork as a social symbolic imaginary with certain posited relations between things, people, events, places, and cultural artifacts, and a literally multi-sited itinerary as a field of movement emerges in the construction of such an imaginary. Literal fieldwork operates within this imaginary, bringing into juxtaposition sites that demonstrate certain connections or relations and the cultural significance that they carry about a world, or worlds, in change.[9]

This imaginary is locally constructed at the scene of fieldwork through ethnographic participation in advocacy, in Fortun's case, which defines relations of collaboration, and both the boundaries of fieldwork and its subject are found in these relations. In addition, the fieldwork is defined and bounded by siting itself in a distinctive concept of present or emergent time as well as place. It is the return of Johannes Fabian's recognition of coevalness with an emphasis.[10] Fortun's understanding of the temporality of being in Bhopal in relation to an event or set of events is as important as being "there," so to speak, as a dimension of her setting the scene of fieldwork. Bhopal was already something more than the literal site when she arrived there in 1990. As a place of disaster, it had symbolic value beyond mere location and site of fieldwork observation. Timing and temporality created a difficult challenge for ethnography.

Many projects today, like Fortun's, find their questions and frames of analysis only by relating the "here and now" of the traditional mise-en-scène of fieldwork to the "elsewheres" in which they are caught up. How to define and work within the imaginary of the "here and now" and the "elsewhere" is what makes contemporary fieldwork multi-sited and redefines the intensities of the scenes of encounter where fieldwork begins these days. One gets caught up in the events of ordinary local life, as always, but one finds there reflexive subjects who stimulate a politics of collaboration necessary for ethnography to proceed in a way quite different from the way anthropologists have enrolled subjects in their projects in the past. The subject and scale of fieldwork are negotiated in a found imaginary out of such collaborations. So for me, the scene of fieldwork today has two key features—working, committed collaborations, and the understanding of imaginaries and their consequences as both the major impetus by which ethnography becomes multi-sited and the medium by which ethnography defines its conceptual and empirical object. Now, what sorts of investigations, researches, have already been operating in terms of such reconfigured scenes of encounter? Where can anthropological fieldworkers find examples and resources to articulate changes that they are half making circumstantially these days in their professional culture of method, what it requires of them, and what they are able to produce as knowledge anyhow? I have sought to find such inspirations in my long-standing interest in the processes of research, with resemblances to ethnography, as they have been practiced and conceived by artists, filmmakers, and theatrical producers, to which I now turn.

If anthropological fieldwork as a method is, as I have argued thus far, both realized and accountable within a distinctive professional culture as the performance of a highly valued aesthetic of inquiry, the material expression of which is the written ethnography—currently at odds, so to speak, with its historic disciplinary exemplars—then practices in the arts, film, and theater are an obvious place to look for affinity and kinship. Quite explicitly, certain practices of "research" resembling ethnographic fieldwork have long been embedded aspects of the complex collective processes that produce film (here I have especially been interested in creating locations for certain films and in the imaginary of the craft of film editing) and drama (here I have interacted with scenographers as kinds of ethnographers as well as specialists in dramaturgy), but there is even a more relevant parallel world of endeavor in the arts with which the fieldwork tradition in anthropology might connect and compare itself. This is the modernist line of installation performance, event-based conceptual art movements with roots in Dada and surrealism, as well as situationism and Fluxus, among others. The scene of spectacle in such artwork, created in the context of real-life situations, is what is imagined rather than the scene of encounter of anthropology, but the two are not unrelated, and it would be interesting to use this affinity to think through what anthropology might learn from such art projects, which I will in fact attempt in a moment.

Indeed, in the same period that anthropology was critiquing its historic method and its performative expression as ethnographic texts, during the 1980s and 1990s, there was a parallel interest in socially conscious artwork in the installation, performance, happenings mode, but influenced heavily by the enthusiasm for culture theory during this period. Nicolas Bourriaud has famously written about this art of the 1990s (into the present) as "relational aesthetics"[11]—the orchestration of sites, settings, social actors, and processes for certain effects that have complex social topologies investigated through background research (like fieldwork) but are realized in a scene of spectacle, where spectacle is conceived as symbolic act, stimulating a critical reflexivity on the part of participants and observers. For example, Rirkrit Tiravanija organizes a dinner in a collector's home and leaves him all the ingredients required to make a Thai soup; Philippe Parreno invites a few people to pursue their favorite hobbies on May Day on a factory assembly line; Maurizio Cattelan feeds rats Bel Paese cheese and sells them as pets, or he exhibits recently robbed safes. In the mid-1990s, Hal Foster, a historian of art and especially of postmodernism, produced an important essay, "The Artist as Ethnographer?" (published in a book that Fred Myers and I edited on the recent traffic between art and anthropology, and its potentialities), which explicitly addressed the pretension to ethnography, to research as fieldwork, in this array of art projects, and he did so with an informed skepticism and acute cynicism.[12] But the limitation in Foster's assessment is that he was measuring the ethnographic pretense and prowess of the artist in terms of the uncritiqued, relatively unproblematic pre-1980s condition of anthropological ethnography—how anthropology is stereotypically known to its publics. Ethnography in its post-1980s and continuing challenges is very different and needs very much, I would argue, the sort of play with its practices that artists have been doing and about which Foster was skeptical. As I will explore a bit more fully, the kinds of research that some artists do are models that anthropologists can think with in articulating manifest changes in their own traditions of fieldwork.

I have found that many of these art projects are concerned either with questions of collective trauma and suffering as a challenge to a smug humanitarianism; with identity and difference among peoples and places in a globalizing world (e.g., the scenes orchestrated by the artistic collective Stalker in various places of a demographically changing European landscape, discussed by the sociologist of art Nikos Papastergiadis as probings into the situated practices and potentials of cosmopolitanism in ethnically diverse situations);[13] or with the material processes responsible for globalizing process: systems of value, exchange, markets, rethinking capitalism in the cultural sphere (e.g., the projects of Neil Cummings and Marysia Lewandowska that deal with art institutions, value, and capitalism, to which I will return in a moment). These are of course the core generic topics and preoccupations of anthropological research as well, making the affinity with the general form of these projects even more suggestive for ethnographers, who, everywhere today it seems, are confronted with a negotiation about reflexivity in order to materialize both an object and a space-time of research. The openness and experimental nature with which artists in the movement that I have been describing are doing fieldwork, so to speak, to occupy the scene of spectacle that art produces are valuable exemplars for articulating systemically changes in the mythic scene of encounter in contemporary anthropological research. In the remainder of this essay, I want to assess the potential of just one example of an art project, that of the "Capital" project of Neil Cummings and Marysia Lewandowska, for articulating emergent changes in fieldwork practices in anthropology.

In September 2003, I attended a large, diverse, and ambitious conference at Tate Modern entitled "Fieldworks: Dialogues between Art and Anthropology." My talk there shared concerns with this one; I was in conversation with Hal Foster's critique of the effort of artists to do something like "ethnography," and I reflected on my collaborative participation with artists from Cuba and Venezuela in the production of a series of installations and performances. Among the supermarket variety of projects and approaches, I was riveted by a thirty-six-minute account by Cummings and Lewandowska of the process by which they had produced an event, an intervention, for Tate Modern in 2001. I thought what I was hearing at the time was an account of the alternative model of fieldwork that I had been conjuring for anthropology. Such a behind-the-scenes account is very valuable, since it rarely appears amid the genres by which artists make their work public or do advertisements for themselves (what stands for this project, for example, besides Web site material, is an attractive and glossy Tate catalog entitled simply *Capital*;[14] there was also a series of Tate-sponsored seminars, plus an intervention in the scene of the museum itself). Fortunately, the conference was Webcast, and I have been able to listen to their presentation several times.[15] I indeed heard what I thought I had, but there were several other nuances in the presentation that made me appreciate how the construction of their project differs from ethnography as well.

Cummings and Lewandowska, who have been working together since 1995, have done numerous projects that required research to create the space for those projects. Most importantly, this research replaces the site specificity of art. Any project of course involves physical locations, but more importantly, the project's site is a social imagination that is conceptually invented and materialized in the practices of research or investigation based on a deeply reflexive motivation. The scene and bounds of fieldwork or of a project emerge through following a set of relations across a social landscape that it is both material and imaginary. Research is a design of collaborations and other sorts of engagements of varying intensity. Regardless of how, and to what critical response, they finally filled in the scene of spectacle as art in the Tate project that they undertook, their conduct of research in this project is immensely important, I believe, as an achieved exemplar for ongoing transformations of the Malinowskian scene of encounter in anthropology.

Cummings and Lewandowska have a Web site where they list and describe their various commissions, and they introduce this list with this manifesto-like statement:

> We recognize that it's no longer helpful to pretend that artists originate the products they make, or more importantly, have control over the values or meanings attributed to their practice: interpretation has superseded intention. It's clear that artworks and artists exist in a larger economy of art; built from an interrelated web of curatorship, exhibitions, galleries, museums, archives, places of education, various forms of funding, dealers, collectors, catalogues, books, theorists, critics, reviewers, advertising, and so on.
>
> In the light of the above, we have evolved a way of working over the last few years which requires an intense period of research with the various institutions of art. We have initiated projects with museums, retail stores, commercial and public galleries, as well as places of education. These collaborations have resulted in a number of different outcomes appropriate to the nature of each project; exhibitions, collections, books, guided tours, lectures, videos, internet browser and a range of promotional or educational material. We are interested in working alongside all of the institutions that choreograph the exchange of people and things.[16]

Cummings and Lewandowska were given free rein to develop a reflexive installation or intervention at Tate Modern. They were very much influenced by the sort of theoretical writings that motivate anthropological research on exchange, value, and material culture, including those of Nigel Thrift (and his important emphasis that the experience of the modern world is increasingly insubstantial, meaning that ethnography about any local condition is always pulled "elsewhere," and that this requires strategies of creating in inquiry social imaginaries that are at least multi-sited) and most interestingly Marilyn Strathern (Cummings and Lewandowska favor and work brilliantly with some of Strathern's New Guinea analogies). They created an imaginary for their project that turned on the analogy and homology between the massive and powerful Tate Modern as the central arbiter of value in the symbolic economy of art and the Bank of

England just across the Thames as the central arbiter of the secular money economy, the lender of last resort, managing the price of debt and the cost of borrowing. Based on their Tate connections, Cummings and Lewandowska were able to conduct interviews in the Bank of England and gain the cooperation of some of its officials. The intensity of their project became centered in this juxtaposition, this back and forth symbolically, conceptually, and literally between the two institutions. The critical probe and resolution of this juxtaposition was resolved in using ideas of "the gift"—a classic foundational theory in the anthropology of exchange, which permeates the work of Strathern, for instance. Cummings and Lewandowska wanted to create an intervention in the museum that would make the otherwise invisible gifting relationships that sustain major cultural institutions visible to museum visitors; they wanted to suggest the symbolic relation between Tate and the Bank of England as well. While the research process itself became the most important part of the research, Cummings and Lewandowska finally did create something, a gesture to fill the scene of spectacle, instead of an art object. At selected times, arbitrarily chosen visitors to Tate Modern were given a limited-edition print, issued by the artists, through a gallery official. This unexpected gesture was meant to act like a detonator, raising many questions about the nature of the gift.

There are many ways in which this project can be questioned. Did its intervention really work as critique on any level? The research was not engaged enough, did not really respect its collaborations perhaps and their generative capacity to generate insight and self-critique. Although the project was very ethnographic at its heart, its thinking was ironically distanced and highly theoretical. It did not take the politics of research that it created far enough. But then why should it? The purposes of art should not be mistaken for the purposes of ethnographic research. Indeed, there was one really strange moment in Neil Cummings's presentation where, in referring to my own prior discussion of Hal Foster's essay in my conference talk, he said that the artist's use of something like fieldwork should not be associated with participant observation (and presumably the Malinowskian model) in anthropology—he presumed that reflexivity in anthropological ethnography is about ethical discipline (actually he is not wrong about this) but that artists are not capable of this function. They are interested in something else, he says.

Indeed, there is something ruthless and manipulative in the management of relations in Cummings and Lewandowska's Tate project—they do not work in the ethics that hovers over and shapes the implicit moral discourse of the Malinowskian scene of encounter. They are after an insight and the production of an effect, an effect of critical reflexive insight, which is its own virtue of doing good. For the sake of this, their research relations are rather instrumental and businesslike. I think this orientation would be both disconcerting and liberating to anthropologists. Finally, then, their research, although set up in ways from which anthropological ethnography could learn much, does not care enough about the politics of the process of inquiry that they set in motion and what kind of unique knowledge it could produce. Instead, they pretty much relied on "theory," and the authority of academics. This is fair enough given their purposes and the real differences of these from those of anthropology, but they have given an achieved and developed sample of what fieldwork is in fact becoming in anthropology.

Let's consider some of the important lessons that they do develop for the refunctioning of the ethnographic project in anthropology. In so doing, one might recall that the anthropological practice of fieldwork is not just a technology of method but an aesthetic of method as well that is powerfully inculcated by professional culture and identity. Accordingly, in reinventing fieldwork for its present conditions, these aesthetics will not be denied, or at least they won't be changed without compensation in whatever idioms. In short, in reinventing fieldwork, it is a certain powerful and established aesthetics that is being addressed in offering a new design, and this is at least as important as the appeal of the techniques themselves. So what is the aesthetic appeal, or rather compensations, of the moves that Cummings and Lewandowska have made?

First, the scene of encounter in contemporary ethnography leads away from a literal site-specificity to fieldwork. The Tate project of Cummings and Lewandowska shows convincingly how this might happen or evolve as a practice of research. Cummings and Lewandowska have a generative sense of the use of reflexivity to generate a field of relations that is more sophisticated than anything in the habit of anthropological fieldwork. Cummings is correct that reflexivity in the classic scene of encounter has been developed in the interest of ethical discipline or moral correctness. For Cummings and Lewandowska, reflexivity is a strategy to generate a space of social imagination that connects an artistic or intellectual discipline to its contexts as its major means and ends of inquiry. The situated collaborative work that is required to generate a social imaginary for fieldwork in which the researchers literally move and operate is the aesthetic compensation for the loss of the Malinowskian scene of encounter.

The encounter here is with a found intellectual partner, a friend, in the face of a more abstract unknown than a literal place—a relation, a system, what Hans-Jörg Rheinberger calls an epistemic thing.[17]

Actually, Cummings and Lewandowksa operate in the historic mode of modernist artistic practice—the space of the experiment—and to some degree their research is encompassed by this idea, investigation materially in an imaginary of a trial, trying something out for a result—here, a performance and intervention as occupying the artistic scene of spectacle. The 1980s critique of the anthropological scene of encounter also introduced something of this artistic idea of the experiment to anthropology—the idea that ethnography is an experiment and that there was even something of this in the originary projects of Malinowski, Raymond Firth, Edward E. Evans-Pritchard, and others. The critique of the tropes of ethnography would not have been possible without this evocation of fieldwork as experimental in the artistic sense.

In recent years, experiment in its natural-sciences sense has been rethought in ways that overlap closely with these art practices and the overlapping sense of experiment in ethnography, especially through the writing of the historian of science Hans-Jörg Rheinberger, who has been very influential among anthropologists working in science and technology studies, a burgeoning arena in which the sort of refunctioning that I have been articulating here has most manifested itself in practice. The account that Rheinberger gives of scientific practice in pursuit of epistemic things resonates with ethnographic inquiry, revised from the regime of conventional empiricism that was its originary model.[18] This overlap of an artistic and scientific aesthetic of practice around the notion of experiment has been one of the more promising background conceptual environments for carrying out the refunctioning of ethnography at the intersection of art and anthropology that I have been trying here. So, then, experiment is the ground of a compensating aesthetic for the refunctioning of the Malinowskian scene of encounter toward a viable idea of multi-sitedness or non-site-specific fieldwork.

Second, within this reflexively evolved terrain of inquiry, the focus or object of study emerges through the intensity of an operation-like juxtaposition as a probe of inquiry and mediation within an imagined and literal space. The intellectual work that led to the connection between Tate Modern and the Bank of England in Cummings and Lewandowska's project suggests the sort of conceptual labor or intensities focused on relations at the heart of ethnographic knowing in contemporary fieldwork. Cummings and Lewandowska give up, they go only so far, they let theory do the work, they impose insights rather than develop sustained collaborations with found counterparts, but they do demonstrate how a different sort of object emerges from fieldwork that is in terms of a multi-sited space or imaginary.

Frankly, the intensity of juxtaposition is about a relation that generates the aesthetic of working in an environment of difference so essential to fieldwork in the anthropological tradition. It is a remnant or residue of the liking for the exotic, where the literal exotic no longer exists and, what's more, has been critiqued to the extent of being unclaimable. In the revised terms of the experiment that I have just discussed, the juxtaposition is the operation that creates the epistemic thing—in Cummings and Lewandowska's project, it is thinking of Tate as an economy in which its relation to the Bank of England is not simply metaphorical but manifest and material in relations of the gift, so to speak, and in the relations that their research produced, made possible pragmatically by the found connections between Tate and the Bank of England, both imaginary and real.

Third, the aesthetic compensation for life in a situated community of the classic scene of ethnography is the partnerships of intellectual collaborations found in fieldwork—mutual aid in pursuit of a common object. Refunctioned ethnography indeed depends on the development of this aesthetic long submerged in traditional ethnography, but now takes to different levels of expression of complexity and expectations of practice. I will have more to say on this dimension in my final comments of this essay.

Fourth, and perhaps most consequentially, what Cummings and Lewandowska's Tate project suggests for the refunctioning of ethnographic research in anthropology is a different modality of purpose and result for ethnography. Mediation or intervention replaces or pushes from primacy the production of conventional description, analysis leading to an ethnographic text of the usual purposes, as a contribution to theory, or as an archive of knowledge accumulated by a collective of disciplinary scholars. Indeed, in this sense, the ethnography may very well be outmoded. Other genres serve these functions better. Others now do the kind of description that ethnography used to do of its old objects just as well, if not more cogently in its new terrains of interests. In any case, there is no representation that is unique to anthropology, and, especially for its new objects of research, there is no collective or specialized disciplinary guild or community for it. It is already the case that ethnography is most important to constituencies that are already found in fieldwork. Yet anthropology does not exactly know yet how to conceive such a function. In the United States at least, there is talk of a public anthropology, and there are claims to activism and activist purpose in its intellectual work. To me, neither of these is convincing; they are symptoms of the uncertainty of purpose of a research practice that once justified itself as part documentation, as part analysis in relation to a growing edifice of general, theoretical knowing about a circumscribed subject matter. The results of ethnographic research today are less clear, certainly more specific, and indeed more ethnographic in quality. This means that ethnographic knowledge creates itself in parallel with and relation to similar functions in the very communities that it makes it subjects. This leads to the more urgent need for modalities of collaboration as method, already mentioned, but also to mediation and intervention as being the primary form and function of the knowledge that ethnography produces. This is similar to what Cummings and Lewandowska attempted in their intervention at Tate, but in a more limited and frankly more superficial way than the more patient, sustained, and ethical relations of ethnographic research in anthropology—something that they rejected as ethical discipline obstructive to their purposes as artists. The clichéd participant observation of traditional ethnography for the archive here is replaced by an aesthetic of collaborative knowledge projects of uncertain closure.

This essay has been an effort to give a sense of what there might be in the research practices of Cummings and Lewandowska's Tate project for the refunctioning of anthropological ethnography, imagined through the systematic redesign of its mythic mise-en-scène—a rethinking of its intensities and its aesthetics through assessing the efforts in contemporary fieldwork projects to morph the Malinowskian scene of encounter and its received norms.[19]

Myth, Performance, Poetics— the Gaze from Classics

Richard P. Martin

Almost thirty years ago, Sally Humphreys, then a member of the Departments of Anthropology and History at University College London, wrote that

> the relation between Classics and Anthropology must be a relation of active debate. It is difficult, if not impossible, to gain an understanding of the methods and critical standards in argument of another discipline without personal contact and discussion. Up to the First World War both classicists and anthropologists took it for granted that their relationship should be one of exchange of ideas and collaboration in developing theory; we have to try to recreate this situation."[1]

Since then, much water has flowed under various bridges in both disciplines. While each side has been occupied eyeing somewhat erratic ebbs and floods of thought by its own embankments, the larger task of making connections between these two disciplines (or disciplinary tribes) has been largely ignored. Humphreys' notion of bringing together classicists and anthropologists continues to be a desideratum. It is my hope that future meetings of workers on both sides can follow the innovative lead given by the organizers' inclusion of classics in the wide-ranging Syros conference, "Anthropology, Now!"[2]

My title alludes to the gaze. It will be worthwhile to ponder, first, this steady one-way stare, as it has been directed for more than a century by classicists toward anthropology.[3] Any gaze can be baleful—like Medusa's head, it can petrify its object—and the object, in this case, has certainly shifted while many on the side of classics have tried to steady it. A list of some magic phrases might characterize the attractions that anthropology has traditionally held over classicists, from Sir James George Frazer until recent times: to cite a few, "fieldwork"; "living informants"; "a fully synchronic view"; "the truly local"; "ethnographic confirmation." A critical look at these elements of the gaze soon strips them of their glamour, however. The fetishization of fieldwork, for one, has certainly become suspect among practitioners, whereas the temptation is still strong for those classicists reacting against the field's text fixation to prize anything *not* derived from books.[4] There is a kind of one-upmanship that can take the form of attempting a "proof" of an argument by citing "real" information from ethnography—in this variation of the gaze, living informants, fieldwork, and the thirst for parallels all combine. Fortunately, this kind of argument has begun to die down, but it can still be found in the footnotes of books and articles, especially on ancient myth and history.

In my own specialization, the study of Homeric poetry—often a lightning rod for broader debates within classics—a variety of "fieldwork" fetishes have brought about a serious and abiding divide between "oralists," on the one side, who have tried to propound arguments about Homer by using Milman Parry and Albert Lord's work with singers of oral epics in Bosnia and Montenegro, and on the other side, purist or "scripsist" classicists, who insist that Homer was a genius transcending his tradition, a Virgil or a John Milton *avant la lettre*.[5] Thus, the former Regius Professor of Greek at Oxford can airily dismiss Serbo-Croatian analogues for epic composition while acknowledging that he does not know how to read a word of the language.[6] But a foothold for his disdain may have been given by the initial stance of oralists who pressed parallels into service as proofs, by mistaking fieldwork as the last word.[7] In recent years, the number and quality of ethnographies of poetry-in-social-use, many of them highly relevant to Homeric epic, have increased; unfortunately, the opposition dwells on the last generation's faults and ignores the new.[8]

As for "living informants"—that desire goes back all the way to antiquity. After all, Socrates himself, in Plato's *Apology*, thought that one of the best things about his being put to death was the opportunity to meet with Homer, Hesiod, and the other great names of the past—in other words, to dispense with books and get his information live, as it were. "Men of the jury, what would a person give to interrogate the man who led the great expedition to Troy or Odysseus or Sisyphus or a myriad other people, men and women? Unbelievable happiness that would be—to converse with, be with, and examine them, wouldn't it?"[9] Neither he nor many classicists since seem to have considered what anthropologists know by experience—live informants in fact can be a real pain. At least the dead, as represented in our texts, do not correct you, take you offtrack, or exhibit the annoying habit of poking holes in your preconceptions.[10]

Finally, there is that double image (itself probably an illusion) that classicists have tended to gaze at with desire, namely, the anthropologist's ability to work with local knowledge at a fine-grained scale and to tease out a "thick description."[11] In the case of the Greeks, especially, this desire must always remain a mirage. For since the eighth century B.C.E., the local, "epichoric" traditions of Greek lands seem to have been regularly reshaped and even repressed by competing versions of "Greekness" in the form of Panhellenic ideology, and later, Athenocentric culture.[12] And since we cannot have the fieldwork experience and must rely on texts, classicists are stuck with a cleaned-up, thin veneer of what may have been going on in any one of the many far-flung Greek-speaking places, from Marseille to the Black Sea.[13]

Here the text-based classicists (philologists and historians) traditionally have yielded to the archaeologists to get an idea, however vague, of what life was like in, say, the Dark Ages, in places outside Athens. The last generation of work, however, in such places as Euboea, Cyprus, Sicily, and the Argolid has revealed more than ever that higher-level affairs, such as the construction of identity, is never confined simply to verbal records. Such institutions as hero-cult or innovations like monumental temple construction represent complicated, ideologically generated responses to various sociopolitical situations. The classical archaeologist deals with these and has as much to learn as the classical text reader does, from good anthropological work about mentalities, ethnos-constructions, and the interplay of center with periphery.

It might be argued that a new postprocessual strain of classical archaeology, emerging from the work of Anthony Snodgrass and his Cambridge students, has taken up this challenge and now in fact offers the lead to other workers within the discipline called classics. This is all the more gladdening since, from its start in the 1870s until recently, classical archaeology had been a problematic stepchild for the prevailing textual interpreters, tightly reined in and focused on high-art objects, lest it give the lie to the usefully idealized Hellenism constructed by the heirs of Johann Joachim Winckelmann.[14] Twenty years ago, Humphreys could write that archaeology in Greece "has still scarcely been touched by the new ideas developing in other fields" and consisted mostly of excavating sites and examining artifacts, rather than studying communities and local culture.[15] That has changed.

So much, then, for the self-deceptions and desires involved in the way classics has gazed at anthropology in the past few generations. As is well known, a gaze can also mirror, so that the desired object sees its own image in return. With this in mind, I offer some reflections on what classics—apart from archaeology—has been doing over the past few years with the results and methods of anthropological work. I exclude from this discussion several rising tides of thought that have floated both our boats but that are not confined to anthropology—for instance, gender studies, new historicism, Bakhtinian dialogics, and varieties of structuralism, post-structuralism, and semiotics. This very personal view will, I trust, make clear several things: first, that there is a real thirst in the field for methodologies that can help us study ancient culture with sophistication and depth; second, that classics, as usual, is about a decade behind the cutting edge in awareness and use of the current work (a gap such conferences as that on Syros can shrink); and third, that classics, in turn, can and should provide both comparative material and methodological help, especially since it has long been involved with philology. This "art of reading slowly" (Nietzsche's phrase for his original field of work) is, after all, a transferable skill that can be applied to any cultural "text."[16]

Before speaking of three special cases, let me sketch the broader changes within the study of classics that we might justly credit to an anthropological outlook. Classicists deal with, or purport to, the entire range of cultural forms and productions stemming from Greece and Rome. Of course, the temporal and spatial boundaries of such study have always been hard to determine. Over the twentieth century, such study fluctuated between an all-embracing *Altertumswissenschaft* (scientific and positivist study of everything from pots to poems) to a more narrowly defined "humanist" core—the study of texts above all, with certain serious poetry and philosophy given privileged position and the "classic" eras of fifth-century Athens and Augustan Rome elevated to special prominence.[17] One welcome sign of progress during the late twentieth century and early twenty-first century is the increasing awareness (though not canonization) of areas that had been considered (sometimes literally) peripheral: late antiquity; Neoplatonism; the transmission of Greek literature in Arabic; the phenomenon of Greek colonization; the local history of Roman provinces, borders, and the role of extra-*polis* sanctuaries; and the status and roles of women, slaves, children, and the elderly, to name a few. Examining these areas naturally involves looking at encounters with the Other (*barbaroi* to the Greeks), questions of ethnicity, and cross-cultural negotiations.[18] Borrowing from *Annales* school history to some extent provided the intellectual underpinning for such investigations, and more straightforward appeals to social anthropology strengthened the effort.[19] Of course, there has been no master figure organizing or inspiring this new acceptance of unfamiliar methodology, no Frazer to lead the way. Instead, scholars have come to the comparative and theoretical materials on their own bypaths, or through word-of-mouth recommendations on what's "out there" worth reading—perhaps a healthier situation, all told.

To turn to some specifics: the first area of concentration worth remarking is the wealth of new work that deals with the study of spectacle and display. The invention of Western drama in Athens in the late sixth century has been subject to reexamination in terms of political acting out, group identity formation, and self-presentation.[20] The origins of this state-theater within the artistic program of the Athenian tyrant dynasty, the Peisistratids (or perhaps Cleisthenes, the succeeding "democrat") is no longer swept aside as an embarrassment—it means something, and a number of scholars have tried to say what.[21] A glance at the recent *Cambridge Companion to Greek Tragedy* will show that a good third of the volume is devoted to locating Greek theater within this and other social structures.[22] Two generations ago, critics like Bernard Knox could read *Oedipus Tyrannus* as a universal tragedy about failure of human intelligence; one generation ago, the play became a tissue of structurally opposed forces.[23] These days, it is about fifth-century Athenian self-image as constructed through the representation of thirteenth-century B.C.E. political disasters in another city-state, Thebes.[24] Oliver Taplin at Oxford, Simon Goldhill at Cambridge, and their students are most concerned with these issues today.[25] In the case of this particular mythic complex, it is a pleasure to see nonclassicists taking a new lead, as in the current work of Neni Panourgiá on Oedipus as archetypal figure of the anthropologist.[26] I expect such work will in turn generate a new wave of interest in rereading, anthropologically, other ancient dramas.[27]

A variation on this brand of research focuses on festivals, processions, athletic games, and public rituals as interconnected means of political and social expression. The names Clifford Geertz and Victor Turner are prominent here, as you might expect. The phrase "theater culture" recurs often. A compendium that might stand to summarize this approach is the volume of papers from a conference at Wellesley in 1990, *Cultural Poetics in Archaic Greece*.[28] Such approaches as those represented in the volume open up questions earlier classicists had not thought to ask: Why are statues of Olympic victors thought to possess magical powers when displayed in the city-state? Why did Athenians choose to play along with the notion that a local girl dressed as Athena was really the goddess, physically accompanying the tyrant Peisistratus back to power? Why was it crucial that eighteen-year-old Athenian warriors got the best seats at the Theater of Dionysus? Answers to such questions center on the intertwining of "reality" and "display"—or to put it another way, in sixth- through fourth-century Athens, "theater" was not the delimited, deracinated phenomenon we watch now but a crystallization of processes one could find throughout culture, from political "acting" to philosophical self-presentation. A populace expected scene setting and drama, whatever the venue. It is not surprising that we find in such sources as pseudo-Plutarch's *Lives of the Ten Orators* the mention of professional actors working as advisers for political speakers like Demosthenes.[29] The material for this sort of study is as old as the texts transmitted from antiquity; what makes the analysis fresh is the newfound appreciation of general cohesive notions, of a set of shared symbols articulating a social "poetics" that generates meaning through gesture and event.

Classicists have also been emboldened of late to move beyond the hot "histrionic" culture of classical Athens.[30] A second key area of research now ongoing has to do with the overarching institutions, beyond the local city-state, that defined what it was to be Greek, starting around 800 B.C.E. Here the role of Delphi has become clearer thanks to comparative data and viewpoints taken from work on state formation, colonialism, and elites. Carol Dougherty has written on the poetics of colonization—how linguistic strategies, dictated by Delphi, "naturalized" Greek expansion into new lands.[31] Lisa Maurizio, through an exhaustive comparative study of oracles, has delineated the complex representations and possible realities behind the Pythia at Delphi.[32] In my work on the Seven Sages—a kind of dream team of poets and politicians sponsored by an elite at Delphi in the sixth century—and on the depiction of Solon, the Athenian poet-politician, comparative work on ancient India and modern Panama helped define the typology and dynamics of such groups.[33] In this area, there seems to be real promise for the collaboration of anthropologists, political scientists, archaeologists, and philologists.[34]

The two areas I have already mentioned deal, inevitably, with the phenomenon of Greek myth. I suspect that this is a term that has slipped out of usage among ethnographers in recent years. Whether or not Greek myth, or "myth" taken categorically, is of any interest anymore to anthropologists, it remains a staple of the teaching that classicists do daily. (Indeed, for many undergraduate audiences "the ancient world" appears to be coextensive with "myth.") The structuralist wave that hit classics in the

1970s and only subsided about 1990 took myth for granted, as a transparent concept and tool, while it explored the way traditional tales interacted with Greek social life. There remained a suspicion among a few, however, that "myth" was an etic rather than emic category.[35]

The evolution of this term, *myth*, which was to become a central category for classics and anthropology, had oddly enough been passed over in discussions of the larger concepts.[36] It had always been recognized that *muthos*, its etymon, appears to function as one of several synonyms for *word* in Homeric Greek. On investigation, the word *muthos* is found to haul much more semantic weight. Taking account of context, it means something like "authoritative utterance, performed at length, before an audience, with full attention to detail and with focus on illocutionary force."[37] Men are almost exclusively the speakers of *muthoi* in Homer. There are three genres of speaking covered by the term: displays of memory, directives, and insults. Women, like Helen of Troy, perform one powerful subcategory (an elaborate and highly stylized one that can intertwine the various genres)—lament.[38]

Homeric poetry no doubt stylizes the *muthoi*, but what it stylizes is something that probably existed as a social reality in the eighth through sixth centuries B.C.E. Here, we can call on the ethnography of speaking, and rich work on social performance—the former represented by Joel Sherzer, Keith Basso, Charles Briggs, Richard Bauman, and others; the latter, for my purposes, by Michael Herzfeld and Nadia Seremetakis.[39] We might consider that *muthos* in archaic Greece was essentially a performance of the self, in an agonistic setting not unlike those described in modern Crete and in Mani. How does this help us understand the category of "myth"?

I suggest that myth—in the sense of a story about gods and heroes of the past—evolved easily from *muthos*, as "authoritative utterance." When, in the *Iliad*, Diomedes of Argos and Glaukos of Lycia meet,[40] we have the first intercultural exchange represented in European literature (which is also, at least in the narrator's view, the first bad bargain). These men proceed to define themselves by nothing less than an agonistic exchange of stories about their own ancestors, people who from the point of view of later Greeks are indexed as "heroes" both in ritual cult and in poetry.[41] *Muthos* becomes myth—in *performance*. Or put another way, *every* myth is a performance of identity. You can extrapolate to arrive at just how such an understanding might change the way we look at political, dramatic, and philosophical mythmaking throughout later Greek history, not to mention how we scrutinize the category when using it with a comparative slant.

Whether or not "myth" in any usable sense exists must remain a culture-specific judgment. Most likely, one will want to file it hereafter under "rhetoric."[42]

It is hard to sum up either a growth spurt or an explosion. They happen, and no amount of hindsight can explain exactly the course of either. What happened when classics opened itself to anthropologically inspired social analysis is somewhere between the two. As my last example, I hope, shows, richly nuanced and accessible anthropological work can help the classicist toward unpacking a concept that itself has played a formative role in anthropological discussion. A similar genealogy of concepts could be—in fact, demands to be—written for other terms and concepts inherited by modern social science from ancient Greek sources. The very notion of a *logos* (a reasoned oral account)—as in anthropo*logy*—assumes, after all, a particular worldview and social setting. The ethnography of Herodotus in the fifth century was a *logos*—but we also know that it was a performance meant to please and advise particular audiences of Athenians at certain historical moments.[43] What are the hidden assumptions behind our own contemporary *logoi*? It is gladdening to see that anthropology today is intent on precisely such interrogations, and I welcome the opportunity for classicists to join the dialogue.

The Birth of Anthropology out of a Pause on Pausanias: Frazer's Travel-Translations Reinterrupted and Resumed

James A. Boon

Alas, poor Frazer: deceased since 1941, yet never at rest. Yes, Sir James George Frazer: repeatedly *revenant*. After World War II, Theodor Gaster eventually pruned *The New Golden Bough*; later Stanley Edgar Hyman gauged Frazer's legacy, along with Darwin, Marx, and Freud; and John B. Vickery saluted Frazer's influence among literary modernists: T. S. Eliot, James Joyce, and others.[1] Meanwhile in 1969, I. C. Jarvie had assessed disciplinary "othering" of Frazer's approach versus Bronislaw Malinowski's functionalism—by then also "historical."[2] Subsequently, I recommended amalgamating anthropological and literary rereadings of Frazer *and* Malinowski (among others), aiming to avoid reductive polarizations that keep reemerging.[3] My hope has been to disrupt hackneyed habits of professional patricide.

Some years after that, Marilyn Strathern returned to Frazer's studies of the Old Testament, her father's favorite; and Marc Manganaro productively situated Frazer in interdisciplinary movements "from fieldwork to text."[4] Soon before, Robert Ackerman's fine biography had appeared in 1987, followed by a scintillating account of the *Golden Bough*'s elaborate spreading by Robert Fraser-with-an-S.[5] I find congenial the latter's slightly arch yet generous ethos of argumentation: "At times the impossibility of knowing anything for certain seems to have inspired in Frazer a sort of twinkling delivery, a sardonic self-scrutiny, a cat-and-mouse game with truth. He was not above playing to the gallery in this respect."[6]

In 1995, George Stocking situated Frazer (a tad grudgingly, perhaps) in a comprehensive history of the discipline "after Tylor," which altered somewhat Stocking's laudable method of "multiple contextualizations" from his earlier *Victorian Anthropology*.[7] Stocking's introduction (in 1996) to a reissue of Frazer's popularized 1926 abridgment of *The Golden Bough*, comments that my construal (in 1982) of Frazer's "irony" was a tad "presentist"—ahistorical, "postmodernist" even (me!—way back then!). I here counter jovially with a contrary insinuation: might it not be "presentist" rather to restrict irony to recent guises, thus implying (questionably) that any "Victorian" could only have been credulous, never ironic?[8] (Strathern inclines this way also, along with Stocking—both friends whom I admire.) Indeed, my interpretive aim in resuming and continuing my reading of Frazer, among others, has been and remains multiple "contextualizations" (in Stocking's historicist sense) of comparative ironies—in which formations Frazer arguably participated (in multiple textualizations!).

Yes, Frazer was manifestly steeped in the "romantic irony" of Jean Paul and Friedrich von Schlegel; he even translated master-ironist Heinrich Heine, his favorite German poet, whose lines he plucked as the epigraph for "The Language of Animals":

> Sie sprechen eine Sprache/ Die ist so reich, so schön
> Doch keiner der Philologen/ Kan diese Sprache verstehn.[9]

I once went so far as to surmise that Ludwig Wittgenstein's lucidly ironic doubts etched in the margins of *The Golden Bough* were conceivably not "ahead" of Frazer's own "language games"—about belief, magic, and their ambiguities; that my opinion has been echoed by R. Fraser makes me (an only occasional Frazer-backer, and partially) feel, for once, more like a "social fact" than a lone voice.[10]

Frazer's comparative task was manifestly Sisyphean. Returning to Frazer (already much revisited) feels Sisyphean-squared, even when this task is tackled sparely, as here. Yes, Sisyphean-squared-yet-spare, this essay forgoes considering retorts by Edmund Leach or remarks by Mary Douglas; nor can I reengage the Cambridge school of mythology (e.g., Jane Harrison), recently revamped by scholars in Victorian-Edwardian cultural studies intent on dragging in "sexual dissidence."[11] Rather, I address arrays of aftermaths to Frazer in token fashion, just enough to launch an interpretive query: can contemporary anthropology harness Frazer's *difficulty* (in George Steiner's sense)—his immense erudition, daunting range, and neglected travels and translations?[12] Might critical comparison today, whose proponents no longer write as long as Frazer, still strive toward reading more capaciously—including him?

To facilitate ironic *rapprochement* with Frazer's cross-cultural corpus making, I list a few germane dates and details—for the convenience of

Birth of Anthropology Out of a Pause on Pausanias 55

readers who either are unfamiliar with this strange-but-true predecessor or, having encountered his prose, have repressed so quaint an ordeal!

Quick Chronologique of Select Frazeriana

1869 — Matriculates, University of Glascow (classical studies).
1878 — Goes to Germany to polish German; buys Heine in Hamburg.
1879 — "Growth of Plato's Ideal Theory," Cambridge dissertation.
1882 — Inns of Court; admitted to bar (never practiced).
1883 — Reads Edward Tylor's *Primitive Culture* on walking tour in Spain.
1884 — Meets Robertson Smith, who assigns him (for *Britannica*) Penates, Priapus, Proserpina, and Pericles; later Totem, Theseus, Thespiae, and Taboo (germ of *Golden Bough*).
— Edits Sallust (Grammar School Classics series).
— Arranges with Macmillan to edit Pausanias.
1885 — *Journal of Philology* piece on vestal virgins via "survivals" in Tylor's sense (germ of *Golden Bough*).
— Anthropological Institute: "On Certain Burial Customs as Illustrative of the Primitive Theory of the Soul."
— Learns of excavation at Nemi; Ernest Renan's *Le prêtre de Nemi*, a philosophical drama (germ of *Golden Bough*).
1886 — Proposes to Macmillan a selection of Heine's poetry in German, with linguistic and literary background.
1887 — "Questions on the Manners, Customs, . . ." (fieldwork survey manual).
1888 — "The Language of Animals," with epigraph from Heine.
1889 — Reads late-seventeenth-century account of ritual killing of king on India's Malabar coast.
— Writes Macmillan about work on legend of the Golden Bough.
1890 — *The Golden Bough* (2 vols.); travels to Greece.
1894—William Robertson Smith dies.
1895 — Fellowship tenable for life, Cambridge; again to Greece.
1896 — Marries widow Lilly Grove, née Adelsdorfer (Alsatian).
1898 — Publishes Pausanias translation and commentary.
1900 — *The Golden Bough*, 2nd ed. (3 vols.)
— ". . .Origin of Gender in Language," nondogmatic theory.
1911 — *The Golden Bough*, 3rd. ed. (12 vols.).
1936 — *The Golden Bough*, aftermath added.
1941 — Blind Sir James dies; deaf Lady Lilly follows suit within hours—perhaps a *kalos thanatos* ("good death"), perhaps not.[13]

Excuses

James George Frazer, whom generations of ethnographers dismissed as a "non-fieldworker," had actually planned research in New Guinea (fell through). Frazer resourcefully backed John Roscoe's efforts in Uganda and indefatigably encouraged fin-de-siècle fieldworkers in Australia (Lorimer Fison, Sir Baldwin Spencer, Francis James Gillen, etc.) whose researches "founded" anthropology as we know it, or used to. Less sedentary than generally supposed, Frazer himself came out (of his armchair) for excursions to Greece—in 1890 and again in 1895. On neither a splurge nor merely a spree, Frazer possibly resorted to travel-research to recuperate from proofing *The Golden Bough* in 1890, and then to assuage the furtively felt loss of William Robertson Smith, who died in 1894.[14]

Officially, Frazer was drawn thither by Pausanias's second-century C.E. *Description of Greece*—the fullest evidence history retains of antiquity's ritual locales. Frazer resolved to retranslate this vital source, despite its (to him) stylistically perfunctory sentences: "Devoid of rhythm and harmony, . . . they do not march but hobble and shamble and shuffle along. . . . The reader is not let down easily by a graceful cadence, a dying fall; he is tripped up suddenly and left sprawling."[15]

Ultimately Frazer produced a kind of *Pausanias*-cum-*anti-Pausanias*: both faithfully "Englished" (for substance) and freshened with eloquence (for effect). Converting flat depictions into rounded prose, Frazer also updated them with later findings (archaeological, literary) meticulously assessed. His immense commentary remains valued today by expert folks—"classicists"—whose business it is to know.[16]

Frazer's Passagen *(an Interruption)*

Our hero's journeys Greece-ward could be compared with those of near contemporaries—Oscar Wilde or Herman Melville, say, picking luminaries at random. Doubtless complex "motives" (per Kenneth Burke) prevailed and still prevail "of and for" (per Clifford Geertz) any philhellenism; that of Frazer deserves construing alongside Nietzsche's, say, or other cases considered by Richard Jenkyns.[17] That worthy project could easily interrupt the one I am pursuing here. Equally distracting are eerie parallels between Frazer and a critic whose interdisciplinary prominence has swelled as much as Frazer's has dwindled. They share a time of death (1940–1941)—Frazer aged and by natural causes; the other one fortyish and by his own hand. Both souls, moreover, based vast projects on Pausanias, or ironic transpositions of his example. (Mystery guest, will you sign in please.)

> [Walter] Benjamin's work on the "mythological topography" of Paris was closely modeled on Pausanias's *Guide to Greece*; he reasoned that like the ancient traveler who "wrote his topography of Greece in the second century A.D. as the places of worship and many of the other monuments began to fall into ruin," so, too, should the modern historian decipher and invoke in the "ruins" of modernity their ancient mythologies. His fascination with the arcades, "being the galleries, which lead into its past existence," was intensified by the sensation that they functioned like the ancient labyrinths that Pausanias had entered. They transferred their visitors from the real world of the street into the "*Passagen* myth."[18]

More precisely, Benjamin had emulated Johann Jacob Bachofen, whom he deemed a "modern Pausanias, a fellow-traveler who actually revisited those 'sites in ancient Greece from which one could go down into the underworld'"[19] Had Benjamin jolted his critical apparatus a few decades further along history's storms, prophecy's winds, and chronology's winks (i.e., reversals), he could have tagged a still more "modern Pausanias." Frazer, I submit, represents something like (1) a slightly later Bachofen (both retranslated Pausanias, Frazer correcting Bachofen's version) and (2) a somewhat earlier Benjamin. Indeed, Benjamin's imaginative rummaging among modernity's "ruins" (via literatures) explicitly recalled the "ancient labyrinths that Pausanias had entered." The same is true of Frazer's spirited sallying among primitivity's "ruins" (via ethnographies).

Yet like Bachofen, Frazer had gone Benjamin one better—had gone so far as to retrace Pausanias's footsteps. Indeed, "being there" (Greece), Frazer tackled "the task of translating" *topoi*—including a renowned one from Pausanias's account of Piraeus that subsequently haunted Benjamin: "Thus the arsenal closely resembled what we should call an arcade, except that the sides were occupied by store-rooms instead of shops."[20] Yes, Bachofen's tombs, Frazer's tomes, and Benjamin's arcades (*Passagen*) are all tied to Pausanias and therefore to each other. Such intricate affinities signal (to me) endless ironies of transhistorical cross-cultural rereading; suggesting so, I also echo Michael Bernstein's cautions against easy parallels between Benjamin and contemporary critical sensibilities:

> Benjamin has frequently been claimed as the inspired predecessor of today's leveling eclecticism, but the impassioned heterogeneity of his approach is very far from the casual irony and unproblematic shuttling among

different eras and models that we think of as "postmodernist." The postmodernist catalogue is seen from the outset as temporary and easily abandoned. Benjamin's, by contrast, is fiercely cumulative and impossible to discard. And this loyalty to all that has been abandoned as worthless, to everything whose loss has not been acknowledged or registered, is Benjamin's abiding legacy.[21]

Abiding too was the "catalogue rhetoric" of Frazer, possibly worth partnering with Boasian readings and comparative writings by authors with kindred affinities (Henry David Thoreau, Melville, and more).[22]

Frazer's Jouissance ("Ivresse en Grèce"): A Resumption

For now let us set aside labyrinths, "arcades," and arsenals to wonder whether Francophile Frazer found bliss in scholarly labors of the hive—such as upgrading Pausanias's dull-as-doorknobs diction.[23] I presume he did, because Frazer confessed as much—albeit in formulaic French, veiled to please readers thereof. His *préface* to *L'Adonis*—in 1921—extracted from *Le Cycle du Rameau d'Or* and translated by his wife Lilly Frazer (*une française*)—deserves quoting at "Frazerian" length. (I "English" it here unroundly, so better to cue snatches of French in my commentary juxtaposed.) *Voici alors*, Frazer—tellingly back-translated:

> This new translation thus debuts smack in the middle of the original work. Why? Because I want [*désire*] to plunge the French reader into the thick of things and not subject him to prolixity [*longueurs*] of an introduction that might well alarm him. In fact, I have tried to seduce him by offering at the outset what would most interest him ... three oriental divinities—Adonis, Attis, and Osiris. In tracing [*retraçant*] the origin of rites, whose aim is to reanimate nature and dress [*revêtir*] her annually in a new cloak of green, one is forced to stray for a while in a gloomy labyrinth [*s'égarer longtemps dans un sombre labyrinthe*] of customs and ideas that are raw, ill formed, and wild. Only after having seen paraded past a crowd of frightful phantoms does the reader experience soothing encounters with gracious figures of these antique deities created by a more refined imagination and profounder sympathy.... The eternal charm of such creations of a fantasy already ripe [*déjà mûr*] and a philosophy still wary [*encore hésitante*] is heightened by the splendor of the landscapes that contain the stories of gods simultaneously mortal and immortal—who died every year with the falling leaves, flowers, and grains, so to live again [*revivre*] in nature's annual renewal. I tried to

depict several such lovely scenes consecrated by the genius of ancient authors and artists, following descriptions of modern travelers who visited these places; for, unhappily, although I have voyaged with delight and, so to speak, intoxication in Greece [*pour ainsi dire ivresse, en Grèce*]—this region of infinite enchantment—I have never visited the Orient, or even glimpsed from afar its coasts and ranges. Nevertheless, having carefully studied and compared what other witnesses more fortunate than I have written about these celebrated shores, it feels as though I myself traversed with them the lands they let us see; cast my own eye on the river reddened with Adonis's blood running in the depths of its ravishing valley; admired . . . cascades of Hierapolis sparkling in the distant sun and dappled in every color of the rainbow; explored the deep *caverne corycienne* yawning abruptly in the stony plateau with all the opulence and freshness of evergreen vegetation. And I believed I heard with my own ears the dreamy lulling murmur of subterranean waters. If I linger overmuch in these landscapes filled with charm, I hope the reader will forgive me and consider such delays as rest stops on a lengthy voyage.[24]

Observe with me, readers, how Frazer's effusive salute to Greece punctuates digressive apologies for never having visited the Orient "proper." Some Scotsman! (That Frazer seldom stuck to the point.) Some rationalist! (Old Frazer always rambled, never navigated a straight line.) Some scholar! (Cagey Frazer, abetted by the missus, repackaged his Augean labors for Gallic tastes.) One might even call them—eventually Sir, and Lady alike—"experimental" in their promotional tactics and textual praxis.

Places (e.g., Greece) Temporally Translated (with Parerga)

Frazer's currying of French favor illuminates his way of writing-for-readers; it may pay to dwell a spell on such solicitous prose. Having "been where," after all, *some* relevant evidence existed, Frazer nonetheless never quite claims even indirect authority. Rather, travels to Greece help him imagine "being elsewhere"—whose *autres témoins* he can therefore compare, and studiously. Frazer recalls his travel-experience (or really, his translating prior travels in Greece by traveling in Greece) to help convey an *Orient* his own eyes cannot attest. And he grafts allusions to his *Pausanias* adventures on French versions of shoots (all these floral jokes are old: recycled) of *The Golden Bough*—which sprang from the Pausanias project, or interrupted it. Probably Frazer's two principal endeavors were more like *parerga*—each to each.

(*Parergon.* "*Parerga*"—*a term I first failed to understand in Arthur Schopenhauer's* Parerga and Paralipomena—*is a keyword in Neni Panourgiá's own* "*description of Greece*," Fragments of Death, Fables of Identity. *Parergon means an effort lying alongside another: a digression, an interruption even; multiple* parerga *could be called labyrinthine. This paragraph is a* parergon *on* parerga: *a* meta-parergon. *I'll get back to substantive* parerga, *and to Panourgiá, later.*)²⁵

Judging from Frazer's French, its well-read writer wanted readers (like voyagers) to savor *lieux* (and *milieux*). Frazer conjured "place" as it might, "being there," be seen *and* heard: "*je crois avoir entendu de mes oreilles le murmure rêveur.*" All Frazer's writing (in English, too) conveyed *polysensoria* of place-names, or "noms-de-pays: le pays," as Marcel Proust might have said. (Proust, by the way, learned to say, or write, such things [in French] by *translating* John Ruskin's English: *c'est une longue histoire!*)²⁶ Frazer's translations, plus cobbled commentary, convey spatial sensoria ("place"): something about the light, the *parfum*, the *fraîcheur de sa vegetation* (aroma? felt moisture?)—that possibly perdures "across" time (note the spatial metaphor!).

Temporal chains of translation thus *carry across* Pausanias's descriptions into Frazer's fin-de-siècle "sites." Now, Pausanias himself had translated into his second century C.E. evidence from antique Attica and from 500 B.C.E. *Péloponnèse*. And Frazer's translations (published in 1898) of that translation subsequently carry across into memories of his prior travel-translations—memories earmarked in French on 23 *juillet*, 1921.

(*Parergon. Nor was that the end of it: Frazer's 1921 remembrance of 1890s experience—retranslating Pausanias's translations [themselves spanning centuries]—was borne ["carried* back *across"] by me, from of all "places" New Jersey, to a conference at Syros in 1999, squeaking in at millennium's end. That occasion was my "excuse" [pretext, "motive"] for Greece-going in these cycling "chronotopes."*)²⁷

But why do I (or my *parerga*) rehash and belabor exponential re-travel-translation? Only because an interpretive pursuit dubbed "anthropology"—diverse *tradition* variously invented and inventive—still entails rereading cultural rites-in-sites. This endeavor may merit intensified recognizing, interrupting, and resuming.

(*Parergon. Hence I hope to tie understanding Frazer not just to Pausanias-then but to Panourgiá-today, to experience his anthropological aftermaths otherwise.*)

As for Frazer, one wonders. Could he, launching his *Lebenswerk*, already have been bent on recapturing over time and space "place" (itself a *topos*)?

Was he pre-attuned to *mi/lieux*, in and as polysensoria-for-readers? *Peut-être*. Regardless, Frazer-in-French (in 1921) kept oscillating between his *Golden Bough* and his *Pausanias*, long after the latter was finalized in 1898, possibly because the former, now overshadowing everything, required renewal of its "MacGuffin"—as Alfred Hitchcock (a still tardier "Victorian" than Frazer, coincidentally born within a year of Frazer's publishing his *Pausanias*) might have remarked.[28]

(Parergon. "MacGuffin" *[the name, like Frazer's, is Scots] is Hitch's celebrated designation of drummed-up pretexts for dazzlingly polysensory assemblages in hybrid arts of narrative film.*[29] Although The Golden Bough *germinated before movies existed, it too sports a MacGuffin [dummy-motive]: the ritual slaying of the priest-king and ex-slave of Nemi [locus: Italia—on which more anon].*)

Frazer's *Pausanias* required no MacGuffin—no *contrived* excuse for strung-along extravagance—because Pausanias really did witness Greece; and Frazer really did retranslate his work and adumbrate archaeological knowledge (largely German) gathered in Pausanias's long aftermath, or wake.[30] (*Plus que Parergon. The German for "after" means "ass"—an important pun in Nietzsche's cases of caustic critique; but that too is another interpretive his-story.*) *The Golden Bough*, I suspect, was less either "mystery" (per Stocking) or "whodunit" (per R. Fraser)—both appealing propositions—than "suspense": the name of the genre *motivated* (in K. Burke's sense) by a *MacGuffin* (in Hitchcock's sense).[31] Detective work on this possibility could yield an alternative aftermath to this essay: a postponed *encore plus que parergon*—which, come to think of it, may be precisely what Frazer's *Golden Bough* and his *Pausanias* reciprocally became, increasingly. Frazer's works, like cultures' histories, kept interrupting themselves and each other. That cyclic quality may explain some scholars' attraction to his still-translating corpus.[32]

Plus que Pausanias

In the meantime, patient readers deserve reminding that Frazer's *Pausanias* scrupulously certified antique Greek sites-for-rites. And his *Golden Bough* inventively imagined one ancient Italian site-cum-rites—(those slayings at Nemi)—that Frazer could not exactly have "translated," because no direct account existed. Still, that same Pausanias professed to having seen what became comparative anthropology's scene-of-scenes: "Pausanias states that the hand-to-hand duel between the priest[-king] and his [slave] successor was held 'in my time'"; and he remains to this day "the only commentator to imply having witnessed the contest."[33]

This business of Nemi as memory-place is wondrously entangled; R. Fraser calls it a "veritable collector's gallery of such fables as Pausanias had found littering the minds of the Peloponnesian Greeks." Manifold "sub-cults" attributed to Nemi include (1) the refuge there of Orestes in the aftermath of killing Clytemnestra and (2) the "translation of the resuscitated Hippolytus" (i.e., his rematerialization there after father Theseus cursed him to die in the aftermath of the episode with Phaedra [Theseus's wife] who was smitten by her stepson [Hippolytus]).[34] All such legendary knots deserve *parerga*, if that is the apt term. Nothing in Pausanias or his own aftermaths (Frazer, Bachofen, Benjamin, Panourgiá, this traveler) is other than digressive!

Indeed, Frazer's introduction to *Pausanias* mentions abundant allusions his predecessor "lets fall to places and objects of interest in foreign lands"; one key *Passage* (arcade?) is flagged by Frazer as follows: "In the neighborhood of Rome the bubbling milk-white water of Albula . . . attracted his attention, and beside the sylvan lake of Aricia he appears to have seen the grim priest pacing sword in hand, the warder of the Golden Bough."[35] Yet, perhaps nervously, Frazer's next sentence questions the reliability of Pausanias's similar allusion: "The absurd description he gives of the beautiful and much-maligned Strait of Messina would suffice to prove that he never sailed through it." Ambiguity was something Frazer apparently tolerated to a remarkable extent. Nor, ironically, did he ever abandon primary sources of inspiration because of it. Some Victorian!

Further Resumptions (Still Saluting Kenneth Burke)

There is nothing whatsoever *new* in my insisting that Frazer was more, much more, than a non-fieldworker; he was in fact a hardworking, place-inscribing traveling-translator. One prior "appreciation" of Frazer merits copious quotation (in Benjamin's fashion):

> In 1898 Frazer published a masterpiece of scholarship, his six-volume edition of Pausanias's *Description of Greece*. . . . Frazer reprinted the introduction and selections from his commentary as *Pausanias and Other Greek Sketches* in 1900 [the year, I might mention, of Nietzsche's and Wilde's deaths and of the publication of Freud's *Traumdeutung*], and reprinted it again as *Studies in Greek Scenery, Legend, and History* in 1917. This little book is not so much a commentary on Pausanias as Frazer's own guidebook to Greece. . . .

The dominant imaginative organization of *Pausanias and Other Greek Sketches* is what Kenneth Burke would call the scene-act ratio, similarly the imaginative core of *The Golden Bough* (Pausanias had *seen* [or wrote that he had, which claim Frazer reported in his *Pausanias*] the grim priest in his sacred grove at Aricia!).... Certain scenes at certain times have fitnesses for certain acts: "It was when the sunset glow was on Humettus that Socrates drained the poisoned cup"; "the scene, if it indeed be so" of the sacrifice of Iphigenia at Aulis "was somewhat bleak and cheerless as I saw it under a leaden sky on a dull November afternoon."... The imaginative reconstruction [in striking distinction to Pausanias's own imaginative reconstruction] of the performance of the mysteries in describing the great Hall of Initiation at Eleusis is typical: "Suddenly the curtain rose and revealed the vast hall brilliantly illuminated, with the gorgeously attired actors in the sacred drama moving mazily in solemn procession or giddy dance out and in amongst the forest of columns that rose from the floor..., while the strains of grave or voluptuous music filled the air...." If Frazer's vision seems to have more in common with the Radio City Music Hall than with anything that could have transpired at Eleusis, it is nevertheless an equivalent for him of the initiatory experience.[36]

Inspired largely by K. Burke's approach to ritual-rhetoric, Hyman's insights nevertheless err (as Burke, I feel, might have agreed) by slighting imaginable analogies between ancient rites and Radio City.[37] Should one glibly discount this possibility? After all, what conceivably "could have transpired at Eleusis" surely surpassed the "esoteric." Indeed, Frazer himself imagined broadly everyday publics in page upon page directed at rites and festivals of Demeter and Persephone:

> On the whole then, if, ignoring theories, we adhere to the evidence of the ancients themselves in regard to the rites of Eleusis, including under that general term the Great Mysteries, the games, the Festival before Ploughing (*proerosia*), the Festival of the Threshing floor, the Green Festival, the Festival of the Cornstalks, and the offerings of first-fruits, we shall probably incline to agree with the most learned of ancient antiquaries, the Roman Varro, who, to quote Augustine's report of his opinion, "interpreted the whole of the Eleusinian mysteries as relating to the corn which Ceres (Demeter) had discovered, and to Proserpine (Persephone) whom Pluto had carried off from her.

With customary, ecumenical intertextuality, Frazer continued:

> Drowning men clutch at straws, and we need not wonder that the Greeks, like ourselves, with death before them and a great love of life in their hearts,

should not have stopped to weigh with too nice a hand the arguments that told for and against the prospect of human immortality. The reasoning that satisfied Saint Paul and . . . sorrowing Christians, standing by the deathbed or the open grave of their loved ones, was good enough to pass muster with ancient pagans, when they too bowed their heads under the burden of grief, and . . . looked forward into the darkness of the unknown. Therefore we do no indignity to the myth of Demeter and Persephone—one of the few myths in which the sunshine and clarity of the Greek genius are crossed by the shadow and mystery of death—when we trace its origin to some of the most familiar, yet eternally affecting aspects of nature, to the melancholy gloom and decay of autumn and to the freshness, the brightness and the verdure of spring.[38]

A plausible hunch is that Eleusis was in part "popular." Conceivably, I would add, no "music hall" (even Rockette-bedizened Radio City), is altogether un-mystery-ous![39]

(*Cancelled Parergon.* Resist *digressing into Hitchcock's "Mr. Memory," his music hall MacGuffin. Silence, Mnemosyne. Forget* The 39 Steps*!*)

Echoes of Excuses and Resonances of Resumptions

Ackerman's biography speculates that Frazer's blend of ethnology and travel-translation had a real beginning—a "cause," perhaps a "birth":

> The intervention of [Robertson] Smith changed Frazer's ideas about Pausanias . . . and led to *The Golden Bough*. . . . By 1885 . . . Frazer had found his subject. . . . Others, most notably [Edward] Tylor and Andrew Lang, had anticipated him here. Frazer's special contribution lay in the use he made of his deep and wide knowledge of classical antiquity, which permitted him to extend greatly the field of comparison. No one had ever before focused so intensively on the "primitive" elements of the religions of Greece, Rome, and the eastern Mediterranean and had juxtaposed these on so large a scale with the religious activity of "savages" (as Frazer and his contemporaries often called preliterate peoples). Frazer seems to have understood early on—in the mid-eighties, while working on Pausanias—that he had lighted upon something unusual and important, and once he did, he never looked back.[40]

This attempt to state facts plainly is admirable; but it is also a fact that Frazerian facts (and facts about Frazer) remain profusely gnarled. Evidentiary intricacy, basic to comparative interpretation, deserves rereading

Birth of Anthropology Out of a Pause on Pausanias 65

"toward the panoply"; Frazer's panoply included "Greece" (not to mention Bali), repeatedly reinterpreted as different eras emerged.⁴¹

So let's review. Frazer first planned "simply" to retranslate-with-commentary Pausanias. He eventually achieved this goal to an extent even his seasoned publisher had failed to foresee: six tomes! The project, Ackerman nicely remarks, wound up consuming "nine and a half years—the length of the siege of Troy"; yes, plans (including successful ones), as they (nearly) say, "ging aft aw'ry."⁴² And Frazer's plans—his Heracles-ian methodicalness and obsessive scholarship notwithstanding—constantly went thataway. With this aspect of Sir James, many readers today—modernist, postmodernist, belatedly either, or post-both—might sympathize.

It is a fetching fact that one of anthropology's touchstone texts, *The Golden Bough*—which helped spawn the writings of Edward Westermarck, Malinowski (a Nietzsche reader too), and more—sprouted (fructified, "rhizomed") in the crotches, as it were, of a *Pausanias* project.⁴³ Yes, the *Geburtz*, if birth it be, of "social anthropology"—whose first professional chair in the world's then-global empire fell officially to Frazer (in 1908, the very year Claude Lévi-Strauss was born)—was induced by interludes (*parerga*) that swelled into a dominant opus. Frazer's hybrid learning, moreover, is manifest not just in *The Golden Bough* but in far tidier items of his bibliography. Examples are (1) "The Language of Animals," a folkloric study that crisscrossed "levels" of civilization and primitivity, yet downplayed that invidious distinction, and (2) "Gender in Language," an evolution-questioning essay with a nondogmatic disclaimer: "How the change from subjective gender to what may be called objective gender took place, if it took place at all, we can only conjecture."⁴⁴ But what might Frazer's transdisciplinary bravado imply *nowadays* for meaning-in-cultures (and meanings-in-death)? Does its unfashionable rotundity preclude any role for his corpus in reasserting comparative anthropology's rightful *place* alongside alternative modes of critical interpretation?

Wondering, I here launch a few "reading navigations" from my little excursion into Frazer's *Grèce* and further.⁴⁵ These skirmishes (which begin to feel as though they portend volumes) are offered as installments on fuller Frazerian "fables." First, I sample smidgens of his *Pausanias*, where documentary data manifestly beget imaginative fling. (The same, I claim, goes for *The Golden Bough*, but in a more riddled way.) Second, I snip sizable slices from his ethnographic assemblages on cross-dressing. Out of the intersensory "force" of Frazer's style, I suggest, its "form evolved"—like a leaf (my metaphor is Goethean).⁴⁶ Nor, I take pains to insist, did Sir James altogether neglect Bali (my own fieldwork area).

(*Parergon. Resolved to emulate Frazer's* Britannica *assignments given by Robertson Smith, I employ the same slice of alphabet ("P" and "T"). Despite this radical restraint, or ascesis, I half hope [like Frazer or Bachofen or Benjamin] to squeeze everything in.*)

Fragment "P": Pausanias

Frazer cultivated an ethic and aesthetic of comparative description less "thick" than lumpy, sensate, and elegiac-yet-ironic.[47] Ackerman ties Frazer's characteristically contrarian opinions to a stylistic tic: "Having begun by denying the authoritativeness of his authorities, [Frazer] proceeds to enforce his ironic position through a number of rhetorical devices. One of his favorites is the strategically placed modifier (e.g., 'The Circassians will tell stories to a sick man, while banging with a hammer on a ploughshare which has been *thoughtfully* placed by the sick man's bed.')."[48]

Another literary commentator, R. Fraser, forcefully denies any superficiality to this rhetorical turn: "The method by which Frazer achieved such refraction of matter into sensibility is his style, which has often been misunderstood. Ackerman . . . refers to it somewhat dismissively as 'literary' without realizing that its literariness is part of the point." For Frazer, Fraser adds, "all discourse was a form of literature, and literature itself no badge of shame even for (perhaps especially for) the would-be empiricist."[49] Indeed in 1982, I used Hyman's similar point to unsettle presumed literary-ethnographic divides in other anthropologist-authors as well.[50] But that was "then-s"; and this is "now-s."

Overlapped intertwining of Frazer's *Pausanias* and *Golden Bough* may help clarify his descriptive sensibilities. To put complex matters in an acorn, Frazer wed (1) positivistic compulsion for empirical compilation with (2) artistic convictions that only imagined flings can inhabit (or become inhabited by) intersensory experience. One could call Frazer's partner-side "Paterian," if only to credit his aestheticist flair when zooming in on clusters of cultural practice.[51] Frazer's alloyed attitude—hard-nosed evidence married to empathetic fancy—is patent in his *Pausanias*'s opening in Piraeus, whose arsenal-arcade (readers may recall) I cited above. Return with me now to that short phrase—"there were ship-sheds there down to my time"—as we scrutinize Frazer's appended commentary: seven packed pages (forty-nine lines each) adjudicating evidentiary disputes:

> Mr. Kalkmann [in *Pausanias der Perieget*] concludes that Pausanias cannot be describing Piraeus as it was in his own time, but must have copied his

Birth of Anthropology Out of a Pause on Pausanias 67

description of it from an old book or books which depicted Piraeus as it had been in happier days before the Roman sack. But between the time of Strabo and the time of Pausanias a century and a half elapsed, during which Greece enjoyed profound peace and basked in the sunshine of imperial favor. It is rash to assume that during this long period Piraeus remained in precisely the same state of ruin and desolation to which it had been reduced by Sulla's sack more than two hundred years before.[52]

No strata of data are neglected: "The colossal statue of a Roman emperor (Claudius?) and a good bust of Augustus have also been found at Piraeus, attesting to some extent the returning prosperity of the port. . . . Extensive remains of Roman baths were brought to light by excavation close to the harbor of Zea in 1892 . . . actually built over the remains of some of the ancient ship-sheds."[53]

Only after two hundred lines of compressed detail does Frazer finally indulge in a comparative aside, *Golden Bough* fashion:

> The only remains of ancient ships which have been found at Zea are some plates of Parian marble representing great eyes. Pollux tells us . . . that the ship's name was painted beside its eye. Philostratus describes the picture of an Etruscan pirate ship painted blue with fierce eyes at the prow to frighten the enemy. . . . Modern Italian sailors sometimes still paint an eye on the bow. . . . Every craft owned by a Chinaman, from a sampan up to an English-built screw steamer, has a pair of eyes painted on its bows, that it may see its way and spy out sunken rocks, shoals, and other dangers of the deep.[54]

That duly noted, Frazer snaps back to the site at hand; he interpolates every intercolumniation conceivably stretching from antiquity to Pausanias's day, down to the sails and canvas gear and slit-like openings "lest the tackle should suffer from damp." Frazer cinches things with uncustomary crispness: "Such was, in outline, the great arsenal of the Piraeus."[55]

Commentary, however, is far from done. With no change of paragraph, Frazer shifts gears into glaring verbiage—conspicuously archaizing (even in 1898). I do not exaggerate how his rhetoric struts its switched registers, jolting readers into the transtemporal scene. To capture Frazer's literary "special effect," behold the full *Passage*: "Such was, in outline, the great arsenal of the Piraeus. *Thither on the burning days of summer, one may suppose,* crowds were glad to escape from the blinding glare and stifling heat of the streets, and to promenade in the cool, lofty, and dimly lighted arcade, often stopping to gaze with idle curiosity or patriotic pride at the long array of well-ordered tackle which spoke of the naval supremacy of

Athens."⁵⁶ This shuddering metamorphosis from circumstantial minutiae to illusions of "being there" (earmarked "one may suppose") is followed by mid-page annotations for all seven pages, plus one last paragraph of text intimately conjoining empirical fact and fancy.

Conjoined as well are traveling *temps* (two of them): Frazer's time of translation ("we may notice") and Pausanias's time of descriptive evocation ("It must have been a heart-stirring sight"):

> Lastly, before quitting the war-harbors of Athens, we may notice the *Choma*, a quay near the mouth of the harbor on which, when an armament was fitting out for sea, the Council of the Five Hundred held their sitting daily till the squadron sailed. When all was ready, every captain was bound by law to lay his vessel alongside the quay to be inspected by the Council. The inspection over, the fleet weighed anchor and proceeded on its voyage. It must have been a heart-stirring sight to witness the departure of a fleet for the seat of war, as gallant ship after ship passed, in long procession, through the mouth of the harbor and stood out to sea, followed by the gazing eyes and by the hopes and fears and prayers of thousands assembled on the shore.⁵⁷

Frazer's "interpretive ethic," as I deem it, crafted duple modalities from assorted scholarships routinely separated since. His virtuoso prowess—accumulating diverse testimony (material, mythological, ethnographic, literary, biblical)—earns, or wins, him the reward, or prize, of convergent aesthetic effect. Frazer therewith grants readers, or bestows on us, the vantage of (in this case) an antique Greek eye (gaze?), nose, ear, and tongue.

By such devices dumb data were made by Frazer to *speak*, so to speak. Yet even in his exponentially archaeology-based *Pausanias* commentary, Frazer's introduction observes that this long-ago traveling expert witness was himself double-voiced—as were those Greeks inhabiting *places* Pausanias inscribed. Thus, from far away and far before, Frazer indeed "translates" duplicitous *anthropoi*. Throughout those *temps perdus*, the natives now interpreted were interpreters too—and possibly ironic as well, in their fashion. Frazer fosters this impression playfully when depicting paintings, themselves representations, that Pausanias had described (represented) along with a "fragment from the comedy of *The Painter* by Diphilus" that portrayed "the long-shore sharks" (figurative ones) "who lay in wait on the quays of Piraeus": "For in the passage in question one of the fraternity tells us how, whenever he spied a jolly tar just stepping ashore, ready for a spree, with a bulging purse and an expansive smile on his sun-burnt face,

Birth of Anthropology Out of a Pause on Pausanias   69

he used to rush up to him, shake him warmly by the hand, drop a delicate allusion to Savior Zeus, and proffer his services at the sacrifice. The bait took, and soon he was to be seen heading for the sanctuary with the sailor man in tow."[58]

Readers, believe me (a more recent traveler than Diphilus, or Frazer), Piraeus, if only in this respect, hasn't changed much: hood*winkers* still abound, as do be-duped "believers" (and possibly "thick describers"). And an "arcade," bulging purses and all, the *place* called Piraeus certainly remains![59]

Fragment "T": The Golden Bough

Again, Frazer's lattice-like *oeuvre* interweaves empirical givens (data) with fact-derived fanciful flings. His detractors like to spread rumors that decades of augmenting the *Bough* merely compensated for absent documentation of the Nemi episodes "ringing" his madcap excursion. Such views have reinforced disciplinary divides of empirical and interpretive from Frazer's day to ours.

With more room, smaller print, or thinner paper—all means Frazer himself urged on publishers to accommodate expansions—I could augment my efforts to quash anew such fruitless divisiveness. Yes, I might then track Nemi's ritual-slaying (Frazer's "MacGuffin") to other *parerga* within the *"cycle de la ramée d'or,"*[60] including (1) its Balder component—anticipated in Walter Pater's "Duke Carl of Rosenmold" of 1887[61]—and (2) its handling of Hippolytus and Phaedra, cued to Frazer's translation of Ovid's *Fasti*.[62] His commentary there offers fresh glosses on that legendary twig plucked by Aeneas "and carried with him as a sort of passport on his journey to the world of the dead." Frazer also foregrounds a Phaedra-factor ("notus amor Phaedrae, nota est iniuria Thesei")—artfully encapsulating truly tangled affairs that are but briefly attested in his *Pausanias*: "Phaedra, wife of Theseus, made advances to his son Hippolytus, which were repulsed. She accused him of having made advances to her, and [Theseus] prayed to his father Poseidon, to punish Hippolytus. Poseidon sent a bull out of the sea to frighten Hippolytus's horses, and the young man was killed."[63]

Ovid elaborates on Euripides by conveying the deceased to Nemi: "Hippolytus fell from the car, and, his limbs entangled by the reins, his mangled body was whirled along, till he gave up the ghost, much to Dianna's rage. . . . Thrice [Aesculapius] touched the youth's breast, thrice he spoke healing words; then Hippolytus lifted his head, low laid upon the ground. He found a hiding-place in a sacred grove and in the depths of Dictynna's own woodland; he became Virbius of the Arician Lake."[64]

This passage underscores how Nemi became for Frazer more than a "survival" in Tylor's sense; rather it represented, legendarily, a gathering place for transtemporal aftermaths of ritual deaths. (To that rhythm of "works and lives" my essay is paying homage.) All roads, times, and resurrections lead to Rome's nearby Arician grove, where translation grows rooted: radical.

Despite my "plan" to defer resuming Frazer's rememorializing of Nemi, readers here are not altogether spared. A similar "sacrificial" ordeal (or opportunity) awaited "wayfarers" venturing into Frazer's mazeways—his labyrinth, as he finally deemed it in *The Golden Bough*'s literal *aftermath*: "At the best the chronicle may serve as a warning, as a sort of Ariadne's thread, to help the forlorn wayfarer to shun some of the snares and pitfalls into which his fellows have fallen before him in the labyrinth of life."[65] That metaphor makes every reader a "Theseus" (*père d'Hippolyte, mari de Phèdre*)—led by the thread of Frazer's prose through tome upon tome saturated with evidence *and* licensed to imagine.

Consider just volume 5 (*Adonis, Attis, Osiris*), with its copious coverage of transvestism and gender ambiguity—topics as alive today as Frazer himself is dead.[66] One relevant section, "Some Customs of the Pelew Islanders" (with thematic subtitles, "Priests Dressed as Women," "Prostitution of Unmarried Girls," etc.) opens by encapsulating J. Kubary's *Die Religion der Pelauer*. From Borneo and Sarawak, it travels over space and time, winding back to Greece, with occasional rest stops: as-if being-theres. The trajectory passes through sundry sources (most strikingly, Lucianic satires), eventually digressing on genital croppings. Let's read!

Frazer guides our "book voyages" with synoptic cues in their margins (a device of English-language comparative compendia at least since *Purchas His Pilgrimes* in 1625).[67] He begins steering us thusly: "In the Pelew Islands a man who is inspired by a goddess wears female attire and is treated as a woman. This . . . may explain a widespread custom whereby men dress and live like women."[68]

Pages range far and wide—Patagonians, "vagabond conjurors" of Rambree, the Vallabha sect—but remain tethered to points of departure: "Among the Ibans or Sea Dyaks of Borneo the highest class of sorcerers or medicine-men (*manangs*) are those who are believed to have been transformed into women. Such a man is therefore called a 'changed medicine-man' (*manang bali*) on account of his supposed change of sex."[69]

This focal case launches another distant leap as far as Northeast Asian shamans, some of whom "become a woman with the appearance of a man, and as a woman he is often taken to wife by another man, with whom he leads a regular married life. Extraordinary powers are attributed to such transformed shamans.... They excel in all branches of magic, including ventriloquism."[70] "Conversely," Frazer notes, "a woman inspired by a god may adopt male costume"—a switch he instantiates with Uganda. We pass to classical enactments of "the theory of inspiration by a female spirit" entailing an "assumed change of sex under the inspiration of a goddess." Variegated evidence consolidates around imitations of Hercules "who disguised himself as a woman to escape the pursuit of his enemies":

> So the Lydian Hercules wore female attire ... as the purchased slave of the imperious Omphale, Queen of Lydia. If we suppose that Queen Omphale, like Queen Semiramis, was nothing but the great Asiatic goddess, or one of her Avatars, it becomes probable that the story of the womanish Hercules of Lydia preserves a reminiscence of a line or college of effeminate priests who, like the eunuch priests of the Syrian goddess, dressed as women in imitation.... Similarly at the vernal mysteries of Hercules in Rome the men were draped in the garments of women; and in some of the rites and processions of Dionysus also men wore female attire.[71]

Frazer advises against assuming that one solution applies to all cases of an "obscure and complex problem": "the religious or superstitious interchange of dress between men and women."

His survey next sketches shifting correlations between transvestism and other customs—for example, circumcision: "Among the Nandi, a tribe of British East Africa, before boys are circumcised they receive a visit from young girls, who give them some of their own garments and ornaments. These the boys put on and wear till the operation of circumcision is over, when they exchange the girls' clothes for the garments of women ... [which] the newly circumcised lads must continue to wear for months afterwards."[72] Such matters, Frazer shows, can be reciprocal by gender: "Girls are also circumcised among the Nandi, and before they submit to the operation they attire themselves in men's garments and carry clubs in their hands." These practices are "intended to disguise the wearers against demons"—an idea that points toward certain usages surrounding not genital croppings (circumcision) but life's cropping (death): "We may compare the practice of the Lycian men who regularly wore women's dress in mourning, for this might be intended to conceal them from the ghost, just as ... some peoples of antiquity used to descend into pits and remain there

... whenever a death had taken place in the family."⁷³ Yet other connections, again reciprocal, grace a Sumatran tribe: "If parents have several sons and desire the next child shall be a girl, they dress the boys as girls. ... On the contrary, when they have many daughters ..., they dress the girls up as boys."

Frazer reiterates that no single explanation suffices; he rejects his own conjecture in *Totemism and Exogamy* "that the wearing of female attire by the bridegroom ... may mark a transition from mother-kin to father-kin." Transvestism, then, attaches to "a variety" of motives, a "principal" one of which gathers force over his pages: "the wish to please certain powerful spirits or to deceive others."⁷⁴

The pervasive theme of fooling spirits may be *The Golden Bough*'s descriptive *Grund*, virtually. Abundant ethnographies adumbrate this topic, and Frazer's distillations of them seem his most assured. Let me cite one instance from elsewhere in the volumes that perchance depicts Bali—whose Hindu inhabitants (I note with an ethnographer's authority) do not circumcise but do (occasionally) cross-dress:

> The people of Bali, an island to the east of Java, have periodical expulsions of devils on a great scale. ... On the day appointed the people of the village or district assemble at the principal temple. Here at a cross-road offerings are set out for the devils. After prayers, ... the blast of a horn summons the devils to partake of the meal. ... Afterwards ... the bystanders ... spread in all directions ... crying, "Depart! go away!" ... hasten[ed] by a deafening clatter on doors, beams, rice-blocks, and so forth. ... When the last devil has taken his departure, the uproar is succeeded by a dead silence, which lasts during the next day also. The devils, it is thought, are anxious to return to their old homes, and in order to make them think that Bali is not Bali but some desert island, no one may stir from his own abode. ... Wreaths of thorns and leaves are hung at all the entrances to warn strangers from entering. Not till the third day is this state of siege raised, and even then it is forbidden to work at the rice-fields or to buy and sell in the market. Most people still stay at home, striving to while away the time with cards and dice.⁷⁵

"To make them think that Bali is not Bali." Frazer's kernel of skillful evocation nicely captures ritual-rhetoric behind ceremonies of Nyepi—drawn from a fine empirical "sketch" in 1879, by Rutger van Eck.⁷⁶ Reliably relaying this best evidence of its day, Frazer also manages to enliven sensory matters anecdotally, much as he did *Pausanias*.

Such augmentation is "vintage" Frazeriana: its veritable "trademark" (both metaphors are apt). It is worth sampling another of Frazer's passes

Birth of Anthropology Out of a Pause on Pausanias 73

at Bali—whose inhabitants (I also note ethnographically) customarily cremate, and extravagantly.[77] In this instance Frazer reports only indirect data—indeed, seemingly superficial "displacements"—pertinent to this key Hindu practice. Yet despite the fact that he never pursues Balinese culture contextually, evidence adduced is no less empirical or apt (or extravagant!). By functionalist standards Frazer inadequately elides Hindu rites with those of noncremating Kangean Muslims. But in this case his notorious skidding across cultures achieves insights that seem (to me) "positively" inspired.[78] Here is a *Passage* of Frazer that I (a Balinist) commend comparatively to any empathetic gaze:

> In the East Indian island of Bali, the mice which ravage the rice-fields are caught in great numbers, and burned in the same way that corpses are burned. But two of the captured mice are allowed to live, and receive a little packet of white linen. Then the people bow down before them, as before gods, and let them go. In the Kangean archipelago, East Indies, when the mice prove very destructful to the rice-crop, the people rid themselves of the pests. . . . On a Friday, when the usual service in the mosque is over, four pairs of mice are solemnly united in marriage by the priest. Each pair is then shut up in a miniature canoe . . . and escorted to the seashore just as if it were a real wedding. Wherever the procession passes the people beat with all their might on their rice-blocks. On reaching the shore, the canoes, with their little inmates, are launched and left to the mercy of the winds and waves.[79]

Yes, I personally have eye- (and ear- and nose-) witnessed similar ceremonies in Bali. Yet, "being there," I failed to imagine the practices so intimately or, despite Frazer's objectionably sentimental manner, exactingly. I also applaud a kind of "contagion effect" (it's almost magical!) when Frazer zooms in on those "little inmates"—we nearly hear them squeak!—left to the "winds and waves." Also magically (perhaps), Frazer's phrases about Kangean rituals help readers feel similarly "up close and personal" to aforementioned rites in Bali. Something subtle resonates here between Balinese and Kangean usages—one in a ritual register of cremation, the other in a ritual register of marriage—both depicted as deflected into prophylactics for a rodent scourge! However antithetical Hindu Balinese and Islamic Kangean doctrines appear, their practices can converge on mock-honorifics of mice. Frazer seems to sense affinities of ritual sensibility between practitioners of two religions whose dogmas alone are asunder. His adroit description juxtaposes playful fragments, as disciplinary functionalism would not.

Final Elipses

So there you have it: a similar style of "imaginative fling," earned rigorously by Frazer in Greece, illuminates cultures selectively distilled in his *Bough*—including Bali. Ironically, Frazer's ungainly corpus can satisfy contemporary tastes for transgressing disciplinary divisions: anthropology, history, literature, classics, religion, media arts, critical theory. (This does not make him "postmodernist," or proto-so, any more than I am that for noting it.) Moreover, attending to Frazer's travels and translations may help cancel stock segregations in patently professionalized "method": for example, Frazer-bookish / Malinowski-outdoorsy; Frazer-derivative / Tylor-primary; British-empirical / French-intellectualist; interpretive/deconstructive; Boasian/Durkheimian/Frazerian/.[80] Diverse epistemological slants—whether modernist, postmodernist, neither, or blends—merit broaching, occasionally at least, in incongruous *rapprochement* (another habit of Kenneth Burke).[81]

Arguably then, Frazer's pursuits—born out of *Pausanias* (with first Persephone and then Phaedra as midwives)—warrant partial resurrection in our "new" millennium: just *after* Frazer's own (juxtaposed to it), and only two past that of Pausanias, whose "description" covered the one preceding. Such spans of time—bridging four [4] millennia!—seem susceptible of travel-translating still. Yes, travel-readers of disparate critical proclivities may benefit from lingering a while in eccentric texts earlier festooned as "Frazerian anthropology" (an official knowledge-*mélange*).

Once upon a *longtemps* ago, well before voyaging Greece-ward, I observed that a certain discipline's root word was not Latin *homo* (singularly this or that) but Attic *anthropos*: "plural, evasive, darkling, paradoxical."[82] Since then, seriocomic *anthropoi* have been profoundly apotheosized in Neni Panourgiá's alluring "anthropography" of Athens—in all that fair city's worldly and historical flows. One day it dawned on this little ole anthropos that Panourgiá's spirited sensibilities resonate with Frazer-in-Greece, supposedly elegiac, but actually ambiguous. That suspicion (or hunch) I now feel called to nurse in conclusion.

With slim space remaining (and no option of smaller print or thinner paper), I thus end amid Panourgiá's intricately contradictory voices, devised to interrogate notions of "native" as radically as any scholar I can remember. Her text engages and enacts *meta-phoren* ["trans-lation," tilted back to Greek] never at rest, never home, even to the *topos* (common-*place*) of the grave [*taphos*]—that is, "death." I might quote Panourgiá's own "description of Greece" at that description's gloamings:

This study, then, has been about two things. First it has explored how the praxis of anthropology and ethnography can be a matter of everyday life.... And it has been a reflection not only on the navigation of the living through a life that can only lead to death, but even more, on the possibility that the *difficulty of incorporating death itself* (much like ethnography and anthropology) into everyday life might be the total and complete [hers is hardly a postmodernist study!] act of resistance [*epimythion*] to its finality.[83]

Greek practices reread by Panourgiá (including herself-translated)— transform stark polarities of death and undeath into true "difficulty." Which, we mortals might mull, is ephemeral: life or death (or birth)? Or which, if any, is existential "wink"—and ironically so. Frazer may well have wondered something similar. As R. Fraser suggests: "For, if in Robertson Smith a ruthless evangelical honesty contrives to undermine the sanctity of the biblical text, in Frazer the idealistic premises of Humean empiricism turn in on themselves to make doubt itself an impossibility. To the end Frazer remained skeptical, even of his own skepticism."[84] Being skeptical even of skepticism may have affinities with "attitudes" (K. Burke) open to difficulties of "incorporating death itself . . . into everyday life" (Panourgiá).

Obdurately reread, Scotsman Sir James provides (or so I propose) premonitions of *Athénienne* Neni. Like Panourgiá's ever-hyphenating identities in many-sided *parerga*, Frazer's comparative Greece-going and globe-girdling encountered *topoi* of "death" alongside many opposites: "birth," "immortality," carnivalized "death of death" (a mainstay in certain "theographies"—my term). Frazer recaptured rites—themselves conceivably not altogether un-ironic—that resist any finality, including death's or life's. This elusive theme is manifest in *The Golden Bough*—which fittingly provides now a final flourish after a "fragment" devoted to it. Citing Frazer here, I hope to lay to rest lingering prejudices that, *properly*, his *Pausanias* and the anthropology (*Golden Bough*) interrupting it would better have been "separated at birth." Toward incontrovertibly blurring and twinning the two, my essay's (nearly) last word emerges from echoey lamentations crowning reflections on "Death and Resurrection":

> There are two kindred sets of observances in which the simulated death of a divine or supernatural being is a conspicuous feature. In one of them the being whose death is dramatically represented is a personification of the Carnival; in the other it is Death himself [the death of Death].
>
>   ... Amongst some of the Saxons of Transylvania the Carnival is hanged. Thus at Braller on Ash Wednesday or Shrove Tuesday.... At the "burial

of Carnival" in Lechrain, a man dressed as a woman in black clothes is carried on a litter or bier by four men; he is lamented over by men disguised as women in black clothes. . . . Similarly in Schörzingen, near Schömberg, the "Carnival (Shrovetide) Fool" was carried. . . . After the procession the Fool was buried under straw and dung.

In Greece a ceremony of the same sort was witnessed at Pylos by Mr. E. L. Tilton in 1895. On the evening of the first day of the Greek Lent, which fell that year on the twenty-fifth of February, an effigy with a grotesque mask for a face was borne about the streets on a bier, preceded by a mock priest with long white beard. Other functionaries surrounded the bier and two torch-bearers walked in advance. The procession moved slowly to melancholy music played by a pipe and drum. A final halt was made in the public square, where a circular space was kept clear of the surging crowd. Here a bonfire was kindled, and round it the priest led a wild dance to the same droning music. When the frenzy was at its height, the chief performer put tow on the effigy and set fire to it, and while it blazed he resumed his mad career, brandishing torches and tearing off his venerable beard to add fuel to the flames.[85]

Join me, readers, in hearing, seeing, and virtually smelling Frazer attesting the "death of death"—especially in Greece, while he was "being there"—well before his own beard grew, figuratively or actually, venerable.

(Parergon. My interpretive plan, gone customarily awry, was to have traced Frazer's explicitly labyrinthine panoply to topoi *of* thanatos. *Alas, having dallied too long in Piraeus [plus* parerga*], I retain scant space for shadowy Phaedra, although her aftermath loops back, via Hippolytus, to Frazer's Nemi, which place* anticipates: Panourgiá, Neni. For, *Nemi became the fancied "grave" [*taphos*] of travel-translation. Here Hippolytus, whose 1962 movie incarnation [Tony Perkins, American] loved Phaedra [Melina Mercouri, Greek] "like they did in the good old days" was reputedly reborn—a fact conceivably fundamental in interpreting Frazer, believe it or not.)*[86]

Regardless, Frazerian skepticism-even-of-skepticism—inspired possibly by flaming effigies of ritual practice (and also possibly by Phaedra)—possibly retains as well considerable promise as critical-comparative ethic-cum-aesthetic. In Frazer's style of constitutive doubt, even death, if dead, can be resurrected! Whether such interpretive irony too derived from Greece is a suspicion (or a hunch) whose confirmation is perhaps best left to experts or to "natives"—Pausanias, Panourgiá, Phaedra, Hippolytus, . . .—dead or alive, or reborn . . . which means "translated."[87]

Anamneses of a Pestilent Infant: The Enigma of Monstrosity, or Beyond Oedipus

Athena Athanasiou

> *I have to build everything from the beginning, homeland, ancestors . . . to invent them, to discover them.*
> —ANDRÉ GIDE, *Oedipe*

> *The revolutionary is the first to have the right to say: "Oedipus?" Never heard of it.*
> —GILLES DELEUZE AND FÉLIX GUATTARI, *Anti-Oedipus: Capitalism and Schizophrenia*

Prologue

The brash skeptic and the defunct hero, the abandoned infant and the triumphant sovereign, the autonomous and the dispossessed, the Hegelian inaugural philosopher, Nietzsche's last human, the Freudian emblematic figure. How do the multiple figures of Oedipus enact and inflect the philosophical, anthropological, and psychoanalytic aporias of modern Western episteme? In this essay, I attempt to tackle this question by thinking through the cleavages of heteronomy and autonomy, belonging and errancy, sovereignty and liminality, the body of the sovereign and the future of the body politic. I suggest a (literally) symptomatic reading of Oedipus's body, one that illustrates a corporeal topography (but also, tropography)—that is, the injured feet, the self-mutilated eyes, and the misplaced sex—that bespeaks the politics of bodily disorder.

The entry points of my inquiry are two threshold moments of Oedipus's itinerary that have remained elided within the Freudian appropriation of the myth: namely, Oedipus's encounter with the Sphinx, the feminine monstrosity, and the eruption of the plague, which served as the prologue of Sophocles' tragic play. In discussing the horror of the pestilence, whereby the polis encounters its own finitude at a moment of a state of emergency, and the mystery of the Sphinx, whereby the masculine hero encounters the sacred enigma about the human condition, as instantiations of the constitutive force of the biopolitical alterity, I will attempt to read the latter as a binding condition for affectability that ensures the cohesion of the social body, while, at the same time, leaving open the necessary possibility of disruption and dismemberment.

The Optics of Memory

In the narrative of Oedipus, the tropes of memory and vision are presented as two interconnected forces synthesizing a "complex" that is dramatized on the horizon of the embodied self, its limits, and its unprocessed traumas. Associated with the symptomatology of hysteria, the optical unconscious is addressed as a dark realm that needs to be surfaced and managed by the normalizing forces of the conscious. In psychoanalytic thinking, memory picture is a significant prompter through which the psychic material emerges out of its latent interiority. Freud has argued forcefully for the psychoanalytic relevance of examining the memory pictures that occupy the patient's inward eye:

> Once a picture has emerged from the patient's memory, we may hear him say that it becomes fragmentary and obscure in proportion as he proceeds with the description of it. *The patient is, as it were, getting rid of it by turning it into words.* We go on to examine the memory picture itself in order to discover the direction in which our work is to proceed. "Look at the picture once more. Has it disappeared?" "Most of it, yes, but I still see this detail." "Then this residue must still mean something. Either you will see something new in addition to it, or something will occur to you in connection with it." When this work has been accomplished, the patient's field of vision is once more free and we can conjure up another picture. On other occasions, however, a picture of this kind will remain obstinately before the patient's inward eye, in spite of his having described it; and this is an indication to me that he still has something important to tell me about the topic of the picture. As soon as this has been done the picture vanishes, like a ghost that has been laid.[1]

The memory picture haunts like a ghost the patient's inward eye. Optical recollection that emerges from underlying latency comes to alleviate the patient's suffering and its embodied enactments. Yet can there be such a thing as a "cure" that does not take into account the multiple and intense interaction of the embodied self with the interrelated fields of social and discursive formations, as well as with the other that constitutes the self by being excluded by it? What follows is a meditation on this question. Taking my cue from Oedipus as "the specimen story" of psychoanalysis,[2] I discuss the specularization and the spectralization at the heart of the affective encounter with the other, whereby the discourse of the other dislocates the sovereign position of the knowing and self-knowing self. I will do so by reading a story written on the marked body of Oedipus—a body floating in the circuit of castration and dismemberment, sovereignty and exile, bare life and power.

Recollecting the Self: Narrative, Memory, Representation

The role of remembering, especially remembering painful and unrepresentable events, is fundamental in the "talking cure" known as psychoanalysis. This rememoration occurs in language and in relation to language; it is a restoration of the historical relation to language. As *parole analytique*, the psychoanalytic process of curing spirits and bodies is founded upon the power of language.

This linguistic, narrational articulation of the psychic material constitutes the *arche* (as both authority and beginning) of the very genealogy of psychoanalysis. "Talking cure" bespeaks the "impure origin" of the psychoanalytic method, its proximity with hypnosis and suggestion. One can trace the therapeutic effects—on both spirit and body—of psychoanalytic narrativization back to the *infancy*, the first steps, of the psychoanalytic paradigm in the era of hypnosis, when the therapy of the "dissociation of personality" aimed at restoring the patient's "real" identity by recovering memories of past traumatic experiences through hypnotic suggestion.[3]

What is significant in our inquiry, however, is the suggestive relevance of psychoanalytic infancy to the infancy of the psychoanalytic hero. In light of the polis affliction (the pestilence that constitutes the inaugural gesture of the tragic play) and the deaths of others, that is, at the very limit of relation to the Other, Oedipus is called upon to refigure his own infancy—the infancy that he has suffered. Such self-figuration would encompass not merely his infancy per se (as lack of speech) but also his passage beyond it to his birth to language—a language that precedes and exceeds him. The entry into language is inevitably founded upon an incomplete and immemorable death: the death of infancy, which marks indelibly every speech.[4]

What is demanded firmly of Oedipus by the plagued body politic is the task of managing his own "dissociation" from his primal experience; what is expected of him is the responsibility of restoring his own real identity and exposing it to the consciousness of the polis's sight and language. In other words, what is demanded of Oedipus is to reconstitute himself in the Symbolic; to restore his relation to language and his relation to the relation between kinship and death. Oedipus is called upon to reinaugurate his unconscious—to recognize what has remained misrecognized—by speaking his life and its most intimate, immemorial, and unspeakable folds. This self-articulation in the polis's language would be a biopolitical undertaking that, if accomplished, would guarantee the polis's life and future. The sovereign is expected to give birth to the body politic through his own birth into language and meaning. The moribund present state of Oedipus's city—the city's radical exposure to finitude and death—becomes the prompter of the sovereign's precarious enterprise of recollecting his own self. Such connection of the dissociation of the subject with a mortal biopolitical exigency of the polis has been important to the literature regarding "multiplex personality": in 1889, the American psychotherapist Frederic W. H. Myers defined *dissociation* as a "city blockaded, like a great empire dying at the core."[5]

It is precisely this dying polis that implicates Oedipus in an impetus to "see." He is enjoined to a performative of making himself present to himself and the community. His restoring the narrational relation to his own self emerges then as restoration of his responsible and responsive relation to the polis: to give himself to the unnarratable adventures of self-narration is to give himself to the body politic. The afflicted polis seeks to gain access to Oedipus's *zoē* and its traumatic enigmas, dissociations, and wounds that have lain dormant for a long time. *Zoē* is never merely one's own.[6]

But isn't this reflective narrativity always a traumatic experience experienced by a certain delay, as Freud has taught us? Isn't this structural necessity for time lapse a critical component of the Oedipal scenario? Oedipus's passage from the exposure of infant temporality to the total exposure of self-blinding occurs step-by-step, in the pace of someone whose feet are wounded and steps are hindered. Oedipus's anguished retrieving of his traumatic origin of language and desire takes place in the common ground of the polis's historicity. Such a search for his own positioning within the family implicates him in a new topology. He steps beyond the grounds of the polis, beyond the limits marked by the mandates of the Law that regulates desire, sexual alliance, and kinship relations. Oedipus is recalled to the ultimate touching of his sight that is the site of the community's knowledge and memory. The absolute revealing comes about as absolute occluding. In the realm of being-in-language, the advent of illumination is in the shape of obscurity. Suddenly, what was invisible becomes too visible, too present. Oedipus's self-blinding, the blinding flash of obscurity that marks the last scene of *Oedipus the King*, signals the moment when the hand (which is specific to humans, according to Martin Heidegger) and the eye (as the navel of episteme in the Western discourse of light and illumination), the haptic and the optic, become coterminous in the human history of the West.

Oedipus is also interpellated by the polis in an impetus to "remember." Insofar as forgetting amounts to absence from the self, Oedipus is urged to "come to himself," to give "its whole meaning to his history,"[7] that is, to accede to a state of conscious restoration of the traumatic truth and its historicity. This is a process that resonates with psychoanalytic rememoration and Freud's theory of reintegration of the mnemonic traces that the unconscious consists of.[8] The curative power of recollection is the driving force of Oedipus's enterprise to convert forgetting into a narrative of self-figuration—indeed, a journey that takes place in a state of suffering and at the limits of language. This is about integrating the dissociated traumatic event into conscious knowledge, memory, and signification. Freud defined this "latency," the time period during which the effects of the traumatic experience are not yet fully assimilated, as a period of repression and forgetting, a time gap between the traumatic event and its ensuing partial return in the form of neurotic symptoms. The trauma's first occurrence is forgotten; after a period of latency, it comes to life again as an outbreak of neurosis ("traumatic neurosis")—an unwitting reenactment of the repressed material.[9] As Cathy Caruth puts it, the historical significance and force of the traumatic event "is not just that the experience is repeated after its forgetting, but that it is only in and through its inherent forgetting that it is first experienced at all."[10]

The traumas of Oedipus's narrative were not fully and immediately perceived as they occurred, but rather were experienced only in the very belatedness and unintelligibility of their occurrence—in the very othering that constituted their occurrence. Hence the historical and political co-implication of Oedipus's personal traumas to the polis's suffering. The assembly's call is for Oedipus to find Laius's murderer (the miasma), but really, the call is for the sovereign subject to "find himself" and to reembody the body politic. Through the discovery of the "name of the father" (the *nom* and the *non* of the father), the son will pass the Oedipal scene as named subject and enter the paternalistic symbolic order.

The polis attempts to overcome the resistance of the amnesiac Oedipus. Oedipus and the polis are implicated in an inextricably mutual demand for insight (Oedipus asks to know about his origin, the polis asks for cure).

The analysand, Oedipus, is urged by the polis—which operates here just like the psychoanalyst who manages the subject's mnemonic restoration—to revive memory traces of his early family life, of the moment that he, as a child, acceded to language and self-other separation. Oedipus's destiny is tied to the law of the city and its authority.[11]

The assembly of the polis is the constitutive background of the Oedipal drama. Taking stock of the cultural master narratives of gender, sexuality, affectivity, kinship, and identity, the polis addresses an Oedipus who is "blind" to the extent to which his own life history is implicated in the polis's affliction. The apolis Oedipus—the one whose origin is abandonment—stands before the polis. Significantly, Oedipus's trauma—or rather, the latency of his trauma—is staged before the polis; it is played out in the topos of suffering that the polis has become. The cure is "suggested" by the convulsions of the body politic. A process of suggestion that "opens his eyes" is underway.

What motivates this process in the Oedipus tragedy, however, is the amphiboly at the heart of discourse, the very uncertainty and misrecognition of its founding moment. It is important to bear in mind in this connection that Delphic oracles are always vague and divergent in the Sophoclean tragedy; no clear and direct response has been given by the mystical authority. Indeed, the force of the oracular language is the openness to its own decentering. The oracle that Laius (Oedipus's biological father) received, or rather, the way he read it—πρός παιδός θανεῖν ("your son will kill you")—signifies the relation of death and kinship that Oedipal generationality impels us to consider. Laius's reading of his own oracle was akin to the way Oedipus read the oracle he had received as foreseeing his murdering his Corinthian (foster) parents Polybus and Merope. In both literalist readings of a phrase that does not necessarily imply literal "murder" (it could have been interpreted as "your son will close your eyes," "will outlive you," "will continue his life after your death"), the child figures as a metaphorical murderer of the parent. In what both Laius and Oedipus read as an ominous prophecy, the child figures as an outliving figure that is ultimately overpowering and murdering.[12]

The Oedipal genealogy of life and death signals the catachrestic readings and recognitions that can erupt within the culturally intelligible familialist and heteronormative "elementary structures of kinship" that organize the reigning model of the unconscious. The agony around the proper object of affectivity and desire (i.e., not related by blood, belonging to the "opposite" sex) plays an utterly important role in depositioning and repositioning the selves in Western culture; and it is upon this agony that both psychoanalytic and biopolitical constructions of pathology and normality are centered.[13]

Let us now turn to Oedipus's own exposure to the biopolitical alterity at the very heart of kinship.

Monsters and Plagues: The Traumas of Biopolitics

The monster and the plague, those specters of abjection that remained residual to the force field of Freudian psychoanalysis, constitute arguably the structuring motifs of biopolitics. The mystery of the vermin Sphinx and the horror of the pestilence evoke limit-manifestations of bodily affectability, which, in introducing a sense of disorder, chaos, and catastrophe, embody the spectrality of a dystopian biopolitical futurity. By interrupting the intelligibility of living organicity, and since human organicity is understood as the very matter of the future, they make the future—or rather, particular manifestations of the future—impossible and implausible.

But how is the polis's stillborn future inextricably connected with Oedipus's traumatic personal past? As a metaphorical reminder of the inaugural trauma, the infant Oedipus's earliest traumatic experience of pierced feet indicates the nature of the prototypical trauma: the Greek *trauma* refers to an injury inflicted on the body (etymologically coming from *titrosko*, to pierce).[14] Therefore, the bodily trauma emerges as constitutive of the subject rather than an external force that befalls the subject. The textuality of Oedipus's scarred body echoes not only the grounded-yet-suspended position of the human but also the traumatic origin of the human. It also impels us to rethink a fundamental relation in psychoanalysis, namely, the relation between the return of the repressed and the temporal delay and repetition. Freud's *Trauma* signifies an injury inflicted upon the mind, having left the body unharmed. (Freud's exemplary scene of trauma is the shocking occurrence of a train collision: the victim leaves the site of the accident apparently unharmed.) What does the textuality of Oedipus's body teach us regarding the relation of the traumatic event to temporality as the condition of the very possibility of narrating?

Indeed, the tragic narrative and the mythic intrigue of the Oedipus narrative are punctuated by configurations of bodily agony whose seriality echoes the repeated flashbacks through which the traumatic event returns. Traumatic events are not fully grasped as they occur, Freud taught us, but return later in a series of repetitive phenomena: the abandonment of an injured infant, the killing of an old stranger at a crossroads, the trauma of inadvertent patricide and incest, the plague epidemic that hit Thebes, the encounter with the Sphinx and the ensuing suicide of the monster, and finally, the self-blinding of the aged and dispossessed Oedipus.

The metaphor of the infectious disease emerges as a key element in all of this, and Thebes, in conditions of the *epi-demic*, emerges as the *demos* par excellence: divided, injured, assaulted, besieged; hit by internecine war, hubris, and curse.[15] The plague epidemic that hit Thebes[16]—a dramatic reenactment of the epidemic that hit Athens in 429 B.C.E., a short time before the writing of the tragic play—constitutes the prologue of the play: the pestilence operates as the inaugural moment of dramaturgy, considering that Aristotle (in *Poetics*) made Sophocles' *Oedipus the King* the definitive exemplar for tragedy.[17] The plague (Greek, *plege*, blow) is also the condition that binds together Oedipus and his polis; it becomes the symbolic language through which the sovereign's unconscious speaks. The sovereign subject's commanding his own memory and bringing it to language occurs in light of confrontation with the finitude of the polis's mortal body; the management of social suffering emerges as the condition of the sovereign's affirmation of subjectivity and power.

As the afterlife of the riddle of the Sphinx, the plague embodies monstrosity at work. It figures as a symptom of the unrepresentability of trauma; it stands for the trauma that is performatively constituted by the breakdown of referentiality. Here is Freud elaborating on "traumatic neurosis," whereby the victim of the railway accident walks away from the site apparently unharmed, only to suffer symptoms of the shock in the course of the following weeks: "The time that elapsed between the accident and the first appearance of the symptoms is called the 'incubation period,' a transparent allusion to the pathology of infectious disease."[18] Similarly, the assembly of the plagued polis is a symptom of the trauma's delayed transmission. It dramatizes the trauma's "contagion" of the ones who listen to the crisis of a trauma, as this infectious traumatic horror, in its unrepresentability and belatedness, necessarily implicates others and is manifested at the related levels of speech and listening.[19] The survivor becomes the "foreign body" that must be expunged, banished. Oedipus is the symptom in the body of the polis, a body foreign to the body of the polis.

In the Oedipus narrative, the inaugural moment of the plague represents the "acting out" of the past traumatic events (of what has not yet been fully known as loss and abjection) incorporated as the "living dead." The polis reenacts the originary trauma that caused its current diseased condition; it seeks to retroactively symbolize it, to represent it, to listen to it. The polis emerges here as analyst whose therapeutic listening intends to awaken the survivor to a new possibility of intelligible narration. The survivor is encouraged to negotiate a narrative delay and to integrate the unrepresentable into the representational order.

The pestilence figures as the lethal threat that has befallen the city's body, and at the same time, somewhat paradoxically, it operates as the constitutive other that substantiates—and sublimates—both the unity of the subject and the cohesiveness of the social body. Entailing the horrors of disintegration and effecting a provisional rupture in the fabric of the *polis*, the pestilence forms the political realm where Oedipus's self-figuration takes place. In its various forms of death, infertility, and stillbirth, the plague is the biopolitical panic that puts the bare life of the polis in a state of exception.

Despite its etymology (ex-capere, "emergency": Greek *ek-taktos*, external to the order), Giorgio Agamben proposes, the exception is not exceptional. The state of exception (a temporal, "temporary" suspension of the law, rather than deviation) is a central structure of the law itself; it is, in other words, the rule of the law that is decided by the sovereign. Drawing on Walter Benjamin, who employed the term "state of emergency" as the very legitimization of power,[20] Agamben writes: "The state of exception, which is what the sovereign each and every time decides, takes place precisely when naked life—which normally appears rejoined to the multifarious forms of social life—is explicitly put into question and revoked as the ultimate foundation of political power. The ultimate subject that needs to be at once turned into the exception and included in the city is always naked life."[21] Thebes's social body is assembled, diseased, traumatized, but above all, homogenized by the commitment to put *blind* trust in the sovereign power, which is founded on the prerogative to proclaim the state of exception.

The Master and the Monster

> *We may call it a border; abjection is above all ambiguity.*
> —JULIA KRISTEVA, *Powers of Horror: An Essay on Abjection*
> (translated by Leon Roudiez)

Oedipus's victory over the monster is the heroic trial that leads to the hero's union with the king's woman (usually daughter; here, wife).[22] Oedipus's victorious confrontation with the Sphinx reads like a hero's experience of alterity. In inhabiting both animality and humanity, the undetermined nature of the Sphinx's monstrous body form upsets the sociopolitical order of bodily intelligibility. The Sphinx is like and unlike a human; like and unlike a woman; originary and derivative, primeval and liminal, both at once: both an archaic mythological figure and a product of technocultural mutation. By being both Same and Other, the sexually indeterminate monster (*teras*: both horrible and wonderful) is, indeed, a "shifter, a vehicle that constructs a web of interconnected and yet potentially contradictory discourses about his or her embodied self."[23] Signaling the para-ontological eventuality of hybridity, the figure of the Sphinx defies categorical taxonomies and pushes past the intelligible order of subjectivity. For all "its" categorical liminality vis-à-vis normal human subjectivity, the Sphinx was, in fact, associated in mythology with *death*—the figure of "psychopompos" (guide of souls) posited as guardian of tombs—but also with undomesticated *sexuality*; as Marie Delcourt mentions, a popular word in Late Greek to designate a prostitute was "sphinx."[24]

The Sphinx's heuristic fiction of not being-one is assigned to the presymbolic, the prelaw, the precultural, the preoedipal, located at the site of the "pre," before gender and sex, before identity formation, before unity and knowledge. The Sphinx is a presubject whose excess remains ungrounded; hence the ensuing suicidal fall, an event utterly paradoxical for a flying entity, an insect, that the Sphinx is: an insect that commits the incest of repetition and discontinuity, of essence and accident. Insects, having been cast as sexless in Aristotle and sexually ambiguous in Pliny, emerge in contemporary critical thinking not only as the exemplar of becoming-molecular (i.e., in Gilles Deleuze's philosophical nomadology) but also as intensely sexualized "queer" beings that disrupt collective constructions of sex and death (i.e., in Elizabeth Grosz's feminist philosophy).[25]

The Sphinx is a winged animal, a bug, that falls. She sat on a high rock near Thebes and posed a riddle to all who passed. As soon as Oedipus responded to her riddle, she flung herself from the citadel and perished, a move that bespoke the ultimate deferral of meaning.[26] The Sphinx's descent into the abyss of groundless nonessence echoes Nietzsche's "dance on the edge of the abyss," a scene that epitomizes the dissimulation aligned with the figure of the woman, as the privileged agent of antimetaphysics; truth is not self-presence.[27] The volatile figure of the Sphinx represents the precariousness that marks the woman's relation to truth-as-presence in Western metaphysics. She falls into the abyss, a *chora* to which women are typically relegated. Furthermore, the tropologies of temporal regression through which homosexual identities are conceptualized in

Freudian psychoanalytic theories of sexual difference are eloquently staged with the Sphinx's suicidal fall, a spectacular turning away from the Oedipus situation, and hence history, sociality, and culture; a returning to the pre-preoedipal—the abysmal semiotic. Diana Fuss has addressed the gravitational tropology in psychoanalysis and, more specifically, the psychoanalytic emphasis on the subject's "fall" into sexual difference:

> In Freud's reading of identification and desire, homosexual desire is not even, properly speaking, desire. Rather, homosexuality represents an instance of identification gone awry—identification in overdrive (or, one might say, oral drive). This overdrive is also implicitly a death drive: *cadere* (Latin for "to fall") etymologically conjures cadavers. For Freud every fall into homosexuality is *inherently suicidal* since the "retreat" from oedipality entails not only the loss of desire but the loss of a fundamental relation to the world into which desire permits entry—the world of sociality, sexuality, and subjectivity. . . .
>
> What Freud gives us in the end is a Newtonian explanation of sexual orientation in which falling bodies are homosexual bodies, weighted down by the heaviness of multiple identifications, and rising bodies are heterosexual bodies, buoyed up by the weightlessness of desires unmoored from their (lost) objects.[28]

The fall of the threatening alterity displaces its subversive potential. The abject other must fall before it flies to acts of subversion; it must be overthrown before it overthrows established order.

But the abject other is not an *it*. The limit-representation of the human requires the medium of female grotesque. The phallic master in the economy of desire summons the woman in the form of the monster. The monster's femininity emerges in the realm of the face—the location of speech but also our visible exposure in the light of the other: "The face, more than any other bodily part, is *for* the other. It is the most articulate sector of the body, but it is mute without the other's reading."[29] In the t(r)opology of Western metaphysics, the face embodies the uneasy dialectic of interiority and surface, recognition and misrecognition, appearance and reality, but above all, self and other. As we know from Emmanuel Levinas, the face is the site of ethics, but also, as "the only location of community, the only possible city," it is the site of the political.[30] One recalls another classical myth, the Medusa myth, whereby the hero Perseus decapitates Medusa, the monster with the castrating gaze.[31] In his essay about Medusa's head, Freud connects the undecidable interplay of fascination and abjection, which psychoanalytic theory takes as fundamental to desire, to the sight of female genitalia. Overwhelmed by castration anxiety, the male gazer decapitates the monstrosity that embodies the feminine object of abjection, this "dark continent" of classic psychoanalysis.

The Sphinx occupies a special position in the monstrous imaginary, however; "she" is the emblematic daemon, *the* face of otherness: daemon as *dianomeas*, the one who divides and distributes, but also—according to the Homeric "daiomai"—as the one who dismembers and swallows. Thus, the daemon inhabits an in-between zone: nomos and para-nomia, *diamerismos* (as division, distribution) and *diamelismos* (as dismemberment, devouring). Above all, embodying the ambiguous semantic intimacy between *nomos* and *nomadism* in Greek language, this polysemy causes us to pose anew the question of how to be a nomad in the house of nomos; how to be a stranger to the nomos of the House, and finally, how to host the economy of difference that you are. The Sphinx is a reminder that the monster does not occur "out there" but *within* the instability of the intercorporeal relation between same and other, within the zone of indistinction between the sacred and the profane, law and life, life and death. As a figure of woman's monstrous excess, the figure of the Sphinx embodies the perennially abject other in Western metaphysics, the beast in the cave—to recall Deleuze's deconstructive reading of difference as monstrosity.[32] The monstrous figure of the Sphinx resonates with the excess of materiality and the persistence of alterity embodied in enslaved black female flesh.[33] The Sphinx, the emblematic native inhabiting the cave on the fringes of civilized humanity, exemplifies the monstrosity of becoming-woman: woman's becoming a phantasmic site of fascination and horror, an eternal irony—and an internal enemy—of the community. The place of the Sphinx is the place where woman is kept in place:

> And so they want to keep woman in the place of mystery, consign her to mystery, as they say "keep her in her place," keep her at a distance: she's always not quite there ... but no one knows exactly where she is. She is kept in place in a quite characteristic way—coming back to Oedipus, the place of one who is too often forgotten, the place of the sphinx. ... She's kept in the place of what we might call the "watch-bitch" (*chienne chanteuse*). That is to say, she is outside the city, at the edge of the city—the city is man, ruled by masculine law—and there she is.[34]

The Sphinx inhabits the obscure edge of the polis; she is captured within the polis by being expelled by it; she thus becomes Oedipus's passageway, where the *nēpios* Oedipus exceeded his insouciance and conquered human speech by differentiating from the other (animal, female, foreign) body. At the passageway of the Sphinx, Oedipus entered the phallic-dominated Symbolic; he was constituted as "man." It was monstricide that inaugurated Oedipus as a Cartesian cogito, a self-knowing masculine human. Through the encounter with the Sphinx, the wound of his infancy (the pierced feet, the suspended body) assumes its political meaning in this co-implication of *being in place* and *being in the place* of the father. His response "Man" performs the very meaning that Jacques Lacan assigns to the phallus: "The function of the phallic signifier touches here on its profound relation: that in which the Ancients embodied the Νους and the Λόγος."³⁵

Things are more complicated, however. I would like to argue that the Sphinx, the questioner, strangles, dismembers, and devours not those who merely *ignore* the "answer" to her riddle but rather those who do not heed the performative call of her enigmatic discourse, those who mistake responsiveness for the quietude of fixed meaning. Let us unravel, then, the devouring figure of the Sphinx as the call of the stranger (the strangeness before the self and within the self): as the performative calling into question the self's claim to unity and knowledge. Devouring here echoes the threat of self-splitting, and this is a threat with profound sexual and racial connotations.

The female monster's oral insatiability bespeaks the Freudian conceptualization of gay sexuality in terms of cannibalistic oral intercourse (i.e., Freud's "oral or cannibalistic phase").³⁶ As an organ of sexual desire, the oral orifice invokes infantile sexuality and sexual perversion in Freud's sexual typology. Orality is a "fixation" that, if not relinquished, is implicated in an ensuing homosexual identity formation. As an organ of sexual desire, mouth must be given up in favor of phallic sexual activity for full sexual maturity to be attained. Recall that Freud associates Leonardo da Vinci's earliest memory of orality—in which while he was in his cradle a vulture opened his mouth and struck him many times with its tail against his lips— with a later homosexual fantasy of fellatio.³⁷ In Freud's thinking, both "the homosexual" and "the primitive" are developmentally arrested in the oral-cannibalistic stage, understood as the earliest phase of libidinal organization. "Perverse orality" provides the site where the classic psychoanalytic association of homosexual oral eroticism with primitive (i.e., cannibalistic) humanity is symbolically constituted. Furthermore, in Hegel's discourse, Oedipus's answer to the Sphinx represents "the solution and liberation of that Oriental Spirit. . . . The Inner Being of Nature is Thought, which has its existence only in the human consciousness."³⁸ Thus, the Sphinx, the sexually ambiguous serial killer, becomes the very incarnation of the emblematic anthropophagite: she embodies the Western fantasy of cannibalism, the fiction of savage anthropophagy that has all too often been deployed as the rationale for biopolitical acts of "humanistic interventions." As Oedipus's passageway, the racialized and sexualized figure of the Sphinx embodies not only the passage (the continuous transition) between human and animal, but also between Greece and Africa.[39]

"The name 'Oedipus,'" as Philippe Lacoue-Labarthe put it, "appears to have been a name for the West."[40] Oedipus, the rational and civilized respondent, resolved the enigma in what constituted a scene of avowal and disavowal, confession and concession, at the same time—above all, a scene of identification through monstricide and matricide.[41] Oedipus is beset with an urge to grasp and a desire to answer, but above all, with an impulse to eliminate the strangling monster-m/other, in order to protect himself from his infantile fear that he will be eaten by the maternal breast (the first sexual object of Freud's libidinal development). Oedipus's was a response articulated by a paradigmatically human subject (male rather than woman, child, or animal) and thus destined to inscribe itself in Western history as the thick narrative that weaves together not only sociality, sexuality, and subjectivity but also primordiality, wilderness, man-eating myth, and perversion. Oedipus, after all, is a man: "he who comes . . . Prince Charming. And it's man who teaches woman (because man is always the Master as well) to be aware of lack, to be aware of absence, to be aware of death."[42]

What the encounter between Oedipus and the Sphinx stages is a mix-up of doubles, a palimpsestuous convergence of identifications and misidentifications, and above all, the blurred space between the self and the other; an intimate and disruptive encounter with a forgotten, yet familiar, stranger. It is a filial and amorous encounter between two different species as well as between two different genders—different to one another and different to themselves at the same time; it is, after all, an encounter between strangeness and intimacy, *heimlich* and *unheimlich*. Freud's theorization of the uncanny derives famously from his night-train journey, when he mistook his own reflection in the looking glass for an intruder in his wagon-lit train compartment. That moment of misrecognition induced in him sentiments of dislike rather than fear: "Is it not possible, though, that our dislike of them was a vestigial trace of the archaic reaction which feels the 'double' to be something uncanny?"[43] At the heart of this disquieting uncanniness, however, there lies the spectrality of delayed recognition.

It was by virtue of the eeriness of sudden recognition that Oedipus's answer killed the Sphinx. Perhaps, as I propose, not merely the response per se, but rather the way Oedipus signed his response, the way in which the Oedipus narrative metaphorized the question as an obstacle to be conquered and the answer as signification to be fixed. What impelled the Sphinx to fall and not fly was Oedipus's drive to outwit unknowability and to harness the nomadic dissemination of meaning—his impulse to reply to a performative address with a cognitive closure. In confirming the primacy of ontology and the dissolution of the undecidable, Oedipus's answer inaugurates the metaphysics of the solution, whereby difference ceases to represent an opportunity and is swept underground, into the abyss. The encounter between the stranger and the strangler stages the hero's necessity to subdue the monstrous and enigmatic feminine alterity in order to demarcate his masculine subjectivity and proclaim his sovereignty.

The end of the myth shows that the Sphinx, this encrypted figure of the other, was hardly defeated by Oedipus, however. The answer was hardly at the disposal of the knowing subject Oedipus and his free agency. The question she posed, the problem of time and the human—or the human's time—came to be fundamental to Oedipus's drama, especially when the riddle returns in the form of the plague. The riddle of the Sphinx articulated the utterly complicated and painfully mundane problem of embodied human time: "What is it which in the morning goes on four legs, at midday on two, and in the evening on three?" (One notices that the emphasis of the riddle is on the low extremities, the legs, thus rememorating infant Oedipus's injured legs and hindered steps.) Questioning is at the heart of the teratological discourse, whereby the other others the same. The Sphinx, the specular other that opposes and constitutes the self, becomes the narcissistic mirror in which Oedipus's cadence of self-discovery takes place.

In the end, at Colonus—where Oedipus's psychoanalysis ends, according to Lacan[44]—the blind Oedipus in exile inaugurates a new tradition of lineage, after wandering urged by the question of origin. Oedipus's becoming into a founding hero (founder of a tradition of kinship as well as a tradition of the unconscious) is induced by the discourse of a teranthropomorphic[45] figure that emblematically defies any question of origin. In the following final section, I will devote my attention to the question of the question.[46]

The Oedipus as Question

> This is, then, the first Oedipal stake of analytical interpretation, whereby the analyst's reply to the analysand is not an answer concerning the initial sexual or incestuous relations of the subject (the Oedipus as answer, as a meaning), but a search for the initial question of the subject (the Oedipus as question, as the constitutive speech act of the patient).
>
> —SHOSHANA FELMAN, "Beyond Oedipus: The Specimen Story of Psychoanalysis," in *Jacques Lacan and the Adventure of Insight: Psychoanalysis in Contemporary Culture*

The Oedipus narrative illustrates, above all, a quest for origin. In Freud's discourse, the drive for knowledge is intimately associated with "the sexual research of childhood": the riddle of where babies come from. In Freud's conception, sexual difference seems to play a significant role in the very structure of the fundamental question that preoccupies psychoanalytic interpretation. And Freud notes in parentheses: "(This, in a distorted form which can be easily rectified, is the same riddle that was propounded by the Theban Sphinx.)."[47]

The Sphinx occupies a parenthetical space in Freud's theory of sexuality. In Freud's language (including, of course, its slips of the tongue), the riddle of life is spontaneously associated with the riddle of femininity, which is introduced in Freud's text as a question ("what is woman?").[48] We have already seen that in the Oedipus narrative, the riddle of human life, a question of platitude and cryptography at once, is represented by a questioning figure of monstrous femininity: the return of the abject. The handling of the question of human nature is figured by the difference articulated in the form of the subhuman, ambiguously female monstrosity in the Oedipus narrative.

Through his appropriation of the Oedipus, Freud attempted to articulate an answer to the question of desire. Shoshana Felman alerts us to the way Lacan understands the significance of Freud's discovery of the Oedipus complex as the ultimate meaning of human desire; Lacan reconstructs the psychoanalytic specimen story not as an answer but as the structure of a question: "What Freud discovered in the Oedipus myth is not an answer but the structure of a question, not any given knowledge but a structuring positioning of the analyst's own ignorance of his patient's unconscious."[49] It is through the dynamic of question and answer that Felman herself understands the analyst's responsibility vis-à-vis the analysand's address: "What [the analyst] gives," she writes, "is not a superior understanding, but a reply. The reply addresses not so much what the patient says (or means), but his very call. Being fundamentally a reply to the subject's question, to the force of his address, the interpretative gift is not constative (cognitive) but performative: the gift is not so much a gift of truth, of understanding or of meaning: it is, essentially, a gift of language."[50] If psychoanalytic interpretation is a gift of language offered in the form of reply, the question then becomes how to read the question—and the quest—that the Oedipus narrative consists in. What is at stake, in other words, is not only the literary narrative within the Oedipus myth but also the différance involved in the narrativity of any insight or interpretation (the psychoanalytic included).

I would like to argue that one of the fundamental issues that the Oedipus narrative impels us to consider is that of response and responsibility to the Other; that of response-ability to the discourse and affect of the Other. Oedipus conquers the autonomy of language by responding to a question posed by an ostensibly perilous alterity: the return of the repressed other, difference, a foreigner, his own unconscious. "The unconscious is," Lacan writes, "this subject unknown to the self, misapprehended, misrecognized, by the ego."[51] In this sense, "the Oedipal question is thus at the center of each practical psychoanalysis, not necessarily as a question addressing analysands' desire for parents but as a question addressing analysands' misapprehension, misrecognition (*méconnaissance*) of their own history."[52]

Oedipus's assumption of his response-ability to the discourse of the Other takes place in light of death: not only the father's death that preceded Oedipus's assumption of his own consciousness, not only his own death as "Oedipus the King" ("Oedipus is no more"[53]) and his biological death that he awaits at Colonus (a death that remains "afanis," unconfirmed and unburied, and undefined, indefinite, and indefinitive), but also his polis's death, for which he is responsible. Lacan—himself exiled, withdrawn from the Freudian limitation and expropriated from the International Psychoanalytical Association—urges that we shift our reading to Oedipus the exile: "You will have to read *Oedipus at Colonus*. You will see that the last word of man's relation to this discourse which he does not know is—death."[54] Explaining that whereas Freud identifies with Oedipus the King, Lacan identifies with Oedipus the exile, Felman reads Lacan's elliptical admonition thus: "What, now, happens in *Oedipus at Colonus* that is new with respect to the recognition story of *Oedipus the King* (besides the subject's death)? Precisely the fact that Oedipus *is born*, through the assumption of his death (of his radical self-expropriation), *into the life of his history.*"⁵⁵

Oedipus's birth into responsibility emerges from the site of his own finitude: "It is from the site of death as the place of my irreplaceability, that is, of my singularity, that I feel called to responsibility. In this sense only a mortal can be responsible."⁵⁶ In discussing the Heideggerian originary responsibility of *Dasein*, Jacques Derrida points out that Heidegger had signaled that death is the place of one's irreplaceability; the origin of responsibility in Heidegger is not reduced to a supreme being, whose onto-theological definitions Heidegger rejects. One is reminded of Levinas's objection to Heidegger with respect to responsibility toward others in their death. Levinas "reproaches" his teacher because his analysis of *Dasein* privileges its own death. In the ethical discourse of Levinas, responsibility is, in the first place, responsibility of oneself for the other, before the other, for the other's death (or potential death).⁵⁷ Implicitly alluding to Heidegger's *Dasein*, he writes: "My 'in the world,' my 'place in the sun,' my at homeness, have they not been the usurpation of the places belonging to the other man already oppressed and starved by me?"⁵⁸ At the time of his death, and after having confronted his own borders, a blind and exiled Oedipus who is not at home in the world asked Theseus not to disclose the place of his burial to anyone. He thus chose an unmourned and encrypted death; he is exposed to a death that no sanction and no rite can redeem. At the nonplace of his death, Oedipus is confronted, once again, with the question of being in place as being in the place of the other.

In a strange way, however, Oedipus and the Sphinx have been in each other's place. It is this life of the exile and this unredeemed death that signal the ambiguous and indissoluble intimacy that eventually ties together the two poles of this fatal encounter: Oedipus and the Sphinx. The heteronomous relation to others that Levinas has written about is figured in the Oedipus narrative as contamination of discourses between Oedipus and the Sphinx and therefore as contamination between the question and the response. In a scene of the self's reencounter with the abject (the abominable alterity that makes subjectivity possible), a scene that embodies the irreconcilably mutual constitution of the other's foreignness (the other as foreigner) and our own foreignness (the stranger-within-us, our own unconscious), Oedipus reiterates the question of the Sphinx. The old enigma announces itself in a state of emergency, whereby the humanist identity and the national language of the *logos* are at stake. The Sphinx addresses herself to the other in the language of the other, in the language of the foreign component of his own psyche; she gives in the law of naming, or she "gives in-to the name of other."[59] The Sphinx's questioning is already a response. The Sphinx is a speaking animal; the *teras* is human. And Oedipus, having passed from his answer "Hu/man" to the questioning of his "I," assumes the position of the teranthropomorphic other—his ontological counterpart—and announces, "That stranger is I."[60]

To put it differently, the Sphinx, the ironic questioner (whereby "question" does not refer to the core concept of enlightenment, the origin of thinking, but rather to the force of the call, the calling forth, and the calling into question), made possible Oedipus's response (which preceded the question—the question of the human). In the manner of the sovereign Oedipus, however, the answer made the force of the question disappear. Oedipus, the demystifier, the authority of literalist response, terminates the deferring of truth and effaces the strangeness of the other; he needs to obliterate difference in order to enforce the (paternal) Law and determine an essential ground for representation and intelligibility.

In all their structural dissymmetry, however, Oedipus and the Sphinx partake in an ethical encounter as a critique of the will to knowledge. Both inhabiting the same realm of expulsion from the community, they are spectrally co-implicated in the incalculable difference and deferral of the self-other metaphysics. Ultimately, the dispossessed Oedipus who finds autonomy in heteronomy and the Sphinx who dwells in the polis by being excluded by it inhabit the same biopolitical realm, where all life becomes sacred and thus perishable and all politics is reduced to the sovereign exception, which ties together bare life and power; they not only abolish each other, but they constitute each other by simultaneously including and excluding each other.[61]

To conclude, then: if read as an affective encounter with the other whereby the other dislocates and disfigures the sovereign position of the subject, the multiple aspects of the Oedipus narrative impel us to question the specular logic that structures the regulatory ideal of the human as male civilized citizen in Western metaphysics. In this essay, I suggested a way to reconceptualize the crucial position that the gendered, sexualized, and racialized monstrous alterity—both alterity within and alterity without the self—occupies in the constitutive fictions (including Oedipal-psychoanalytic ones) of "sexual identity" (having versus not having the phallus), "representation" (gazing versus being gazed at, as well as blinding versus illuminating), but also "signification" (signifier versus signified) and "discourse" (question versus answer).

The enigma of the Sphinx, although answered, remains always open; it persists as a spectral presence, constantly posing anew the disquieting ethical and political question of the stranger, the one who cannot be recuperated within representation and remains outside—or beyond—the representational order of Oedipus's triumphant answer, "Hu/man":

> Long afterward, Oedipus, old and blinded, walked the
> roads. He smelled a familiar smell. It was
> the Sphinx. Oedipus said, "I want to ask one question.
> Why didn't I recognize my mother?" "You gave the
> wrong answer," said the Sphinx. "But that was what
> made everything possible," said Oedipus. "No," she said.
> "When I asked, What walks on fours legs in the morning,
> two at noon and three in the evening, you answered,
> Man. You didn't say anything about woman."
> "When you say Man," said Oedipus, "you include women
> too. Everyone knows that." She said, "That's what
> you think."[62]

Fragments of Oedipus: Anthropology at the Edges of History

Neni Panourgiá

> *The Oedipus is essentially a critical analysis. Everything is already there, so it needs only to be extricated. This can be seen in the simplest action and in the briefest segment of time, even if the events themselves are still very intricate and dependent on particulars.*
> —Letter from Schiller to Goethe, October 2, 1797, quoted in Karl Kerényi and James Hillman, *Oedipus Variations: Studies in Literature and Psychoanalysis*

This paper was originally written differently, argued differently, and presented differently, before the clouds and drums of the unspoken and undeclared war and occupation that surround us now. However, this same war, whose absence produced a different discourse, makes imperative the reflection on what follows. The events of 9/11 forced upon us the radical reevaluation of the ways in which we engage in critical discourses. Not that we need to invent new ways of addressing the events around us, because, as Schiller already noted in his letter to Goethe, "everything is already there, so it needs only to be extricated." Instead, because it has forced us to reconsider the assessment by the empire's sovereign that criticism after 9/11 is tantamount to treason as nothing but the perverse contortion of the thought that is behind Theodor W. Adorno's melancholy phrase that "writing poetry after Auschwitz is barbarism."

We tend to rest comfortably on the notion that the project of humanity is to understand the world around us; I would actually argue, with Yiorgos Cheimonas, for the opposite: that we, humans, are trying to make ourselves understood by the world that surrounds us, that each of us is crying out to be heard, agonizes over the process of translation of this cry,[1] a process that often takes a violent form—the more violent the more desperate. And I would further argue that if that is the project of humanity, then the project of anthropology is to make this translation process intelligible.

It is in this context that a reading of the myths that have participated in the construction of "Western" systems of subjectivities—reading, interpretation, and representation—demands itself anew, and there is hardly a myth more definitive of the ways we have come to understand subjectivities than the myth of Oedipus. And it is also in this context that the reflection on the mythical as commensurate with the political becomes imperative.

Myth

To say that the space of signification occupied by Oedipus has been colonized by the Freudian analysis would be a truism at best. To say that the myth has been reduced to its bare bones by both Freud and Claude Lévi-Strauss would be a platitude. To say that what has become of the myth is the slaying of a father and the coupling with a mother would be more than self-evident. So, to start at the beginning, we need to go back to the myth itself, always keeping in mind what Lévi-Strauss told us (but never did himself), namely, the fact that the myth of Oedipus which first appeared before the Homeric texts is still being produced today. In other words, I take *Oedipus* as a myth, portions of which belong to antiquity, other portions to modernity, and yet other portions to postmodernity; hence Sophocles and the medieval scholiasts; Freud, Ernest Jones, Edward Westermarck, and Bronislaw Malinowski; Lévi-Strauss, Jean Cocteau, and Pier Paolo Pasolini; Gilles Deleuze and Félix Guattari, Gayatri Chakravorty Spivak, and Judith Butler are all part of the production of the myth, not its elaboration, explanation, interpretation, theorization. So, let's do what is rarely done: take a look at this myth.

Oedipus, after leaving the Delphic oracle, killed a man at a crossroads. This is the crucial event of the myth. The myth tells us that Oedipus did not know who the man at the crossroads was. As a matter of fact, when he killed the man at the crossroads, he knew as little about anything in his life or outside of it as could be possible. Before arriving at the oracle Oedipus knew that his father was Polybus and his mother was Merope, the royal couple of Corinth. But that (ephemeral) knowledge had been shaken when, as a young man, Oedipus was taunted by a drunkard who told him that he was not his father's son. He asked his parents if that was true, and they, outraged, denied it. But Oedipus was not satisfied. So, without telling them anything, he set off to Delphi, to the oracle, to ask the god who exactly he was. Apollo sent him away saying nothing about his lineage but delivering the famous oracle: "You are fated to couple with your mother, you will bring a breed of children into the light no man can bear to see—you will kill your father, the one who gave you life." From there he ran away—as far away as he could from Corinth; he wandered around until, on his way to Thebes, he came upon a crossroads, where in self-defense he killed a man on a carriage coming from the opposite direction. A little farther away he came upon the Sphinx.[2]

Parergon 1[3]

The Sphinx was a monster known from Egyptian mythology who had the body of a bull, the nails of a lion, the wings of an eagle, and the head of a woman. In Egypt, the Sphinx was male; in Thebes, female. In Greece, the Sphinx herself was the product of the unconventional and incestuous union of two natural elements who were, structurally, a mother and a son: Echidna, the chthonic worm or snake, and her son Orthus, the dog of the monstrous hound Geryon. According to Hesiod, the Sphinx was the daughter of Chimera and Orthus (Dawn). According to Apollodorus (in the version presented here by Athena Athanasiou), the Sphinx was the daughter of Echidna and Typhon. In either case, she was the sister of the Nemean lion, which had been slain by Hercules. According to yet another version of the myth, the Sphinx is the illegitimate daughter of Laius (born before Oedipus).

Myth

The Sphinx was sitting on a stele on top of Mount Phicium (Sphinx Mountain) and posed the famous riddle, taught to her by the Muses, to everyone who passed by:[4] "There walks on land a creature of two feet, of four feet, and of three; it has one voice, but sole among animals that grow on land or in the sea, it can change its nature; nay, when it walks propped on most feet, then it is the speed of its limbs less that it has ever been before?"[5] Oedipus guessed correctly. "*Anthropos*," he said, which means human—man and woman—and the Sphinx flung herself from Mount Phicium. Upon his arrival in Thebes, Oedipus was proclaimed the savior of the city and was given Jocasta to marry. He and Jocosta eventually had four children: two boys and two girls—Polynices, Eteocles, Antigone, and Ismene.

Jocasta had recently been widowed; her husband, Laius, had been killed—reportedly by a band of thieves at a three-road crossroads on the way to Delphi. Jocasta was the daughter of Menoeceus, one of the sons of Cadmus, the founder of Thebes, who was also the ancestor of Laius. Laius was the son of Labdacus, grandson of Cadmus, and king of Thebes. When Labdacus died, Laius was still young and his existence was threatened by his uncle, who became the viceroy. According to Pausanias, Laius was given safe passage by "those who had in their best mind not to allow the genos of Cadmus become unknown to the coming generations."[6] Laius was offered safety in Corinth as the guest of the king of Corinth, Pelops. While in Corinth, Laius fell madly in love with the son of Pelops, Chrysippus, whom he abducted and brought to Thebes, where Chrysippus, ashamed, committed suicide. Pelops placed a curse on Laius either to die childless or to be killed by his own son.

After the death of his uncle, the viceroy of Thebes, Laius assumed the throne of his dead father and married Jocasta. Because Jocasta failed to become pregnant, Laius consulted the oracle in Delphi and received a warning: "Better off without children," the oracle said, "because if you do have a son he will eventually kill you." Laius kept the oracle secret from Jocasta (who didn't much believe in oracles and seers, anyhow), but after a night of revelry and desire, coupled with her and got Jocasta pregnant (or Jocasta got him drunk, coupled with him, and became pregnant, unbeknownst to Laius). When she gave birth to a boy, Laius pierced the ankles of his son with a pin and gave him to Jocasta to dispose of. She gave the boy to a shepherd to expose on Mount Cithaeron, but the shepherd took pity on the child and instead of exposing he gave him away to another transhumant shepherd from Corinth, who took the baby to his master, Polybus, and his wife, Merope, who were childless.

It is to Corinth that Oedipus was taken when saved from the mountain, a generation after his father had been taken there to be saved from the usurpations of the sovereign, and it was from Corinth that Oedipus fled when he came full circle, back to Thebes, unknowingly retracing the steps of his father, through the fateful encounter at the crossroads. One day, however, when Oedipus was the king of Thebes, a plague broke out in the city, and despite the purification rites that everyone performed, the plague did not go away. So Oedipus fetched the old blind seer, Teiresias, as Jocasta's brother, Creon, consulted the Delphic oracle. The oracle came back with the command to rid Thebes of the miasma, Laius's murderer.

As Oedipus vowed to find the murderer and drive him out of the city, Teiresias identified Oedipus as the murderer after a messenger from Corinth came to say that King Polybus was dead and that Oedipus was the rightful heir to the throne. But Oedipus refused to go back to Corinth out of fear of fulfilling the old oracle about marrying his mother. Oh, he shouldn't worry about that, the messenger said, since Merope was not his real mother; she had been given the baby by this same messenger who had received it from a shepherd on the mountains of Boeotia. The moment comes when Jocasta is convinced and convinces Oedipus also, despite the logical objections he raises initially, that he is the son she had abandoned.[7] She runs to their chamber and hangs herself as Oedipus runs after her. When he sees that she is dead, he brings her body down and with her garment pins strikes his eyes again and again. According to the myth, he remains as king in Thebes, where he dies and is buried with great honors. Sophocles, however, in the Athenian version of the myth, a version that owes to the experience of the Peloponnesian War, gives us another ending: thus blinded, Oedipus is allowed to live in Thebes until, many years later, Creon expels him and his own sons make no attempt to keep him there. Outraged at the indifference of his sons, Oedipus curses them to die from each other's hand. He leaves Thebes blind but a seer now, with Antigone as his guide, and wanders around until he arrives in Athens. There he finds refuge in the garden of the Furies and is given asylum after he foretells the future for the city. He dies there and is buried in a secret place that only Theseus, the king of Athens, knows.

Parergon 2

The Sphinx's sexual indeterminacy is not the only example of sexual indeterminacy in the narrative. Equally confusing is the constitution of Teiresias, who, although born male, was transformed into female when, as a child, he watched two snakes copulating at a crossroads on Mount Cithaeron. He killed the female with his shepherd's staff and was immediately transformed into a woman. Teiresias spent seven years as a woman, during which time she had intercourse with men, until she witnessed two snakes copulating again. She again killed one of them—this time the male—and was transformed back into a man. Teiresias was asked to testify during a quarrel between Zeus and Hera about which one of the sexes experienced greater sexual pleasure. The woman, opined Teiresias, and not by a little but ninefold. An enraged Hera, determined to prove to Zeus that women had been shortchanged in their sexuality, blinded Teiresias, but Zeus gave him his unique powers in divination and prophecy and seven times the life span of mortal men.

The question of why Hera would be outraged with such an answer has been raised in the past, most notably by Nicole Loraux.[8] Loraux notes that what enraged Hera was the fact that Teiresias's response (based on personal experience and not mere speculation) went against the position that

Hera (as "guardian of the orthodoxy of marriage" in Loraux's words[9]) held, namely, that women ought to be content with the level of sexual pleasure afforded to them within the context of marriage and reproduction. Loraux further argues that the specific response given by Teiresias underlined the fact that women, experiencing nine times the sexual pleasure that men did, paid more attention to the qualities of Aphrodite than to the demands of Hera. Loraux's reading of Teiresias is a highly unorthodox one. Rather than following the myth given above regarding the blinding of Teiresias, Loraux focuses on a version developed by the Hellenistic librarian and poet Callimachus. In Callimachus's version, Teiresias was blinded when, as a child, he accidentally got a glimpse of the naked body of Athena as she was undressing to bathe in a stream. In either case, Teiresias is blinded as a man for having witnessed the scene of the woman. It is through the Callimachus reading that Loraux can place the soma of the woman within the field of vision of the man as the dangerous object that will cause the deprivation of sight and grant the gift of seeing, thus complicating not only the already existing analyses about female sexuality in Athenian social life but also (and, perhaps, more importantly) the question of knowledge.

What possibilities does this myth animate, then?—the myth of Oedipus, in fact the character of Oedipus, this paradigmatic man who looked for a truth and accepted many, whose courage, perseverance, and intelligence guided his peripatetic life and made him a native and a stranger everywhere he went, the man who loved his wife more than he loved his mother and strove to find humanity in law and structure. What possibilities become apparent when this character is invoked in cases and under circumstances when all humanity seems to be all but forgotten, and how could this character be usefully appraised as a paradigm for anthropology?

Question

Oedipus, then, is the emergent point of the interdisciplinary reflections that follow. Oedipus is a mythical character who has constituted the pivotal moment not only of the modern subject, as read through Hegel and Nietzsche, but also of anthropology as an interdisciplinary project. The myth of Oedipus, received by Freud (through Nietzsche, even though Freud never acknowledged that he had read any of the circulating discussions on Oedipus)[10] and transformed into the universalist Oedipal complex with the aid of Jones, Sándor Ferenzci, and others, made the debate between Malinowski and Westermarck, on the one hand, and Freud, on the other, imperative. It also authorized fieldwork as the anthropological method that would become the nodal point on which a theory of humanity, a meta-knowledge of human action, could be articulated in the triangulated relationship of knowledge, truth, and method.

I do not argue that this is the beginning of fieldwork. What I argue is that this is perhaps the first time that specific ethnographic knowledge was presented as a critique of a theory and method (a theory of human behavior that emerged through the methodology of psychoanalysis) that used anthropological and ethnographic material to support itself (as Freud had done in *Totem and Taboo*) and the theoretical conclusions that he arrived at through the theory of the Oedipal complex. James Boon, in discussing the process of translation from ethnographic experience to anthropological writing, has mapped out the difficulties that are there on how to read, navigate through, negotiate, the unmanageable contradictions, self-contradictions, self-cancelations, deep questionings, and trenchant aporias (that ought to be) present in the exercise of fieldwork. Boon moves back and forth looking at the certainty of fieldwork as "empirical" (naming this certainty "fallacy") to the view ("mistaken") that "cross-cultural interpretations happen empirically."[11] Centering on the process of translation, he sets the object of anthropology (one assumes by engaging with fieldwork, but not only and exclusively with it) as being able to "make explicitly exotic populations appear implicitly familiar and explicitly familiar populations appear implicitly exotic."[12] Freud's Oedipalism and the Malinowskian matrilineal "facts" against the Freudian Oedipal universality (and all who got caught up in the battle of the two) engage in the exact opposite: they maintain the exoticism of the exotic and the familiarity of the familiar.

I approach the myth of Oedipus from a number of different perspectives, attempting to articulate a discourse on the political commensurate with the gestures of Oedipean specificity: questions on the fragments of the body, the emergency of biopolitical power, technologies of self and technologies of alterity, the problem of autonomy. The nexus of this interrogation of Freud's Oedipus is located in a specific tortured place: the concentration camps for Marxists, Leftists, and Communists in Greece after the Second World War.

Oedipus, as a persona, as a character, and as a text, is (still and again) appealing to the extent of authoring new renditions, translations, and adaptations of the play and the myth, continuing to appear in the beginning of the twenty-first century. In a time when the knowledge and truth sought in the modernist experience gets progressively translated into apocalyptic and messianic terms (not least of all in the current discourses developed as responses to 9/11 and in the articulations of the new Empire), what are the key issues being managed and negotiated in this text that make it relevant to us now? What is the type of knowledge sought through *Oedipus* nowadays, and how can it be culturally situated and epistemologically located to make *Oedipus* of interest to anthropologists and to anthropologically informed productions of knowledge? *Oedipus*, as a comprehensive text that spans space and time from its pre-Homeric formulations to the present, constitutes a reflective moment on the human condition that coincides with the project of anthropology. The knowledge and the aporias negotiated in *Oedipus* correspond to the fundamental principles that guide the process of anthropological investigation. In this respect, Oedipus is the first anthropologist,[13] insofar, and only insofar, as this mythical text contains the basic questions that have come later to be associated with and posed by the discipline of anthropology. Enveloped within this fictional encounter with the Oedipean text is also the gesture of anthropology as it attempts to answer questions always already formulated outside the epistemological confines of the discipline. With my reading of the Oedipus myth as a narrative[14] (hence, as a text that exists in a dialectical relationship to its storyteller), I look for the sites where discourses on technologies, philosophical investigations, anthropological epistemologies, and their interstices can be located and where formulations such as kinship, divinity, fate, experience, and sovereignty can be revisited. *Oedipus* has engendered vocabularies that have produced critical discourses in thinking about the political and the social, such as the question of the sovereign in reference to cultural praxis (in the encounter between Oedipus and the oracle). Furthermore, the philosophical foundations of the anthropological project become transparent through the questions that the Oedipean project has set for us (and as we have inherited it from Sophocles through Hegel, Sir James Frazer, Malinowski, Luce Irigaray, or Judith Butler), as do the idioms that anthropology has inherited from the epistemologies that surround the character of Oedipus, such as categories of kinship, friendship, the monstrous and the human, and understandings of the divine.

Aporia

One of the fundamental questions that *Oedipus* sets for us is that of the constitution of the social subject as a product of the dialectical tension between the self and the other. In other words, the fundamental question that *Oedipus* asks us to consider is not *whether* we know who we are but *how* we know who we are, how we know who the other is, and how we negotiate these categories as they participate in the processes of identity production. When this question is posited as part of the attempt to define and delineate cultural and political formations, it acquires the urgency of political praxis. "Who is an American?" we have been asked daily since 9/11; and why some Americans are recognized as such whereas others are not is the disturbing question posited by the relatives of the 1,500 interned Americans of Middle Eastern descent who were summarily interned after 9/11, some of them still in custody or unaccounted for.

My inquiry, then, is not concerned with the Freudian analysis of Oedipus, not only because the inordinate volume of work devoted to it has managed to dislocate the centrality of the myth, but also because the psychoanalytic emphasis on Oedipus has limited the scope of other analytical possibilities to which the text lends itself. The anthropological literature on Oedipus has thus far, with minor exceptions, dealt with responses not only to Freud's claim of the centrality of the Oedipal complex to the process of identity formation but also to Freud's claim of its universality. Although responses to this analytical aspect of Oedipus are still being produced, they are not of the present concern. The latest such undertaking is by Suzette Heald.[15] Heald engaged in a critique of the Freudian theorization of the Oedipus complex by presenting alternative material from the Gisu ritual male circumcision. Heald's gesture is not unlike that of Malinowski, who tried to prove that the complex presupposes a patrilineal descent system and foreclosed its possibility within a matrilineal one, or of Anne Parsons, who, in 1969, proposed the triangulation of Freud's and Malinowski's positions by presenting yet another complication in kinship structure, the one that she saw in Naples (Italy). Unlike Freud's late-nineteenth-century Vienna, where the patrilineal family rested on the distance between the parents, on one hand, and the son and the father, on the other, or Malinowski's early-twentieth-century Trobriands, where the matrilineal family rested on ignorance about the father's contribution to reproduction and the closeness to the mother's brother, Parsons showed that in working-class Naples, kinship was experienced through the proximity between the mother and the son and through the distance between them and the son's wife. Melford Spiro's work on Oedipus in 1982 tried to synthesize all the existing anthropological responses to the Freudian universalist model by crediting Malinowski for having singularly managed to teach "every (anthropological) schoolboy" that the Oedipus complex "is not found in the Trobriands and, by extrapolation, in other societies whose family structures do not conform to that of the Western type."[16] Allen Johnson and Douglass Price-Williams attempted an anthropological approach (which became a folkloristic enterprise) to the Freudian position on Oedipus, supplying folktales from around the world that deal with incest. The main problem with this collection, of course, is that instead of looking at the myth of Oedipus as a culturally specific narrative and engaging in its analysis as a cultural text, the two authors (the former an anthropologist-psychoanalyst and the latter a psychiatrist) took Freud's reading and looked for other folk tales around the world that refer to incest, thus reducing Oedipus to something that is far more restrictive and narrow than what even Freud has produced.[17] The problem, however, with both Freud's use of the myth and the responses to it (from Malinowski to Parsons to Lévi-Strauss) is that none looks at the myth or the play in its entirety, as a narrative. The only responses to both Freud and Lévi-Strauss that critique this solipsistic look at Oedipus are those articulated by the French classicists Jean-Pierre Vernant and Pierre Vidal-Naquet when they argue (convincingly) that if the Oedipus complex exists it does not come from Oedipus.[18] Of particular interest is Lacan's comment on the Freudian Oedipus, in *Seminaire I*, that the Oedipus complex cannot be sustained if the myth is considered in its totality, precisely because the complexity of the myth is such with multiple details that the question of what becomes the complex is overshadowed. Certainly this position by Lacan is not autonomous from the importance that he himself placed on the questions of visuality and verbality. But what I am primarily interested in is the corpus of theoretical responses to Oedipus produced outside the space occupied by psychoanalysis: notably, the philosophical debates produced by the reading of the text and their importance in engaging in anthropologically informed analysis. In other words, the anthropological response to questions posited by philosophy.

This myth that has been central to the theory of psychoanalysis and to the early practice of the methodology of anthropology, however, has not been addressed exhaustively either in psychoanalysis or in anthropology. Both disciplines have eschewed the study of the myth and have engaged in mythic analyses. It is particularly startling for anthropology, a discipline uniquely positioned to engage in the analysis of myth as a cultural text, to note that starting with anthropologists in the late nineteenth century (principally Frazer) and ending with the structuralists (not only Lévi-Strauss but also his critics, from G. S. Kirk and Clifford Geertz to Peter

Munz), anthropology has looked at Oedipus rather reductively, only responding to the challenges posed by Freud's interpretation. It is interesting to note that both the Freudian Oedipalism and the Lévi-Straussian structuralism of Oedipus rest on a scant four pages of analysis each. The usual practice has been to look at single, isolated mythemes in it and to approach them ethnographically. The few attempts toward such a direction have centered on the following three topics: (1) *kinship*, first by Frazer and his evolutionism alongside his mythic analysis, prompting a critique by functionalists such as A. R. Radcliffe-Brown and Malinowski, and later as part of the structuralist study of myth by Lévi-Strauss, which prompted the consequent critique by Munz and Geertz; (2) *fate*, first by Meyer Fortes in his analysis of notions of fate in *Oedipus* and Job, in West Africa, and in Terrence Turner's analysis of time and structure; and (3) *incest*, primarily by William Arens and Richard Fox. Fox is the only anthropologist to actually engage in an analysis of two of the plays of the Theban cycle, namely, *Oedipus Rex* and *Antigone*, but still within the parameters of the triangular formulation of kinship, incest, and parricide.[19] In a text as rich as that of *Oedipus*, however, there might very well be found as many thematic approaches as there are epistemological, methodological, ideological, and analytical problematics. *Oedipus* manages to complicate everything that is taken for granted and demands that it be reconsidered. Undoubtedly, the issue of incest and that of parricide[20] is emblematic of the analysis of the myth. *Oedipus*, though, asks that we acknowledge and void the collusion of political power and the responsibility it demands. In other words, it demands the preservation of the responsibility that ought to be constitutive of political power. It is a reflection and a complication on the issue of the native/autochthonous and the stranger/foreigner; of home and away; of illness/disease and wellness; of dream analysis; of memory and time; of the development of the subject and its struggle with the divine; of ambivalence toward adoption; of the relationship to death and the dead; of class relations; of vision, truth, and authenticity; of the relationship to the state; of inheritance; of violence on the body, as in infanticide, parricide, suicide, rape, self-mutilation, and execution; of the violence done in power relations; of selfhood; of truth and reality; of fate, chance, and destiny; of catharsis/miasma; of purity and danger; of the construction of the biological and cultural category of the father and of the mother; of the role of the body in the formation of subjectivity; of private and public; of personal and political.

Above all, *Oedipus* is a metaphor on responsibility and accountability. *Oedipus* is a text that betrays society's abstraction of the process that has constituted it as such. In this sense I read *Oedipus* not as the symbolic text facilitated in structuralism (from Freud to Lacan and the feminist responses to it, from Spivak to Irigaray and Butler) but as a *metaphorical* text that emerges as it participates in the process of its own metaphorization and that manages to complicate everything that it metaphorizes. What *Oedipus* shows us is not that "culture" (as that social formulation that engages in myth making) can think but that "culture" actually thinks on the level of the conscious, producing its own metaphors. I focus on this particular dimension of *Oedipus* as a text that constitutes a reflective moment upon the relationship of the mind and body, upon problematizations of categorical thought on life, self, other, enemy, friend, kin, authority, truth, chance, structure, the divine, the bestial, and the human. In this time of global cultural postmodernity, a time of movement of vast numbers of people, a time that repeatedly challenges the constants of our subjectivities, movements that are translated to different technologies of being by producing different technologies of the body—it is at this particular moment that Oedipean questions on the political emerge. Who is constituted as self and who is constituted as other? is the question that *Oedipus* asks us to ask constantly; and it is a question that has had a pressing importance in the history of modern Greek articulations of the political self and that right here, right now, in the shadow of Guantánamo Bay, in the darkness of the Patriot Act and the articulations of the neo-imperialist project, demands to be revisited anew.

The question that emerges, thus, is that of the fundamental coincidentality of the experience of the fragmented body with the multiplicity of idioms that the (Oedipean) subject *is*: adored yet exposed, sovereign but fugitive, dispossessed in his hubris and autonomous in his suffering, willing but unwitting savior, Hegel's first philosopher, Nietszche's last philosopher, Freud's paradigmatic ego. And also Freud's remnants, all the points in the myth and the play that Freud ignored (consciously or unconsciously, knowlingly or unknowingly): the plague in the city, the Sphinx, Oedipus's intentionality and lack thereof, the importance of actions taken and gestures made in the midst of a state of emergency, namely, the pestilence that demands that the foreign body—the miasmatic regicide—be removed from the city.

Parergon 3

John Ross traces Freud's discovery of Oedipus to the famous letter that Freud sent to Fliess in 1896, ten days after the death of the old Herr

Freud—what became the famous four pages in *The Interpretation of Dreams* in 1900. Ross rightly brings into the discussion of the Oedipus complex what Freud refused to consider, namely, the responsibility borne by Laius for the actions of Oedipus. Ross looks at the myth and its background and brings about all the details that have been largely ignored by the psychoanalytic and anthropological approaches to the myth. He considers the history of the place (Mount Cithaeron) and the "crimes against nature" that had been committed there long before Oedipus was born, by women in the line of Cadmus: Semele, who gave birth to Dionysus (himself "orphaned and forced to wander Greece," as Ross notes), and her sister Agave, who dismembered her son Pentheus in a Maenadic frenzy, thus committing the "first filicide at a *mother's* hands."[21] Oedipus, Ross notes further, escaped the fate of Pentheus only to fall in the hands of an "indifferent" mother and an "ignorant, weak, authoritarian, and . . . homosexual father."[22] Ross concludes that before the Oedipus complex is considered, one ought to examine what he calls the "Laius complex," the complex of a father who is narcissistic, self-centered, self-serving, hubristic, self-denying homosexual pedophile, jealous, misogynist, and superstitious.

In Ross's deft hands Oedipus has nothing to do with Jonathan Lear's unthinking and impertinent mythic hero but is the virtuous contrast of his father, bearing, alas, all the markings and effects of this father: "neglect as an infant, a sense of discontinuity as an adult, lost origins, identity confusion."[23] Ross manages to bring into the open the question that the Oedipus myth posits in accounting for kinship: kinship as responsible not only for the person as a social entity but also for the dialectical relationship between the social person and the polis, in other words, for the constitution of the social person as a political entity. It is in this discussion of the horrors of an altered body, a pestilent polis, and their historicity, where biopolitical alterity is instantiated, that the (predictably failing Aristotelian and Durkheimian) discourses of cohesiveness of the social body are interrogated.

Conceit

Lear has called our age "the age of Oedipus," a time that is marked by the sense of abandonment and the certainty of "knowingness," both of which he sees developing in the myth of Oedipus.[24] To the Socratic conceit of "the only thing I know is that I know nothing," Lear erects what he sees as the fallacious idiocy of Oedipus in thinking that he knows everything, all the while misrecognizing the fact that "the only thing I know is that I know nothing" and "I know" are nothing but the opposite announcements of the same. Lear is a most astute thinker, so it is impossible that the Socratic conceit eludes him as such or that he really considers Oedipus as someone who "knew it all." One must think that Lear is offering this reading of Oedipus (and the accompanying admonition to the Chicago graduating class of 1998 to be as Socratic as possible, steering away from Oedipus) only as a "teaching moment" in his attempt to get the graduating students to acknowledge the fact that a first university degree does not really give them but fragments of the knowledge that they need in order to continue. And one could have been such a generous reader had this not been Lear's sustained argument on Oedipus from his 1997 paper (that he presented at a conference organized by the New York Psychoanalytic Society) to his 1998 *Open Minded*, where he later included the paper.

Lear sees in *Oedipus* a text that transcends the Freudian complex, as he does not concern himself with the questions of parricide and incest. And rightly so. Lear dives in to the fundamental question of *Oedipus*, which is the question of knowledge, and comes up for air announcing that there is no real knowledge in this text, just the performativity of it. Hence the heights of hubris that Oedipus achieves by claiming throughout the play "I know." And it is through the exposure of hubris that Lear sees in *Oedipus* a text that can help us understand the politics of today when he attempts a reading of the Clinton era through the text of *Oedipus*. But as much as he names his reading a cultural one, it is a fundamentally psychoanalytic reading, a reading based on talking and listening. He mentions that he has "found a way to reinterpret the Oedipus myth" by "listening to the culture,"[25] a reinterpretation of the myth that he is able to do in order to analyze the pathologies of modern politics. But there is nowhere in his text even a nod to the fact (or the possibility of such an existence, a glimpse of which he might have seen) that there is an explicit or implicit reference to *Oedipus* in modern politics. Lear might say that such a reference is not necessary to be present, which is precisely what makes his reading a psychoanalytic one.

But if Lear feels compelled to see psychoanalysis through culture (a most welcome gesture), he does so by walking though the Oedipus complex as if it wasn't there (another most welcome gesture) and exposes the possibilities that *Oedipus* has as a cultural text through a profoundly wrong reading of the questions of the myth. The political, in Lear's hands, becomes a matter of manhandling political power that begins and ends with the hubris of the sovereign, be that Bill Clinton's White House scandals or the certainty of Oedipus that he knows the answers to the questions posed to him. But there is no adequate explanation in Lear for Oedipus's contrition, an explanation that would show that it takes into consideration that "the psyche of the individual and the psyche of the city are not to be separated"[26] in *Oedipus* as they are so glibly separated in modern politics. And in his haste to follow the ever-so-common and trite reading of Oedipus as the embodiment of hubris, Lear refuses to recognize Oedipus for the deeply wounded human that he is exactly at the cleavages where his existence *exists*: human but exposed to nature as an animal, wounded as a child by the actions of his parents that bear the imprimatur of prior *hamartiai*/errors; kin to a half-human half-animal creature; wounded as the suppliant who is denied the knowledge of the divine; wounded as the sovereign who seeks relief for his people that cannot be found outside of himself; and self-wounded at the moment of knowledge of his having wounded nature and culture.

Anti-Myth

Exiles on the Greek islands where concentration camps were established for the Leftists in 1947, as the Civil War was raging, saw Oedipus from a different light, so to speak.[27] Beaten, tortured, and pressured to sign declarations that they were not what they maintained to be (Leftists) but something that they were not (Christian nationalists), they found themselves somatically in the place of Oedipus: with swollen feet from bastinado,[28] gouged eyes from strikes on the head, being asked to answer the unanswerable question, are you (with us) or are you not?[29]—all the while being told the same thing, you will become human (*ánthropoi*) or you will die. So "in order for them to make us human they first made us into King Oedipus," says Yiorgos Yiannopoulos, a pediatrician who was confined to the islands for over three years.[30] The riddle of the Sphinx is reversed in this context: Who is human? asked the liberal state engaged in the first acts of the Cold War, to construct itself as the only correct answer: human is that animal that recognizes the power of the state as the maker of the human. What is the point where the torturers of the Greek Leftists could not hear the response that they were given: we are already humans, we are already *ánthropoi*. Where did the mythological break down in that most unmythological, nay anti-mythological, existence?

The establishment of the modern Greek state, predicated upon the ideality of an unbroken organic history of Greece that spans ten millennia, has produced a historicity of political forms of life that in the early twentieth century demarcated the possible and the desirable from the impossible and the undesirable. The Left, from the moment of its inception as an Agrarian Party to its eventual materialization as a Communist Party, and all the hues of the Leftist spectrum in between, fell under the second category of the impossible (within the context of the Greek psyche) and the undesirable (within the context of the Greek imagination). During the Civil War (1946–1949), the torturers on the islands (Makronisos and Yaros for the men, Trikeri for the women), engaged in a program of returning the (considered as) wayward and lost Leftists to the common imaginary of Greece as a capitalist entity. The bamboo sticks that fell on heads, backs, arms, legs, feet, testicles, carried the voices of the torturers with them from the first moment that the Leftists arrived on the islands: you will become human or you will never leave this island alive (*tha ginetai ánthropoi i den tha fygete apo 'do zontanoi*). Human or dead became the dialectics of existence on the islands, where the wounded bodies (some of them permanently), the wounded minds (all of them permanently), and the wounded psyches of the Leftists made the metaphor of *Oedipus*, in the hands of Yiannopoulos, a possibility. No, this is not naked life (either in Walter Benjamin's or in Giorgio Agamben's sense). This is a tag of war for the recognition of the human.[31]

What makes *Oedipus* recognizable to Yiannopoulos, then, is what ought to make *Oedipus* recognizable to the anthropologist: a text on *ánthropos*, the human, and how this human makes itself intelligible to the world.

MAN

This is my father! And he is not alive. His own people slaughtered him during the civil war because he went out with a woman from the opposite side who danced *zeibekiko* like a man and her own people slaughtered her too because she went with my father, and I don't know, if you ask me, who is Zeimbeko—as I found out later that they called her—but my mother she is not, I was six years old then.

—MARIOS PONTIKAS, 2004, Laius's Murderer and the Crows[32]

Carnal Hermeneutics: From "Concepts" and "Circles" to "Dispositions" and "Suspense"

Eleni Papagaroufali

From the Students' Point of View

To give my students a sense of the incomplete and elusive character of interpretive anthropology, I use two images drawn from Clifford Geertz's *The Interpretation of Cultures*.[1] One is the "Indian story," which is "about an Englishman who, having been told that the world rested on a platform which rested on the back of an elephant which rested in turn on the back of a turtle, asked . . . what did the turtle rest on? Another turtle. And that turtle? 'Ah, Sahib, after that is turtles all the way down.'"[2] The other comes from Geertz's assertion that "the culture of a people is an ensemble of texts, themselves ensembles, which *the anthropologist strains to read over the shoulders of those* to whom they properly belong."[3]

Every year, the students' reactions are, for better or worse, the same. With respect to the Indian story, first, they seem to enjoy the possibility of this mythical reversal, and laugh. Then, having realized that this is an analogy to reality, they seem puzzled, annoyed, even threatened, by the real possibility that the analysis—no matter how "deep" it goes—may not "get anywhere near to the bottom of anything ever written about."[4] Except for one or at most two out of twenty students, no one seems ready to buy this story! There *must* be a *bottom* where the very, very, very last turtle *must* rest! There is an argument accompanying this collective assertion: it is contradictory to say that there is no end in cultural analysis and yet to care so much about "the meaning" of "readily observable" or "actually occurring" symbolic forms, that is, words, images, institutions, and behaviors tied as closely as possible to "concrete, social events and occasions, [and] the public world of common life."[5]

The students' responses to the second image are similar. First, they seem puzzled and impressed by the ethnographer's presentation as a clandestine reader of cultures-as-texts. Then, recalling that this is an analogy to reality, they feel insecure at finding that "participant observation" in fieldwork may be such a distant and fleeting experience. Finally, insecurity and awe give their place to relief-generating assertions: if cultural phenomena are like texts, then they are somehow grounded things the fieldworker can not only observe—it doesn't matter how fleetingly—but read, converse with, translate, write about, make "meaningful." Students' familiarity with these "mental activities" makes them feel secure about their future job and helps them understand the presentation of cross-cultural translation or interpretation as a "hermeneutic circle": a continuous dialectical tacking between natives' "experience-near" and ethnographers' "experience-distant concepts."[6] Nevertheless, the notion of experience confuses them. To their minds—as to ours?—"experiences" are immediately and really lived, yet internally sensed and unselfconsciously practiced. On the contrary, "concepts" are abstract and symbolic (somehow nonreal) and yet self-consciously and meaningfully used. The former are closer to one's body, so to speak, whereas the latter are closer to one's mind. If interpretive anthropology involves "poking into another people's turn of *mind*,"[7] as opposed to "putting oneself into someone else's *skin*,"[8] then, the students ask, what's the use of our including "experience" instead of sticking to "concepts"? The point underlying this question is familiar to most interpretive anthropologists: *verstehen* is more feasible, reliable, and useful than *einfühlen*.

The next step in my lecture about interpretive anthropology is to convince students that this separation is impossible. To do this I use the image of "*carnal* hermeneutics."[9] This is not a shift in stress from spiritual mind to material *carne* and thus to a renewed search of a more tangible "bottom." On the contrary, it is another complementary way to explain why the interpretation of cultures is incomplete and elusive. It is suggested that the "symbolic means"—words, images, actions—through which both natives and ethnographers represent themselves to themselves and to each other are as experiential as the experiences supposedly represented. Yet the so-called *immediate* nature of experience is denied here: it is the always already *nonimmediate* character of experience (e.g., of comprehending or writing about Other cultural experience) that is responsible for its incompleteness and indeterminacy. Time, rather than space (*near*-, *far*-experience), is the name of the game.

Carnal Hermeneutics

I use the metaphor *carnal* hermeneutics to suggest that the act of both ethnographic and native *interpretation* is not simply a "mental" or "cognitive" function but a sensory and emotional engagement in the world. This means that cultural interpretation (seen as either "text reading" or "conversing" or "translating" or "writing about") is not a conceptual re-presentation of experiences, understood as immediate and thus more real and prior to their representation. It is itself an experience, understood as a historically and temporally, and thus culturally, informed somatic intersubjectivity: instead of "points of *view*" or "*visions* of the world," participant cointerpreters, physically or imaginatively copresent,[10] juxtapose, contest, negotiate, realize, socially informed embodied, and bodying forth, knowledge that includes "from *silence* and *gesture* to *language*."[11] In Geertz's terms, this knowledge would be natives' "near-experience concepts," namely, the unselfconscious and spontaneous local definitions of feeling, thinking, imagining.[12] In carnal-hermeneutics terms, a more apt category, covering both near- and far-experiences, could be Pierre Bourdieu's *habitus* or *dispositions*, understood as historically informed, lasting "manners of feeling and thinking,"[13] "embodied" through sensory mnemotechnics, extremely general in their application, yet responsible for agents' "*intentionless invention* of regulated improvisation."[14]

Shifting from "concepts" to "dispositions" implies that natives and ethnographers produce knowledge as sentient agents—through our always already socially informed senses and emotions rather than through our "minds." It also implies that knowledge becomes constantly embodied and bodying forth through past, present, and future practices, sensorily and emotionally shared with persons, objects, and institutions—actual or imagined, seen or unseen or never to be seen. Finally, and for all these reasons, it implies that the meaning or truth claimed by any interpreter is never entirely contained nor constructed in the ethnographic present of the interpretive process. Seen as a juxtaposition of dispositions, rather than concepts, interpretive ethnographic process becomes a temporally and spatially decentered and decentering "coexperience,"[15] that is, one much less localizable, visible, cyclical, and intentional than cognitive synchronic approaches, such as "text reading," "dialectics," and "dialogue," imply. This happens because in this approach, the "sources" of data collection and interpretation include more than interlocutors' "minds" and go beyond their face-to-face ethnographic present. In other words, meanings are not simply "conceived" but "sensed"—touched, smelled, tasted, heard, seen. During research this multisensory production of meanings proves to be always taking place in time-bound intersubjective milieus: in surroundings including conversing interpreters *and* "offstage conversation partners"[16]—living or dead, actual or imagined—with whom each interpreter has consciously and unconsciously shared, shares, might share, negative or positive sensory-emotional relations.

The people I have been studying for many years are so-called prospective organ or body donors living in Athens, Greece.[17] Contrary to the teachings of the Orthodox Christian Church and transplant-policy rhetoric about altruism and Christian love, these people decided to sign donor cards because they feel disgusted by the "idea" of being buried, eaten by worms and thus decomposed, and finally exhumed.[18] Only some have actually observed burials and exhumations, whereas others have only heard about them. However, they all feel that those rituals are "burdensome," because, as they say, instead of familiarizing Orthodox Christians with death, the rituals cause fear and repulsion—"It's like watching a Dracula film." Almost all my interlocutors say that they feel repulsed by the smells smelled on such occasions (the smell of cologne spread on the dead body by undertakers, of the incense used by priests, of flowers, and of the damp soil in the open grave); the tastes tasted (of coffee and brandy as well as boiled wheat distributed); the things and persons seen and touched (the wooden coffin, the icon placed upon it to be kissed, people kissing each other); the sounds heard (relatives' crying, priests' hymns). Prospective donors do not want to "*see* themselves" suffering these "barbarous, aesthetically abusive and meaningless tortures," despite the fact that "by then, they won't be able to feel what is done to them." Having excluded a world with whom they have apparently shared unpleasant feelings (from the Church or priests to undertakers to relatives), donors have turned toward another world: that of doctors specialized in extracting and transplanting body parts, of medical students practicing anatomy lessons, of terminally ill people living all over the world waiting for transplants. Although they don't know and will never get to know these people, donors seem to trust them more and to already experience their relations to them in a pleasant way.

A woman organ donor, now in her early forties, told me that she has been afraid of being buried and decomposed since she was around six years old. Almost every night, she would wake up and touch one hand with the other to see if she was alive. During the day, she would make her mother tell her the Snow White story: that young girl, though laid dead in the coffin, never decomposed, because the prince came in time and kissed her and resurrected her. What a relief! The prospect of donating all her organs and tissues after her death causes her the same relief: she knows that some day she will die but will not decompose within the grave—at least not totally. There is a long list of princes (doctors and organ recipients) waiting to kiss her and save her! In that case, why didn't she donate her whole body? For two reasons: out of respect for her relatives' right to get her body as a whole, even organless, to bury it in a concrete place, and to be able to "see" it and "speak" to it and "communicate" with it; and out of fear of being endlessly mutilated by doctors and thereby decomposed in a different way. How about whole-body donors? Are they so disrespectful to relatives and so liberated from the fear of being mutilated? Body donors wish to get rid of what is felt as burdensome altogether: "While my body will be traveling to the dissection room, priests and my relatives will be performing a parody of my funeral in front of a picture of mine," said a man, laughing. Instead of being partially decomposed within the damp soil, body donors prefer to expose their naked bodies on the anatomical table to be consumed by formalin, as well as by medical students' gazes and hands, and what is left, to be thrown into the garbage or burned—or so they imagine.

Given the temporally and spatially dispersed and indeterminate nature of "offstage partners," as well as their determining role in the production of dispositions, *intuitive empathy* and *imagination* (understood as "somatic modes of attention," rather than "psychological" or "mental" functions)[19] become the inevitable means for the ethnographer to get not inside her interlocutors' heads but inside the seen and unseen or never to be seen worlds embodied by them. Ethnography, in this case, becomes imaginatively "multi-sited."[20] To capture the knowledge produced beyond the confines of a dialogical communication in a specific location, anthropologists may travel, with or through their informants' narrated experiences, to "different locales, even different continents," the political, economic, and cultural systems of which "are registered in dispersed groups or individuals"—in this case donors—"whose actions have mutual, often unintended, consequences for each other, as they are connected by markets and other major institutions that make the world a system."[21] This sort of "sympathetic" or "empathetic" involvement between ethnographers and their subjects may seem to be what George Marcus calls "traditional ethnography": "I *know* because 'I *was there*'—I *saw*, I *sympathized*, etc.";[22] or, I know because I am studying "cultural formations . . . encompassed in the everyday lifeworlds of a limited set of subjects concentrated in an easily defined place."[23] This is not the case, because attending to dispositions not only avoids the "ocularcentrism" implicated in the cognitive "pursuit of clear and distinct ideas"[24] but undermines fast and easy attribution of "certainty," "domesticity," and "significance" to the so-called "ordinariness of everyday life."[25] Put another way, for carnal hermeneutics, there is no place easily "seen" thus defined, nor sets of subjects limited to themselves, nor cultural formations encompassed in the supposedly visible and thus seemingly accessible daily life.

Long before signing a donor card, most of my informants had already prepared the way to protect their fleshly bodies from decomposition and exhumation. Some had officially declared themselves atheists in the hope that the Orthodox Christian Church would not allow the burial of their dead bodies. Others had denied their Christian identity—more or less definitely—to join Hindu-oriented groups in the hope that their souls (identified with their "selves") would be reincarnated into new bodies. At the same time, through their travels to India, they had been convinced that the "body" perceived by Christians as material flesh may not really exist: "This is why meditating yogis can feed themselves on a biscuit per year!" Some others, while studying or working in foreign countries, had observed the practice of cremation—which is not allowed in Greece—and had decided to make, or had already made, a will asking relatives to carry their dead bodies abroad and have them cremated; one of them, an ex-mariner, had already bought the urn for his ashes. Finally, others had joined recently established pro-cremation groups in Athens, in the hope that this practice, legitimate in other countries of the European Union, could be also established in Greece. In fact, almost all donors wish to have their bodies cremated after having donated parts or the whole of their bodies. Apart from having a "fast and dignified death," they believe that combining the two practices is the perfect way to undermine black markets for organs that, "from what they *know*," flourish in Brazil, China, India, Albania, Turkey, and even Greece! Does this mean that they would be willing to donate and cremate their relatives' bodies and body parts? Yes and no! They would probably donate certain organs (eyes or heart) but not whole bodies; they would be skeptical about cremating them. In general, they would have preferred to bury them in a concrete place so that they could go and "see" and "speak" to them!

Listening to all these stories, I found myself in a very difficult position. I was prepared, from my prior readings, to locate donors' meanings attributed to their body, to death and donation, to Christian love and altruism, in the Greek context. I never thought that I would meet Hindus, atheists, or pro-cremationists among Greek donors, or that signing a donor card in

Greece involved so many people—other than donors themselves—spread in so many places other than Greece. The "social context," supposed to guarantee the "content" or "meaning" of donors' concepts about donation, proved too indeterminate and elusive. I *knew*, more or less, what these people were talking about because I was born an Orthodox Christian, had observed most of the above-mentioned rituals, and had read or heard about cremation, body-parts commercialization, and so on. However, I did not *understand* them, because, in the beginning, I felt that I shared neither their fears nor their images of escape from rituals. More specifically, I am an atheist myself but have never related it to the consequences of my death. Although I find Hindu philosophy interesting, I don't care about it concerning myself. I have become an organ donor myself only because during fieldwork I felt compelled to do it. Nevertheless, I intend to remain so because, as my Hindu and atheist informants say, I don't care what happens to this "piece of meat" after my death. On the other hand, although it has occurred to me to become a body donor, I will not do it; I share my interlocutors' position that relatives should not be deprived of the right to bury my body and communicate with it. Finally, I refuse to be cremated; I saw my father getting burned in an accident and do not want to "see" this happening to my—dead—body!

Paradoxically, through this empathetic, rather than simply conceptual or dialectical, juxtaposition of similar and different somatic knowledge, I felt familiar with the donors' world and comfortable with, rather than frightened by, its indeterminacy. More specifically, by discovering and *attending to*, rather than neglecting, my own unconscious fear of being burned even after my death, I came closer to the donors' kinds of fears—initially incomprehensible to me. *Einfühlen*, or sensing a similar feeling, which however came from a completely different experience, made me realize that we both shared a common concern about our carnal bodies' destiny and a common fear of losing the way we sense our embodied selves with respect to embodied others. This common feeling gave further impetus to my culturally informed intuition and imagination and somehow introduced me to a legacy or *habitus* that, until then, I was unconscious of but that my informants had already reworked into practices meaningful to themselves and their relations to many others. In other words, whereas I was just discovering "how *corporeal* [rather than spiritual] a dogma Greek Orthodoxy is,"[26] my informants had already attended to this local somatic knowledge and had integrated it with more global practices imaginatively experienced as more pleasant and useful than the ones promised by Greek Orthodoxy: almost none of them will wait for the Second Coming of

Christ to have their bodies resurrected because all abhor the idea of decomposition and exhumation intervening between (their) Orthodox Christian death and (their) resurrection. Instead, through the institutions of donation, imported from the United States, and cremation, to be imported from the European Union, they will skip these two horrifying experiences and retain the "image" of their embodied selves the way they will be *immediately* after death, that is, as "semi-alive"—neither fully dead nor fully alive.[27] The more "intact" their bodies are to be kept (i.e., the more protected from decomposing within the grave), the more (semi-)alive they are imagined to stay and the more tangible, visible, audible, their relations to the living are imagined to remain after death. Is this one reason I wish to remain a donor myself even after fieldwork?

None of these empathetic realizations or co-experiences provided me, the ethnographer, with "an almost preternatural capacity to think, feel, and perceive like a native,"[28] namely, like a person who became a prospective donor only after having gone through so many and such long, conscious and unconscious, painful and pleasant experiences. Instead, they made me fully aware of the co-experiential character of *all* practices (including ethnography) and familiarized me with the always already non-immediate, and thereby elusive and indeterminate, nature of all "experiences"-as-dispositions (including the disposition to practice ethnography). This means that I have been liberated from the fear of "losing," or the illusory hope of "finding" ways to "rescue" the "raw" material of fieldwork—a concern usually ending by locating cultural formations that seem to be "nearer" to native experiences and therefore more "central" to the local society.[29] Does this mean that substituting dispositions for concepts eschews the problem of "representing" the cultural Other, especially when the time comes to write about it, that is, to transform the "active" and uncontrollable—because "immediate"—dialogical or sensory co-experience into "static" yet neat and controllable texts? The ethnographer who juxtaposes his or her own disposition to others' dispositions is particularly sensitive to the embodied and bodying forth tempo(rality) of such co-experiences. This means that the ethnographer is aware of their irreversibility, and hence non-re-presentability and partiality; he or she considers "losses" in comprehension and interpretation and representation of cultural otherness inevitable, not only because of cultural differences or their final transformation into "written" text, but because of their temporal nature: of the time constantly intervening and defining—not definitively—the meanings of all past, present, and future practices, including writing about the Other. Thus, instead of trying to *center* analysis by *privileging* (and hence *detemporalizing* and *disembodying*) certain cultural forms or concepts versus others, this ethnographer accepts the somatic and intersubjective (and thus dispersed, indeterminate, nondefinitive) nature of her own and her informants' interpretations. She knows that, not only during but also after fieldwork, "the domain of interpretive possibilities is continuous between those of observer and those of observed."[30] In other words, writing at "home alone" (no less than conversing in fieldwork or text reading or translating or dancing or dreaming or keeping silent) is a somatic mode of attention: a *culturally elaborated* way of attending to and with one's body to surroundings that include the embodied (actual or imagined) presence of others. In this new intersubjective milieu ("home") to which colleagues' comments should also be added, nothing will be "lost" or "found" or "rescued" in order to be "re-presented," as "near" as possible to natives' experience and the co-experience of fieldwork. New meaningful yet indeterminate realities will present themselves in written form, and no one will know exactly whose property they are. The ethnographer who is conscious of this will undertake the responsibility of telling readers that the faults of the book are of course the ethnographer's alone, so that readers feel free to add their own interpretations to it. This is another way to conceptualize Geertz's assertion that,

> in the study of culture, analysis penetrates into the very body of the object—that is, *we begin with our own interpretations of what our informants are up to, or think they are up to, and then systematize those*.... In short, anthropological writings are themselves interpretations, and second and third order ones to boot. (By definition only a "native" makes first order ones: it's *his* culture.) They are, thus, fictions; fictions in the sense that they are "something made," "something fashioned" ... not that they are false, unfactual, or merely "as if" thought experiments.[31]

Words as Dispositions

Every time I expose these thoughts to an audience—be it students or colleagues or others—the majority ask me whether "in the long run" I perceive and represent informants' dispositions "by means of *words*." This question echoes Geertz's asking, in all honesty, "Are we, in describing symbol uses, describing perceptions, sentiments, outlooks, experiences? And in what sense? What do we claim when we claim that we understand the semiotic means by which, in this case, persons are defined to one another? That we know *words* or that we know *minds*?"[32]

Despite my assertion that socially informed embodied knowledge or dispositions include "from silence to gesture to *language*," my audience not only identifies dispositions with nonverbal gestures but considers the latter not "expressive" enough to be read and interpreted. Apparently, dispositions are identified with "experiences," understood as inner, spontaneous, unmediated, and therefore unobservable and anterior to outer, observable, culturally mediated typifications such as "words." This stance reproduces the perennial distinction between experience and language; the latter is seen as not "experiential," because related to mind, thought, consciousness. Consequently, verbal language is approached as linear, logical, predetermined by social conventions, and therefore more "constructed," more social or "public," than experiences, perceptions, sentiments, outlooks. For all these reasons, however, discourse is considered the most useful tool to represent nonverbal experience "scientifically,"[33] and simultaneously, the expressive means that most distorts and belies the vital significance of lived experience, including body language.[34] Anthropologists who adopt this position constantly face the dilemma of how to "close the gap between descriptive language and the actions described."[35] One proposal has been to read action as (if it were) a text; another is to read language as (if it were) polyphonic or dialogical action; neither one bridges the gap between *body*-action and *mind*-language. Another approach, coming from carnal hermeneutics, could be to read words as dispositions or *habitus*, that is, as socially informed "verbal gestures" or "one of the possible uses of our [socially informed] body,"[36] as one of the many "experiences" we live with others within nonlinear time. Here, then, unlike Bourdieu, who distinguishes *habitus* from discourse, words, and consciousness,[37] we see language as one's embodied, multisensory, and emotional knowledge or skill made up and shared with others both unconsciously (when we think we are literally speaking by means of "dead metaphors"[38] and we do not feel the need to explain) and consciously (when we objectify it, we invent and perform new metaphors, neologisms, and seemingly new realities—not simply objectifications) if, of course, we are similarly *predisposed* to it, that is, we (have learned to) share similar embodied knowledge or experiences; if not, we feel we speak different languages.[39] Because *language* is *habitus*, the words used in our conversations with informants "contain an 'objective intention' . . . which always outruns [interlocutors'] conscious intentions";[40] this is why "the truth [or meaning] of the [verbal] interaction is never entirely [constructed] in the interaction."[41] Each interlocutor participates with his or her own culturally informed verbal images, indexes, and symbols that do not represent inner ideas seen with the mind's eye but constitute sensory and emotional estimations of sociopolitical relations, experienced in the past and present or to be experienced in the future, with real and imagined, embodied or seemingly disembodied, others—dead persons, objects, institutions. The many metonyms upon metonyms, metaphors upon metaphors, and similes used neither obscure nor distort nor immobilize nor de-historicize experiences—especially when they project experiences impossible to be lived in the future, such as decomposing within one's grave! Being themselves experiences or dispositions, these tropes disclose how verbal gestures are as historical, temporal, and fluid as nonverbal ones.

Many potential donors, "framed" by my ethnographic interviews, were made to delve, so to speak, into their *habitus* and describe or "word" how they feel or "see" their bodies with respect to their future plans to donate them. According to a woman organ donor,

> it is the material cover of my soul which is me, something like a temple, or a box. . . . It is the image of my soul on earth . . . something like my house, so if I gave it away to medical students I would feel like selling off my furniture . . . . Although I know that when I die my body will be a piece of meat . . . nothing . . . nothing worth of making all these expenses, etc. . . . but this [donating organs versus body] is a way to leave my parents something of me to see and speak to.

No definitive definition of "the body" is given. The indeterminate character of native interpretation obliges me to become equally indeterminate and leave my "key words" aside. Nevertheless, this "tropic movement . . . from pre-objective [yet not precultural] indeterminacy to inexhaustible semiosis"[42] makes me feel anxious about how to control it, to communicate it. I feel confused with a body image (which I thought I knew), that *is* (now) or *would be* (after death) a "house," and that *will be* (after death) "meat" or "nothing" but also "something of me." I feel both familiar and unfamiliar with these "views": I live the same as my informants' society but do not perceive my body—now and after my death—as they do. A stranger in my own land, I feel tempted to follow the traditional path: to isolate donors' strange concepts, order them into antithetical pairs, and connect them with "deeper," more "central" concepts of society at large. Our conversation does not allow me to do so. While speaking, my interlocutors enter various past, present, and future relations and emotional states—only generally known to me—and depending on how they feel them, they "word" the body "house" or "nothing" or "something." When they speak positively about the religious choices they have made, they feel like calling the body "house," "temple." When they criticize the Orthodox Church priests for imposing barbarous rituals, the undertakers for exploiting people's pain, and the Greek state for refusing to pass the cremation law, the body is felt as "meat" or "nothing." When they get enthusiastic about the advantages of donation, the body organ becomes the "Olympic flame" to be transferred all over the world. When they get angry with organ dealers, the body becomes "flesh," and the organ, "flesh of my flesh." When they feel sorry imagining their relatives burying and crying over the "empty" body, then the latter is felt as "something of me." Finally, when they speak of their plans to be cremated or of their plans to modernize Greek society by claiming their civil right to cremation, they speak of the body as "energy."

I find my informants' vocabulary unfamiliar. The only word that I share is "meat": like them, I perceive my dead body as a mere "piece of meat," and yet, unlike them, I don't want it to be cremated! I would prefer it to be buried and eaten by worms. Juxtaposing "words" cross- and intra-culturally proves to be a complicated experience, as it goes beyond matters of different grammar and syntax and into the "mysteries of incarnation."[43]

What, then, are all these "words" the moment they are uttered? Are they the "conceptual means" by which "experiences" or "minds" are "re-presented," depending on the "social context" in which speakers find themselves? Are there multiple meanings attributed to "the [one] body" by "multi-positioned" actors' selves? These *spatially* oriented views not only detemporalize verbal gestures but neglect the positive or negative feelings felt by "observers" when they do or do not share their informants' "vocabulary of motives."[44] An alternative view, suggested here, would be to approach words with an emphasis on *time*: as dispositions or as "emotional engagement[s] with social and political realities."[45] Through this path, the ethnographer discovers and attends to the nonlinear nature of language, compatible not only with the "deeply rooted emotional component[s] of identity" but also with the processes of their "integration" with actual (seemingly "present") and dreamed of (seemingly "past" or "future") experiences.[46] Experienced in this way, the process of "making sense of the foreign and [of] communicating the very foreignness"[47] is felt as a hermeneutic "suspense" rather than as a "circle," and this feeling should be fearlessly disclosed in our "writing" about cultural otherness, including our own. For example, writing about certain people's decisions to become so-called prospective donors should communicate to readers this emotional state of potentiality or prospect, the more so when it concerns donors who have the right to countermand this decision—and they often do!

In case my informants did, would they have lied to me, since words are easy to use because of their "externality" to "real" dispositions? Or, for that matter, would their own conscious words have belied their own unconscious feelings? By the same token, my own words toward informants may prove otherwise—some day I may decide to be cremated. Also, my ethnography may prove "false" when read by readers who happen to be donors. Well, this is the destiny of ethnographies exposed to time-bound *dispositions* rather than space-bound *concepts*. Carnal hermeneutics is another rather complementary way to convince my audience—be it students or colleagues or even myself—that "in finished anthropological writings . . . what we call our data are really our own constructions [i.e., dispositions] of other people's constructions [i.e., dispositions] of what they and their compatriots [in this case myself] are up to."[48]

"Real Anthropology" and Other Nostalgias
Kath Weston

Imagine it. You are there, in the Department of Anthropology on any one of a number of college campuses in the United States, circa 1974. Clifford Geertz's recently published *The Interpretation of Cultures* has made it past the standard-bearers of political economy, past the guardians of waning structuralist truths, and into a graduate-student reading group.[1] No one knows yet whether the discipline will turn in the direction of meaningful explication or veer off in search of more easily replicable projects.

Students emerge from the reading group intellectually invigorated, duly impressed, but as nervous about their career options as you have ever seen them. "If this is the future of anthropology, what is to become of us?" one of them asks. "After all, we can't all write like Geertz." As, of course, we can't.

In those corridors of circumscribed power, the halls outside the faculty offices, other objections are raised: What separates thick description from phenomenology? From literature? From good journalism? Is this (really) anthropology? Objections that double as a warning: beware the interpretive method, for it has the power to entice you away from the kind of "real" ethnographic inquiry that drew you to anthropology in the first place.

Today, when uncertainty about the field's labors and prospects still reigns, it is worth remembering these early attempts to locate what would later be called "interpretive anthropology" outside the boundaries of the discipline. Perhaps those early critics mistook anthropology's impending turn to meaning for a rhetorical twist, their anxieties inflamed by an Aristotelian understanding of rhetoric as an art of seduction.[2] In the late 1990s, Renato Rosaldo still had to argue against the facile literalism that would reduce interpretive ethnography to the notion that "all the world's a text."[3] Interpretation requires an intimate grasp of empirical context. Like peripheral vision, context is notoriously difficult to narrate, since once sustained examination nudges the peripheral toward the center, there is no longer anything con(tra)textual about it.

Whatever interpretive anthropology's shortcomings, it never proposed to be a strictly rhetorical move. Yet there may have been more than a grain of insight in the association of interpretive anthropology with rhetoric and with the necessary seductions that separate a well-conceived argument from a compelling one. Interpretive anthropology has engendered a new respect for modes of presentation, modes of intellectual production, if you will, as well as widespread recognition of the inevitability that the ethnographer will have a hand in shaping and selecting "data."

However one may differ with the questions, the emphases, and the theoretical apparatus embedded in the interpretive turn, its impact on the discipline is no longer in doubt. If nothing else, it has certainly *become* anthropology. These days, the phrase "real anthropology" seeks other targets, when it does not dissolve into irony altogether. Are studies of television "real anthropology"? Studies of shopping? Advertising? Postcolonial fiction? Migration in search of work? Protests against the latest round of World Trade Organization meetings? The emergence of "gay" organizations in Jakarta? The emergence of a technology-driven bourgeoisie in Bangalore? Or is it, as I have argued elsewhere, the study by a person whose body is understood to have a naturalized, "native" connection to the topic at hand that often tends to elicit such doubts?[4]

More than a quarter of a century after the publication of *The Interpretation of Cultures*, a colleague who employs the term "real anthropology" is now more likely to elicit a rolling of the eyes, an exchange of knowing glances, perhaps even a chuckle. After all, anthropology has entered an era that requires the discipline to respond to changing circumstances by developing a range of new specialties, each of them vying for legitimacy, none with any particular purchase on the real. Or has it?

These days, many of us would like to consider ourselves intellectually sophisticated about the high stakes that people invest in claims to authenticity. Ethnographers jockey to position themselves at some remove from any allegiance to "the real." If the real world is symbolically mediated, everywhere and always, so must be the compartments of study that historically have organized the field.[5] But when it comes time to retool the discipline, how far gone is that allegiance to authenticity, really?

There is a certain nostalgia embedded in the phrase "real anthropology," a nostalgia that references an earlier (not just more authentic) time in which anthropologists understood their work and went about it with an almost utopian clarity of purpose. "Real anthropology" is a backward-looking term, floated on beliefs, however vaguely or well substantiated, about the way things used to be for practitioners of the discipline. As such, the term encodes a certain historical consciousness, a particular understanding of the way anthropology was done in the imaginary era when Big Men were Big Men and ethnographers were ethnographers, when expeditions were well funded, when Self and Other stayed separate and stayed put.

That bygone (if never quite existent) world, for all its flux, is imagined to have granted a stability to the discipline that presumably is absent today. In those good or bad old days, the globe could be neatly demarcated into discrete societies without the pesky areas of overlap and confusion introduced by the space-time compression of jet travel and satellite communications. In the old days, people under study were supposed to be too preoccupied with their own alleged vanishing (i.e., the colonial assault) to offer critiques of the latest monographs written about them. In the old days, the authority of the anthropologist remained intact, his or her identity secure in the grasping individualism that informed claims to "my village" or yours. Topics of specialization lined up in an orderly fashion: kinship, politics, religion, economy, and any other structural-functionalist categories required to exhaust the possibilities of human endeavor. Or so the story goes.

Shadowing this imagined disciplinary past is a vision of the contemporary, no less oversimplified, no less the product of a volatile mix of political economy and memory. Today's areas of specialization appear more transient: this year, intellectual property; next year, biotechnologies; the following year—who can tell? The "trans" in this "transience" begins to organize topics of inquiry: transcultural symbolic forms, transracial adoption, transnational capital flows, transgender communities, translocal movements of resistance, each with an implicit emphasis on historical discontinuities.

Embedded in the contrast between the simpler time represented by "real anthropology" and the seemingly wider range of studies that now fall within anthropology's purview is an element of mourning for the orderliness, the predictability, indeed the discipline, presumed to characterize the field in days gone by. Or the reverse: an element of celebration that forgets to consider the possibility that anthropology's current expansiveness—its apparent readiness to embrace all and sundry—may be overrated. In either case, nostalgia filters out irony. Imagine attributing stability to a field at the very phase of its development when it had undertaken as its project the study of forms of living that appeared to ethnographic eyes to be rapidly passing from this world! Such are the dangers of sentiment, be they of loss or self-congratulation.

"Real anthropology" was, and remains, a disciplinary term. Its invocation implies that in recent times, when anthropology has stumbled from grace, some policing of the boundaries of the discipline is necessary to separate acceptable from unacceptable topics or methods of study. And although the overt injunction to pursue "real anthropology" seems to have fallen out of fashion, the backward-looking glance encoded in the phrase is very much alive. The policing embedded in the phrase too remains very much an ongoing, everyday occupation in an occupation that has come to perceive itself as embattled. Even as colleagues appear to abandon "real anthropology" to contemporary sophistication and wit, even as the laughter that greets the phrase is offered up to the gods of change, the notion of real anthropology reemerges as a more generalized nostalgia that continues to afflict the field.

In the United States at least, nostalgia for the golden era of anthropology must be placed in the context of a wider fascination with all things retro at this latest turn of a century. From wooden roller coasters to martinis, from the rehabilitation of aging disco stars to the renewed popularity of Harley-Davidson motorcycles, yesterday's passé has become chic. But to treat the infusion of nostalgia into discussions of the remaking of anthropology solely as a matter of style would stop short of a fuller understanding of the dynamics entailed. For there is also a political and economic context to the debates about what is to become of this field.

In the United States, such debates are often informed by the perception that anthropology is engaged in a struggle for institutional survival. Within the North American academy, anthropology is considered a small field, relegated to the margins by administrators and publishers alike. Even in periods of economic expansion, departments regularly face funding cuts and have difficulty securing authorization for new hires. Some of this can be attributed to the restructuring of higher education more generally, but anthropology still seems to lose out relative to many other disciplines. Times have changed since 1877, when the secretary of the Smithsonian Institution characterized anthropology as "the most popular branch of science."[6]

In a development that shows that history does not lack for humor, anthropology would now appear to have traded ideological places with its onetime subjects of study. The fear that fuels nostalgia is precisely this:

what if anthropologists themselves have joined the ranks of the vanishing? Even those, such as Marc Augé, who beg to disagree, seek to assuage this concern. "The idea defended here," writes Augé in *An Anthropology for Contemporaneous Worlds*, "is that social anthropology, by the very fact of its self-critical tradition, is fully capable of adapting itself to the accelerated change."[7] In the shadows of such passages hovers a threat to the discipline that must be repelled, whether through "adaptation," innovation, or disavowal.

If ever there was evidence that a cursory review of Talal Asad's collection *Anthropology and the Colonial Encounter* has proved insufficient to dispatch anthropology's entanglement with colonialism, it is this: observe the means by which many of us have attempted to fight these disquieting trends.[8] Two ghostly reminders—remainders—of colonization come to mind. Call the first flag-planting; the second mapmaking.

The flag-planting approach asks anthropologists to stake an exclusive claim to particular methodologies or concepts, all, of course, in the name of saving the discipline. Ethnography becomes a distinctively anthropological practice with a long academic pedigree, and pity the poor sociologist who has only lately discovered it. Culture is "our" concept, and damn any cultural-studies type who tries to claim it for his or her own.[9] This is a possessive idiom with a history of rough service in land conflicts and trademark disputes, given new life in the fields of intellectual inquiry.

The mapmaking approach to disciplinary salvation mobilizes colleagues to map out a host of new topics with bright red boundaries and then rush to christen them subfields. Mapmaking can carry its own nostalgias: for systematicity, for organic harmonies, for the comprehensiveness of conquest. There are good arguments to be made, of course, for arriving at categories of convenience to demarcate intellectual labor. But why the rush?

To date, there has been relatively little discussion of the advantages and disadvantages associated with the reifications required to produce specific subdisciplines. Nor have we as anthropologists bothered to distinguish carefully between emergent nodes of inquiry, where scholarly interests coincide, and a more rigid organization into subfields, which tend to have a long half-life in job ads and thus in the organization of departments. Subdisciplines, once disseminated and legitimated, require time to dismantle. (Witness the hardiness of "international development" in the face of the withering critique of modernization theory.) When it comes to reification, it behooves anthropology to take its institutional time.

Two cases in point that bear upon my own scholarship involve the inauguration of "the new kinship studies" and "sexuality studies." The implication that today's study of familial ideologies, reproductive technologies, and so on is a new variant of the old, or at least a departure from something already established and well known, sidelines some of the more productive aspects of the critique that David Schneider and others leveled at the concept of kinship itself. At its best, that critique opened possibilities for thinking afresh about the forms of human solidarity, not to mention thinking across the lines of received analytic categories.[10] Perhaps kinship is not a given, much less a subdivision, the sort of "thing" you can follow through its changes because you know it when you see it. Perhaps the assumptions that qualify certain topics for study under the rubric of "kinship" bear further scrutiny, now as then. Why not suspend closure long enough to build creatively upon that disciplinary break?

Likewise, the establishment of a settled something called "sexuality studies" relies upon an Anglo-European category (sexuality) of relatively recent vintage that incorporates a plethora of assumptions about gender, practice, and personhood. To be sure, "sexuality" is a term now widely used outside Europe and North America, but often with very different semiotics and syntax. What does that subdivision give us and what does it demand, especially in terms of its regulatory effects?

To be clear: I am thrilled to see scholarship flourish in these areas, a development that I have supported at some professional cost. What becomes problematic is a preemptory haste to reorganize the discipline in lieu of engaging in the necessary interrogation of the terms used to map out a subfield's borders. That sort of reification can lock down inquiry, leading analysts away from precisely the kind of thick description and even thicker explanations required. Any rush to christen subfields accordingly risks falling into ethnonostalgia, a naive alliance of relativism and empiricism that asks how the So-and-Sos conceive of sex, how the Such-and-Suches do kinship "these days," still safely ensconced over there, even if "over there" now takes the shape of a fertility clinic in Bangkok or an ecotourism project in Mozambique. Ethnonostalgia will place any fledgling subfield at odds with the work required to theorize border crossings.

Both flag-planting and mapmaking ride the wave of nostalgia by attempting to reinscribe boundaries at the very historical moment that celebrates the hybrid and the "trans." Both flag-planting and mapmaking rest their case on the preservationist conviction that foundations, administrators, and the like will treat things old and preferably unique (culture, ethnographic method) as something worth conserving. Should that not come to pass, with the marketing of a limited number of concepts and methods as "anthropology's," perhaps brand recognition can do the rest: "Coming soon, for a limited time only, from the folks who brought you 'culture' . . ."

Like all nostalgias, this yearning to develop strategies that will return us to an age of remuneratively employed ethnographers and neatly bounded disciplinary objects cannot be satisfied. It represents an unattainable desire, in part because, as Gilles Deleuze reminds us, repetition yields difference, not sameness.[11] Today's candidates for the title of subfields do not represent parallel categories even to Euro-American ways of thinking. The scarcely intuited yearning for return is also unattainable because, like all nostalgias, it is based on an airbrushed reading of the past. Anthropology has never been so stable nor hardly so neat.

At the same time, there is reason to take these nostalgias seriously, both for their instigation—after all, the moves to withdraw institutional support are real enough—as well as for the specificity of the longings they entail. Not all aspects of disciplinary history have come into view with that backward glance.

Where have the current nostalgias tended to focus? As discussed above, on the re-creation of subfields, on the search for distinctive concepts and methodologies, buttressed by reverential nods to the unprecedented complexity of it all. (A lingering narrative of modernity, surely.) One might equally well ask where the current nostalgias have hesitated to roam. At one time, appeals to "science" provided considerable institutional leverage: anthropology is real science, hard science, our forebears argued, and thus worthy of financial support. Among sociocultural anthropologists today, one sees little desire to go back to that way of self-styling the discipline.

By the last quarter of the twentieth century, the association of science in anthropology with sociobiological reductionism had largely relegated interest in the theoretical contributions of math and science to biological anthropology. I am not speaking here of the many insightful ethnographic studies of laboratories and scientific communities, of course. Nor do I mean to overlook the growing number of studies of the ways that medicine and technology figure in popular culture. I have in mind something rather different: the noticeable lack of interdisciplinary dialogue across the lines of anthropology, science, and mathematics for the purposes of elaborating analytic frameworks. Our latest nostalgias have not carried us there.

Within sociocultural anthropology, the historical reaction against modeling the discipline on "hard" science included a move to break away from systemic accounts, replicable generalizations, and rule-bound analyses, as well as the formal mathematical symmetries encoded in structuralist analyses. In this sense, the turn toward interpretive anthropology also represented a turn away from science and mathematics as such. Yet this refusal targeted a kind of science that was then already outdated. The science that sociocultural anthropology rejected was thoroughly Newtonian in its search for generalizable rules or laws.[12] The mathematics that sociocultural anthropology rejected was thoroughly Euclidean in its restriction to two or three dimensions. Yet the same kind of discredited or at least superseded geometric space that allowed Claude Lévi-Strauss to chart his mythemes continues unobtrusively to shape avant-garde social science metaphors: borders, lines, intersections, levels, scales, points, grids, and of course the "trans" that introduces transverse and transept as well as transnational.

While anthropology set its interpretive course, the scientific and mathematical disciplines were experiencing a qualitative turn of their own. Rather than casting the universe in the image of law, their students had to grapple with the implications of non-Euclidean geometries and post-Einsteinian physics. What to make of broken symmetry, closed timelike curves, twists in spacetime, boundary conditions, wormholes, infinite speeds, four-dimensional creatures, or a runaway universe? What would, could, anthropology make of the same? Rejuvenated metaphors, to be sure, as well as an opportunity to move interdisciplinary scholarship in rather different directions.

In some of my own work, for example, I have gone to the history of mathematics to trace the diasporic travels of the concept of zero, and then used the zero to develop a less fetishized, more temporally situated approach to gender than those most prevalent in gender theory. Time-travel paradoxes allowed me to attempt to articulate the relationship between the production of gender, historical memory, and modernity in new and less naturalized ways.[13]

More generally, a dialogue with science provides a useful way of identifying Newtonian and Euclidean categories that tacitly continue to structure our thinking. No need to be a math whiz to cross this particular line or, as Euclid's successors might say, to double back upon the discipline like a Möbius strip. Some of the most revered scientists of this generation have taken the time to set down accounts of their fields in words accessible to a numerate but not necessarily number-crunching audience.[14] The concepts that inform contemporary scientific theory remain culture-bound, no doubt, equally entangled in bids for institutional funding, but for all that, the ears of most anthropologists are less accustomed to them. That is why I often find these concepts valuable for augmenting a sense of what anthropology would and could be.

There are other tundra zones besides science where lightly equipped nostalgias cannot long endure exposure. Anthropology's colonial history is one. When it comes to colonialism, a sense of "been there, critiqued that" reigns. Few hurry to make a pilgrimage back to what are now commonly understood as sites of disciplinary shame. In an eagerness to put the nasty business of the discipline's implication in colonial regimes behind "us," many current practitioners assign colonialism to the past. But anthropology's colonial history is also current history, in the sense that the discipline has work left undone in the wake of only partially realized colonial critiques. These critiques are partial in the sense of necessarily remaining incomplete, yet their incomplete realization is also partial in the more problematic sense characterized by split and attenuated political loyalties.

To understand such partiality, consider David Scott's tripartite division of colonial critiques into problem-spaces of the anticolonial, the postcolonial, and "after postcoloniality."[15] By *problem-spaces*, Scott means a set of historically linked questions and answers that emerged in response to changing political and economic circumstances. Within anthropology, anticolonial critique incorporated an account of Anglo-European expansion framed in part by the discourse of nationalist movements. Ethnographers who colluded with colonial administrators in Africa, researchers who worked for the CIA in Vietnam, a discipline institutionally rooted in the metropole—these were the targets of anticolonial critique, sometimes coupled with the political demand that anthropologists "go home," in effect opening up the space for subalterns to offer (or refuse) accounts of their "own" societies.

Postcolonial criticism brought with it a revaluation of rhetoric and representation that in many cases still begs to be applied.[16] As anthropologists recognized the subordination built into a term such as *informant*, for example, they began to speak of collaborators and coparticipants, newly allotted a "voice" in the text. The monumentality accorded to this shift was clearly not the product of war, since as anyone in wartime will tell you, there is an invisibly fine line between informing and collaboration. Rather, the postcolonial critique within anthropology emerged during the years following the nationalist wars for independence, when nation-states set about establishing and consolidating their polities. Subsequently, ethnographers have had to come to terms with the fact that anyone in a position to give textual shape to a voice remains positioned as a presiding officer of a sort, to the detriment of any pretensions to equality between researcher and researched. And if, after so much experimentation, ethnographic modes of writing are still so very often found uncongenial by those they purport to describe, then the field still has some work to do to figure out why. "Virtual anthropologists" have much to teach in this regard. As the ethnographers that well-meaning colleagues judge to be "natives studying themselves," virtual anthropologists have no chance to become "real anthropologists" in the nostalgic sense of the term. Yet they too are implicated—albeit differently—in colonial discourse.[17]

As for a critique "after postcoloniality," it has barely begun. To pursue such a reformulated critique would require the discipline to open more inquiries into the ways that colonialism helped generate the terrain on which collaboration, resistance, and indeed ethnography become possible.[18] One example can be found in Mel Tapper's study of the race politics of sickle-cell anemia.[19] Tapper could simply have exposed the collusion of doctors, anthropologists, and government administrators in setting up the testing programs that transformed sickle-cell anemia into a marker of racial or ethnic identity (an anticolonial critique). Or he could simply have set about identifying the assumptions embedded in representations of sickness, ethnicity, and so forth that furthered colonial domination (a postcolonial critique). The critique "after postcoloniality" develops when Tapper goes on to consider the ways that technologies, research programs, colonial administrative practices, and the isolation of "sickle cell" as a disease entity combined to shape a terrain on which nationalist movements as well as contemporary discourses of modernity would later build.

In the broadest sense, a critique of the field after postcoloniality would have to supply historical context for the kinds of questions that have preoccupied anthropologists who do not define themselves as working on colonialism per se. And what kind of politics would follow from that?

In addition to nostalgias ventured and nostalgias abjured, there are latent nostalgias that are no less powerful because they elude naming as such. Methodological discussions are loaded with assumptions about what constitutes ethnography, even at its most innovative. Embedded in many usages of the term *ethnography* is a certain reverence for the way things used to be, when face-to-face meant a few strides away rather than Webcams at two ends of an Internet hookup, when fieldwork meant immersion in a fixed place rather than a series of mobile encounters strategically designed to create a research space. Pick up any university-press catalog with a significant anthropology list, and you will see advertisements that play on this longing: "For those who still believe anthropology means ethnography . . ."

Techniques developed to study across boundaries—disciplinary or otherwise—still often assume a relatively stable form of ethnography that can be conducted in manifold sites. In George Marcus's perceptive schema, multi-sited ethnographies can be grouped according to what they follow from place to place or space to space: the people, the thing, the plot, the metaphor, the conflict.[20] What and where the anthropologist follows seems to overshadow discussion of what he or she might do differently having "arrived" at multiple destinations.

Even as such ethnographies depart from older fieldwork designs, some of the best exemplars of this trend continue to rely on a site-specific, community-based model of ethnography. Not that these studies are unimportant. Anthropology would be the poorer without Roger Rouse's ingenious conceptualization of transnational migration circuits and Brenda Jo Bright's work on the ways that Chicano lowriders customize the mass-produced commodities that are their cars.[21] Perhaps, though, multi-sited ethnography offers only a bridge from the bounded communities of an imagined past to a future that seems much harder to dream. These ethnographies rest, after all, on an operation of multiplication that keeps the notion of field sites, if not a field site, intact, even unto the metaphor of the global village. So how far have we moved, methodologically speaking, from "village anthropology" by way of an exercise that leaves the terms of investigation undisturbed, yielding village-as-villages, village-as-corporate-boardroom, village-as-scientific-lab?

If we as anthropologists take a more critical stance toward the nostalgic impulse to make the discipline "real" again, we can do so in the confidence that what really makes something anthropology is neither a certain object nor a certain method, but rather a kind of *engagement* that can have been produced only by the history of a discipline, this discipline. Such an engagement applies equally well to a conversation, an observation, an interview, a text. It represents knowledge of a sort unlikely to be ventured by the historian or, if you like my vision of interdisciplinarity, by the physicist sitting beside you in a study group. The engagement that is anthropology is a matter of the framing of topics and questions brought to bear, a matter of that unfinished colonial critique, a matter of recognizing the desire to return for what it is when it beckons. To borrow a phrase from a mathematician, Ian Stewart, the distinctiveness of this engagement is what continues to give anthropology an "unreal reality" all its own.[22]

Above all, the intellectual legacy of anthropology—itself already impossibly hybrid—needs to be placed in historical rather than nostalgic perspective. For it is this legacy, not unique methodologies or concepts, not closely defended terrain, that makes us anthropologists. History is no more or less symbolically mediated than longing, and like other forms of heritage in today's world, the legacy of anthropology may have to be marketed as such. But secure in the value of an intellectual inheritance, anthropologists can extend the critiques of the discipline that need to be extended and venture interdisciplinary dialogue without adopting a proprietary stance. To do so requires that we periodize our longings with greater historical specificity. The alternative is to submit to static contrasts between past and present or to modernization narratives about the discipline catching up with an increasingly complex world. Nostalgia has its pleasures and its place, but it goes down better slightly chilled, at a remove from historical accounts.

Canonical and Anticanonical Histories
Antonis Liakos

Plurality of the Local Meanings of History

The purpose of this paper is to propose an interpretation of national historiography(-ies) as a specific way of making sense of the past, within a framework of tensions in the making of a global sphere of production of history. The term *history* is a linguistic and cultural indicator of diverse ways of understanding social temporality. These ways of understanding are different in time and space. In some cultures, the concept of history and more generally the understanding of chronology were entirely different from the meaning of history in Western tradition. In Polynesia, for instance, historicity unfolds as an eternal return, the recurrent manifestation of the experience of ontogeny, which recapitulates its ontology.[1] What in Western tradition is called *history* exists as the "*Spring and Autumn Annals*" (attributed to Confucius) or the "*Tso* tradition" in China, as "*Rikkokushi*" or the "*Six National Histories*" in Japan, as "Itihasa" in India, as short histories in Arab and Islamic tradition, as the Bible in Jewish tradition, and as eschatology in Christian tradition.[2] In preclassical Greece, neither the concept of time nor reference to reality was contained in the term *logografoi*, used to describe the recorders of oral tradition.[3] Writing about the past was part of rhetoric. The use of the term *historia*, in the sense of investigation and inquiry, was connected with Hippocratic semiotics. What was expected from history was not a representation of something fictitious but an investigation of the invisibility of reality.[4] The term *history*, placed between medicine and rhetoric, was at the crossroads of two semiotic systems, investigation and representation.[5] The dynamics of this semantic transformation were connected with the emergence of citizenship.[6] Both terms, *history* and *citizenship*, were the result of an awareness of the changing nature of society and the active role of human agency. However, Greeks employed the term *history* only in relation to the recent past, a space of still living experience. For the remote past they employed the term *archaeology* and were quite uninterested in investigating it.⁷ The inclusion of the past in its entirety within history was a consequence of the Roman expansion to the whole of the then known world. The absence of any sense of investigation in medieval historiography was expressed by the employment of the term *chronicle*. Historical writing was reduced to a simple description of the temporal sequence of events, and the meaning of the term *historicize* (ιστορώ) was extended to visual representation and the painting of icons. The painter of icons was described as *historiographer* or *historiotechnitis* (i.e., the maker of holy images).⁸ *History* retained this double meaning of history (*Geschichte*) and image until the sixteenth century. In the following centuries, *history*, in the sense of the representation of the past, was employed alongside the concept of *res gestae*. The emphatic singular of the term (*historia*) derived from seventeenth- and eighteenth-century philosophy, as the inherent sense of a unified world history. For this reason, when history was first taught in German universities and Jesuit colleges, it was taught as universal history.⁹

The conception of history and the meaning given to the term depend on the historicity each culture produces. The way in which society sees itself determines both the historical view and vice versa: culture is historically determined not only because of its formation in time but also on account of the perceptions over time that constitute part of the warp and weft of culture. As a consequence, it is difficult to describe what history is or what it is about in terms common and recognizable in different cultures. Rather, to understand what history is in each case, we have first to penetrate the cultural connotations. What we call *history* is strictly woven into each cultural environment. The meaning of historicizing therefore depends on "local knowledge."

The Transplantation of History

Since the nineteenth century, the term has acquired a stricter meaning, epitomizing principles and values that had been elaborated in Western Europe up to then. Historicism transcended German borders and became a philosophy, theory, and method of history. According to Friedrich Meinecke, "historicism is only the application to history of the new life principles conquered by the great German movement from Leibniz to Goethe's death."¹⁰ As a consequence, what we now recognize as history has spread across national cultures over the past two centuries. It took the form of written text and not of oral stories; it was written in prose and not in verse; it described linear and not circular time; it aimed at verisimilitude and not fiction; it constructed narratives that claimed evidentiality; it used footnotes and provided references for its sources; it conformed to the norms and the standards of historical research; and so on. The type of thinking and writing that we call history is a product of modernity, a plant of Western culture, transplanted all over the world, obscuring and substituting for other forms of History. Although elements of historical writing, such as the criticism of sources, the sequence of cause-effect relationships, and the like, were common to Arab and Chinese historiography, an epistemic rupture took place, which transformed all other histories into the pre-history of History. This sharp change is visible inside and outside Europe.

When and where did this rupture happen?

- During the formation of nation-states in Central, Southern, and Eastern Europe and East Asia (from the nineteenth century through the first half of the twentieth century)[11]
- During the era of colonization in the same period
- During the period of postcolonial nation building in the post–World War II era

Each period has specificities and common elements, and the encounter between the different ways of writing history and their consequences to the formation of historical consciousness is worth studying. The formation of nation-states was the more efficient vehicle for the worldwide transplantation of the Western concept of history. An example of this transplantation is the Greek case. Although there was a tradition of historiography in Greek language from Herodotus to Eusebius and then to the Byzantine historians of the fifteenth century, modern Greek historiography was the product of the establishment of an independent state at the beginning of the nineteenth century. The postindependence Greek historiography was closer to its contemporary German, French, or English historiography than to the ancient and Byzantine tradition of historiography. Similar was the case with the Balkan states that were created in the nineteenth and early twentieth centuries. Historiography and statecraft were interconnected.

The newly created states tried to organize their historiographical enterprise by imitating the genre of historical writing and the methods of historical compilation, founding archives and historical departments in their universities, publishing textbooks, and so on. The difference between the noncolonial countries of the European periphery and the postcolonial countries of Asia and Africa is that the former had to imitate and transplant models from Western Europe, whereas the latter had first to oppose and then to transform models imposed by the colonial powers.[12] During colonization, Western missionaries, officials, and scholars undertook the task of writing down the history of *peoples without history*. The meaning of this engagement with history was the translation of the knowledge of the (non-Western) *other* into the (Western) intellectual and cultural framework. The representation of non-Western histories and cultures by Western scholarship has been explored since Edward Said's *Orientalism* in 1978, mainly by postcolonial, subaltern, and black studies.[13]

The relationship between history and nation was, and still is, one of the most productive fields as well as a fashionable theme in historiography. But the main emphasis was put to the internal aspects of the history-nation relationship. What was neglected is the textualization of this relationship to a broader, supranational context. If the idea of the nation is a pattern of social organization with claims to universality, its universality depends on the enhancement of the individuality and particularity claimed by each nation. To be recognized universally, newly formed nations required a common language to convey their individuality. This common language was to be found in history. But in this case, under the term *history*, two meanings were hidden: *historia rerum gestarum* and *res gesta*. The first meaning refers to historiography as a recognizable form of treating the past. The second meaning refers to the content, to the manifestation of the national individuality during the historical time.

The diffusion of historiography runs parallel to the diffusion of the novel. Since the end of eighteenth century, the novel was a place where West European patterns met the local reality. The first gave the pattern where the local experience as a raw material was melting in. The idea of the plot and of the simultaneity of disperse actions belongs to the pattern. The social characters belong to the local reality.[14] But unlike in the novel, in history writing, the content is not a raw material indifferent to the form, because history writing is not only referring to the past, but it has also a strong comparative component. Writing history is part of a broader practice of comparative activities that intensified during the eighteenth century in Western Europe and have grown to embrace the rest of the world ever since. These activities, including travel literature, correspondence, missionary work, diplomatic activities, and research, were forms of rendering the European experience of the world familiar to European home audiences. They were stimulated by the spread of commerce, capitalism, technology, emigration, and navigation; by intellectual movements such as the

Enlightenment; and by political aspirations such as those embodied in nationalism. Comparative activities in brief were created by every movement that was not confined to local and national borders. History belonged to these comparative activities, even before it was conscious of being comparative. Historiography could be seen as a grammar of representation with a twofold function. It represented the history of the particular community to the outside world, and at the same time, it represented the worldly to the local. National historiography was its main and outstanding example. It spoke on behalf of the nation to the world, and it familiarized the world history to the national audience. Imagining the nation was impossible without a comparative series of activities. Not only the sameness of the national identity was founded on making manifest the differences from other national, supernational, or subnational identities, but the whole project of nation building was shaped on an interplay of imitation and competition. Nationalism is a "ground of comparisons."[15] On this ground even national historiography grew up as a comparative historiography, and that was true for the set of national disciplines: philology, anthropology, law, political and social sciences, folk studies. National historiographies were constructed not only as a nation's self-image but, at the same time, as a representation of the nation to the world. Both instances constituted a performance of the nation in which it shaped its own image of the past. Even when addressing an internal audience, national histories were to give an account of the reputation and the place of the nation as part of the world. As a consequence, they could not neglect other societies and had to adopt a comparative perspective toward them. They had to give an account of the nation's place in the imagined line of progress and civilization. From this point of view, interaction with the canon was one of the formative elements of national historiographies.

The making of comparisons in history is today an issue of debate because of the skepticism about how national histories come to terms with the complex realities of the past. Cross-national history, transnational history, *histoire croisée*, entangled history, are methods and theories aiming at the definition of what and how we are comparing and how we get cognitive value and deepen our understanding from these comparisons.[16] My argument is that comparison is not a method à la carte but a given and even coercive framework that was historically formed and imposed from within the historical discipline beginning in the nineteenth century. What I am arguing is that together with historical theory and method, and inside the description of the world past, a *canon* of world history was shaped as an implied code in writing history. It grew up like an invisible worm in an apple and became shallowed with the apple! This implied code imposed a canon of how history was evolved, and imprinted a hierarchy of nations and civilizations on the concept of history. Writing history means interiorizing the canon, and being ascribed in a mental geography prescribed by the canon. As a consequence, each nation, in writing its own history, was constrained to deal with the problem of its implied place in the mental global map. Writing history, whatever history might be, means a mediate or immediate encounter with this historical canon. That was true for world, European, and national histories, as well as for local history and social history. Through encountering *canon*, a comparative framework was established, which produced and determined the scope, the conceptual tools, the meanings, and the purposes of comparison inside national knowledge. This framework is traceable in history writing, but has also transcended its borders and is manifest in the national historical culture.

Canon and Exclusion

Since the eighteenth century, the tradition of history writing in Europe involves not only a description of the past, but also the imposition of a hierarchical view of the world, with Western Europe perched at the top. This hierarchical view has taken the form of a description of a linear course of civilization in time, space, and values. The center of history was moved from the Middle East to Greece, then to Rome, and then to Christian Europe.[17] It moved from the Renaissance to the Reformation, the Scientific Revolution and the Enlightenment, and then to modernity. Modernity and progress, taken as the capacity of society to fashion and refashion itself, lies at the core of the canon.[18] This course of history, implicit or explicit in historiography, philosophy of history, and social theory, identified the concept of "civilization" with the concept of "European civilization." This identification was first made in the epoch of the Enlightenment. As a consequence, all other civilizations were conceived in negative terms, or as deviationary currents from this main course. This form of thinking of universal history as bifurcated between the main trajectory and the unfinished or deviating paths could be described as "canon." When, for instance, Italian unification was characterized by Antonio Gramsci as *"rivoluzione mancata"* and this idea became a central idea in post–World War I Italian historiography, the underlying idea was a comparison between the "complete" French and the "incomplete" Italian revolutions. A comparison with Britain and

France was the presupposition of the German *Sonderweg* debate. Other societies were described using the negative terms of incompleteness and absence.

Canon is a Greek word. Its Latin equivalents are *regula* and *norma*. During the Hellenistic years, the canon was the collection of ancient writers. In the fourth century of the Christian era, *canon* was used with the meaning of a collection of the "authentic" books of the New Testament. The first Ecumenical Council of the Church under the Roman Emperor Constantine in 325 C.E. in Nicaea established the *"Canon of Faith,"* a short but highly normative text defining and codifying the Christian faith. Deviation from the canon was considered heresy. In the 1980s, the term was employed metaphorically in literary criticism. The tradition of literary works that were considered to embody the main aesthetic values—the European high culture from the Bible and Homer to twentieth-century literature—was called "canon." This canon took the form of a collection of literary works and of a normative history for the education of Western elites. Erich Auerbach's *Mimesis: The Representation of Reality in Western Literature* is a good example of this canon in literature. In the 1980s and 1990s the literary canon was criticized for imposing a hierarchy of values and for excluding non-Western and minor literatures.[19]

The formation of the historical canon starts with the corpus of Greek, Latin, and Hebrew texts, available to the emerging European scholarship at the end of the Middle Ages. The stories of the Bible and the Trojan War (Homer and Virgil) were the source of inspiration for the national myths of origins of the European nations. Even more the ethnic names of antiquity and Middle Ages were used to define modern nations.[20] Three elements were needed to transform this written tradition into a historical canon:

- The secularization of history and its weaning from the divine Providence
- The reordering of time: the periodization of the world according to the Bible's schema of the four empires, which corresponds to four epochs, was replaced by the triple schema of antiquity, the Middle Ages, and modern times
- The reordering of space: the center of history was transferred from Asia to Europe, and Eurocentrism became a constant feature for history and historiography

Under this deep transformation, the historical agency was transferred from the use of the peoples as vehicles of the providential will to their civilizing contribution. European historians, like Leopold von Ranke, and philosophers of history, like Hegel, developed the idea that universal history was the sequence of nations contributing to civilization. The French historian Jules Michelet, in his *Introduction a l'histoire universelle*, wrote that the whole history was a struggle between man and nature, spirit and material, freedom and fatalism. Man, spirit, and freedom were thought of as belonging to Europe, and nature, the material, and fatalism as belonging to Asia. Christian faith and morality, Greek philosophy and art, Roman law and statecraft, made up the core of this tradition, which was enriched and extended by the Renaissance, the Scientific Revolution of the seventeenth century, the Enlightenment, theories of evolution and Darwinism, social theory from Marx to Max Weber, and theories of modernization in post–World War II Europe and the United States.[21] From the point of view of this tradition, other nations of the European periphery, other continents, and non-European countries and cultures were considered negative aspects or previous stagnant stages or deviations from this course. The founder of eugenics, Karl Pearson, wrote that "the path of human progress is strewn with the decaying bones of old nations, everywhere we can see the traces left behind by inferior races, the victims of those who have not found the narrow path to perfection."[22] Even in 1965, Hugh Trevor-Roper argued that Africa has no history, merely "the unrewarding gyrations of barbarous tribes in picturesque but irrelevant corners of the globe."[23] And in the 1990s, John Vincent was still writing of Asian history as an impossibility: "We don't understand Asia and will not need to."[24] Even Karl Marx, though critical of British imperialism, concluded that the colonization of India was ultimately for the best because it brought India into the evolutionary narrative of Western history.[25]

All these theories of exclusion from the canon were spread in mentalities and political cultures fueling high national aspirations like France's *"mission civilisatrice,"* Rudyard Kipling's "The White Man's Burden," the United States' doctrine of "manifest destiny," and Adolf Hitler's notions of racial superiority. For the excluded it was impossible to be represented in the Western framework, and they were denied the capacity to represent themselves within the discipline of history.[26] The history of the non-Europeans was forged on a master narrative, the History of Europe, but as a variation of what did not belong to the master narrative, as a series of negative imprints of the main pattern. These negative imprints took the form of various disciplines such as Orientalism, Indology, Africanism, and areas studies. We could say that the European historical canon was an ideological construction equivalent to the hierarchies of power and colonization of the nineteenth and twentieth centuries.

Dealing with Exclusion

The adoption of the modern concept of history writing, by the rest of the world, was not only a matter of methodology. For the national elites, writing their national histories involved dealing with the problems of exclusion, deviation, or negativity toward this European canon of history. This confrontation became the central idea of each national history. The case of Greece is an exemplar. Modern Greece developed its own national history after its establishment as a nation-state in the beginning of the nineteenth century. The strong point of this history was the appropriation of classical Greece. In this aspect, modern Greeks could identify with the strong core of the European canon. But the medieval period of Greece (called "the Byzantium") and the modern period of Greece under the Ottoman Empire were excluded from the course of European history and considered deviations from it. For Voltaire, Edward Gibbon, and Hegel, and for the majority of the eighteenth- and nineteenth-century historians and philosophers, the Byzantine Empire represented a sequence of crimes, an epoch of religious fanaticism, that was deprived of creativity in the arts and literature and was sterile in culture—the twilights of the Roman Empire.[27] So the Greek history was partly identified and partly excluded from the canon. What possibilities of response were available to modern Greek historians?

There were three main strategies, reflecting the time period and political exigencies.

- The suppression of the undesired period: modern Greeks reclaimed the legacy of ancient Greece, dismissing their medieval legacy
- The inclusion of the medieval period in the national narrative, with the insistence that it contributed to the Western course of history
- The sublimation of the excluded period, with emphasis on its differentiation from Western cultural elements, that is, the dismissal of the Western "canon"

A common denominator of these three strategies was to claim the right for Greeks to write their own history and not to leave it to the foreigners, that is, to the European scholars. Writing the history of the nation was considered a national task not only in the Greek case. There are striking similarities between intellectuals of different countries and different epochs who acclaim the exclusivity of writing their own national history:

> Greece: Spyridon Zambelios (1852): "The Past? Alas, we allow foreigners to present it according to their own prejudices and to their own way of thought and interests."[28]
>
> Egypt: Mahmud al-Sharqawi (1975): "[Islamic history] is influenced by Western education, [which is unable] to understand Islam.... The mind that will judge Islamic life must be Islamic in its essence."[29]
>
> India: Bankim Chandra Chatterjee (1880): "We have no history. We must have a history."[30]
>
> Algeria: Mohammed Chérif Sahli (1965): "The peoples liberated from the colonial rule have to re-write their history from the inwards, in terms of colonial as subjects and not as objects."[31]

The response of the Greek historiography was not a unique one. Several national historiographies conceived of their exclusion from the Western canon as a "stigma," and they developed various strategies for dealing with it. The first strategy was to suppress and conceal the stigma from the national narrative. This suppression was facilitated by the adoption of the threefold division of the historical time according to the European pattern of antiquity, the Middle Ages, and modernity.

The Turkish case is indicative of the use of a combination of strategies to overcome the "stigma." For the Turkish Republic, the stigma had its origins in the Ottoman Empire. Ottomans were considered a nomadic people who invaded and destroyed the civilization of the Eastern Mediterranean.

The first strategy was to dismiss the Ottoman period and to invent a classical past in remote prehistoric times in Central Asia (the Sun-Language Theory).[32] The Ottoman period was considered the Turkish Dark Ages, and the establishment of the Turkish national state was viewed as a cultural and political "Renaissance." This transformation of the historical perspective paralleled a huge cultural transformation, which aimed to show, as Kemal Atatürk declared, that "no difference existed in the manner of thought between the Turkish nation and the whole family of civilized mankind."[33]

The second strategy was to include the immediate past of the Ottoman Empire in their national history, but as a period in which the differences between the European and the Ottoman history were diminished and common elements were emphasized. As the French school of *Annales* and

Fernand Braudel shifted the focus toward social and demographic history and the history of the Mediterranean world, the Turkish historiography found an opening to enter as a partner in a unified European historical space. As a consequence, the main trends in the postwar Turkish historiography were inspired by French social history, and their main task was to contribute to a unified historical space. The third strategy was the sublimation of the initially excluded past. In the postwar debate on feudalism, Turkish historians participated in the celebration of the Ottoman state as the protector of the independent peasantry of the empire. Thus, these specific elements of the Turkish social tradition were emphasized as offering (by Ömer Lufti Barkan in 1937) a solution to the social problem of the peasant and as the third way between capitalism and socialism![34]

In the Turkish case, as in the Greek case, there are two elements to consider. The first is *the invention of a classical period* beyond historical memory that was used as a source of national pride and inspiration in contrast to the attached stigma.[35] This was the case in modern Greece, in Iran (regarding the Persian past of the era of Cyrus),[36] in Egypt (regarding the Pharaonic past), in India (regarding the Vedic culture), in Israel (regarding the era of the Bible), in Ireland (regarding the Celtic past, which preserved the classical heritage in the early Middle Ages), in Italy (regarding the early modern period of communities and the Renaissance), and in the Balkan states (regarding their medieval kingdoms).[37] The essential point in the invention of a classical period was its *contribution to the world civilization* and, as a consequence, to the canon. This was the Arab case, with an emphasis on the period of expansion and on the transmission of ancient Greek and Middle Eastern knowledge to modern Europe.

A different case was that of African historians. They developed the idea of Black Africa as the birthplace of civilization. Long before the publication of *Black Athena* by Martin Bernal in 1987, they invented the "Black Pharaohs." Thus, they tried to undermine the canon and to displace it from the north of the Mediterranean to the south and from the high culture to the Neolithic agricultural revolution.[38]

The second element is the individualization of a period as the *dark interim* between the classical past and modernity. The use of the Ottoman period as a shameful historical period was not confined to the early stage of the Turkish historiography. This alienation from the past was much stronger in the Balkan and Arab nationalisms that emerged from the ruins of the Ottoman Empire. In the modern Greek historiography, this period was called the "Turkish yoke," and the four or five centuries of Ottoman sovereignty were considered a dark period of servitude and the principal cause of backwardness compared with Europe. In India, the dark interim was the age of the Mongol conquest, and in postcolonial Africa, it was the colonial period. In the structure of national histories, the counterbalance to the dark interim was the concept of *revival*. Several names were used for this concept: Celtic cultural revival in Ireland, Risorgimento in Italy to describe the nineteenth-century nation building, Palingenesia in Greece to describe the new birth of the nation, Bulgarian Renaissance to describe the making of the Bulgarian nation in the nineteenth century. The pattern of the European periodization of history was manifest in these three stages of the construction of a national history. Underneath was the interpretation of the biblical stories of paradise, the Fall of man, and salvation in secular terms. Despite its Christian origin, the threefold periodization of historical time was adopted by Indian,[39] Chinese, and Japanese historians[40] during the period of imitation of European historicism in the early twentieth century. According to Chatterjee,

> for Indian nationalists in the late nineteenth century the pattern of classical glory, medieval decline, and modern renaissance appeared as one that was not only proclaimed by the modern historiography of Europe but also approved for India by at least some sections of European scholarship. What was needed was to claim for the Indian nation the historical agency for completing the project of modernity. To make that claim, ancient India had to become the classical source of Indian modernity, while "the Muslim period" would become the night of medieval darkness.[41]

The exclusion from the canon was productive because it provided the framework for a comparison between the excluded and the canonized. Besides reordering the past, national historiographies responded to the canon by playing with the elements of differences and similarities in two ways: first, by seeing the difference in a traumatic way and by trying at the same time to indicate strongly the hidden or neglected similarities with the canon; second, by seeing the difference in a positive way and handling it as an alternative to the canon and thus turning it upside down.

Difference as "Negative Consciousness"

The convergence with and the divergence from the "civilized" Europe have been transformed into a foundational concept that defined the modern and the traditional, progress and backwardness, the moving and the static. The European past constitutes the future of the excluded. The first is made up of condensed history. The second is an empty place and time. This idea of *emptiness* is central to this polarity between European and non-European histories and creates a consciousness of absences and failures that could be described as a "negative consciousness"—negative in the sense that the consciousness is defined not by *what the subject is* but by *what the subject is not*, by the adoption of a point of view of self-exclusion.

An extensive criticism has been addressed to this way of implementing difference in a national historiography in the case of Indian history, which was read in terms of lack, failure, absence, incompleteness, and "inadequacy." "Instead of tracing the particular course of the indigenous history, therefore, the practice has been to see the history of "backward" countries as a history of 'lack,' a history that always falls short of true history."[42] For modern Greek historiography, there was no Renaissance, no Reformation, no process of secularization, no Industrial Revolution, no bourgeois or working class, no civil society in Greece. Thus, although the Greek state had the form of a Western nation-state, it was understood as suffering from a serious deformation. Negative consciousness is a constant feature of the history of the Balkan nations, and the term "Balkanization" has been used inside and outside the Balkans with a scornful or pejorative meaning.[43] Other societies were described using the negative terms of incompleteness and absence. This negative consciousness was stronger in the eastern and southern portions of Europe. The invention of the term *Central Eastern Europe* and the categorization of history within this regional conception was a consequence of this encounter with the canon. Central Eastern European historiography describes this region as not completely European but more European than Eastern Europe. The deviation from the canon was attributed to external factors, such as the Russian occupation of Eastern Europe and the Ottoman Empire's occupation of the Balkans.

A further consequence of this negative consciousness is the internal division within noncanonized societies between a modern and a traditional part, which acquires a dynamic dimension as a matter of choice. The post–World War II modern Greek historiography offers an example. Greek society has been viewed through the framework of a dichotomy between the "inertia" of the masses and the intellectual vibrancy of the elites. This interpretive framework was influenced by social theories that characterized the social change as the clash of a modernist elite with the inactive masses, as renewal versus tradition.[44] This framework was consumed, enriched, and expanded over time by a series of interrelated concepts: on the one hand, renewal, Europeanization, Westernization, rationalization, and modernization; on the other hand, inertia, conservatism, anti-Westernism. This dichotomy in various ways penetrated intellectual, political, and economic history from the eighteenth to the twentieth century. The central question, why the Greek backwardness? points to a history of absences, to the comparison between a model and its shadow. Even more this history describes its object-shadow with the terms, the methods, and the underlying value system of the model. From this point of view, recent historiography has kept apace in the formulation of the basic dilemma of Greek society, following a bipolarized conceptualization between *modernity* and *traditionalism*.

The dilemma regarding *tradition* versus *modernity* is a founding concept that reorders the historical facts and recasts them in a binary logic. This dichotomy structures the social and historical disciplines, their methods, and their theories. It is difficult to escape from this polarity of concepts and values because the analytical tools were forged in European historiography and social theory for the European realities. The historian, standing in between, speaks for the excluded, but on behalf of modernization.

In this approach, the historian resembles Janus. Looking inward, historians indicate the differences from the canon. Looking outward, they indicate the elements of sameness to the canon. Looking inside the nation, historians are critical of backwardness, advocating modernization. Looking outside the nation, they indicate in each national or regional history the elements in common with the canon that have been remained hidden or neglected, "belated" or "distorted."

The resemblance to the West and the difference from Eastern Europe in terms of civil society is a cornerstone of the historiography of Mitteleuropa.[45] The invention of a Balkan enlightenment in the eighteenth century and the Western origins of the national movements are central ideas in the historiography of Southeastern Europe. A recurrent theme in Indian historiography is the preexistence of the elements of capitalism in Indian society.

Sublimated Differences

The consciousness of the difference is not the unique cause of the division between tradition and modernity. The inner logic of the construction of a national history imposed the need to celebrate differences, particularities, and exceptionality. As a consequence, the internal division between the modernized and the traditional has been reconstructed as two domains:

the "inner" and the "outer." The inner was identified with the spiritual; the outer, with the material. Language, religion, literature, aesthetics, family life, identity, were considered to belong to the inner and the spiritual. Economy, technology, statecraft were considered to belong to the outer and the material. In the inner domain, historiographies were in search of authenticity, advocating a policy of preservation. Imitation was condemned as a parody. In the outer domain, the issue was efficiency and compatibility. The problem of compatibility has been long discussed for social institutions that stand between the inner and the outer (democracy, human rights, education, etc.). Through this division, the "inner" domain and the difference from the canon have been celebrated as the "essence" of national identity. Historiography, because of its long apprenticeship with historicism, was prone to define its task as the study of the *unique*, of the particularity, of the specific, and of the nonrepetitive.

The celebration of the differences took several forms. In some cases, differences were used as exceptionality, incompatible, but coexisting, with the canon. In other cases, they were exalted to the detriment of the canon. In the latter, the criticism of modernity by European intellectuals was used to undermine the canon and to reevaluate the excluded. According to Léopold Sédar Senghor:

> Negritude ... is a response to the modern humanism that European philosophers and scientists have been preparing. ... Africa has always and everywhere presented a concept of the world which is diametrically opposed to the traditional philosophy of Europe. The latter is essentially static, objective, dichotomic. ... The African, on the other hand, conceives the world, beyond the diversity of its forms, as a fundamentally mobile, yet unique reality that seeks synthesis.[46]

The othering of the West is manifest in the book by the influential Iranian intellectual Jalal Al-e Ahmad titled *Plagued by the West*, or *Westoxication*.[47] The significance of this book for the Muslim world was compared to the significance of Frantz Fanon's *The Wretched of the Earth* (*Les damnés de la terre*), first published in Paris 1961, for the postwar, anticolonial movements of Africa. The central idea is to reverse the *othering* of the canon. The accused or scorned *Oriental* subject was transformed into a subject proud of his *Orientality* and the difference from the West. This movement was part of a greater historical revisionism in the Arab-Muslim world. Its first target was the secular modernists. According to the Egyptian intellectual Umar al-Tilmisani, "He [Gamal Abdel Nasser] falsified

Egyptian history in a way no one would believe. He erased the history of Islam in Egypt and removed the history of Egypt in recent centuries."[48] Another Egyptian intellectual, Tariq al Bishri, explained the meaning of the "Islamic approach to history": "The Islamic approach to history . . . does not mean a new criterion for judging the objectivity of facts at hand. When we carry out historical research, and set up criteria to evaluate events, we should simply keep in mind the weight and influence of Islam, as a concept and as a culture, in shaping historical events"[49] David Gordon has noticed that these approaches underestimate the scientific standards of historiography, considering it as part of the colonial-rule apparatus.[50] The problem is not to juxtapose scientificity and anticolonialism but to see these attitudes as part of the framework of the encounter with the canon and of the strategies to overcome it.

All the adaptations of or the reactions to the canon are grounded in a comparative discourse, the concepts and categories of which were defined by the canon. Although in most cases the canon of European history was implicit in historical narratives and not explicit, it created the categories and the concepts with which we comprehend the very sense of modern history. Concepts such as culture and civilization, nation, civil society, citizenship, public sphere, and others cannot be used without imagining a comparative framework comprising both the societies in which these concepts were forged and the societies in which they were applied. This conceptual substratum determines the canonical discourse of European history, beyond the chronological structure of the historical events themselves. As a consequence, to write history means to regard these concepts as an imaginary backbone of an ideal model against which we measure delays, deviations, deformations, or particularities. In most cases, this ideal model is nothing but an image of Europe as "seen through an inverted telescope." European (and American) history observed in such a way appears highly schematic. These responses to the canon gave an all-embracing structure to the historiography of national histories, but also give rise to internal tensions. The canon and the responses to it were decisive in shaping national histories because they have decided the form and the content of national history. Should there be an apology for missing the canon or an adaptation to it? The whole process constitutes what Hayden White has called the prefiguring of the object of study: "the poetic act which precedes the formal analysis of the field [where] the historian both creates his object of analysis and predetermines the modality of the conceptual strategies he will use to explain it."[51]

Alternative Equivalence

The canon of European history, with its inclusions and exclusions, depicts the inequality of power that existed in a world climax during the long period of colonization and the rise of the supremacy of the West. It is a structure of ideas that depicts, duplicates, and goes along with this enormous reallocation of power in the world. What happens with the cultural areas outside the European colonial territories? The question regards East Asia and its two main pillars: China and Japan.

The invention of China's culture in the seventeenth century by the Jesuits was one of the stronger external earthquakes for the European historical tradition. It was described as the "death of Adam"[52] because it spread the idea that Chinese civilization was older than the world of the Bible. The awareness of the Chinese past resulted in the abandonment of the Christian pattern of the universal history and contributed to the secular reordering of historical time. Despite the shaking of the canon, Chinese history was considered an external negativity—neither inferior nor inadequate, but the negation of the progress. Johann Gottfried von Herder said that the Chinese empire "is an embalmed mummy, painted with hieroglyphs . . . in a corner of the earth, remote from stimulating contacts between other nations." For Hegel, China had "really no history." Ranke numbered the Chinese among the "races of eternal stasis." Marx in his early writings regarded China as a "carefully preserved mummy in a hermetically sealed coffin."[53]

The response to the banishment of the East Asian history from the European canon was not possible before the transplantation of Western historicism in the East in the late nineteenth and early twentieth centuries. But the response was not unique, because of the difference between China and Japan in their encounters with the West. In both countries, it was not the colonials who introduced the modern history writing. Thus, the modern writing of history was not the result of describing the past of a subaltern subject, as in India or in the Arab Orient.[54] As a consequence, the response was neither to internalize the stigma of exclusion nor to sublimate it. The response was to construct an alternative universality equivalent to that of the West. Japanese elites, outside the orbit of Western colonial power, were able to question the categories of civilized and barbarian as well as the organic bonds between modernity, development, and "Westernness." *Toyo* was constructed as an alternative to *Sheiyo*, imposing its own space and time, its own values and hierarchies. The same elements used by Westerners to explain Oriental inferiority were turned into positive characteristics of Japan's uniqueness.[55]

Summary

During the past two centuries, through various cultural encounters resulting from transnational movements related to colonialism, nationalism, and imperialism, there developed a distinctive approach to writing history that was tied to the project of modernity. The spread around the world of this modern concept of history writing was not exclusively a matter of knowing how to do modern history. It was the result of the transplantation or the adoption of historicism as a new method for turning the past into history. This tradition of history implicitly included a worldview that placed Western Europe atop a hierarchy of nations and cultures. Embedded in modern historiography from its inception was the idea that there was a single linear developmental course of civilization in time, space, and values. This perception, implicit or explicit in historiography, philosophy of history, and social theory, identified the concept of "civilization" as synonymous with the concept of "European civilization." As a consequence, all other civilizations were conceived of in negative terms as being debased, retrograde, or evolutionary deviations from the correct developmental path. Modern historiography, then, not only created a metanarrative that imposed the European experience as the true path of historical development, but it also enshrined a specific ideology and methodology as the *only* way to write history, which became the "canon" of modern history.

Although not always explicit, this canon of European or Western (in the twentieth century) history created categories and concepts out of which the discourse of modern history was constructed. European historians developed and deployed concepts, such as culture and civilization, nation, civil society, citizenship, and public sphere, as the foundation for writing the history of Europe, and by so doing they enshrined them as the central props of the canon. This had two consequences. First, it essentialized these concepts as universal elements of modernity, and since Europe experienced modernity first, it ensured that European history would be the yardstick against which all other nations would be measured. Second, when scholars and writers outside Western Europe attempted to write their nations' histories and adopted the canon as the basis for doing so, they donned an intellectual straitjacket that compelled them to narrate their nations' stories with a conceptual vocabulary drawn solely from the European experience. To do modern, scientific history, then, meant adopting a canon that invariably resulted in the writing of histories of non-European nations that explained why they were inferior to Europe—even though the canon itself was based on a very schematic, oversimplified image of Europe.

Consequently, beginning in the nineteenth century, making national histories implied a comparison with a pattern of evolution and a system of values. Scholars and writers outside the West were entangled in a dialogue that was decisive in shaping national historiographies. For each nation, writing its own history meant dealing with the problem of exclusion or deviation because the canon prioritized, marginalized, or excluded certain aspects of national histories. As a consequence, accommodating European history was a constant concern for national histories. With the same gesture, the canon was accepted, contested, or modified by national histories. The implied canon of European history created the categories and the concepts with which the very sense of modern history is comprehended and by which historians are engaging in comparative activities with or without their will and awareness. The encounter with the implied canon and the strategies of overcoming it have produced a derivative discourse by which the "spectres of comparison" (according to Benedict Anderson)[56] have been grafted onto historical work.

Anthropology at the French National Assembly: The Semiotic Aspects of a Political Institution

Marc Abélès

In the conclusion of his book *Negara: The Theatre State in Nineteenth-Century Bali*, Clifford Geertz writes: "What our concept of politic power obscures, that of the Balinese exposes; and vice versa. And so far as a political theory is concerned, it is there in exposing the symbolic dimensions of state-power."[1] Commenting, a few pages later, on the classical conceptions of the state, Geertz notes also that "in these views the semiotic aspects of the state remain so much a mummery."[2] What seems to me very stimulating in these reflections, as in the whole analysis of *Negara*, is that it opens new perspectives for the scholars who try, like me, to understand the political process from an anthropological point of view.

From these two quotations I will extract two main ideas. The first one deals with our ethnocentric conception of politics. When we think about politics, there is a sort of spontaneous association between power, violence, hegemony, and domination. These concepts are circulating all along the spectrum of political philosophy, from Thomas Hobbes to Max Weber and Antonio Gramsci. Geertz, by contrast, emphasizes the symbolic aspects of politics; he refuses to consider the equation between symbology and ideology. He produces a critique of these reductionist theories for which state ceremony is no more than mystification, hiding the real conflicts, creating an artificial consensus. But it seems to me that there is a second idea in the conclusion of *Negara*, one that posits a challenge to me, working as I am on European and French institutions. Is it possible to study the semiotic aspects of the state in occidental societies? And what do these "semiotic aspects" mean in the context of modernity or postmodernity? Trying to answer these questions, I will use some of my own data and I will argue that what Geertz calls *semiotic aspect* plays a central part in the political process if we examine all the meanings of *semiotic*.

Semiotic dimension connotes, first, the theatricality of power, the strong association between governance, ritual, and symbolism. In contemporary political institutions, the meaning of *semiotic aspects* is far more extensive, as it deals with the complex imbrication between orality and writing. We must not forget that one of the aims of politics consists in the production of the law. My study of the French National Assembly engages with the importance of the texts and the speeches.[3] This semiotic dimension of political agency has often been underestimated by political scientists. I will further suggest that a specific contribution of anthropological work on politics deals with what I would call the semiotic acting out of the politicians.

To begin, I would like to give some details on the French political system. Members of the National Assembly are elected by a majority election system in which the candidate who receives the largest number of votes wins. Normally, there are two rounds in the election. Candidates who receive less than the specified percentage of the vote in the first round are not allowed to stand in the second round, and the other minor candidates usually withdraw after the first round and offer their support to the winner or the runner-up of the first round. In France, the majority system has usually been uninominal: there is one seat to be filled per election district and voters choose a single candidate.

To be elected, a candidate must be well known at the local level, within his or her constituency. A candidate's electability depends on two different parameters: the candidate's political party and the candidate's personality and local influence. For instance, in the Paris suburbs, such as Saint-Denis and Ivry, the Communist Party has always been very powerful, and it is nearly impossible for an outsider to be elected. In the western province of Vendée, since the Revolution and the revolt of the royalist peasants against the republican order, a majority of the votes have been in favor of the rightist parties. Under such conditions, it would be very difficult for a Socialist candidate to win in those electoral areas. The historical specificity of France explains why there is a sort of political inertia in these areas (Vendée, Saint-Denis, and Ivry). French politics is still marked by three founding events: the Revolution, the separation of church and state, and the World War II Resistance. These were turning points in French history, periods of intense conflict that continue to form the collective imagination. These founding events have left their mark on the behavior of voters, which is strongly affected by the sort of imprint transmitted from generation to generation.

Legitimacy is certainly one of the key words in the French political vocabulary. To enjoy legitimacy means to belong to the world of eligible individuals to whom responsibilities can be entrusted. As I have shown in *Quiet Days in Burgundy*, the French political system places a high value on regional roots.[4] The first question asked of a candidate concerns his or her origins: whether the candidate is from the district will be a major influence on his or her future. Professional politicians take great pains to emphasize their roots and their local connections with their constituencies. Everyone places great importance on local activity. Yet I do not wish to minimize the importance of national political parties, notably in the selection of candidates. A number of candidates are sent to provinces where they have no link. This phenomenon is tellingly called "parachute landing." Some of the newcomers are successful in the election. But once elected, they will spend a lot of time promoting their local networks. An elected representative is never simply the embodiment of an idea or a party. What wins for the representative the support of his or her fellow citizens is above all the incarnation of a series of qualities that make the representative similar to those citizens. An elected representative is simultaneously a person and a symbol. Politicians are not only men or women of action; they also have the power of evocation. Many rituals are intended to express in material form the continuing identification of the elected representative with his or her community. Some rituals commemorate events that have marked significance for the community, and here the elective representatives must speak and behave in a way that magnifies their personalities, the incarnation of their common heritage. Others, such as the ceremony of inauguration, permit the display of improvements or the common heritage to which the elected representative has contributed.

One of the essential activities of the deputy consists in repeated weekly journeys to meet with his or her constituency. Part of a deputy's time is dedicated to management of economic and social problems, a task that involves numerous meetings with local elected representatives, as members of the state administration. The deputies also spend much time in ceremonies of inauguration and commemoration that are not so different from those that anthropologists have observed in non-Western societies. There is, of course, no ritual sacrifice; instead, monuments are unveiled, a minute's silence is observed, and so on, but the meaning of the ceremony, the affirmation of local roots and a common territory, are equally basic rituals. Those who refuse to devote the required time to these political rituals will sooner or later learn, to their detriment, that it is a mistake to neglect this aspect of political representation. All deputies, whatever their political affiliation, divide their week into two almost equal parts: from Monday afternoon to Thursday night, they work in Paris at the National Assembly; from Friday morning to Monday afternoon, they stay with their constituency. For a deputy, the best way to enforce his or her local influence is to be at the same time a local representative, a mayor, or a member of the departmental assembly, the conseil général. Until the 1980s, there was no restriction on what we call the *cumul des mandats*. I knew a deputy who was simultaneously a member of the European Parliament (MEP), president of the departmental assembly, mayor, and conseiller régional. Nowadays, one may not hold more than three political offices. But it is very difficult to fight against this tendency of monopolizing political functions. A deputy I interviewed, referring to this centralization, explained that a representative will be more influential in Paris if he or she is simply the mayor of the main city of that representative's constituency or president of the conseil général.

Another reason for the French phenomenon of the *cumul* is that a politician will be reelected more easily if he or she is also a well-known local personality. We have a specific word for these people: we call them *les notables*. France is the kingdom of the notables.

Inside the National Assembly we find two kinds of people: deputies who have no other elected functions or who have only a small local responsibility (a very small group) and those who also are mayors or chair their departmental or regional assemblies. Politicians such as François Mitterrand, Jacques Chirac (who was mayor of Paris and deputy in Corrèze), Philippe Séguin, Pierre Mauroy, Jack Lang, and François Bayrou are what one would call "typically French." The younger ones, such as Martine Aubry and Elizabeth Guigou, try to conquer local positions, the first in Lille, the second in Avignon. There is an official discourse that consists in denouncing the *cumul des mandats*. But the truth is that there are only a very few politicians who would willingly resign one of their elective functions. Even the French citizens are ambivalent on this matter: when surveyed, they answer that they are against the *cumul*, but at the local level, they like to identify a personality as their mayor and their deputy. A new restrictive law concerning the *cumul* has not yet been voted on.

Among all the political groups in the Assembly we find a cleavage between the "big men"—those who are sorts of provincial lords—and the rest of the deputies. Some of these "big men" are so involved with their local constituencies that they have almost no time to spend in Paris. When they come to the Palais Bourbon, their main motivation is to meet ministers and cabinet members—especially for purposes of local lobbying. During the year I spent in the Assembly, I saw only a few times the deputy-mayor of Montpellier, Georges Freches. This kind of politician, I was told, knows that the people will reelect him or her not for the work done in the Palais Bourbon committees but for what he or she does at the local level.

The position that one occupies in the national hierarchy represents another cleavage. There is a distinction between the *députés de base* (the backbenchers), on the one hand, and two other categories of deputies, on the other hand: (1) those who have a leading role inside their party and share the most prestigious functions inside their political group and, if they are part of the governmental majority, are appointed as chairmen of the committees or of the working groups and (2) the deputies who are well-known in the media. Politicians such as Édouard Balladur, Jack Lang, and Nicolas Sarkozy, even if they don't get a governmental position or a special responsibility in their group or in their party, are much more influential than most of their colleagues. When something important happens, journalists are eager to interview these personalities. It is very easy, in the lobby of the Palais Bourbon, to identify the few people the media view as political leaders.

There is also a distinction between the elders (those who have been elected two or more times) and the newcomers. It takes almost one year to understand the diverse inner workings of the Assembly. Diversity of motivation is also observed between those who devote most of their energy to the local affairs and define themselves mainly as the representants of their constituency and those who are involved in the lawmaking process, participating in the committees and the general discussion in the hemicycle. But there is also diversity of generation in terms of allegiance. For instance, one could distinguish three generations of Socialists: those who were first elected in 1981, when Mitterrand became president; those who came to the National Assembly during Mitterrand's second term and were a minority fighting against the Balladur government; and those who were elected in 1997, when Lionel Jospin was elected prime minister (the Jospinist generation). This last generation presents two key characteristics: (1) their discourse insists on the necessity of a moralization of politics; and (2) the proportion of women is much more important (and higher) in this generation than in others, and this generation tries to be more connected to the daily problems of civil society. There is a common issue raised by the new generation of deputies, and not only among the Socialists; it concerns the modernization of political life in France. Many young members of parliament (MPs), both from the Right and from the Left, highlight the gap between politicians and the rest of the citizens. For them, the workings of the Assembly are too much embedded in old rituals; the way of speaking is too difficult to be understood by the common people. The media are not able to reflect the sophistication of the political debate inside the National Assembly, and they report only superficial aspects of the political activity. These MPs would like to simplify the procedures of the National Assembly, but after two years they realize that it is very difficult to transform the institution.

In fact, the Palais Bourbon is one of the key places of French political life. The National Assembly has two different responsibilities: the main one is to legislate; the second consists in control of the government. When Charles de Gaulle became president in 1958, his first initiative was to give more power to the president and to the prime minister and the cabinet, and to limit the prerogatives of Parliament. During the Fourth Republic, any government could fall by a single vote of the National Assembly. Also, initiating legislation was in the hands of the deputies. De Gaulle changed the rules of the political game, so that the government would write the texts to be discussed by the deputies. The Assembly has to follow the agenda prepared by the government. The president can also dissolve the Assembly. It is impossible for the Assembly to limit the government, because the prime minister is the leader of the parliamentary majority. The National Assembly is mainly an institution dedicated to the discussion, in order to amend the texts that have been elaborated by the government. As an old MP told me, "When you are part of the opposition, your influence is very limited, because you will never obtain a vote for your amendment. When you are part of the majority, you have to follow the government. So you will not be able to bring forth some original contribution." This statement has been checked many times. But if there is no consensus between the different components of the majority, the work of the deputies becomes much more exciting. For instance, in October 2006 the Socialist minister Martine Aubry had to accept some of the Communist amendments to her proposed legislation on the thirty-five-hour workweek.

The political role of the French National Assembly is restricted in comparison with that of the U.S. Congress. When French deputies visit the Congress in Washington, they return with a certain nostalgia. They would like to be as autonomous as their American colleagues. Nostalgia notwithstanding, the Palais Bourbon plays an important role. Every day, members of the government are obliged to spend hours in the National Assembly listening to the deputies' propositions and debating with them. A law could not be adopted without this process, during which the majority and the opposition discuss and debate for hours. Sometimes it takes all night: the Assembly is one of the few institutions that is open around the clock. If you want to read a book in the library, no problem, there will be somebody to bring it to you. Members of the government do not just participate in the debates concerning their legal texts. They also have to answer questions asked by the MPs during special sessions: two of these sessions are broadcast on France 3, one of the public television channels, for one hour on Tuesday and Wednesday afternoons. Usually, the hemicycle is full because the MPs know that the session can be watched on television by their constituencies. They have to present an image of assiduity. After the hour of oral questions, most of the deputies leave the hemicycle, and only a minority stay there for the continuation of parliamentary activity.

When I did my fieldwork at the National Assembly, I adopted a strategy of defamiliarization. I was confronted with the very general assertion, which I found among journalists but also among intellectuals, that the Assembly is no longer a central place as before, but only a kind of theater where a parody of political struggle is enacted. Two main reasons were offered. First, the French political system has been completely transformed by de Gaulle: during the Third and Fourth Republics, the National Assembly was the true basis of political power; in 1958 the new constitution promoted by de Gaulle gave preeminence to the executive. Decisions come from the president and the prime minister, leaving to Parliament a deliberative function. More recently, François Mitterrand, who had often shown contempt for presidentialism, did not modify the constitution when the opportunity presented itself. On the contrary, his reign was characterized by a reinforcement of the authoritarian practices. Second, the consumption of mass media throughout the country has had devastating consequences for the political process. Until the end of the 1960s, the Assembly was a central place for political communication. It was the temple of a kind of oratory that has now completely disappeared. More important now are one-minute speeches on television and participation in any type of talk show.

In this context (with changes in the political system and the growth of mass media), the National Assembly ought to be considered an out-of-date institution. Moreover, there are many discourses that announce the end of politics within a world entirely dominated by the media constraints. We find this thesis in the writings of Guy Debord and Jean Baudrillard.[5]

Both Debord and Baudrillard consider that politics has become a sort of spectacle. Politics take place in a global universe of simulacra. Antagonisms have lost any consistency. The media-driven game reproduces or recreates the opposition between the Right and the Left because confrontation is more attractive to spectators. What is interesting to me is that politicians who have not read Debord or Baudrillard speak of the crisis of politics as a consequence of the reign of the "société du spectacle." From this perspective, it did not seem very interesting to study the workings of the French National Assembly. It would have produced one more book on the crisis of politics. Or maybe a description of an archaic form, a way of doing politics as it worked a long time ago. When I spoke with MPs, many of them thought that, being an anthropologist, I would be interested almost exclusively in the protocol and rituals. As an old institution, the Assembly has cultivated its own rituals. That is what would typically interest an anthropologist, they told me. But I did not want to gather the folklore of the institution. Moreover, I refused to be an archaeologist looking at an archaic political structure.

I decided to consider politics at the National Assembly as a form of production, a way of producing intangible goods. I would deal with the elected representative as I would deal with workers in any other organization. I had to identify which type of production resulted from this organization. It was not very difficult: the Assembly produces laws. What are laws? Everybody can answer: laws are texts that contain norms that apply to the whole society. Most of the activity of the MPs inside the Palais Bourbon was dedicated to the production of laws. When we say that the MPs deliberate, most of the time we forget the true aim of these debates. Now I had to investigate something very precise: the fabrication of the laws. I tried to note very precisely the daily activity of the MPs, each one a member of one of the six committees that examine the legislation proposed by the government. Every week they have to attend committee meetings and meetings with their parliamentary group. They spend part of their time in the hemicycle participating in the plenary meetings, where legislation is discussed and voted. The Assembly's agenda focuses on the making of laws. At the end of the annual session, the government will give the result of the parliamentary work; for instance, 1999 was a good year—thirty-four new texts were proposed.

This result notwithstanding, one cannot forget that every project presented by the government creates an opportunity for confrontation between the two opposite camps. I tried to shed light on the complexity of the lawmaking process. Indeed, part of the lawmaking activity is carried on by the parliamentary committees. The main work is devoted to the discussion of the text (the draft legislation) and its amendment. I was struck by the extraordinary creativity developed by the MPs in suggesting a lot of amendments. Adding a word (or cutting one), for instance, can completely change the meaning of a provision. One may also change part of a sentence or propose a completely different formulation of the same idea. In the lawmaking process, we could find an illustration of the "semiotic aspects of the state." Inside the committees, the parliamentary work is exegetic. Each text, or part of a text, gives birth to several interpretations. For instance, I attended the discussion of the *pacte civil de solidarité*, or PACS, a form of civil union that will give legal status to homosexual couples. During the 1999 session, this was the most controversial project of the government, giving rise to a tough confrontation between the Right and the Left. The Right did not accept the legalization of homosexual unions. Its representatives used all their procedural power to delay the adoption of the legislation.

A more sophisticated way of going about this subject was to contest the semantic choices of the government. For example, the proposition included the word *agreement*. Some of the right-wing MPs proposed replacing *agreement* with *contract*. The aim of the Right was to point out the contradictions of the majority: the word *contract* is used to designate marriage. But the government and its majority did not want to create equivalence between the PACS and marriage. They always asserted that the PACS would not modify the institution of family and marriage. In the end, the majority won and the MPs maintained the definition of the PACS as an agreement. What appears very clearly in this example is the importance of textual production as part of political action. Text is also a pretext, a pretext to semantic elaborations: sometimes I attended negotiations between the two camps in their attempt to find a more satisfying formulation of the future law.

Amendments are discussed not only inside the committees but also publicly in the plenary meetings. We find again this semiotic contest, but something else can be noted. The atmosphere is not the same in the hemicycle as in the committee rooms. One could speak of dramatization to emphasize the specificity of the public debate. For instance, the discussion of the PACS, which was relatively courteous inside the committees, took a very violent form in the hemicycle. Insults are not uncommon. Once, Lionel Jospin addressed a comment to his main opponent, a female MP from the Right, which she interpreted as an insult. She began to cry and ran to the government bench; the ushers kept her from striking the prime minister. This incident gives an idea of the tension that characterizes this kind of public debate. Speeches are punctuated by jokes, shouts, and insults. Sometimes when one of the camps wins a vote, members of that camp stand up and applaud.

What must be kept in mind is that the lawmaking process includes two different components. One is what I called the semiotic contest. The other component is the theatricalization of the conflict during the plenary meetings. But the idea of theatricalization must not be misinterpreted. Many times it has been said or it has been written that the public debate is something artificial. Theatricalization would mean that MPs give a performance; they play their part and after that, out of the hemicycle, members of the two camps can be friendly together. In other words, the hemicycle would be like a stage—it would be the reign of the appearance, not the true reality. We find again the idea that political activity deals more with simulacra than with the real. In this interpretation, politicians are playing their part on two complementary stages—in the Assembly's theater and on television's permanent political show, the second one being more attractive to the people than the first one, which is often described as something a bit obsolete.

I cannot agree with this conceptualization of the political, which, in my opinion, underestimates the true consistency of this political process. I think the public debate can be interpreted as a ritual struggle. By *ritual struggle*, I mean an effective and sometimes violent confrontation between people who incarnate intellectually and physically different segments of civil society, as can be observed in the debates dealing with controversial texts like the PACS. The confrontation of MPs on the topics of homosexuality was nothing but a tough one. The word *struggle* means exactly the sort of interaction I witnessed. When I talk of ritual struggle, I mean that the confrontation is from the beginning to the end codified by a specific procedure. No one can claim the floor at will. Just as in any parliament, the regulations are included in a special book and address, among other things, the organization of the plenary meetings and speech time. The MPs must all be aware of the protocol; for instance, there is a repartition of the hemicycle between the Right and the Left, with each segment going in and out through different doors. The MPs cannot speak with the ministers when they pass by the bench of the government: this protocol symbolizes the separation between executive and legislative powers. As the French classical tragedy, the parliamentary debate has kept its own specific tempo, which does not follow the temporality imposed by the media. The discussion of a law may take more time than was expected. Often, the final text includes important modifications.

This is not the place to give more details on parliamentary activity. I only want to shed some light on the specific interest that contemporary politics might hold for anthropology. Many things have been written by philosophers and sociologists on the topic of "public space." But most of these writings do not focus on the concrete modality of political action and discourse inside these public spaces. For instance, the main thesis of Jürgen Habermas's *Die Einbeziehung des Anderen* concerns the conditions required to make possible a better intercomprehension realized through the creation of new forums emerging from civil society.[6] The ideal of transparency plays here the central part in this analysis of public space. An opposite thesis has been developed by the postmodernists, like Baudrillard, who assert that in the société du spectacle, the simulacrum is omnipotent, not the political communication. I think that these two opposite conceptions of the public sphere have something in common. They deal with politics in terms of communication: for Habermas more democracy could be achieved through intercomprehension; to Baudrillard this ideal of transparency does not mean anything. Postmodern communication is essentially perverted, and the only way of thinking must be a radical critique of the simulacrum of democracy. In these two positions what becomes transparent is that they are grounded in a normative and reductionist position, confusing politics and communication. The point of view adopted by Habermas and Baudrillard is one adopted by those who pay attention to the political spectacle and its actors.

By contrast, the anthropologist gives another interpretation of what happens in the political space. This is an interpretation that focuses on the point of view of the actors. Referring to the "semiotic aspects" of contemporary politics, I have tried to deconstruct the complex process in which they are involved. From this perspective, my analysis is focused on the making of the law. There is an exegetic activity, a semiotic contest, from which the text of the law emerges. Almost simultaneously there happens a ritual struggle, and it is the combination of these two modalities that can produce at the same time a political event (that will be echoed by the media) and a textual production (the law itself that everyone must respect, independently of its conditions of production). This anthropological way of thinking about politics contrasts with the approaches in terms of simulacra or intercomprehension. Not far from interpretive and textual anthropology, it offers new grounds for constructing the political object, breaking away from the idealistic dominant conceptions and promoting a realistic approach of the public space.

"Life Is Dead Here": Sensing the Political in "No Man's Land"

Yael Navaro-Yashin

Triggered by references to "death within life" by informants in Northern Cyprus, this paper is an attempt to write against the grain of what I would like to call normalizing representations of "the political" in anthropology. If I have picked what could be called an "abnormal" context for ethnographic research, the territory of Northern Cyprus carved out of international recognition, I intend this "facing [of] the extreme," in Tzvetan Todorov's terms,[1] of an exaggerated context, to accentuate the "abnormal" in contexts that are usually considered politically "normal." The purpose is not to normalize, by default, the abnormal (i.e., the illegal state in Northern Cyprus and experience in what I metaphorically call "no man's land") but to invite reflections on the abnormal qualities of "normal" states that are recognized by the international system. I employ the term "no man's land" not as a literal description of a no-access or dead zone[2] but as a metaphor that accentuates the abjected quality of space in places,[3] like Northern Cyprus, that fall out of the recognized domains of the international law and system.[4] I use the metaphor "no man's land" to refer to the absence of Northern Cyprus from recognized transactions of the international system (its pariah political status and structure) and to the marks of such political rejection on space and subjectivity. Can ethnography in such a space be used to estrange ourselves from what is considered politically normative (legal) or "normal"? Northern Cyprus is one of the most fruitful grounds I can think of to facilitate this kind of critical project.

The philosopher Giorgio Agamben writes about "the concentration camp as paradigm of the modern," rightly wondering why theorists of power, like Michel Foucault, although sitting in the middle of the last century in the middle of Europe, have not theorized "the politics of the great totalitarian states of the twentieth century."[5] Just as such thinking on the concentration camp challenges current conceptions of "modern power," so would I like to explore what an ethnography of "no man's land," the term I use for this manner of abjected space (here, Northern Cyprus), might have to tell us about what is too easily called transnationalism or globalization in ethnographies of the contemporary.[6] There is a normalizing discourse in ethnographies of the transnational that tends to miss the multiple exceptions: that which falls out of the international system. But doesn't the exception have something to tell us about the rule, totalitarianism about democracy, the camp about modernity, the illegal about the law, the abnormal about the "normal"?[7] Anthropologies of globalization in the model of Arjun Appadurai's work fail to study the ways in which the very processes of transnationalism, which supposedly promote mobility and flexibility,[8] also engender the opposite: immobility, entrapment, confinement, incarceration. The bordered and militarily patrolled area of Northern Cyprus is not a remnant or relic from a time past (a monument to history) but a contemporary political formation coeval with what is often sketchily theorized as the border-lifting forces of globalization. What follows, an ethnography of subjectivity under a state of siege, must be read as a critical commentary on theoretical work in the anthropology of transnationalism, which would do away with bordered existences, violating the experience of people who inhabit confined spaces in the contemporary period.

The analytical rubrics of "everyday life" and "the life cycle" could easily gloss over the disaster that is immanent (latent or dormant) in many of the contexts that we study. What is everyday experience? asks the anthropologist. Or, how would you study the life course? One could very well write an ethnography that depicts everyday experience in Northern Cyprus. But how can one write using the concept of "everyday life" for a zone that has been trapped outside the international system for the last twenty-nine to forty years? In Northern Cyprus, people often say, "Life is dead here." Here we are referring to a zone that has been carved out and sealed off on a small island. Anthropological framings of "the life cycle" could end up naturalizing or normalizing (by culturalizing) a context that, in the subjective experiences, lies betwixt and between life and death.

Rather than asking what "everyday life" is about (an ordinary object of anthropological analysis), I attempt to draw out the disaster that underlies a seeming pretense to normality. Certain of my informants at times wanted to pretend that things are normal in Northern Cyprus, to carry on with their everyday lives. It may be asked, what is it for an anthropologist to point at the fault lines underneath such strategic attempts to normalize disruptive experience? Is it to imply "false consciousness," in the Marxist sense, in the native's point of view? Talal Asad has cautioned us against conflating our informants' ideologies with "their culture."[9] I would agree with him that the anthropologist must work against the normalizing discourses even of his or her informants. The native's point of view might direct us to perceive a context as "normal everyday life." Living and livelihood in "no man's land" demands that one forget its "no man's" quality, that one numb oneself to it. The native's point of view might at times reflect this alienation. But the anthropologist can do more than understand the native's point of view.[10] This requires not just depicting context but sensing it as well, sensing the catastrophe that underlies the pretense (or ideology) of "normal everyday life." In Northern Cyprus, it is the administrators of the illegal state guided by the military who would like to argue that "everyday life goes on."

In the ethnography that follows, I make some suggestions about how we anthropologists have imagined our "research," how we have consciously *looked for* the sites and spaces that could be identified as the sources of the issues we were investigating. I would like to propose that "the political" cannot be "searched" or "found" within the systems and methods handed over from a positivist tradition of research. In an older tradition, in what used to be called political anthropology, the political was tangible, "citable in all its moments," in Walter Benjamin's depiction,[11] as though the analyst or the writer could study a context in its fullness and totality. Indeed, in that Judgment Day imaginary of research, the researcher was trained to look *for* something. "Only a redeemed mankind," Walter Benjamin suggested, would be able to study a context in its totality.[12] Benjamin's aphorisms might inspire us, instead, to look away from the sites and sources identified for research, to be purposefully misguided, to be carried away.

I wonder whether the rationalizing training of anthropologists desensitizes us from the very issues we set out to study. Fully conscious, always rational, never lost. I wonder whether another sort of sensibility may keep us within the domain of the subjective experience that the political generates so that we may sense it, catch hold of it as it fleets by or before it is normalized, and write about it without flattening it into the rationalizing discourse of the social sciences. What follows is an attempt to approach such a political context with this different sort of sensibility.

Entering No Man's Land

In his novel *Pedro Paramo*, Juan Rulfo writes about descending to Comala, his mother's village, after her death, as heat and mist engulf the landscape and an apparition in the shape of a man shows him the way down to the ruins of a place devastated by the political power of Pedro Paramo, the protagonist's father.[13] Metaphors of hell shape Rulfo's narrative, where we are drawn to a liminal space between life and death. The protagonist encounters a world of ghosts and villagers fading into one another. Villagers seem dead, ghosts appear alive. In this "town of death," where Pedro Paramo, Landlord and Father (as a metaphor for the state), has loved as well as devastated all, the distinction between life and death does not hold.

"I wonder what could have happened to the town?" the protagonist asks the man-ghost who shows him the way. "It looks so deserted, abandoned really. In fact, it looks like no one lives here at all." The villager responds, "It doesn't just look like no one lives here. No one does live here."[14] Further on, as he enters the world of ghosts, our protagonist discovers that here, there is another order of living and death; he has to immerse himself to understand. In the village, he encounters a woman who is worried about being seen with the purplish spots, the stigmata of sin she feels on her skin. "But who is going to see you if there's no one here?" our protagonist asks her. "I've been through the whole town and not seen anyone." "You think you haven't," she replies. "Nights around here are filled with ghosts. You should see all the spirits walking through the streets. As soon as it's dark they begin to come out. No one likes to see them. There's so many of them and so few of us that we don't even make the effort to pray for them anymore, to help them out of their purgatory. We don't have enough prayers to go around."[15] Is she in the space of life or of death? our protagonist wonders, still distinguishing the two. He finds out, later, that she too is a ghost. Death has seeped into everyone's cells, into molecules in the air. All live betwixt and between two worlds, this and the other, but in a zone recognized by neither.

Following Rulfo's man-ghost, I would like to guide you to another such "no man's land" where linear metaphors for the life cycle don't apply. A place outside the bounds and off the records of the international system, administered by an unrecognized state, or what I call "a phantom state." The reference is to "Northern Cyprus," coined, constructed, and implemented as a separate "place" through the agencies of a local guerilla group (the TMT) that organized Turkey's military invasion in 1974. This "zone" has to be historically studied and situated, for it did not exist, either as discursive category or actuality, without the imaginary of "partition" (in Turkish, "*taksim*") and war, which created it.

Official discourses in "Northern Cyprus" have marked "1974" as a millennial turning point, constructing the "before" as a period of suffering for Turkish Cypriots under attack by Greek nationalists and the "after" as one of "Peace and Freedom," as the anniversary of Turkey's invasion (July 20) has been named. Even the mental hospital has been officially assigned the name "The 20 July Peace Hospital for Mental Diseases," after the very war that caused the extreme distress for many of its patients.

The year 1974 is indeed a landmark. But it is a turning point in terms unspecified in official discourses. Since 1974, Cyprus has been practically carved in half by an ad hoc imposition of barricades and wires between a makeshift "North" and "South." The capital city, Nicosia, was bisected after the arrival of the Turkish army, with an intermediary area that belongs to the United Nations and a border dividing "the Greek side" from "the Turkish side," heavily guarded by armies on both parts. Banned from access to the other side of the island and from contact with Greek Cypriots, Turkish Cypriots have been living in a zone of spatial and temporal surreality. Estranged from places formerly known to them through enforced migration from the south to the north of a small island, the drawing of no-trespassing areas, the changing (Turkey-fication)[16] of village names, and so forth, Turkish Cypriots often say that "we feel as if we are being strangled." Expressing a feeling of entrapment in a slice of territory, a man described his brief visit out of Northern Cyprus as "the permitted stroll of the prisoner in the courtyard to take in some air." In what is now the "Turkish side" of Nicosia, I frequently visited a public park that was built by the municipality over a hidden storage of ammunition and right beside the barricades and fences that divide the city from the middle. Every time I went there, there were people—Turkish Cypriots, settlers from Turkey, and soldiers off duty—holding onto the wires and looking curiously, through the little squares and holes, at "Life," writ large, on the other side. In turn, "Life is dead here," said a man who worked in a restaurant right beside the ruins of a house on the northern side of the border.

The making of "Northern Cyprus" was a declaration, on the part of Turkish Cypriot officials, of (at least partial) secession from the Republic of Cyprus. Territory and borders, as such, were carved through an imagination of state formation.[17] Today, this cornered area of the world is administered by "the Turkish Republic of Northern Cyprus (TRNC)," declared as a separate "state" in 1983 but not recognized by the international community. Heavily controlled by the Turkish army and foreign ministry, the "TRNC" operates as the contemporary outpost of a postimperial state, Turkey.

The entity "TRNC" was manifested through several stages and constructions of "statehood." An account of these is an illustration of the energy, investment, and efforts geared toward "statehood" in this zone. Of course, Ottoman-Turkish Cypriots were already involved and associated with administrative practices. In fact, if anything differentiated "Muslim" from "non-Muslim" subjects of the Ottoman Empire, it was the easier access of the former (sometimes through conversion to Islam) to political (i.e., state and military) power.[18] When the British took Cyprus over from the Ottomans, they used the Muslim Cypriots' special skills in statecraft, to a certain extent building on existing practices and hierarchies.[19] Hence, they employed a disproportionally larger number of Muslim Cypriots as police officers. The tide turned in the 1950s with the rise of Greek nationalism in Cyprus under the organization of the armed EOKA group (National Organization of Cypriot Fighters [*Ethniki Organosis Kyprion Agoniston*]). EOKA members not only fought against the British, soliciting unification with Greece, but specifically targeted the Muslim population of Cyprus, whom they identified as "Turks."

During and in the aftermath of British colonialism, and through the times of conflict with Greek Cypriots, Turkish Cypriots were administered by such administrative constructions as the "Cyprus Turkish Minority's Association," beginning in 1943; the "Turkish Resistance Organization," an armed nationalist guerilla army founded to fight its Greek counterpart EOKA in 1957; the "Cyprus Turkish Associations Federation," formed in 1958; separate Turkish councils in big towns (like "the Nicosia Turkish Council," created in 1958) that incited further intercommunal conflict; "the Republic of Cyprus," recognized as a bicommunal state by the United Nations in 1960; "the Turkish Cypriot General Committee," announced when Turkish Cypriots were living in ghetto-like enclaves between 1963 and 1974; "the Provisional Turkish Cypriot Administration," which was created in 1964 and dropped its provisional status in 1967; and "the Turkish Federated State of Cyprus," declared in 1975 after the Turkish army's invasion of "Northern Cyprus" in 1974 and imagined as a component of the proposed "Federal Republic of Cyprus." State practices in "Northern Cyprus" were managed through this series of administrative constructions until "the Turkish Republic of Northern Cyprus (TRNC)" was declared a separate state in 1983.[20]

Those trapped in "no man's land" have been governed by these transitory administrations, which have been recognized by no member of the international community other than Turkey.[21] According to the Security Council of the United Nations, the "TRNC" is "legally invalid." Greece and the Republic of Cyprus refer to the "TRNC" as the "pseudo-state."[22] Since 1983, Turkish Cypriot officials have been involved in all sorts of lobbying, soliciting, and propaganda activities to gain "international" status as "a state" for the "Turkish Republic of Northern Cyprus." Rauf Denktash, the president of the "TRNC," has been at the center of these activities geared for recognized "statehood."[23]

Here, I would like to draw attention to the excessive interest in the subject of "the state" and international recognition among officials and supporters of the "TRNC." The vocabulary of "statehood" and its numerous constructions ("federate," "confederate," "sovereign") imbues public discourses in "Northern Cyprus." The topic of "statehood" predominates in international meetings and conferences abroad about Cyprus, as well.

In "Northern Cyprus," an official discourse of Turkish Cypriot "independence" glosses over political and economic dependence on Turkey and the absence of international recognition. This ambiguous situation has produced an indeterminate and complicated language of "statehood" among Turkish Cypriots. The "ethnography of the state"[24] in such a context in between the absence and presence of "statehood" deserves its particular analysis of the everyday imaginary of "state."[25]

Turkish Cypriots' references to their "state" alters and switches between the "TRNC," "the Republic of Turkey," and "the Republic of Cyprus." In school textbooks and lessons in Northern Cyprus, children are presented with contradictory references to their "state." On the one hand, they are taught to revere the "independence" of the "TRNC." But on the other hand, they encounter ordinary references to "Turkey" as their "state." For instance, I saw the statement "Our state was founded on October 29, 1923" written on the blackboard of an elementary-school classroom in Lefke. This schoolteacher had not thought it necessary to distinguish between the foundation of the "Republic of Turkey" and that of the "TRNC." "It is confusing," one mother said. "Sometimes they teach the Republic of Turkey as our state and sometimes the TRNC. But in time children grasp the situation." In schools today, Turkish Cypriot children, as well as children of immigrants from Turkey, are taught two separate history classes, one named "National History," using the standard history textbooks published by the Ministry of Education in Turkey, and the other entitled "History of Cyprus." Such lessons serve to reify Turkish statehood.[26] Children are taught to identify with a vague "idea of state"[27] and as descendants of generations of state makers over the centuries. "History" is constructed as a succession of state-entities. It is often called the "History of Turkish States" and includes chapters on what are called "the first Turkish states in Central Asia," with references to the Hun and Gokturk empires; leading next to the Seljuks, the lordships in Anatolia, the making of the Ottoman state, the foundation of the Republic of Turkey; and culminating in the declaration of the "TRNC." Identity is constructed in close association with the presence of "statehood," here, in spite (or perhaps because) of its legal absence. With the official term "infantland" (*yavruvatan*) that is used for the "TRNC" in relation to "motherland" (*anavatan*) used for Turkey, Turkish Cypriots are taught to identify their supposed "statehood" with the statehood of Turkey. Strongly militaristic in content and imagery, narratives of history recount "Turkish" conquests of territory, where "Northern Cyprus" figures as the last such achievement. Generally, if a subtext of identification with "Turkey" underlies official discourses and administrative policies in contemporary "Northern Cyprus," so is any willing identification with "the Republic of Cyprus" banned on the threat of punitive measures.

In these conditions of possibility, in the context of a pervasive reification of "the state" and its symbols, Turkish Cypriots have no singular, unambiguous, or homogeneous loyalty to "Turkish statehood." Finding themselves subjects of an unrecognized state in a zone of unsettlement and temporariness, Turkish Cypriots have been pragmatically shifting their loyalties between the alternative constructions of "statehood" and "citizenship" presented to them. They feel the stigma of international nonrecognition. Subjects of this pariah state, caught in the discriminating discourses of nationalism and internationalism, Turkish Cypriots have been attempting to bypass or subvert their entrapment by soliciting, through any means, their way out of "no man's land." Papers of the "TRNC" do not always allow them such access away.

In 1995, there was a passport scandal in "Northern Cyprus," when it was discovered that many Turkish Cypriots held or obtained passports of "the Republic of Cyprus," that is, of the Greek side. President Denktash announced that police would be sent to peoples' homes, ad hoc, to search and check whether they held Cypriot passports. The "Republic of Cyprus" does not recognize the "TRNC," and the "TRNC" does not recognize the "Republic of Cyprus" in return. The Denktash administration announced through semiofficial newspapers that anyone caught with a

Cypriot passport would be subject to five years' imprisonment and a large fine. Under the citizenship laws of the "Republic of Cyprus," anyone who can prove that both of his or her parents are indigenous to Cyprus or anyone married to a Cypriot can receive a Cypriot passport. This is how the "Republic of Cyprus" works against the legitimacy of the "TRNC," claiming Turkish Cypriots as its own citizens. For Turkish Cypriots with or without nationalist loyalties, a Cypriot passport is the gateway to access to Europe with a recognized passport and without a visa. Of course, during the passport scandal, it was discovered that top-ranking ministers in the Denktash administration also held and occasionally used "Republic of Cyprus" passports.

Finding out that he is registered as "dead" in the census books, the character Yashar Yashamaz (whose given name can be translated as "Lives and Doesn't") in the novel of Aziz Nesin,[28] reflects that "one must be alive in government notebooks to be living. Unless government officials say that you are alive, you may go on forever screaming that you are alive, only to console yourself.... [But] just because the notebook writes 'dead,' can someone be counted 'dead'?" In practices of the international system, "existence" is linked with the appearance of membership in a reified, recognized "state." The lack of adequate representations—papers, symbols, and practices of statecraft—prevents international access, connection, and privilege. Many Turkish Cypriots do not identify with the "TRNC" that purports to represent their ethnically defined interests. Those who are critics of this polity are doubly or triply marginalized on all fronts. In other comparable contexts, anthropologists have communicated the sense of "a place on the side of the road"[29] or of "marginality."[30] In Northern Cyprus, people speak of "being in the abyss" or of "hanging in the middle."

Being a subject of a pariah state, an inhabitant of "no man's land," means being politically liminal. Marginalized because of their critiques of Turkey's military presence on Cyprus, Ayse and Okan have been trying to get out of Northern Cyprus. But which papers would grant them passage to a place outside the perimeters of Turkey? The "passports" of the "TRNC" that they hold do not allow access to the hallways of international airports. The Republic of Cyprus passports they have obtained through their "rights" as natives of Cyprus do not allow them the privileges reserved for the Greek Cypriot citizens of Cyprus. On their Republic of Turkey passport, likewise, the citizenship page is empty, withholding from them the right to work and of residence in Turkey. In a series of applications, as a means to get out, Ayse has applied to Fulbright and other foundations for higher studies abroad. However, every application asks her what country she is a citizen of. When she writes that she is a citizen of "TRNC," she, like the unrecognized state, is not recognized and her application is filed. When she applies as a citizen of "the Republic of Cyprus," she is not able to benefit from funds reserved for the "Greek" citizens of Cyprus. Like the "TRNC," as a subject of "no man's land," Ayse is off the records of the international system, too. She has no "identity" that can properly be translated into the accepted terms of international practice. Stuck in Northern Cyprus, Ayse and Okan have been shuffling, searching, and switching papers in order, in their words, "to be able to take some air." In this breaking point of a context between the absence and presence of state practice, where "the phantom state" follows your whereabouts through its symbolic effects and actual practices and the international system shuts its doors, experience is about political liminality.

The not-merely-constructed, but, indeed, "phantom" ("lives and doesn't"), quality of the "TRNC" is obvious to most of its subjects, whether supportive of the administration or not. I am interested in asking why and how, despite Turkish Cypriots' consciousness of and ability to analyze their subjection in Northern Cyprus, there is a continuous, even compulsive, interest in the topic and symbol of "the state." Why has there been such a proliferation of discussion on "statehood" in Northern Cyprus? To use Slavoj Zizek's terminology, we could analyze the recurring concern with "statehood" in this historical context as a "fantasy"—a symptom that repeats despite analysis or deconstruction.[31] This "fantasy" of state-centricity does not emerge from an isolated cultural context handy for anthropological study. Though one can study a particular and peculiar reverence for "the state"[32] in contexts of Turkish nationalism,[33] particularly in the aftermath of a history of Ottoman bureaucratic practices, the "fantasy" in contemporary Northern Cyprus is, more than cultural or historical, international and political. The obsessive interest in the subject of "statehood" in this "no man's land" has to be situated in the broader context and conditions of possibility of the state-centrism of international discourses where "livelihood" is associated with and facilitated by belonging to a "state" that has a seat in the United Nations.[34] I would suggest that it is within the context of international law and its discourses that such an acute interest in "statehood" has developed in Northern Cyprus. The "TRNC" is not a product of an isolated imagination. "No man's land" cannot be studied in self-referential (or cultural-culturalist) terms, re-reifying the makeshift maps and borders. The "TRNC," a nonnormative state, is a product of the very international discourses that produce "normal" (or "recognized") states at the same time.

Peripheral administrative entities and "no man's lands" like this exist, more and more, in other parts of the world as well—in Abkhazia and South Ossetia within the Republic of Georgia, in Nagorno-Karabakh between Armenia and Azerbaijan, in Chechnya, in Kosovo, in the West Bank and Gaza, and so on. What interests me is the poignancy of the experience of existence in such areas that can be called (not literally, but for analytical purposes) "no man's lands." What can a study of the experience of being trapped in such a zone and the subject of such an administrative entity tell us about statehoods that we take for granted? The study of the peculiar ought not to lead us to reify its strangeness against the so-called normality of existence under recognized states.[35] The state-centric international system operates through a normalizing discourse. The study of zones of illegality should, I think, help us become aware of "the abnormal" that underlies what is presented as "normal" in such discourses. This study of Northern Cyprus should thus be read as a narrative that will, in anthropological fashion, lead us to estrange ourselves from political practices, such as "legal states," that we tend to associate with "the normal." Of course, the purpose is not to legitimize the statehood of the likes of the "TRNC," run by a military order. I am interested, rather, in highlighting the eeriness of living in "no man's land" in order to convey the "no man's land" qualities of zones, in Britain, the United States, and Turkey, that we "normal" citizens of the world inhabit. The purpose of such an inquiry is to ask more poignant anthropological questions about the international "legal" system itself.

Living in Ruins

It is 10 p.m. in north Nicosia. A hot summer evening when, as is customary, everyone should be sitting outside. But we are walking through a half-dead city, the capital of "the phantom state." Many houses and flats in the neighborhoods of Yenisehir and Kosluçiftlik are empty. Homes that belonged to Turkish Cypriots, Greek Cypriots, and Armenian Cypriots are abandoned. Shutters are tightly closed as we walk past five-story skeletons of buildings standing erect as markers left from a time of liveliness.

Because we are the only souls walking through empty streets and spaces, it is hard to distinguish living houses from dead ones. We continue walking in the dark. We are the only ones walking in a neighborhood where evening strolls used to be habitual. A couple of cars whiz by, as well as a motorcycle carrying someone at a fast pace. Further ahead, a house of yellow stone, which used to belong to Turkish Cypriots who left, is now inhabited by immigrants from Turkey. There are no curtains, nothing to cover the floors. The house is practically empty. A large extended family has set cooking pots on the ground, in the garden. Trees, burned from the sun, surround the evacuated place that they inhabit.

Next door, a living house can be detected from the watered plants, bushes, and trees that have grown to hide and surround it. An old Turkish Cypriot woman has attempted to keep a spot of paradise for herself in the midst of ruins and piles of debris all around. She sits on her one-person sofa, behind pots of living geraniums. With a frozen gaze and in silence, hand pasted to palm, she looks without seeing through the window. Framed portraits and photographs of her relatives crowd the wall behind her. All gone. In the stalled gaze and posture of this woman, I sensed that moment of emergency: an image from a world annihilated. Here, disruption, tentativeness, and temporariness seemed permanent.[36]

In this place, living in ruins is the condition that has been normalized. "X" is the mark that the Turkish military inscribes in red paint on places deemed politically "suspect" or spaces "canceled" or "erased" from the records. Like the Kurdish areas of Turkey, certain parts of Northern Cyprus are "X-ed." Space here is full of X marks blotted on houses, buildings, and graveyards assigned a second death after the enforced expulsion (from life) of their inhabitants. Tension is particularly high in the spaces where "minorities" have been allowed to remain. A small Maronite (Christian) community has been given leave to remain in Northern Cyprus until death, as have a few Greek Cypriots. These X-marked subjects appear in the official archives of the "TRNC" only as numbers in police records. Because Maronite citizens are not allowed to leave property to their children, when they die, their houses die with them. They are red-marked.[37] Living Maronite houses stand, full of framed portraits, paraphernalia, crosses, and photographs, beside the dead houses of neighbors. Dark-dressed widows carry the double burden of death on their shoulders. There is no space salvaged here, where death is not political.

As we attempted to find the way to the Maronite village through the changed village names, we were asked, "Have you not found a better place to go?" by Turkish Cypriots in neighboring villages. Fearing being X-marked for visiting the Maronite region in Northern Cyprus, many Turkish Cypriots have X-ed this region from their everyday itineraries, just as they have blotted out the southern part of Cyprus, as well as the numerous military zones where entry is forbidden. The way to Kormacit, one of the only Maronite villages left in the north of the island, was amassed with blocked-off barracks and soldiers on duty. But on arrival to Kormacit, now called "Koraçam" in officially Turkified fashion, the scene was different. Beside the village church, members of the village were preparing to celebrate a wedding, with tables set out on the little square. Children were running around, calling to each other in Greek. Young girls, dressed up for the occasion, appeared in groups from the basement of the church. Televisions were tuned to news from the Greek side of Cyprus, broadcasting loudly through the windows. How striking it was that life and liveliness went on in this village, with festivity and sound, in the middle of X-marked ruins, debris of war, military bases, and a marginalized position in a pariah state. This was a place on the precipice of life and death.

Turkish Cypriots too live in such spaces, assigned to inhabit houses evacuated by Greek Cypriots with the arrival of troops and parachutes from Turkey. The vision of bodies floating in the water catches the imagination of Turkish Cypriots now and again. The ground, the fields, the air, the heat of the place, is swollen with such memories. Southern Cyprus, which pretends to be a corner of Italy in the popular and ethnographic imagination,[38] must be like this as well, the Janus of "no man's face." The army that claimed to protect Turkish Cypriots from being massacred, as a "minority," by the Greek Cypriot "majority" has now turned Turkish Cypriots into strategic indexes, number points in a territorial outpost. Keeping the photo albums and other belongings of the Greek Cypriot owners of their dwelling in the basement, Rasim, in a classic fashion, did not repair the house. "This is the Greeks' house," he said. "If things change, they will surely want it back." The sense of temporariness, of the capture of time in uneasy space, was paramount. In the village of Argaki, previously studied by Peter Loizos,[39] no one has erased or painted over the numbers marked on the houses that have been assigned to refugees after the forced exchange of populations. Turkish Cypriots seem in a certain way to be resisting the normalization and appropriation of other peoples' belongings. In the village of Argaki, now trapped in the north, Turkish Cypriots don't want to forget that this, since 1974, is abnormal time. No one whitewashes over the numbers. Let us not pretend that these are ordinary times.

In Nicosia, likewise, space is kept unkempt, ruins of war are unrepaired, wrecked buildings are left intact, garbage sits uncollected, as though purposively marking and re-marking memory. As I walk through the city, I keep an itinerary of items that I see. The list contains broken glass, rusted iron rods, a burned pine tree, spilled garbage, an old oven stuffed with newspapers, a tree growing in what used to be a kitchen, a roof that has collapsed into a house, the skeleton of a bed on the street, a mattress turned inside out and chewed up by the cats, a half-dangling balcony, clothes hung on electric wires, shrapnel holes in walls, windows filled with sacks of sand to make shooting targets, wires marking off a military zone, white barrels lined up as barricades, a sign marking "the border," poles carrying the flags of "Turkey" and the "TRNC,"... The list continues. The items of ruins are intricately related to the items of militarism, internationalism, and politics. They belong in the same itinerary, the same politography.[40]

"The houses here are like candles," said Erdal, who lives here. "Everyone has left." "Nothing has changed; everything remains the same here. There will never be a solution." Erdal was referring to the Cyprus problem, a symptom of political discourse here. Erdal was laughing and laughing and telling jokes around the few candles lit under eucalyptus trees in the semi-deserted neighborhood. "What happened to the house you were building for yourself?" I asked him. He said, "That house will never be completed."

In this place that was transformed into "no man's land," time is caught, like the flip-second of a camera shot, in between. Somewhere in the middle, life was frozen, trapped, held on hold. Twenty-nine years (after 1974), forty years (after 1963) fled by, half a lifetime: the cycle does not turn. One experiences death within life in "no man's land." This place is already off the records. Already inhabiting an afterlife (the other side of the border, the other world), death arrives here only as a second call.

"Before, we used to die of war," Emine said. "Now we die of cancer and heart attacks." Emine's younger brother had just died of a heart attack, in his late thirties. She was devastated. As we spoke to her, she didn't know that one evening before, in a conversation we had with Anna over the phone between London and South Cyprus, Anna had said, "So many people have died recently. It feels like everyone is dying." Anna was referring to the sudden death of a friend in his thirties from a heart attack in south Nicosia.

A wall does not erect a boundary on the narrow line between life and death. Cypriots, whether in the North or the South, are "coeval" in Johannes Fabian's terms;[41] they share a time. They live in enforced division. Partition. But they are subjects of the same history, the same historical context. If encoded, imagined, and written official histories have been bisected through barricades and flags, erected by men in uniform, an excess, an uncommunicated sense of history, a structure of feeling, is shared.[42] There is much that cannot be put into rationalized language. Consciously articulated words do not communicate the effect of history that is shared by Turkish Cypriots and Greek Cypriots. What the anthropologist has to catch is not the formalized narrative of identity, the tamed memory, or encoded oral history. More revealing of the experience of the Janus faces of suffering are the passing comments, exclamations, statements made out of despair, sighs, interrupted sentences, ironic phrases, laughter, and the like.

Emine and Anna had shared an experience of history, waiting on either side of the border, for something to change. Both are involved in bicommunal activities. Change didn't happen. Now it felt like everyone was dying. Somehow, Emine's and Anna's youths too had evaporated through the waiting. Something inside them died with the sudden death of young friends. It was not the first time that they were struck by the poignancy of death. Death lay on the flip side of each site and memory in Cyprus. But the sentiment of these new deaths, now, was different. This was a time of neither life nor death. A stasis, a stall, a paralysis. Though divided by makeshift borders, the excess, or unarticulated sense, is the same in a history that is shared on either side of the fence.

Facets of Authoritarianism

"Northern Cyprus" has a television station that operates as the voice of the self-declared "state." BRT 1 and 2 (standing for Flag Radio and Television) operate much in line with Turkey's state-owned TRT 1 and 2 (Turkish Radio and Television). The difference is that in Northern Cyprus, the president appears on television almost every evening to give a state-of-the-day interview or speech. On one such characteristic evening in the summer of 1999, Rauf Denktash appeared on BRT in prime time as he posed accepting visitors in his palace in north Nicosia. Sitting across from his silent visitors and staring at the television camera, addressing his "people," the president spoke with implicit messages of threat to the opposition in the "TRNC," to the Greek side, as well as, generally, to all subjects of the "TRNC." What was most striking in Denktash's speech, more than its content, was the tone, particularly as he ended with the phrase *anlasildi mi?* in Turkish, meaning "understood?" or "has it been understood?" This was not a question, but a reminder to the viewer of the consequences of dissent, disagreement, or opposition. Similarly, "Those who speak in opposition to Turkey are not our fellows; understood?" he said one summer evening, as though a general in a military base ordering lower-level soldiers. Denktash continued his monologue in front of the journalists who could do nothing but keep silent. "No one can say that life was better before 1974; understood?"

"He is out of his mind, this guy," said eighty-year-old Ibrahim Bey, watching television again one evening and pointing at the "president" on the television screen with his finger. "I turn on the TV and every evening it's the same thing." "Enosis,"[43] he says. "The Greeks killed us," he says. "Every evening, he repeats the same thing. He knows nothing else." Ibrahim Bey paused and said, "In this place nothing changes."

Militarism applies not only within army barracks. In this particular space, a whole territorial zone is treated like a base. Such was the feeling, once again, on the arrival of the president of the Republic of Turkey in Northern Cyprus, five days after the celebrations of Turkey's invasion in the summer of 1998. In the days of preparation for the arrival of the "TRNC's" most revered guest, inhabitants of Nicosia woke up, in the early hours of the day, to the sound of loudspeakers pointed toward the residential areas of the town telling people to clean up the garbage from in front of their homes, in order to receive properly the president of Turkey. Loudspeakers played the anthem of the tenth year of the Republic of Turkey. "We came out with a clean forehead," cried the marching soldiers, "in ten years from every war. In ten years we produced fifteen million youth in every age." Sitting in their homes and in their gardens, inhabitants of north Nicosia could not but hear this beating sound that interrupted the buzzing of cicadas in that quiet (part of the) city in "no man's land." One wondered whether these broadcast orders to welcome the president were also heard on the Greek side of the city, only a two-minute walk away.

In Famagusta, a Turkish army general had invited the mayor on a tour over the city with a helicopter. The general was preparing to receive the president of Turkey for the celebrations. Pointing to a few areas that disturbed his gaze, the general ordered the mayor to have them cleaned immediately. Then he asked the mayor, "But what are those beds on the rooftops that I see, and those beds on the streets and in the gardens?" "It's a custom here, my general," replied the mayor. "In Cyprus, people sleep outside in the summer because it's very hot." "In that case," said the general, "ask them to cover their beds at least, every morning, after they wake up."

In north Nicosia, all the main roads were blocked to civilian drivers on days of preparation for the president of Turkey. Cars of diplomatic and military protocol, marked with symbols of authority, passed by. As I walked to the center of town, every hundred meters was guarded by police. All the roads were colored with flags of Turkey and the "TRNC," in red and white. Two cloth portraits of Kemal Atatürk, the founder of the Republic of Turkey, and Süleyman Demirel, the (then) standing president, had been hung over apartment buildings. But despite all the broadcast orders to join the peoples' line to welcome the president of Turkey, there were only about thirty civilians, all immigrants from Turkey, standing on the side of the road, clapping at the dignitaries' arrival. News in Turkey's newspapers on the following day read: "The people of Nicosia flocked to the streets for Demirel."[44] In fact, on that weekend, most Turkish Cypriots of Nicosia were on the beaches of Kyrenia.

The road to contemporary Kyrenia, formerly used predominantly by Greek Cypriots, is now driven by Turkish Cypriots as if it were an escape route. It was worth keeping an itinerary, once again, of items on this path across the Besparmak Mountains to the sea. Attempts to "take some air" on the seashore of Kyrenia were blocked at every point by facets of authoritarianism. On the road were wires marking off either side as military bases; there were red signs indicating that military vehicles may pass, a run-down and abandoned oil factory (that belonged to Greek Cypriots), the wreck of a house with a rotten roof and burned doors, garbage on the sides of the streets, a burned forest with the inscription "Ataturk Forest" on the hill, and so on. Finally, on a public beach close to Kyrenia, two students attending university in the "TRNC" said, "We are dying; we are bored to death here." A retiree in his fifties, Erol Bey, had brought his grandchildren to swim on this beach. As he threw his fishing pole into the sea, he said, "The point is to loiter. What else can we do but loiter in this place?"

As one enters Kyrenia in the late evening, the signs of casinos, hotels, and gambling houses flash in many colors. However, it is forbidden for citizens of the "TRNC" to enter the casinos. The casinos are made for the entertainment of foreigners and visitors from Turkey. At the center of the harbor is a military house. It is forbidden to park in front of it. At 10:30 p.m. on that Kyrenia summer weekend, the harbor area was almost silent. Groups of people, couples and families, strolled through the little port. But there was no music in the restaurants and cafes in the marina. Not even much light. Waiters were standing with signs in their hands ironically reading, "Fun is forbidden!" "Be silent!" "We have been sleeping for twenty-four years; is it not enough?" "Should we send youth to retirement homes?" It turned out that the military house on the port had ordered all music and entertainment on the marina to stop at 10 p.m., when soldiers were due to go to bed. "Civilians" in the marina were protesting and collecting signatures. Here, military discipline had infiltrated into the most private moments of public entertainment. Like soldiers, young people in their teens, couples, and families with children were ordered to stop their socializing at a certain hour. The militarism was not confined to the barracks. The whole space was treated like a military zone.

Here, there was a sense of no escape, of entrapment. After the undeclared curfew in Kyrenia, we drove to Bellapais, on the mountain, hoping to find a place to sit. Again, we were stopped, this time by traffic police, who asked, "Where are you going? What are you going to do there?"

Back in Nicosia, sitting out in the garden in the quiet of the evening, eighty-year-old Ibrahim Bey complains. "No goodness has been left in this place. You can't pass here, you can't pass there. Here soldier, there police. On this side [referring to the Turkish side of Cyprus] they strangle people. They fear that if the borders open, people on this side will rejoice. If the borders opened, let me tell you, no one would remain on this side. Everyone would go to the other side [the Greek side] to live."

Sensing the Political

"To articulate the past historically," Walter Benjamin wrote, "does not mean to recognize it 'the way it really was.' It means to seize hold of a memory as it flashes up at a moment of danger."[45] My wish within this ethnographic project is to capture just such expressions of disarray and disruption as they fleet by—an image of a deserted place, a blank stare, nervous laughter—cutting through seemingly normalizing discourses of stately or quasi-stately order. "The tradition of the oppressed teaches us," Benjamin emphasized, "that the 'state of emergency' in which we live is not the exception but the rule. We must attain to a conception of history that is in keeping with this insight."[46] An ethnography of authoritarianism, like this one, asks that we sense the emergency, as uncitable as it may be. Like the Paul Klee painting *Angelus Novus* cited in one of Benjamin's aphorisms, the idea is to keep one's face turned backward to that "catastrophe which keeps piling wreckage upon wreckage and hurls it in front of his feet."[47] To perceive that gripping silence of the ruins that surround and make the everyday spaces of inhabitants of "no man's land," "Northern Cyprus," one indeed needs to maintain that sense or sensitivity that works against the grain of normalizing discourses, including those of anthropology. The experience that "no man's land" engenders in its abandonment and military devastation must be properly retained in any ethnographic depiction. We must hold onto that strangeness, that eeriness, in the writing, so that we can employ it to defamiliarize ourselves and grasp the political in contexts that present themselves as "normal," whether they be under pseudo- or proper states.

Orin Starn had written about anthropologists "missing the revolution" in Peru when they culturalized the Andes and depicted static, structural contexts, as though there were no movements for change there, right there and then.[48] It is my wish to attempt to perceive what is between the lines, to work on what appears to pass unnoticed, and to depict those expressions of emergency and desolation in what could otherwise have been studied as "the culture" or "social structure" of Turkish Cypriots, rationalizing a situation that is historically contingent. This is not a "place" that is natural and in place. This is "no man's land," carved out as "place" through specific historical agencies. Here we are studying a contemporary experience unrepresented in ethnographies of transnationalism and globalization.[49] In such celebratory accounts of movement across space and time written in critique of bounded anthropological imaginaries of "culture," the walls erected by those very same processes to dissect place and divert access have not been grasped. The "TRNC" phenomenon that I have attempted to describe is no anomaly within a normal international "order of things." It only accentuates the process, call it global or transnational, that is transforming many parts of the world into such "no man's lands."

When I write about sensing the political, am I referring to "the senses" in the ways analyzed by Nadia Seremetakis?[50] I don't think so. In the collection edited by Seremetakis on the anthropology of the senses, there is much to be learned from the unpacking of "sensory organs" and the domains that they reach—the scent of an orange, the taste of pomegranate—for the making of more tactile ethnography. I perceive an inherent (perhaps modern) alienation or a basic estrangement, by default, in this particular call, shared with Paul Stoller and others, to anthropologists to perceive the "sensory" memories of our informants. The sensing that I would like to write about is more akin to Walter Benjamin's grip of what he calls that moment of "emergency" as it runs by and away, or as it boils underneath what appears to be a quiet sea. In "no man's land," the meaning of existence must be sensed in the unkempt places, the evacuated buildings, the wrecks of war, the loud silence, in order to be grasped.

Am I speaking about the "anthropology of the emotions," as suggested by Lila Abu-Lughod and Catherine Lutz?[51] Once again, I am unsure. What has been written on the "anthropology of the emotions" is quite a different project interested in depicting the relativism of emotions across cultural contexts. That formulation assumes an essential cultural sieve preceding and determining the political. In contrast, in the experiences in which I have immersed myself in Northern Cyprus, there is no space where "culture" is not already and all the time politicized. This is not to displace an essentialist notion of "culture" with an essentialism of "the political." Though "the political" appears in symbolic form in the flags and papers of the pirate state and in physical form in the military barricades and fences, it is not possible to locate, cite, or corner "it" for analysis. "The political," here, as arguably in other contexts, never shows itself in the holistic form in which it is often depicted in political anthropologies. It rather appears, often in phantasmatic form, between absence and presence (in this case of "state"), or in the recurring imaginaries and fantasies of "statehood." Here, the meaning of existence, betwixt and between life and death (a subversion of the opposition), must be sensed to be grasped, in the subdued tentativeness of time, in the fleeting or cursory remarks, in the weird surroundings.

Betwixt and between life and death, hanging in the middle of time, living in interruption. An ethnography of a context in limbo,[52] as Northern Cyprus is, requires that we center "disruption" in our analyses,[53] since it is central to the lived experiences of our informants. Disruption, since 1974, since 1963, appears permanent to those caught in Northern Cyprus. In fact, there is now what could be called a culture of disruption or interruption. The frozen time, the time interval, has become the consciousness of temporality in this bisected space. It is not, therefore, possible to write yet another anthropology of "life cycles" or of "death" here, in the model of Bloch and Parry or of Loring Danforth.[54] This disruption, arguably like others, undermines any structuralist or culturalist rationalizations of concepts of life through death. There is, once again, no space here (in war or under cease-fire) where death is not tangled with "the political." The life cycle does not turn. Nor is it linear. Life is kept on hold.

Text and Transnational Subjectification: Media's Challenge to Anthropology

Louisa Schein

In the brief space of this essay, I want to stage three relationships and delve into their implications for anthropological ethnography. The first concerns the paradigm agonisms precipitated by the encounter of anthropology with cultural studies. These "culture wars" have been a source of much heat in recent years, of acrimonious vilifications and reciprocal otherings, and I want here to query where the fires are coming from.

The second relationship is that of the much-discussed interconnection between media and transnationalism. On the one hand, I hold that media produce a kind of transnational subjectification. That is, in the consumption of media, people may develop social imaginaries and senses of community and identity that are supralocal—*even when they are not mobile themselves*. On the other hand, media production and circulation also generate certain forms of transnational mobility and new types of transnational relations. Importantly, then, television, videos, and other media are not only about meanings harbored within the actual texts: media's webs of significance are immanent in their social consequences and their relations of production and reception, as well.[1] A fieldworker, then, needs to be attuned to what could be called media's social effects, to "the translation of cultural texts into contextured texts."[2]

The third linkage that I want to develop is that of the constitutive role of gender and erotics in the formation of certain transnationalisms. Gendered relations and erotic longings, likewise, may be the substance of transnational imaginings, and may structure transnational mobilities.[3] We need to go further, though, than merely asserting that transnationalism is often gendered, to be able to assert that gender and eroticism in fact drive some forms of transnational practice. To get at how this works, we need to turn back to meaning—toward the contents of the media texts that are implicated in a kind of transnational subjectification.

My exploration of these relationships draws upon ethnographic research in two related aspects. I touch on cultural politics and media consumption in post-Mao China, especially among the Miao ethnic group of China's southwest. And I investigate media practices of Hmong refugees from Laos, co-ethnics of the Miao in China. These immigrants to the United States have become avid producers and consumers of their own ethnic videos, in multiple genres, and some have traveled back to Asia and have transfigured those voyages into the contents of their media productions. Both the immobile Miao villagers in China and the world-traveling Hmong Americans are implicated, through their deployments of media, in multifarious forms of transnationalism.

Anthropology, Ethnography, Cultural Studies, Media: Some Polemics

Although explications of just what the difference is between anthropology and cultural studies continue to be churned out,[4] what I want to pursue here is what makes that difference seem unstable to me, the blurring of boundaries that has, despite proclamations to the contrary, been taking place in practice. I think anthropologists are actually doing more cultural studies than they are willing to acknowledge—what is this about? To be sure, it is largely explicable as an artifact of institutional divides, of the corralling of resources, prestige, and students by the literary disciplines—a process that has embittered so many anthropologists. But I think it is also about what I call the "dread textualism," the impression on the part of anthropologists that cultural studies has favored texts, popular as they may be, privileging semiotic readings to the neglect of contextualized ethnography.

Is text to ethnography as cultural studies is to anthropology? Yet another boundary has been anxiously marked in the embattled American academy where the political-economy-inspired insights and methods of Birmingham were imported first—albeit selectively—by the literary disciplines. In English and comparative literature, the pressure toward textualist methods has precipitated a decided reshaping, what some would call a hijacking of what—to traffic in canonicity—could be termed the British cultural studies canon. There is the inevitable inertia of the disciplinary conventions that fawn over the textual object, and there is what Stuart Hall noted some time ago already, the swift and heady institutionalization and professionalization of cultural studies in the United States, which spawned all manner of careerist aspirations, of academics doing "what they think of as critical political work... while also looking over their shoulders at the promotions stakes and the publication stakes," and often digressing, under the constraints of still-disciplinary gatekeeping practices, from the initial problematics of British cultural studies.[5]

But, returning to U.S. importing practices, as Hall put it, with an implicit sigh: "I don't know what to say about American cultural studies."[6] The beauty of being an anthropologist, and, yes, I am speaking with irony here, is that *I* don't really have to say much. I could just rail against it as a corruption of a more ethnography-based investigation of culture, one that anthropology has long cordoned off as its turf. Somehow, though, I cannot seem to be convinced of the grounds for—to say nothing of jumping on—that bandwagon. It would require too much forgetting of the specific history of how cultural studies made its transatlantic passage. Call me a Birmingham fundamentalist. I think Paul Willis's *Learning to Labor*, for instance, was a classic of theory-relevant ethnography that revealed the centrality of culture to working-class reproduction.[7] I *can't* forget it. But neither can I forget Paul Gilroy's *Black Atlantic*, a classic of synthetic cultural critique that finally put race and modernity squarely on the same page—and the arguments were made through close analysis of cultural processes without fieldwork.[8] In the end, as Renato Rosaldo consoles, "Losing a monopoly need not be such a bad thing; maybe there is something to be gained from working in more rough-and-tumble arenas where conflict and misunderstanding reign alongside innovative transformations brought by fresh applications and the remolding of familiar terms."[9]

I want to turn for a moment, then, to the media object, that incontrovertible presence in so many of our field sites, the same one that it is still de rigueur for so many anthropologists to dismiss as outside our bailiwick. I want to suggest that it is the specific route by which media as research objects made it onto so many of our radar screens, through the imperialistic power of moneyed, strong-voiced literary disciplines' claims about "culture," rather than what our fieldwork was relentlessly demonstrating to us, that made the media object such a demonized fetish, deserving only of queasy avoidance. Meanwhile, we have for the most part dodged coming to terms, in any real probing mainstream fashion, with whether and how media make a difference in our work, no matter, in my case for instance, if that work is in Fresno, California, or in the highlands of southwest China. This is not a statement to the effect that all anthropologists should turn toward scrutiny of the media presence in our data. To the contrary, I want to risk making the statement, so that I can subsequently unpack it, that media—movies, television, print, music, advertising—

cannot be an anthropologist's primary object. This would appear to be launching a salvo directly at some of my heroines (hmm, are they all women?) who have done groundbreaking work in theorizing media and reception—Faye Ginsburg, Lila Abu-Lughod, Purnima Mankekar, Lisa Rofel, Mayfair Yang—but that is not what is meant here. I want instead to focus on methodological considerations and another reason dread textualism has remained so intolerable to certain anthropological sensibilities.

What I am intimating, perhaps, is that it is not the diabolical texts that are the problem in and of themselves. More likely it is the centering of them at the heart of research—whether it is to study and interpret them or to strenuously expurgate them as tangential or supplemental to one's data—that trips us up. Nor is the remedy to situate media products with reference to a context that is by implication not yet mediated. That separation is increasingly hard to make. Lila Abu-Lughod tells a story of an initial field encounter that makes this point eloquently. She talks of arriving in a village and of the "pleasure of recognition" that a local woman and her children evinced when she professed an interest in television. "They brought out their little television set. . . . They invited me to come watch with them any evening, pitying me for not having access to a television set of my own. Television," she recalls, "bonded us. And this bond began to separate me from other foreigners, people who generally, as the villagers knew, did not follow the Egyptian television melodramas they loved."[10]

It is not, then, that media need to be contextualized; it is that media *are* the context: for most of us media are an ineluctable part of our field encounters and we make authorial choices *at the level of interpretation* as to how much to excise media from what we write up. I am not talking about selection of this data or that in the construction of ethnographic texts—I am talking about taking epistemological positions as to whether media products are constitutive of the social formations and subjectivities we purport to evoke. What is entailed here may be nothing more than an extension to media of what our very own Clifford Geertz suggested with regard to "art forms" almost three decades ago: "Because . . . subjectivity does not properly exist until it is . . . organized, art forms generate and regenerate the very subjectivity they pretend only to display. . . . They are positive agents in the creation and maintenance of such a sensibility."[11] Yet the subjectivity–art forms suture is not where we want to stop. I am talking about going further, about also unsettling the text-context distinction, by situating media simultaneously within both, as does Faye Ginsburg when she suggests, "If we recognize the cinematic or video text as a mediating object—as we might look at a ritual or a commodity—then its formal qualities cannot be considered apart from the complex contexts of production and interpretation that shape its construction."[12] What would it mean—in terms of research design and methods—to respond to this quandary by taking the phenomenon of media saturation seriously? We have barely begun to entertain this question.

This may appear to be a disciplinary polemic for the recuperation of grounded ethnography, now retooled to be media friendly, a play for the rectification of anthropology's special domain of expertise. Yet as early as 1988, Janice Radway, critic extraordinaire of the reception of the romance novel, was saying, in the journal *Cultural Studies*, "I have begun to wonder whether our theories do not impress upon us a new object of analysis, one more difficult to analyze because it can't be so easily pinned down—that is, the endlessly shifting, ever-evolving kaleidoscope of daily life and the way in which the media are integrated and implicated within it."[13] Is this a simple convergence between anthropology and cultural studies, then, a collective recipe that glibly calls for a large measure of ethnography of the everyday and a dash of media—stirred vigorously? Not for me at least, for I am also compelled by another literary critic, Tania Modleski, who impugns ethnography for its positivist pretensions, its masculinist gaze, and its assumptions of a stark line in the sand between observer and observed.[14] Wouldn't it be less disingenuous, she suggests, to assume our roles as critics, as activist members of interpretive communities who do things with what they receive as do those we study? Indulge me in an anecdote that allows me to work through some of these questions.

Is It Ethnography or Is It Celluloid?

I am doing fieldwork in rural China in the 1980s. The site is a community of the Miao minority in the mountains of the southwest. These are the mountains farthest from the glittering centers of China's putative economic miracle, and these are the people on whose backs the much-touted prosperities of the coastal regions are being acquired. As evening falls, I call upon a family, an elite family in which each of the young parents has done a stint living in cities—she for teacher training; he for forestry education. I hope to talk about all the things we have been discussing for months, but talking is not happening that night. The room is darkened, and a tiny black-and-white television with snowy reception commands the living area of their three-room abode. Tonight there is a rare broadcast of an American movie: it is *Crocodile Dundee*, the story of a roughhewn chunk of white masculinity from the Australian outback who so entrances a blonde American reporter that she contrives to bring him to New York to get a sexy sensation out of his savage-meets-the-city experience.

I sit down and we watch together. As the New York scenes begin to play through the techno-snow—the dubbed Chinese-speaking voices superimposed on white bodies and only partially audible through the crackle—the room becomes more highly charged. The film becomes a chronicle, which my viewing companions take very seriously, of a first encounter with the Western metropolis. There, cataloged for them—in a text that uses humor to mitigate the discomfort, but at the same time spoofs the alien initiate as he discovers the city's charms—are the technologies, the conveniences, the displays of affluence, that had once been vilified by Maoist asceticism but under Deng Xiaoping had become the objects of a most acute envious desire. It is a place they do not envision themselves ever going, yet in my presence, somehow, imagining a visit there in the company of a sympathetic American native, becomes more, well, imaginable.

Is this the kind of imagining that Arjun Appadurai urges attention to when he asserts that "more persons throughout the world see their lives through the prism of the possible lives offered by mass media in all their forms . . . as the ironic compromise between what they could imagine and what social life will permit"?[15] This sort of translocal subject formation is critical, but it cannot be bounded, confined, to the dyadic articulation between media texts and viewer positionings. As Mankekar has pointed out in her analysis of television reception in India, "the viewer is positioned not simply by the text but also by a whole range of other discourses, with those of gender and nationalism being dominant in Indian television."[16] Assuming multiple forces effecting subject positionings, how can I get a sense of *how* an American movie means to certain Miao in southwest China, of the forms of imagining that it inspires or stifles?

I can surmise these things not because I could, through a mechanical interview methodology, elicit from informants a narration of their viewing subjectivity, but rather because I am familiar with the shape of their worlds, the images and structures that constrain and incite their fantasies. I can sense this because I lived with them, because we talked about all manner of things, because the kinds of things that matter to them were deeply impressed on me through myriad encounters and engagements. In some ways these things came to matter to me too, but not because of a kind of naive identification with Miao villagers, a going native, but rather because of the structures that made our worlds proximate. It is not so much because I got inside their heads, because, to cite a fieldwork great-grandfather, I obtained the "native's point of view."[17] It is, more accurately, because I too lived in the ambience of China's post-Mao public culture, that kaleidoscopic mass-mediated era in which the growth of material disparities spawned a thickening of desires, quests, and frustrations. Watching *Crocodile Dundee* together in China at that historical juncture was not so much about getting at how it played for the other but about the way it played *for us*, and about the intersubjective space in which its reception took place. Elsewhere, I have called this an "ethnotextual" approach to media research.[18]

Does invoking the intersubjective make me one of Modleski's critics, who, rejecting the pseudo-positivism of ethnography, delves into her own subjectivity to make sense of fieldwork encounters as if they were but other texts? Or, more pernicious, does it implicate me in a sort of power evasion in which my putative mingling of subjectivities with those I have the privilege to travel the globe to learn about amounts to an elision of the privileges that put me in that living room in the first place, standing for whiteness and prompting envy? Is it a dodge for me to emphasize the media object in reflections such as these, displacing my own implication in the orders of difference that put me there and that actually render *me* a text of another yearned-for world? Possibly; and I am not going to attempt a definitive resolution of these questions here. Rather, I want to return to the issue of the disciplinary border transgressions implied by attending to the media-saturated character of these field encounters, and of the kinds of "knowledge" they might produce.

Field moments such as this one defy a forceful expurgation of their media contents. Moreover, they shake what is meant by the field, if the text of *Crocodile Dundee* is partially constitutive of it. Again, the quandary is not new but harks back to earlier struggles over subjectivism and the literary: "In a discipline nurtured in the hothouse of positivism, where 'to see' was more than a metaphor, to admit to the literary was tantamount to admitting to the subjective, and the subjective was, unlike the objective, essentially blind."[19] To confound the metaphor of blindness and sight, then, might we think in terms of a kind of second sight for anthropologists, one nurtured in the age of mechanical reproduction and savvy about the subtleties of representation?[20] Here I would think of the recasting of the notion of the field by Akhil Gupta and James Ferguson: "Genres seem destined to continue to blur. Yet instead of attempting to . . . seal off the borders of anthropology from the incursions of cultural studies and other disciplines, it might be a far healthier response to rethink 'the field' of anthropology by reconsidering what our commitment to fieldwork entails."[21] Likewise, I may be reiterating what Sherry Ortner advocates as a reappropriation of "a larger anthropology in which ethnography, theory and public culture are held in productive tension."[22] At a minimum, my citing of these strategic reflections effects another way of hinting that what the cultural-studies anthropologists have been so assiduously othering is already here, and may have been for quite a while.

Transnationalism in and through Media

I come to a concern with the very media that have raised anthropological hackles through the concrete conditions of my fieldwork, through the specific types of practices I encountered and my attempts to make sense of them in historical and social context. In 1978, I started working with Hmong refugees in the West, beginning in the years when they were just arriving from over-bombed, war-ravaged Laos, after having become political exiles from a regime they opposed. They had assisted the CIA in a secret war to block the North Vietnamese from stealing through the Lao jungle and to deter the rise of the Communist Pathet Lao. They had hoped in the process to protect a fragment of territory for their own politico-economic autonomy in the Southeast Asian highlands. Instead, when the United States withdrew, they were rendered involuntary migrants, acutely concerned about the depths of their losses—of land, loved ones, lineages, and lifeways. It was in response to Hmong American urgings, spurred by their bereft sense of dislocation, that I had been persuaded to go to China, the wellspring of all Hmong migrations, questing after their cultural roots, their origins. This quest turned so complicated because of the difficulties of recuperating authentic ancestors in the homeland—and I say this with intended irony—that it became my central project instead to understand and position the Miao, co-ethnics of the Hmong, in the specific milieu of *China's* cultural politics. The particular vagaries of China's social and political history were such that the indigenous Miao to be found there had defied appropriation as straightforward emblems of a fading Hmong ancestral past.

Meanwhile, Hmong migrants continued to live out their lives and their identities in a diasporic space—one that increasingly involved participation in an imagined, and highly media-constructed, supranational community.[23] As I was completing the China project,[24] a few Hmong Americans were also becoming transnational border crossers, regularly voyaging to Asian sites, especially Thailand, Laos, and China, on the strength of their first-world capital and their U.S. citizenship. They were going for tourism and to visit relatives; they were going for business ventures and to import goods especially longed for by Hmong Americans; and they were going for other types of social alliances. A search for homeland brides, mistresses, and girlfriends was key for many of the primarily male Hmong travelers. In the 1990s, there was also a boom in camcorder-toting, world-traversing Hmong Americans who in turn involved many less mobile others in their privileged travel by means of the circulation of images garnered from their Asian voyages. Media practices, then, had become pivotal in securing, generating, and collectively processing Hmong transnationality.[25]

There are now well over 200,000 Hmong in the United States, with other large refugee populations in France, Canada, and Australia.[26] In different communities, they have pursued different strategies for livelihood, including skilled and unskilled wage labor, social-service provision, and reliance on public assistance. Among these strategies, for not a few, is the taking up of technologies of cultural (re)production—for music recording, newspaper publishing, or video making.[27] A burgeoning production of Hmong media is not only by amateurs who produce such media recreationally but also by entrepreneurs who have made it their livelihood.[28] Videos—shot, edited, and marketed all by Hmong—are in the Hmong language and, like all Hmong media, are targeted exclusively for intraethnic consumption. Shrink-wrapped and usually copyrighted, they sell for up to $30 a piece. Although usually produced for profit, they are not backed by corporate or other advertising interests.

What has struck me most about these new Americans questing simultaneously for roots and opportunities is that so many are engaged in creating representations of their homelands. There are videos that portray Laos, the birthplace of almost all Hmong Americans and the scene of the Secret War orchestrated by the CIA in which Hmong fought as guerillas during the Vietnam War. There are those set in Thailand, where Hmong sojourned in refugee camps before being granted permission to migrate to the West. And there are those that document a mythologized land of origins in the mountains of southwest China. Several types regularly appear on the market: narrated travelogues on the order of homemade tourism videos; stories and folktales enacted in "traditional" homeland sites; historical reconstructions and tracings of migration routes; dramatic re-stagings of war and flight; martial-arts action stories; contemporary (melo) dramas concerning Asian lives; documents of festivals, pageants, and other events; and an avalanche of music videos. In some cases, the attraction of the tape is precisely in its traversing of untraveled but oh-so-familiar territories—the mountains of China, Vietnam, Burma (now Myanmar).

These tapes invite, or perhaps interpellate, Hmong Americans into a globally diasporic sensibility, one in which they can sense a connectedness to newly fashioned ethno-kin not only in the lands they themselves left behind in their own lifetimes but in more distant Vietnam, Burma, southwest China. Describing immigrant literature, Azade Seyhan has suggested that "by remembering, reappropriating, and allegorizing into language, the ethnic immigrant subject invents a new cultural space for her personal and communal self."[29] This cultural space, media generated for Hmong, is not in the form of a discrete subnational niche but rather sprawls over the globe. To capture the reception effects of viewing such wide-ranging images, I refer to the process of transnational subjectification. But, to go further, I maintain that the transnationality that Hmong media effect is not only at the level of subjectification but also at the level of social relations, of actual mobilities. I sketch here four dimensions that need to be considered in grasping this dialectical character of media and transnationality: production, distribution, consumption, and contents. Like media, transnationalism has also been a subject of much disciplinary and methodological anxiety in recent anthropological practice, and this stems in large part from the elusiveness of fixed research sites. What is called for in tracking these processes is what I call a siteless or itinerant ethnographic method that extends beyond the multisite approach outlined by George Marcus.[30] It entails a highly mobile approach to fieldwork, one that permits rapid movement between a range of sometimes ephemeral venues, and one that builds in deep engagement with the texts embedded in these circuits.

Production

Hmong media with homeland themes involve decidedly transnational relations of production. Not only are Hmong American producers themselves traveling to Asia with their camcorders and crews, but they are also involving many local Hmong and Miao in their enterprises. These involvements take many forms. Hmong American producers may hire crews and actors on-site in Thailand or Laos. They may choose a popular Hmong/Miao singer or dancer in any of these countries and promote that performer as a phenomenon with special allure for nostalgic Hmong American consumers. Of late, one of the most lucrative ventures in the industry is that of Hmong entrepreneurs buying the rights to feature films out of Hong Kong, Thailand, China, or even India and dubbing them into Hmong language. In some cases, they also subcontract the translation and voice-over work to their co-ethnics in Asia to save labor costs. Video pioneer Su Thao of ST Universal Video, who studied in Hollywood and has produced dozens of videos in Asia, actually maintained an office in Thailand near Wat Tham Krabok, a large settlement of relocated Hmong from Laos. This way he could take advantage of the regular involvement of locals and also expedite his projects. Transnational Hmong media, then, is unthinkable outside of these complex supralocal production modalities.

Distribution

Although so many of the most consumable images in Hmong video are from Asia, the circulation of the products is within a decidedly Western sphere. Here, the asymmetries of production relations so conditioned by global geopolitics reemerge in stark relief. Hmong in Asia, although providing the stuff of much of video contents, and the labor for much of their creation, rarely access VCRs on which to view videos. They are not only relatively immobile but also almost entirely excluded from consumer participation in their own intraethnic media flows. Doreen Massey's notion of "power-geometry" is evocative of the discrepant regional and national positionings of Hmong in relation to what otherwise might appear simply as a unifying communicative medium: "Different social groups and different individuals are placed in very distinct ways in relation to these flows and interconnections. This point concerns not merely the issue of who moves and who doesn't, although that is an important element of it; it is also about power in relation *to* the flows and the movement."[31]

On the other hand, within Western sites of Hmong settlement, distribution is highly elaborated and follows the circuits of long-standing kin, clan, and other kinds of relations. From the United States, where most production is situated, videos are shipped in bulk to France and Australia, where there are smaller aggregations of Hmong, and then ethnic brokers peddle the videos to people in their networks. Occasionally, tapes are sold through ethnic shops as well. Often friends and family members buy the videos and send them directly overseas. Meanwhile, the bulk of sales remain within U.S. borders, where the Hmong population is largest. The most sizable U.S. aggregations are in the California Central Valley and Minneapolis–St. Paul, where the presence of tens of thousands means that Hmong ethnic businesses thrive. Not surprisingly, these are the locations of much of the Hmong media production and of the outlets for most direct sales. In every large Hmong community, ethnic groceries have sprung up that market not only a range of Asian consumables but also Hmong media products—cassettes, CDs, and videos. In Fresno, St. Paul, or even Wausau, Wisconsin, there are video shops exclusively for Hmong, offering sales, but mostly rentals, of hundreds of movies. Hmong American festivals, especially large-scale festivals such as Fresno Hmong New Year in late December and the Fourth of July Soccer Tournament in St. Paul, are glutted with open-air stalls where producers and their agents set up tables to display and sell media products. The air at these gatherings of tens of thousands is filled with the blaring noise of competing vendors blasting their best music and videos over huge speaker systems to lure customers by drowning out their neighbors. Video monitors run continuously, showcasing the latest products. Hmong consumers pride themselves on establishing long-standing collections and regularly exchange videos between friends and family. One can thus think of the Western countries in which Hmong are settled as dotted with key nodes through which messages and images of remote sites across the globe are relayed to them.

Consumption

I have spent a good deal of time hanging out at various sales venues, watching people consume and talking to them about their choices. I also spend time in Hmong living rooms around the United States, noting peoples' media collections, watching videos with them, and talking to them about their consumption tastes. The Hmong ethnographer Jo Ann Koltyk gives an extended evocation of these disparate living-room modalities, beginning with the atmosphere prior to a shamanic ritual:

> The air is thick and humid from the smoking joss sticks and the steamy pots boiling on the stove. In the living room, a group of men gather around the television set, watching a videotape filmed in Laos. They chat about the homeland as they watch New Year images flit across the screen. Down the block, another Hmong family is entertaining relatives visiting from St. Paul and Fresno. A video of their family reunion is being made while, at the same time, they watch another video taken of the funeral services of a deceased relative. . . .
>
> In the late afternoon a group of female relatives gather at the oldest relative's house to talk and sew. . . . One of the women plays a Hmong video filmed in Laos about a man kidnapping a bride. . . . They watch the video three times—with repeated rewindings of the bride capture scene. . . .

In the evening another family sits in front of their television watching a video made in India.³²

Among the many genres and viewing modalities, I have particularly followed the videos with homeland themes, whether documentaries, dramas, or music tapes, with an eye toward understanding what difference they made in what I have called the forging of transnationality. What desires, what identities and identifications, what alliances, are generated in the Hmong reception of homeland images? The following vignette illustrates some of the viewing subject positions, the range of ways in which Hmong Americans engage homeland material, emphasizing that although its appeal is highly differentiated, video is nonetheless a powerful agent in creating transnational presence in immigrant spaces.

In 1999, I visit a Hmong American grandfather in Philadelphia to find two big crates of videos next to a large-screen television, the focal point of his living room. "This is my history collection," he tells me. "I am thinking of getting all my videos on DVD, and my tapes on CD, so I can keep them longer." As he places the first box on the floor for me to sort, his two-year-old granddaughter rushes over to do her own sorting. She extracts tape after tape, strewing them across the living room carpet, glancing with a discerning eye at each one she discards. Finally, she finds the one of her choice. It is *China Part 3* by ST Universal Video. Wordlessly nudging her grandpa, pleading to him with her eyes, she insists that he play the tape. She plunks down in front to watch a kaleidoscope of dancing, singing, and costumes with narration in her first language, which she is only beginning to understand.

The elder tells me that the toddler's favorite videos are the China dancing tapes and those of Hmong beauty contests. "All the Hmong babies like this kind of video," comments the toddler's twenty-eight-year-old father, returning from his class with a quizzical look on his face. His younger sister, a twenty-two-year-old Temple University student, has just told me that she enjoys every genre of videos *except* the cultural documentaries. "I don't know . . . I wasn't born there," she demurs, defending her disinterest. Her brother concurs, emphasizing that the China tapes are simply not engaging. He watches his daughter sit riveted before the swinging skirts of dancing Miao girls, the crooned melodies of old-time courtship songs, the virtuoso dancing of bamboo-reed-pipe players. He is not drawn toward the screen but speaks directly to me, imputing a nascent ethnic identification to his daughter with a touch of incredulity: "It's the culture, I guess." Later I observe that the toddler will throw tantrums if she is not allowed to dress up in Miao costumes from China. And she is most elated when family members affectionately refer to her by the name of Mee Hang, one of the most famous Miao singers from China. As is typical in so many Hmong households, though the young-adult generation remains nonplussed, both grandparents and young children are employing homeland videos to effect a sense of unity with the most distant of their peoples.

Reading Homeland Romance

This kind of devoted fandom is one type of consumption, but I want to turn now to another type, one structured around gendered spectatorship. In the bulk of Hmong American media, homeland desire is distinctly gendered, and here we venture into the imponderables of erotic subjectification. Videos range over the youthful faces and ornate adornments of homeland women, they strategically place attractive women in nostalgia films as a focal point for the gaze of the homesick viewer, and they fashion scripts of courtship, sexual trysts, and marriages to homeland brides. How specifically does the costumed, singing, smiling, traditional woman get constructed as an object of longing? How might her incarnations in media incite forms of eroticism not present, or only latent, before the moment of watching her in so many genres of text? Here I take up the fourth aspect of mediated transnationalism, that of textual contents. The semiotics of homeland representations and the dense intertextuality that characterizes Hmong migrant media become crucial sources of insight. To explore the dimension of textual interpretation, and to make the case for its imbrication with other aspects of media study, I turn to the consideration of one video.

Dr. Tom, parts 1, 2, and 3, is a text in transnationality—and I mean that in all its ambiguity, polysemy, and inscrutability. In the late 1990s, the video was, by almost all accounts, the "most popular" of hundreds that were being produced, circulated, and consumed among Hmong from Southeast Asia now living in the United States.[33] Hanging out in a Hmong-run beauty salon in Fresno, I first heard of the then two-part drama *Yuav Tos Txog Hnub Twg*, colloquially referred to as "*Dr. Tom*." Shot in Thailand on the spur of the moment with a shoestring budget and an improvised script, the blockbuster is the creation of Ga Moua, formerly involved in the Hmong music scene and a frequent traveler to Asia. The story combines time-honored Hmong folklore motifs—including the tragic orphan boy and the exquisite torment of unconsummated love—with newfangled themes of transnational relationships gone wrong.

Set in a refugee camp in Thailand, part 1 showcases a beautiful saronged young woman who is falling in love with a young man who was raised as her stepbrother after the horrible murder of his parents by a predatory Thai gang as they crossed out of Laos. In jets "Tom," a Hmong American man, with slicked hair, sunglasses, a cowboy-booted swagger, a camcorder, and claims of being a highly paid "doctor." Tom immediately begins wooing the girl's family with money, and convinces them that it would be best for everyone's future if she marries him. Despite her broken heart, the family gives her away, just in time for her new husband to run out of money and flee to his vindictive first wife in the United States, leaving the girl to wait, wasting her life indefinitely. It is the pain of this waiting that is evoked in the title of the video, which translates roughly as "When will be the day that I am waiting for?"

The more didactic part 2 reveals the gradual demise of the evildoer Dr. Tom, who turns out to be nothing but a janitor in an American doctor's office. Lying to an uncle-in-law that he needs a loan to start a farm, he garners enough cash to race back to Thailand where he learns that his second wife has abandoned her marriage to him and returned to her original boyfriend. Having been resoundingly rebuked by her now-savvy parents, he tries in vain to impress many other women, all of whom let him know that they are no longer to be duped by men from America. Humiliated, he returns home and violently vents his frustration on his wife, who in turn reports him for domestic abuse; he ends up, in a dramatic climax, arrested, handcuffed, and carted off to jail.

What is the social life of this story as it circulates in Hmong America, focalizing issues of gender in transition, of sexual exploitation? The wide consumption of the text makes of a relatively small-scale practice of male homeland sexual adventuring a near-universal concern that touches both men and women in the Hmong diaspora. When I first began watching and thinking about this video, I was intrigued with the question of why the director, a Hmong man and a regular traveler to Asia, would have produced such a morally didactic text. Why would a Hmong man with the potential to access the gender power that homeland touring has offered to male returnees produce a text that comes off as feminist critique? There are, I think, at least two ways of looking at this question.

First, the creation of this story, and its wrenching treatment of the tragedies of the accumulation and abuse of patriarchal power in its border-crossing modality, plays to a feminist market. Some Hmong I talked to told me that women are the primary purchasers and viewers of the videos, since they are more likely to be at home with limited English and idle time. This seemed plausible for a couple of reasons. For one, the director is in ongoing conversation with his audiences. He says that Dr. Tom was jailed in part 2 because women wanted to see justice done. Meanwhile, he was berated by Hmong men for creating such an unfavorable portrait of them. Indeed, as he tells it, the script for part 3 was designed to make people "happy"—to give them a good message. In part 3, Tom gets out of jail and immediately borrows money to go back to Thailand, where he again strikes out before realizing that he must now go deep into the mountains of Laos to find a family who will fall for his money and his bragging. There he procures another bride, but because he fails to put a halt to his compulsive woman-hunting, she leaves him. Finally accepting his defeat, he returns to the United States to make amends with his first wife, who welcomes him back despite having taken up illicitly with a real Hmong doctor in Tom's absence. In the closing scene, they are shown reembedded in Hmong American community and morality, walking arm in arm among the crowds of an ethnic New Year festival. Ga Moua's professed aim to please notwithstanding, disparate readings of his text persist. Some women I have talked to are particularly displeased with part 3, saying, "I would never take him back . . ."

The director's attempt to placate a female viewership is one possible explanation for why *Dr. Tom*'s message should come off as so didactic, but there is another way of thinking about how such a gendered critique could emerge from the editing room of an American man. I want here to fuzz up the comfortable categories of production, circulation, and consumption that have been so helpful in cultural-studies method to unsettle any facile binary between authorial intent and audience reaction. Can *Dr. Tom*, the movie, be thought of instead as a node and a site of condensation for the intersecting concerns of Hmong in discrepant social locations, all nonetheless confronting the desire to forge unities out of radical disparities and finding pleasures and agonies along the way?

The idea of such a video text as a site of condensation rather than a product of a specific authorial intent is supported by the polyglot and collaborative way in which *Dr. Tom* was made. As the director tells it, it was a Thai driver who suggested the central premise for the film while chauffeuring Ga Moua, camcorder on his shoulder, to visit family members. Ga Moua availed himself of his relatives' help, recruiting a niece to act opposite him as the beautiful yet reluctant bride.[34] Other friends and relatives played the other roles, and they improvised the story and the lines as they went along. After the release of part 1, audience members, as we have seen, also played a role in the creative process. Their feedback was in large part what, according to Ga Moua, propelled the design of the subsequent scripts. Dilemmas over how the transnational relationship with co-ethnics in Asia was to be carried out, and in turn represented, as well as fractures over gender and geopolitical positioning, all came into consideration as the text grew, not only through the creation of parts 2 and 3, but also in the communal conversations that began to ensue with widening viewership. Indeed, part 3 ends with letters on the screen, a direct address to viewers in the first person *plural*: "Thanks to all the people who have helped us put this video together and to those who have financed it. If we've done anything that's offensive, please everyone forgive us." Beyond thinking of this as simply an author's mechanical response to audience demands, we can think here more concretely of the kind of social space inhabited by the text—one in which the story itself is imbricated in social life—rather than thinking of it as a text in a dyadic relation with audience reactions.

Stealth Erotics

The *Dr. Tom* story, and its resounding reception within the Hmong American community, shows that ethnic media has a role not only in bringing the images of co-ethnics in distant Asia into Western living rooms for entertainment but also in working through current concerns in the ongoing development of Hmong transnationalism. To read *Dr. Tom* for its didacticism about ethnic community and morality is to read it only at one level, the level of its overt message. There is, however, an inescapable polyvalence to the text, which issues from the knitting together of its story line with its rich visuals, its extratextual references, and its social life at a particular moment in Hmong transnationality. What I want to explore here is the unmistakable eroticism that these videos incite, a particular structure of desire that is inextricably bound to the figuring of homeland nostalgia in a romance of lost sexual culture, a cult of the very young woman, and the memory of the most highly charged moments of a distant past, the moments of tender courtship and of the excitement of youthful yearnings. *Dr. Tom* is never without this doubleness in which contemporary concerns with the ethics and improprieties of transnational practice coincide with the intensity of an almost-palpable nostalgic longing, one imbued with the most elemental sorts of passions. Hamid Naficy has written eloquently of what he calls "independent transnational film" produced by immigrants making texts of their exilic lives:

> By linking genre, authorship, and transnational positioning, the independent transnational genre allows films to be read and reread not only as individual texts produced by authorial vision and generic conventions, but also as sites for intertextual, cross-cultural, and translational struggles over meanings and identities.... More, this genre considers the relationship of the transnational filmmakers to their subjects to be a relationship that is filtered through narratives and iconographies of memory, desire, loss, longing, and nostalgia. Memories are fallible, playful, and evasive, and the narratives and iconographies that they produce—in whatever type of film—are palimpsestical, inscribing ruptures, fantasies, and embellishments as well as ellipses, elisions, and repressions.[35]

Thinking about the polyvalence of *Dr. Tom*, then, also means disaggregating gender and erotics as two distinguishable inscriptions in Naficy's palimpsest.[36] There is without doubt a clear exploration in the film of the problematics of discrepant gender privilege and its exacerbation by transnational asymmetries. But there is also that not-so-subtle evocation, the prodding toward desire that the film relentlessly effects. Listen to these two Hmong responses to the social impact of the film: "The movie warns men about what they shouldn't do when they go to Thailand or Laos" is voiced commonly by women and men. By contrast, one middle-aged man suggested a fantasy effect to explain the video's popularity: "It's what many men want to do, but know that they can't." Both responses acknowledge a similar moral message, yet the second allows for a simultaneous indulgence in the pleasure of fantasy.

Let us look more closely, then, at the modes by which eroticism is kindled in *Dr. Tom*. In the process, I develop a meta-argument about method. The erotic dimension is one that is so elusive, so difficult to research in any more than a partial way through interviews and conversations, that it demands of us a reconfiguration of interpretive approaches, an activation of that second sight I described earlier. I am not speaking of an optional supplement to more positivist social science analysis; rather, my premise is that desires and fantasies are so socially consequential that they cannot be ignored and that their incitement through media is so ubiquitous that it must be studied head on. Anthropology must not shrink from deploying a range of reading techniques to get at the kinds of subtleties that are intrinsic to this domain. Some of our tools might be attentiveness to visuals as distinct from but complexly linked to narratives, awareness of cultural referentialities that potentially condition reception subjectivity within an ethnic population, and close analysis of intertextual devices and conventions that thicken the meanings of any particular text. Moreover, erotics need to be situated in complex and flickering subjectivities, not privileged as dominant structures of feeling that eclipse other sensibilities. As Mankekar, describing Indian women's television consumption, put it: "Viewers' semiotic skills were shaped by their positions along multiple axes of power. I posit that not only are texts polysemic, but subjectivities are multifarious as well. Since the position of the subject is an unstable, temporary one rather than a static sociological ascription, she is located in an interdiscursive space."[37]

No matter how ineffable the process, how unspeakable the effects, then, I have little doubt that *Dr. Tom*, despite its overt didacticism, is also rich material for fantasy, that it traffics in and generates eroticized homeland longing. The visuals in the film convey a luxuriant sensibility: they ooze with the nuances of a special desire. The central female figure epitomizes a reconstructed Hmong femininity—her long hair flows down her back, and she never appears without a sarong and the mincing steps that accompany that narrow-skirted attire. Despite impoverished camp conditions, she is rounded and healthy; incessant close-ups of her face showcase her drop-dead beauty no matter what is going on in the plot. She always speaks demurely, contriving the softest of voices, while rarely looking Dr. Tom in the eye. The lure of this girl is the lure of nostalgia mingled with men's longings, longings *not only* for that feminized icon of home but also for that remembered sexual culture, the courtship of very young girls, the heart-stopping need for one's object of obsession and the privilege to make one's conquest.

And conquer he does, for Tom partially achieves his end, procuring a few nights of bliss in bed with his new wife—nights only enhanced by her initial reluctance and her eventual passionate surrender to his embrace. No matter that the film ends with a parting and a judgment at the level of the metatext against Tom as exploiter. Along the way, the bride, having dallied in the conjugal bed for a few nights, has come to profess her love for Tom. In a farewell scene after he has announced his imminent departure, she bashfully confesses her sorrow, her regret, at having underestimated him, and an affection that hints at passions awakened by his virility alone.

At the same time that *Dr. Tom* works through concerns about community, there is this other aspect, that intangible domain of incitement, the filmic framing of the homeland beauty, her irresistibility. For the many men who have not returned to Asia, or are contemplating it, the video is the stuff of fantasy, the intimation of romantic possibilities. It is not only reading the images of the object of desire in this one text that makes me so certain about this, but rather reading them intertextually in relation to other images and also in relation to social practice.

One aspect of *Dr. Tom* that makes the homeland woman such an object of longing in the film is that the early part of the text lingers lovingly on her courtship with her local boyfriend. He is an eminently sympathetic character, hardworking, modest, attentive, and upstanding. His impeccable social credentials are signaled by a longstanding Hmong folkloric trope for the good young man, hero of countless tales: he is an orphan. His look is simple, and compared with Tom's almost campy affect with ill-fitting clothes, neckties, and oversized shades, his is unassuming and almost effeminate. He always puts family welfare first. With Hmong love songs playing softly on the soundtrack, he talks tenderly and with bashful restraint to his new love, daring only to hint at his feelings, although it is evident that they extend to the depths of his soul. His holding back only makes her want him more. When her parents have told her that she must marry Tom, she comes to her boyfriend in desperation, offering her virginity to him first, but he defends virtue, insisting that sexual relations would be detrimental for her imminent marriage.

This dream of reciprocal romantic love is central to Hmong men's longings for the country from which they have been separated. It is as if the passions of bygone youth are conflated with the affection for their lost land. The rituals of courtship come to constitute a quintessential facet of culture that is imperiled by flight to the United States. Illuminating Anne-Marie Fortier's assertion that "memory and forgetting work together in the struggle over differing histories and geographies that construct the identity of a place," it is a situated culture, one that sutures certain memories to specific locales while eliding the present unevenness that characterizes current homeland relationships.[38] This theme comes home strongly in other videos, both fictional and documentary, on homeland topics. One widely sold video entitled *Vib Nais*, after the main Hmong refugee camp in Thailand, is a nostalgic revisit to a site that many Hmong American viewers remember as the place they came of age.[39] Contrary to the mainstream image of the grimy and demeaning squalor of a holding settlement where Hmong were forced to sojourn, this tape explores the feeling tones of the highly charged locales that remain so deeply engraved on the memories of those who made the camp their home, sometimes for over a decade. Having cinematographically surveyed key sites such as the school, the

United Nations office, and the water pump, the tape devotes an especially ample amount of time to the relatively deserted road where young people used to court. The male narrator talks softly, describing with affection the niceties of holding hands, playing, flirting. In a poignant rehearsal of loss, he laments, "Now, I don't know where my lover has gone. Maybe she still remembers when I was holding her hand and we were together." The effect is enhanced by the placement of a popular Hmong beauty, Cha Mee Xiong, a stylishly dressed Hmong Thai singer and star of the transnational Hmong music scene, who voicelessly accentuates whatever is the focus of the image.

Intertextual perspectives on romantic-erotic video themes also reveal a nostalgia for a particular kind of male privilege. It is not only gender power but also an intensity of desire that is captured in the evocations of longing for first loves. *China Part 3* is a widely circulated video that documents the voyage of a group of almost exclusively male delegates from the United States to attend an ethnic festival in Yunnan. Along the way, they pick up some exotically dressed Miao women (of the Hmong dialect group), who ride their bus with them to the festival like escorts. On-site, the producer and other Hmong American men are seen in their Western trench coats and athletic wear opposite a seemingly endless number of ornamented women much younger than they are. The camera zooms in close, peering voyeuristically at the women's faces, and depicts them with the men playing a customary ball-toss game traditionally reserved for courtship among unmarrieds. Some scenes even show flirtatious dialogues between the middle-aged men and the demure women.

In another video, the idiom of courtship is even more explicit. Three rural young women are arrayed on a hilltop, colorfully dressed, before a backdrop of panoramic scenery. The cameraman asks: "Will you sing a song for me to take back to America to find you a man?" And then: "Are you girls still young and unmarried?"

The girl who is apparently the eldest, but still appears to be in her mid-teens at most, utters: "Yes, we don't have 'it' yet."

"Thank you very much," he replies. The camera hesitates, zooms in on the face of the speaker, then pans to the other two girls. They smile awkwardly, like would-be picture-brides, and smooth their skirts and aprons self-consciously. The cameraman, now self-appointed matchmaker, narrates: "These are three of our Hmong girls. They are going to sing, and I'm going to record a couple of songs to take back to our men in America." He chuckles audibly, then asks one of them a key question for the determination of potential marriage partners in the Hmong/Miao clan-exogamous social system:

"What clan are you?"

"Zhou clan," the eldest offers.

Then they proceed to sing, not knowing where to cast their eyes. They appear disoriented at the staging of what, in face-to-face courtship, would have been a dialogue but now has been rendered as a one-way self-marketing opportunity, concerning which their faces convey primarily ambivalence. Like catalogue brides, they communicate, but only from a position of what Ara Wilson has called "rhetorical vulnerability" in which they are commandeered to present themselves in codes not of their own making to audiences not visible to them.[40]

We can speak, then, not only of transnational subjectification but also of erotic subjectification, as male viewers consume, along with images of homeland beauties, representations of an entire sexual culture that includes such specificities as access to very young women and marriage by capture (both of which are out of bounds in the U.S. legal code).[41] Interestingly, in *Dr. Tom*, part 3, once Tom has reached the highlands of Laos, he is able to procure a bride through one of those traditionally sanctioned methods, a method that would have been transgressive even in the Thai refugee camps and towns depicted in parts 1 and 2. After courting a Hmong village girl to no avail, he assembles some clan members to abduct her as she walks on a deserted path. Once she has been "with" Tom for a short period, presumably losing her virginity along the way, her parents agree to the union. Although for Tom this may be a desperate measure, Hmong viewers know that the video rehearses a time-honored mode of acquiring a bride, one that many remember from their own or their parents' personal histories but that is now legitimate only in remote places such as the Lao countryside. What I am suggesting is that there is a special aura of desirability that surrounds the homeland woman, an aura born of the culturally particular forms of conquest to which she is subject. In other words, it is precisely these cultural particularities, in an atmosphere of loss and nostalgia, that accrue to the homeland woman's allure. What plays at one level as pleasurable indulgence in images of courtships past serves at another level as intimations of pleasures yet to be had for the traveler who makes his way to sites of cultural intactness in Asia.

Conclusions

A decade ago, two anthropologists sparred over what was then framed as the postmodernism controversy. Elizabeth Traube did a reading of the film *Ferris Bueller's Day Off* in terms of what it told us about American social life.[42] Michael Moffatt rebutted with an avowedly antipostmodern counter-reading of the text.[43] His conclusion, however, is in favor of a kind of disciplinary rectification in which he impugns Traube's authority by asking, "What . . . is an anthropologist doing publishing an article in a journal of anthropology about the meaning of certain cultural artifacts which is based on no ethnographically rooted evidence of what these artifacts mean to 'the natives'?"[44] Despite Traube's quip in retort, to the effect that Moffatt is guilty of an "overvaluation of reception," we are left with a quandary, the still-nagging dilemma as to what, methodologically and interpretively, would constitute a viable encounter with the mediated form.[45]

The debate continues to revolve around the binary of textualism versus social context. In making the case for figuring media as an anthropological object, Abu-Lughod, discussing a television show, makes a bold statement in favor of textualism: "How can we study the encounter between some Upper Egyptian village women and this television serial? With television programs, one is forced to talk not so much about cultures-as-texts as about discrete cultural texts that are produced, circulated, consumed."[46] Indeed, only by encountering media texts inquisitively, deploying with impunity the reading strategies that have been used for literary and other filmic texts, can we engage them with the depth required to situate them in social life. But my point for the purposes of this discussion is that anthropologists need not privilege the textual per se but rather the sign-saturated social life of which media is one element. In the case of Hmong Americans, and of transnational Hmong community, media is implicated in so many ways—from the economics of transnational production and domestic distribution to the actual relationships forged in production relations to the involvement of audiences in shaping the scripts they want to consume to the incitements to travel and sometimes to pursue erotic attachments across borders. Theorizing social practice, in so many instances, then, cannot be undertaken with the enforced exclusion of media.

Hmong American media can thus be seen as a polyglot enterprise that reveals itself to be a major force in Hmong social life, identity formation, and economic strategies. It emerges out of the historical moment of the camcorder revolution and out of the particularity of Hmong positioning within U.S. ethnoracial stratification. How do immigrants negotiate their cultural practice while undergoing U.S. minoritization? Viewed in the context of dominant media, and a culture of Americanism that disciplines immigrants as particular kinds of subordinated subjects, we might think of

Lisa Lowe's tenet that "the subject that emerges out of Asian American cultural forms is one in excess of and in contradiction with the subjectivities proposed by national modern and postmodern modes of aesthetic representation," that "the current social formation entails a subject less narrated by the modern discourse of citizenship and more narrated by the histories of wars in Asia, immigration, and the dynamics of the current global economy."[47] In this light, Hmong could be seen to be making space for their very particularized narratives, ones that enunciate their own cultural memories, war genealogies, sentiments of loss, and struggles of resettlement. Not only in explicit texts such as war docudramas but even in pop music formed out of the sojourn in Thailand the traces of their specific pasts can be retained and processed.

I hold, however, that it is not the politics of the American site that is the primary shaper of Hmong media, and this is how it differs from case studies in specifically national contexts.[48] Fruitful anthropological work has been done on the kinds of transnational imaginings enabled through the consumption of media products from within particular localities,[49] but the peripatetic character of Hmong media demands more complex methodologies. Generated within webs of diasporic linkage, such media are produced in, circulate in, represent, and structure relations across national borders. Yet such media are far from being generically cosmopolitan. Benedict Anderson has pointed out that "not least as a result of the ethnicization of political life in the wealthy, postindustrial states, what one can call long-distance nationalism is visibly emerging. This type of politics, directed mainly towards the former Second and Third Worlds, pries open the classical nation-state project from a different direction."[50] This is why I emphasize the imbrication of media with transnational subjectification. "Globalization and image culture do not exist separately first and then interact with each other," asserts Mitsuhiro Yoshimoto. "Image culture has not merely been globalized, nor is globalization merely characterized by the ubiquitous dissemination of transnationally produced images. . . . On a fundamental level globalization and image are inseparable from each other."[51] It is not only that the relations precipitated by Hmong media—from the transfer of dollars to the transfer of wives to the movement of travelers back and forth across the Pacific—are materially consequential at the supranational scale. It is also that the specific meanings embedded in so many of the texts that are produced can be seen as interpellating Hmong consuming subjects into a kind of border-crossing sensibility, one that sites their identity in no one nation-culture but only in the interstitial spaces they have carved out through millennia of wars and conflicts with dominant others. This becomes the substance of Hmong collective memory and the focus of all manner of pained reflections on the differences that their dispersal has generated and exacerbated.

A text such as *Dr. Tom*, then, has a palpable social reality for those it addresses. It inhabits and enunciates the transnational space in which Hmong Americans live. Asked about *Dr. Tom*, most Hmong I spoke to chuckled or smiled, with a glimmer of irony. Why did they think it was so popular? "Because it's true," most of them said. "It's a real story." Not that this particular story actually happened, they hastened to explain, but that this kind of thing happens all the time. Some talked disapprovingly about the calculations of Hmong and Miao families situated in the Third World and willing to offer their daughters to secure that transnational alliance that would magically transform their economic fortunes. What the text condenses is a collective concern over emerging cleavages, a painful awareness that beyond horizontal solidarity, Hmong/Miao transnationality is fraught with pitfalls for identitarian aims—a minefield in which those from the West suspect those in Asia of economic opportunism and those in Asia see their Western counterparts as sexual predators. Read at the level of its social life in transnational space, *Dr. Tom* might be seen as a call for ethnic self-scrutiny in which the wrenching realities of internal exploitation could be brought to light and expelled.

Yet even as the Hmong sense of collectivity spans the globe, augmented by media messages, those same media messages may also play a role in refashioning the most intimate of interiorities. Transnational erotics, such as we see in Hmong media, remixes sex and space, revealing that physical distance and proximity are complexly intertwined in the contours of homeland desire. Elizabeth Povinelli and George Chauncey reflect on these types of configurations by suggesting the way that intimacy and closeness are being reworked: "Globalization studies ask a fundamental question: where are the intimate and proximate spaces in which persons become subjects of embodied practices and times of desire? . . . The reconfiguration of the intimate and the proximate poses a set of interesting problems to theories of sexuality."[52] And likewise to studies of transnationality. My object is to situate erotics not simply in the personal or the psychological but in a transregional cultural economy in which national, ethnic, and racial identities are always implicated and in which global geopolitics participates in shaping longings and fantasies. Such longings and fantasies in turn spur practices that become the stuff of certain transnational linkages.

AFTERWORD

The Ethnographer's "Gaze": Some Notes on Visuality and Its Relation to the Reflexive Metalanguage of Anthropology

Maria Kakavoulia

Since commentary seems to be both a questions-raising and an interpretive practice, I would like to bring into discussion an issue that I think relates in an immediate way to the preceding papers in this volume. We already have an overabundance of theoretical metalanguages informed by powerful interdisciplinary movements (semiotics, linguistics, textual theory, postcolonialism, etc.) that attempt to master issues concerning representational modes. Here, for reasons of terminological economy, I would like to bring into the discussion the verbal-visual distinction and its importance in cross-cultural research. Reminding us of Michel Foucault's distinction between the seeable and the sayable, this semiotic division may even take the form of the oral-written divide.[1]

The discussion concerning the dominance of written culture over the culture of the spoken word dates from Aristotle's *Poetics*, and the debate concerning the priority of seeing over hearing, the priority of optics over acoustics, has been related to the definition and understanding of tragedy. "Hearing did not develop into the guide metaphor for thinking,"[2] whereas vision embodied the faculty of critical judgment. Moreover, orality has been attributed to nonliterate societies, whereas visuality dominates in the scopic regime of writing.[3]

Sight is regarded in Western society as giving us immediate access to the external world. Visual ability is conflated with cognition in a series of complex ways. As Nicholas Mirzoeff has pointed out, the paradox is that the biology of vision has remained more or less constant, on the one hand, whereas, on the other hand, the resulting perception and interpretation of visual symbols is variously experienced as culturally and socially embedded or contingent.[4]

Philosophy itself has relied on a vocabulary heavily loaded with metaphors originating from the domain of vision. Hence, vision has been both philosophically and historically considered the most reliable source for truth. Philosophical discourse has systematically adopted the language of vision to construct itself.[5] Moreover, academic and scientific terminology is heavily based on metaphors related to vision; knowledge and cognition are metaphorically related to notions of light, "clear" vision, enlightenment, sight, insight, and so on. Ocularcentrism has been related to cognitivism. Ocular metaphors, examples, and analogies pervade everyday language, as in the expressions "Just use your eyes!" or "Do you see my point?"

Vision-centered interpretation of truth and knowledge has characterized the Western philosophical tradition, and ocularcentrism reached its highest point in late-eighteenth-century rationalism. Furthermore, the privileging of sight has been a vehicle for the achievement of modernity's projects.[6] Conscious manipulation of images and the notion of "gaze" are two practices by which modern systems of power and social control are exercised. The modern world is very much a *seen* phenomenon. Moreover, the dichotomy between "self" and "other" in sociological and anthropological work has settled into the methodological form of "observation." "Observation" has become a root metaphor within social and cultural research, and an extensive vocabulary of "visuality" is instrumental for gaining access to and understanding practices of human communities.

The "observer" has an external *perspective* in relation to the participant's *gaze*. Foucault's notion of the *sovereign* gaze connotes God's omnipotent vision and panoptic power (*panopticon*),[7] and words such as *theory* and *idea* are etymologically rooted in the morphology of the Greek verb *to see* (ορώ), thus pointing to the gaze that becomes knowledge, ideology. Jürgen Habermas too points out the objectification taking place under the gaze of a third person, under the *philosopher's gaze*: "Everything gets frozen under the gaze of the third person."[8] Thinking of ourselves as seers, we imply a certain capacity that connotes not only the free sense of sight, but also a deep understanding of what really matters, an ultimate concern. As Irit Rogoff succinctly puts it, "Spectatorship as an investigative field understands that what the eye purportedly 'sees' is dictated to it by an entire set of beliefs and desires and by a set of coded languages and generic apparatuses."[9]

Interpretive anthropology involves visual practices as both a source domain (seeing) and a target domain (objects to be seen). What are the preconditions of the anthropologist's interactive gaze? To what extent is anthropology's self-critique based on forms of self-observation? In what ways, then, could interpretive anthropology benefit from a theory of visuality that would transgress the observer-observed divide or the real-virtual dichotomy?

Visualism has been related to mentalism, dividing the world of senses from the world of the mind. The familiar rationalist distinction between the "eye of the mind" and the "eye of the body" establishes fundamental parallels between the visual and the cognitive domains. In the history of Western thought, the Enlightenment is characterized mostly by the ocularcentric construction of the subject and object of knowledge, and René Descartes is the philosopher whose work is dominated by the metaphor of knowledge as spatio-visual.[10] The domination of sight as the most reliable and the most universal of senses—in the sense that perceiving subjects are assumed to see the same thing—informed also the methodology of sciences. However, anthropological studies have quite clearly shown that the Western association of knowledge with sight is not at all universal.[11] Different sensory models and hierarchies are found in different cultures. There have been a number of approaches that do not focus on visual symbolism or the analysis of visual hegemonism and other "Western sensory biases."[12] Rather, these approaches propose a "survey" of the "archaeology" and history of the senses, given that the senses are not merely physical mechanisms but are also subject to social conditioning.[13] In the last decade, heightened interest has led to a focus on sensory perception; for instance, touch has been broken down into three different specialized senses: kinesthesia, movement, and perception of temperature and pain.[14]

Among the objectives of cross-cultural anthropological research is the exploration of the embedding of a "sensory" order in the "social" order of society. Sensorial anthropology studies various cultural systems of sensorial symbolism, contrasting Western perceptual models with orality and aurality in other cultures. In this line, Tim Ingold's work proposes an integrative approach of the body that unites experience and skill, involving all senses and especially movement through space.[15] Bodily movement is the process of building up knowledge. In this sense, Ingold shifts away from the ocularcentric model of perception to an integrative approach that rethinks "sight, hearing and human movement in an environment" and provides a persuasive new theory of the perception of the world around us. However, aspects of vision and visuality such as *imagination* have failed to capture the attention of anthropological study. Thomas Csordas finds it noteworthy that *imagination*, "as a modality of human creativity and a powerful self process . . . is virtually absent as a topic of anthropological interest."[16] In my opinion, there is still a need for a systematic theory of visuality that would (1) address cultural ocular conventions, (2) explore the visual dimension within anthropological practices, and (3) inform cross-cultural research of power and its representational practices.

At a time when "culture" and related notions of social "difference" and "identity" are becoming the master concepts for the humanities and social sciences, it would be useful to have conceptual counterweights that examine cultural formations. There is a need for a self-reflexive (note the visual metaphor) theorizing of vision that would simultaneously treat and study the contradictory fact that Western society legitimizes the practice of eye-witnessing (believing is seeing) and at the same time destabilizes visual evidence with rhetorical manipulation. Ethnographic narrativization is already a part of the methodologies used in revelations and explanations of "unseen" or "hidden" discourses, cultures, power relations, and so on. Visual practice seems to submit everything that is seen to a specific representational order.[17]

Our attempts to explain what we see in words are ways of symbolically reimagining the basis for identification, belief, cognition, and interpretation. The visual is entailed within the rhetorical. How is this relation involved in the literary production of anthropologists themselves? In other words, in what way does visual practice inform, for instance, the rhetoric of autoethnographic representations of experience? Is the issue of mediated and mediating visuality specifically addressed in the ways that it enters ethnographic discourse? How is vision discursively embedded within anthropological or ethnographic narratives? Vision as sight, visual perception, imagination. It is precisely in this line of argument that Neni Panourgiá criticizes the limitations of the ocular-optical metaphors people employed to interrogate her autoethnographic project.[18]

Different subject positions relate to different "views" and approaches to ethnography's postmodern object of study. Exclusions and inclusions operate according to the multiplicity of "viewpoints," of "positions." As Kenneth Burke put it long ago, "A way of seeing is also a way of not seeing—a focus on object A involves a neglect of object B."[19] Donna Haraway's notion of "positioning," her quest to reclaim the embodied nature of all vision, "to reclaim the sensory system that has been used to signify a leap out of the marked body and into the conquering gaze from nowhere,"[20] supports contemporary ethnography's need to renegotiate the ethnographer's identity within a mobile and multi-sited fieldwork.[21]

NOTES

INTRODUCTION
George Marcus and Neni Panourgiá

1. Renato Rosaldo, *Culture and Truth: The Remaking of Social Analysis* (Boston: Beacon Press, 1993), 93.
2. Sherry B. Ortner, introduction to *The Fate of "Culture": Geertz and Beyond*, ed. Sherry B. Ortner, Representations Books (Berekely: University of California Press, 1999), 11.
3. Theodor W. Adorno, *Minima Moralia: Reflections on a Damaged Life*, trans. E. F. N. Jephcott (London: Verso, 1974), 38.
4. Edward Said, *Representations of the Intellectual: The 1993 Reith Lectures* (New York: Vintage Books, 1996), 58.
5. Adorno, *Minima Moralia*, 74.
6. Ortner, introduction to *The Fate of "Culture,"* 4.
7. Adorno, *Minima Moralia*, 74.
8. Michael Jackson, *Minima Ethnographica: Intersubjectivity and the Anthropological Project* (Chicago: University of Chicago Press, 1998), 3.
9. Michael Jackson, *At Home in the World* (Durham, N.C.: Duke University Press, 2000).
10. Adorno, *Minima Moralia*, 39.
11. Said, *Representations of the Intellectual*, 56.
12. Ortner, introduction to *The Fate of "Culture,"* 1.
13. Clifford Geertz, *The Interpretation of Cultures* (New York: Basic Books, 1973), 69.

INTERVIEW WITH CLIFFORD GEERTZ
Neni Panourgiá and Pavlos Kavouras

NOTE: Originally published in a slightly different form in *Anthropological Theory* 2, no. 4 (2002): 421–431, © 2002 Sage Publications (London, Thousand Oaks, Calif., and New Delhi). Reprinted by permission.

CONTEMPORARY FIELDWORK AESTHETICS IN ART AND ANTHROPOLOGY:
EXPERIMENTS IN COLLABORATION AND INTERVENTION
George E. Marcus

1. See, e.g., Douglas R. Holmes and George E. Marcus, "Cultures of Expertise and the Management of Globalization: Toward the Re-Functioning of Ethnography," in *Global Assemblages: Technology, Politics, and Ethics as Anthropological Problems*, ed. Aihwa Ong and Stephen J. Collier (Oxford: Blackwell Publishing, 2005), 235–252; and Douglas R. Holmes and George E. Marcus, "Refunctioning Ethnography: The Challenge of an Anthropology of the Contemporary," in *The Sage Handbook of Qualitative Research*, 3rd ed., ed. Norman K. Denzin and Yvonna S. Lincoln (Thousand Oaks, Calif.: Sage, 2005), 1099–1114.

2. Clifford Geertz, "Deep Play: Notes on the Balinese Cockfight," in *The Interpretation of Cultures* (New York: Basic Books, 1973), 412–453.

3. Bronislaw Malinowski, *Argonauts of the Western Pacific* (New York: E. P. Dutton, 1961), 46 (first published 1922).

4. Kim Fortun, *Advocacy after Bhopal* (Chicago: University of Chicago Press, 2001), 1.

5. James Clifford and George E. Marcus, eds., *Writing Culture: The Poetics and Politics of Ethnography* (Berkeley: University of California Press, 1986).

6. Paul Rabinow, *Anthropos Today: Reflections on Modern Equipment* (Princeton, N.J.: Princeton University Press, 2003).

7. See, e.g., Marilyn Strathern, *Commons and Borderlands: Working Papers on Interdisciplinarity, Accountability and the Flow of Knowledge* (Oxford: Sean Kingston, 2004).

8. I should also note here another similar sort of effort ongoing in U.S. anthropology by Chicago-trained students of George Stocking, the historian of anthropology; they are reinventing fieldwork from within merely by reinvoking and reinterpreting for present conditions the fieldwork style of Franz Boas, who was prominent in the institutionalization of U.S. anthropology, but whose style of ethnography lost out as a model of method to that of Malinowski. The so called neo-Boasian revival of Matti Bunzl and others is so suggestive because, inspired by Michel Foucault, it effectively shifts the coordinates of the Malinowskian scene of encounter to reflect the realities of changed circumstances of fieldwork today, mainly from the anthropologist's crossing the boundary of cultural difference to encounter the subject as informant, as source of data on a culture for which is a token, to the anthropologist's establishing collaborative relations with others who establish mutual curiosities and interests in a common object of knowledge. The Boasian pursuit of research requires a collaborative social imaginary in which to do its work that does not depend on the fixed coordinates of the way culture presents itself as a puzzle in the Malinowskian vision and relation of fieldwork.

9. Fieldwork is no longer site specific in a literal sense. It has become multi-sited not in the sense of making Malinowskian scenes of encounter many times over but through a different strategy of materializing the field of research at certain locations—these are questions of scale-making, a located, situated logic of juxtaposition in which fieldwork literally and imaginatively moves and is designed as such. The object of study is not a particular cultural structure or logic to be described, analyzed, and modeled but the exploration of the anthropologist's relations to social actors who are both subjects and partners in research.

10. Johannes Fabian, *Time and the Other* (New York: Columbia University Press, 1981).

11. Nicolas Bourriaud, *Relational Aesthetics* (Paris: Les Presses du réel, 1998).

12. Hal Foster, "The Artist as Ethnographer?" in *The Traffic in Culture: Refiguring Art and Anthropology*, ed. George E. Marcus and Fred R. Myers (Berkeley: University of California Press, 1995), 145–170.

13. Nikos Papastergiadis, *Spatial Aesthetics: Art, Place, and the Everyday* (London: Rivers Oram Press, 2006).

14. Neil Cummings and Marysia Lewandowska, *Capital: A Project by Neil Cummings and Marysia Lewandowska* (London: Tate Publishing, 2001).

15. *Fieldworks: Dialogues between Art and Anthropology*, http://www.tate.org.uk/onlineevents/archive/fieldworks.

16. ChanceProjects, http://www.chanceprojects.com (accessed February 8, 2006).

17. Hans-Jörg Rheinberger, *Towards a History of Epistemic Things* (Stanford, Calif.: Stanford University Press, 1997).

18. In Rheinberger's view, experimental systems are to be seen as the smallest integral working units of research. As such, they are systems of manipulation designed to give unknown answers to questions that the experimenters themselves are not yet able clearly to ask.

Experimentation as a machine for making the future has to engender unexpected events.

Epistemic things are material entities or processes—physical structures, chemical relations, biological functions—that constitute the objects of inquiry. As epistemic objects, they present themselves in a characteristic, irreducible vagueness. This vagueness is inevitable because epistemic things embody what one does not yet know. Scientific objects have the precious status of being absent in their experimental presence.

19. How this revised aesthetics of method emerges in different projects will be diverse. For example, in 2005, I published an initial account of a collaboration with a Portuguese aristocrat, Fernando Mascarenhas, the Marques of

Fronteira and Alorna, who was, at once, patron, partner, and subject in this research. See George E. Marcus and Fernando Mascarenhas, *Ocasião: The Marquis and the Anthropologist, a Collaboration* (Walnut Creek, Calif.: AltaMira Press, 2005). It is called *Ocasião*, a term rich in meaning both for Fernando's house and our experiment in ethnography. This account is a transcript of our initial discussions via e-mail. Although superficially resembling a reflexive account of fieldwork in the Malinowskian mise-en-scène typical of the genre that followed the *Writing Culture* critiques, in fact it is an account of the development of a different architecture or design from our collaboration that involves creating a multi-sited imaginary for this particular project, materialized as a system of nested dialogues and discussions with orchestrated reflexive commentaries on the corpus of material as it was accumulating in this form. The climax of this study was a conference of Portuguese nobles held at Fernando's palace in 2000. This was a rather rarified subject, but finally it incorporated many of the aspects of the practice of fieldwork explicit in the project of Cummings and Lewandowska and implicit in many contemporary projects of anthropological research. In short, it was a theater of reflexivities modulating nested occasions of discussion, increasingly enriched by a recursivity that comments on earlier materials. This was a project full of mediations, interventions, reactions, and receptions within its bounds; for anthropology, the academy, and others there are a set of publications that reflect its contents in the conventional genre tropes of anthropological writing, analogous to the way in which Cummings and Lewandowska resolved their project into the genre of the glossy, theoretical, semi-academic museum catalog publication as just one of its publicly expressive forms. In this publication of Cummings and Lewandowska, the processes of producing the project were hidden, made available only in the informality of the conference presentation at Tate; in the case of our Portuguese project, the comparable publication—the ethnographic work—was entirely devoted to the process of the research and thinking it through collaboratively. Surely this says something about the state of ethnography in anthropology—where its process inside out is of more immediate or priority interest in a general way than its results. Indeed, the most interesting ethnographic works today have this inside-outness quality where quite substantive results, understandings, analyses of processes, things in the world, are woven into a reflexive account of how the project itself as an act of research comes into being or evolves. This is far from the charge of narcissism and so-called self-indulgent reflexive ethnography so frequently written and even more feared after the 1980s critique. Such an account is actually relevant to its intellectual function and scope.

Anthropologists such as Kim Fortun, with her work *Advocacy after Bhopal*, are attempting to escape the narrowly configured ethical discipline that shapes the traditional ethnographic narrative rejected by Cummings and Lewandowska for the sake of working at ethical plateaus of the emergent, where there is no firm ground in the multi-sited imaginary that Fortun constructed for herself out of the obligatory Malinowskian mise-en-scène of fieldwork, impossible to constitute from the very beginning of her work.

MYTH, PERFORMANCE, POETICS—THE GAZE FROM CLASSICS
Richard P. Martin

1. S. C. Humphreys, *Anthropology and the Greeks* (1978; paperback reprint, London: Routledge, 1983), 21.

2. I am especially grateful to Neni Panourgiá, George E. Marcus, and the *Ethniko Idryma Erevnon* for the invitation to represent classics at the sessions in Hermoupolis in July 1999. As a *xenos* in several regards, it was my privilege to attend, learn, and contribute toward a sharing of ideas between two not-so-distant intellectual encampments. It should be said that the intervening years have seen some progress in the directions observed within this paper; rather than try to provide a full update, I have selectively noted useful works.

3. Humphreys, *Anthropology and the Greeks*, 1–30, remains the best overview of the ways in which scholars of Greek and Roman culture used and abused anthropological ideas. She takes account of more recent work and renews the call for a more self-aware critique of classics methodologies, aided by anthropology, in S. C. Humphreys, *The Family, Women and Death: Comparative Studies*, 2nd ed. (Ann Arbor: University of Michigan Press, 1993), ix–lii. For turn-of-the-century views on the link between the two disciplines, see R. R. Marett, ed., *Anthropology and the Classics* (Oxford: Clarendon Press, 1908). On the pivotal role of Frazer, see Robert Ackerman, *J. G. Frazer: His Life and Work* (Cambridge, U.K.: Cambridge University Press, 1987); and Stanley Edgar Hyman, *The Tangled Bank: Darwin, Marx, Frazer, and Freud as Imaginative Writers* (New York: Atheneum, 1962), 189–291.

4. On anthropology's identification with fieldwork and the problems involved, see for a start, James A. Boon, *Other Tribes, Other Scribes: Symbolic Anthropology in the Comparative Study of Cultures, Histories, Religions, and Texts* (New York: Cambridge University Press, 1982), 4–9.

5. Parry, in his University of Paris *thèses* of 1928, developed his position regarding the deeply traditional nature of Homeric verse on textual grounds alone. See Adam Parry, ed., *The Making of Homeric Verse: The Collected Papers of Milman Parry* (Oxford: Clarendon Press, 1971), 2–239. Only in 1933, with his assistant Albert Lord, did Parry compare Homeric poetry with the results of fieldwork among Serbo-Croatian singers. In the remaining years before his tragic early death in 1935, Parry concentrated on comparing technical aspects of Greek and South Slavic verse, rather than on the social contexts of the

respective poetries. Lord went on to develop and expand Parry's findings, while stressing the fieldwork aspect of the investigation. See Albert Bates Lord, *The Singer of Tales* (Cambridge, Mass.: Harvard University Press, 1960). Lord's role and the innovative aspects of Parry and Lord's methods have been obscured, however, by anti-oral critics, including Parry's son and literary executor, on which see Gregory Nagy, "Irreversible Mistakes and Homeric Poetry," in *Euphrosyne: Studies in Ancient Epic and Its Legacy in Honor of Dimitris N. Maronitis*, ed. John N. Kazazis and Antonios Rengakos (Stuttgart, Germany: F. Steiner, 1999), 259–274 (esp. 265–268). On the "scripsist" position, see Oliver Taplin, *Homeric Soundings: The Shaping of the Iliad* (Oxford: Clarendon Press, 1992), 335–338. Ironically, Taplin, in seeking to find a middle ground, is forced to appropriate the privileged term, giving the title "poetic fieldwork" to his attempt "to work out the mental and social structures of the *Iliad* by accumulating and comparing the evidence from within the poem"—in other words, doing what has usually been called philology. Ibid., 48.

6. Hugh Lloyd-Jones, "Becoming Homer," review of *Epic Singers and Oral Tradition*, by Albert Bates Lord, *New York Review of Books*, March 5, 1992.

7. Lord insisted on the importance of fieldwork data (see esp. Albert Bates Lord, *The Singer Resumes the Tale*, ed. Mary Louise Lord [Ithaca, N.Y.: Cornell University Press, 1995], 104–105, 187–202; see also Albert Bates Lord, *Epic Singers and Oral Tradition* [Ithaca, N.Y.: Cornell University Press, 1991], 38–48), without making the experience a shibboleth. His follower James Notopoulos appears to have been less careful about this. Cf. James A. Notopoulos, "Studies in Early Greek Oral Poetry," *Harvard Studies in Classical Philology* 68 (1964): 1–77.

8. A good sample of new work, with further bibliography, is provided in Margaret Beissinger, Jane Tylus, and Susanne Wofford, eds., *Epic Traditions in the Contemporary World* (Berkeley: University of California Press, 1999). See also Philip Lutgendorf, *The Life of a Text: Performing the Ramcaritmanas of Tulsidas* (Berkeley: University of California Press, 1991); and Dwight Fletcher Reynolds, *Heroic Poets, Poetic Heroes: The Ethnography of Performance in an Arabic Oral Epic Tradition* (Ithaca, N.Y.: Cornell University Press, 1995). Gregory Nagy, *Poetry as Performance* (Cambridge, U.K.: Cambridge University Press, 1996), 87–103, draws on fieldwork among the Navaho in reimagining contexts for the lyric poetry of Sappho (seventh to sixth centuries B.C.E.).

9. Plato *Apology* 40b7–c4 (my translation).

10. As a referee for this volume kindly reminds me, the same point was made a number of times by Paul Ricoeur. See, for example, "The Model of the Text: Meaningful Action Considered as a Text," *New Literary History* 5 (1973): 91–117, in which he stresses the necessity for distancing in order to expand the horizon of understanding.

11. The two abilities tend to be blurred, in the desiring vision, although there is nothing in practice that guarantees a highly localized viewpoint—even if available—will automatically generate an analysis carefully aware of the sort of framing and distancing effects noted by Clifford Geertz, *The Interpretation of Cultures* (New York: Basic Books, 1973), 3–30.

12. On Panhellenism, see Gregory Nagy, *The Best of the Achaeans*, rev. ed. (Baltimore: Johns Hopkins University Press, 1999), 115–142; and Catherine Morgan, "The Origins of Pan-Hellenism," in *Greek Sanctuaries: New Approaches*, ed. Nanno Marinatos and Robin Hägg (London: Routledge, 1993), 18–44.

For the effect on studies of religious cults, see Robert Parker, *Athenian Religion: A History* (Oxford: Clarendon Press, 1996), 1–9.

13. Recent work has begun an explicit attempt to recover epichoric history and tradition. See, e.g., Thomas J. Figueira, *Excursions in Epichoric History: Aiginetan Essays* (Lanham, Md.: Rowman & Littlefield, 1993); and Roger Brock and Stephen Hodkinson, eds., *Alternatives to Athens: Varieties of Political Organization and Community in Ancient Greece* (Oxford: Oxford University Press, 2000).

14. See the cogent historical analyses of the discipline in Ian Morris, *Archaeology as Cultural History: Words and Things in Iron Age Greece* (Malden, Mass.: Blackwell, 2000); and Michael Shanks, *Classical Archaeology of Greece: Experiences of the Discipline* (London: Routledge, 1996).

For further good examples of the work coming out of a new convergence of historians, archaeologists, and philologists, see the collection edited by Nick Fisher and Hans van Wees, *Archaic Greece: New Approaches and New Evidence* (London: Duckworth, 1998).

15. Humphreys, *The Family, Women, and Death*, 6.

16. On culture as an assemblage of texts demanding close reading, see the conclusion of "Notes on the Balinese Cockfight," in Geertz, *The Interpretation of Cultures*, 448–453. On the applicability of notions of "text" and thus hermeneutics to living events, see Ricoeur, "The Model of the Text."

17. The roots of the polarization are earlier, reaching back to the very establishment of classics as an academic discipline in the early nineteenth century. See R. Steven Turner, "Historicism, *Kritik*, and the Prussian Professoriate, 1790 to 1840," in *Philologie und Hermeneutik im 19: Jahrhundert*, vol. 2, ed. Mayotte Bollack and Heinz Wismann (Göttingen, Germany: Vandenhoeck & Ruprecht, 1983), 450–477.

18. The work of Jonathan Hall has been especially valuable in examining notions of Greek social affiliation. See Jonathan M. Hall, *Hellenicity: Between Ethnicity and Culture* (Chicago: University of Chicago Press, 2005); on borders and frontiers, see François Hartog, *Memories of Odysseus: Frontier Tales from*

Ancient Greece, trans. Janet Lloyd (Chicago: University of Chicago Press, 2001).

19. Humphreys, *Anthropology and the Greeks*; and Humphreys, *The Family, Women, and Death* offer reliable guides through the earlier literature.

20. See especially the essays in J. Peter Euben, *Greek Tragedy and Political Theory* (Berkeley: University of California Press, 1986); Alan H. Sommerstein and others, eds., *Tragedy, Comedy, and the Polis* (Bari, Italy: Levante editori, 1993); and Simon Goldhill and Robin Osborne, eds., *Performance Culture and Athenian Democracy* (Cambridge, U.K.: Cambridge University Press, 1999). An important early contribution on the social context of a predramatic form, female choral performance, is Claude Calame, *Choruses of Young Women in Ancient Greece: Their Morphology, Religious Role, and Social Function*, trans. Derek Collins and Janice Orion (Lanham, Md.: Rowman & Littlefield, 1997) (originally published in French in 1977).

21. On the possible political backgrounds, see W. R. Connor, "City Dionysia and Athenian Democracy," *Classica et Mediaevalia* 40 (1989): 7–32; and Gregory Nagy, *Pindar's Homer: the Lyric Possession of an Epic Past* (Baltimore: Johns Hopkins University Press, 1990), 382–414.

22. P. E. Easterling, ed., *The Cambridge Companion to Greek Tragedy* (Cambridge, U.K.: Cambridge University Press, 1997) prefaces the volume by referring to Clifford Geertz's question, "How is it that other people's creations can be so utterly their own and so deeply part of us?" and Paul Cartledge, in a similar gesture, titles his contribution (pp. 3–35) "'Deep Plays': Theatre as Process in Greek Civic Life."

23. Bernard M. W. Knox, *The Heroic Temper: Studies in Sophoclean Tragedy* (Berkeley: University of California Press,1964); and Charles Segal, "Greek Tragedy and Society: A Structuralist Perspective," in *Interpreting Greek Tragedy: Myth, Poetry, Text* (Ithaca, N.Y.: Cornell University Press, 1986), 21–47 (originally published in 1981).

24. See Froma I. Zeitlin, "Thebes: Theater of Self and Society in Athenian Drama," in Euben, *Greek Tragedy and Political Theory*, 101–141.

25. See essays and the bibliography in Easterling, *The Cambridge Companion to Greek Tragedy*. Ironically, little more than twenty years ago classicists could be described as prone to thinking that Greek philosophy and tragedy lay outside the province of anthropology. Humphreys, *Anthropology and the Greeks*, 4. At that time, the work of the so-called Paris school was only beginning to make its mark. For an introduction to the work of this group of structuralist interpreters and their academic forefather, Louis Gernet, see Louis Gernet, *The Anthropology of Ancient Greece*, trans. John D. B. Hamilton and Blaise Nagy (Baltimore: Johns Hopkins University Press, 1981); R. L. Gordon, ed., *Myth, Religion, and Society: Structuralist Essays* (Cambridge, U.K.:

Cambridge University Press, 1981); Jean-Pierre Vernant, *Mortals and Immortals: Collected Essays*, ed. Froma I. Zeitlin (Princeton, N.J.: Princeton University Press, 1991); Pierre Vidal-Naquet, *The Black Hunter: Forms of Thought and Forms of Society in the Greek World*, trans. Andrew Szegedy-Maszak (Baltimore: Johns Hopkins University Press, 1986); Nicole Loraux, *The Children of Athena: Athenian Ideas about Citizenship and the Division between the Sexes*, trans. Caroline Levine (Princeton, N.J.: Princeton University Press, 1993); and Humphreys, *Anthropology and the Greeks*, 76–106. Jack Winkler, who worked to a large extent independently of the Paris scholars, was one of the first to bring social analysis to bear on problems of gender in Greek society and literature. See Jack Winkler, *The Constraints of Desire: The Anthropology of Sex and Gender in Ancient Greece* (New York: Routledge, 1990). The foundational era of the school has now passed with the deaths of Loraux (2003), Vernant (2007), and Vidal-Naquet (2006).

26. See the essay by Neni Panourgiá in this volume.

27. This desideratum remains unfulfilled, unless one considers modern adaptations of drama from overt comparative angles (like Wole Soyinka's Oedipus) to be analogous to anthropological readings.

28. The influence of Geertz on it is explicitly acknowledged in Carol Dougherty and Leslie Kurke, eds., *Cultural Poetics in Archaic Greece: Cult, Performance, Politics* (Cambridge, U.K.: Cambridge University Press, 1993), 2–3. The Princeton bias of the collection (seven out of ten contributors once studied or taught at the university) has its own genealogy involving the numinous presence of Geertz a short walk away through the woods, at the Institute for Advanced Study. His influence was mediated through the wide-ranging work of W. R. Connor. See especially W. R. Connor, "Tribes, Festivals and Processions: Civic Ceremonial and Political Manipulation in Ancient Greece," *Journal of Hellenic Studies* 107 (1987): 40–50; and W. R. Connor, "Early Greek Land Warfare as Symbolic Expression," *Past and Present* 119 (1988): 161–188. It is significant that the sequel volume, marking the tenth anniversary of the Wellesley conference, takes a turn familiar also to current anthropology, toward questioning the notion of cohesive, unitary "cultures," as can be seen even in the title: *The Cultures within Ancient Greek Culture*, ed. Carol Dougherty and Leslie Kurke (Cambridge, U.K.: Cambridge University Press, 2003). In an interesting twist, Josiah Ober's concluding essay argues for the virtues of "thin" description.

29. Plutarch, *Moralia* 844F, 845B, in *Plutarch's Moralia*, vol. 10, trans. Harold North Fowler, Loeb Classical Library (Cambridge, Mass.: Harvard University Press, 1949), 416–418.

30. This is Gerald Else's term. See Dougherty and Kurke, *Cultural Poetics in Archaic Greece*, 1.

31. Carol Dougherty, *The Poetics of Colonization: From City to Text in Archaic Greece* (New York: Oxford University Press, 1994).

32. Lisa Maurizio, "Anthropology and Spirit Possession: A Reconsideration of the Pythia's Role at Delphi," *Journal of Hellenic Studies* 115 (1995): 69–86.

33. Richard P. Martin, "The Seven Sages as Performers of Wisdom," in Dougherty and Kurke, *Cultural Poetics in Archaic Greece*, 108–128; Richard P. Martin, "Solon in No Man's Land," in *Solon of Athens: New Historical and Philological Approaches*, ed. Josine Blok and André Lardinois (Leiden, Netherlands: Brill, 2006), 157–172.

34. Special mention must be made of the work of Marcel Detienne in this connection, whose *Comparer l'incomparable* (Paris: Seuil, 2000) usefully interrogates our assumptions about the boundaries and even arrogance of comparison. His special interest in comparative political systems, and their spatial expressions, offers a powerful new method for historians who have so far resisted the lessons of non-Greek comparanda.

35. Bruce Lincoln, *Theorizing Myth: Narrative, Ideology, and Scholarship* (Chicago: University of Chicago Press, 1999), traces the gradual demystification of the concept.

36. Marcel Detienne, *The Creation of Mythology*, trans. Margaret Cook (Chicago: University of Chicago Press, 1986) (originally published in French in 1981), broke the silence.

37. For what follows, see Richard P. Martin, *The Language of Heroes: Speech and Performance in the* Iliad (Ithaca, N.Y.: Cornell University Press, 1989), esp. 12–26.

38. Careful work has been done recently using modern Greek ethnographies in tandem with ancient texts embodying laments. For a good application of the method, with further bibliography, see Sheila Murnaghan, "The Poetics of Loss in Greek Epic," in Beissinger and others, *Epic Traditions in the Contemporary World*, 203–220. On comparative Irish and Greek texts, see Richard P. Martin, "Keens from the Absent Chorus: Troy to Ulster," *Western Folklore* 62 (2003): 119–141.

39. See Richard Bauman and Joel Sherzer, *Explorations in the Ethnography of Speaking*, 2nd ed. (Cambridge, U.K.: Cambridge University Press, 1989); Keith H. Basso, "'Wise Words' of the Western Apache: Metaphor and Semantic Theory," in *Meaning in Anthropology*, ed. Keith H. Basso and Henry A. Selby (Albuquerque: University of New Mexico Press, 1976), 93–121; Charles Briggs, *Competence in Performance: The Creativity of Tradition in Mexicano Verbal Art* (Philadelphia: University of Pennsylvania Press, 1988); Michael Herzfeld, *The Poetics of Manhood* (Princeton, N.J.: Princeton University Press, 1985); and C. Nadia Seremetakis, *The Last Word: Women, Death, and Divination in Inner*

Mani (Chicago: University of Chicago Press, 1991). For more on Greek oral performance as it merges with literacy, see Jesper Svenbro, *Phrasikleia: An Anthropology of Reading in Ancient Greece*, trans. Janet Lloyd (Ithaca, N.Y.: Cornell University Press, 1993) (originally published in French in 1988).

40. *Iliad* 6.119–236.

41. On the phenomenon of hero-cult and its interaction with epic, see Carla Maria Antonaccio, *An Archaeology of Ancestors: Tomb Cult and Hero Cult in Early Greece* (Lanham, Md.: Rowman & Littlefield, 1995); Robin Hägg, ed., *Ancient Greek Hero Cult: Proceedings of the Fifth International Seminar on Ancient Greek Cult* (Stockholm, Sweden: Svenska institutet i Athen, 1999); and Nagy, *The Best of the Achaeans*.

42. Politically savvy work on myth is exemplified in Christiane Sourvinou-Inwood, *"Reading" Greek Culture: Texts and Images, Rituals and Myths* (Oxford: Clarendon Press, 1991). A brilliant analysis of the working of "myth" in Roman culture is provided in T. Peter Wiseman, *The Myths of Rome* (Exeter, U.K.: University of Exeter Press, 2004). It must be confessed that the bias of the foregoing paper is toward Greek studies; Roman studies offer an even broader, faster-growing field for the application of anthropological approaches, and have in fact since the 1990s outpaced the scholarship on Greece in several key areas.

43. See Nagy, *Pindar's Homer*, 214–73; and Rosaria Munson, *Telling Wonders: Ethnographic and Political Discourse in the Work of Herodotus* (Ann Arbor: University of Michigan Press, 2001).

THE BIRTH OF ANTHROPOLOGY OUT OF A PAUSE ON PAUSANIAS:
FRAZER'S TRAVEL-TRANSLATIONS REINTERRUPTED AND RESUMED
James A. Boon

NOTE: Deep and playful thanks to Neni Panourgiá, Stathis Gourgouris, and participants in and around our conference, especially Pavlos Kavouras, George E. Marcus, and Cliff Geertz. Cliff had relished Syros and fondly remembered this company of scholars in many conversations until soon before his death. I also thank Dimitri Gondicas and Princeton's Program in Hellenic Studies for support.

1. James George Frazer, *The New Golden Bough*, ed. Theodor H. Gaster (New York: Mentor, 1959); Stanley Edgar Hyman, *The Tangled Bank: Darwin, Marx, Frazer, and Freud as Imaginative Writers* (New York: Grosset & Dunlap, 1962); and John B. Vickery, *The Literary Impact of the Golden Bough* (Princeton, N.J.: Princeton University Press, 1973). For supplements to Theodore Besterman's 1934 bibliography of Frazer, and for commentary on Robert Angus Downie's biographical study, see Robert Ackerman, *J. G. Frazer: His Life and Work* (Cambridge, U.K.: Cambridge University Press, 1987). My essay samples sources tactically.

2. I. C. Jarvie, *The Revolution in Anthropology* (Chicago: H. Regnery Co., 1969).

3. James A. Boon, *Other Tribes, Other Scribes: Symbolic Anthropology in the Comparative Study of Cultures, Histories, Religions, and Texts* (New York: Cambridge University Press, 1982), chap. 1. Other anthropologists I have reread this way include Boasians (Ruth Benedict, Robert Lowie, Margaret Mead, Jane Belo), Claude Lévi-Strauss, Marcel Mauss, A. M. Hocart, and Louis Dumont. See indexes in Boon, *Other Tribes*; James A. Boon, *From Symbolism to Structuralism: Lévi-Strauss in a Literary Tradition* (New York: Harper & Row, 1972); James A. Boon, *The Anthropological Romance of Bali: Dynamic Perspectives in Marriage and Caste, Politics and Religion* (New York: Cambridge University Press, 1977); James A. Boon, *Affinities and Extremes: Crisscrossing the Bittersweet Ethnology of East Indies History, Hindu-Balinese Culture, and Indo-European Allure* (Chicago: University of Chicago Press, 1990); and James A. Boon, *Verging on Extra-Vagance: Anthropology, History, Religion, Literature, Arts . . . Showbiz* (Princeton, N.J.: Princeton University Press, 1999). Relevant too are my recent studies of Edward Sapir, Clifford Geertz, and Max Weber: James A. Boon, "Accenting Hybridity: Postcolonial Cultural Theory, A Boasian Anthropologist, and I," in *"Culture" and the Problem of the Disciplines*, ed. John Carlos Rowe (New York: Columbia University Press, 1998), 141–169; James A. Boon, "Showbiz as a Cross-Cultural System: Circus and Song, Garland and Geertz, Rushdie, Mordden, . . . and More," *Cultural Anthropology* 15 (2000): 424–456; James A. Boon, "Geertz's Style: A Moral Matter," in *Clifford Geertz by His Colleagues*, ed. Richard A. Shweder and Byron Goode (Chicago: University of Chicago Press, 2005), 28–37; and James A. Boon, "Also 100 Years Since Weber Flirted with Ethnography," in *Max Weber's 'Objectivity' Reconsidered*, ed. Laurence H. McFalls (Toronto: University of Toronto Press, 2007), 322–350.

4. Marilyn Strathern, "Out of Context: The Persuasive Fictions of Anthropology," in *Modernist Anthropology: From Fieldwork to Text*, ed. Marc Manganaro (Princeton, N.J.: Princeton University Press, 1990), 80–130; Marc Manganaro, "'The Tangled Bank' Revisited: Anthropological Authority in Frazer's The Golden Bough," *Yale Journal of Criticism* 3 (1989): 107–126; *Myth, Rhetoric, and the Voice of Authority: A Critique of Frazer, Eliot, Frye, and Campbell* (New Haven, Conn.: Yale University Press, 1992).

5. Ackerman, *J. G. Frazer: His Life and Work*; Robert S. Fraser, *The Making of the Golden Bough: Origins and Growth of an Argument* (London: Macmillan, 1990).

6. Fraser, *The Making of the Golden Bough*, 210.

7. George W. Stocking Jr., *After Tylor: British Social Anthropology, 1888–1951* (Madison: University of Wisconsin Press, 1995), xiv; George W. Stocking Jr., *Victorian Anthropology* (New York: Free Press, 1987). See James A.

Boon, review of *Victorian Anthropology*, by George W. Stocking Jr., *Science* 237 (1987): 1516–1517.

8. George W. Stocking Jr., introduction to *The Golden Bough: A Study in Magic and Religion*, abridged ed., by James George Frazer (London: Penguin Books, 1996) (hereafter cited as *The Golden Bough* [1926 abridgment]). This is a reissue of Frazer's own "compendious" 1926 abridgment (edited with Lady Frazer for "uplift"). For Frazer's controversial full third edition, readers should rely on R. Fraser's historically alert condensation: James George Frazer, *The Golden Bough: A Study in Magic and Religion*, a new abridgment, ed. Robert Fraser (New York: Oxford University Press, 1994) (hereafter cited as *The Golden Bough* [new abridgment]). I note here ironies of "multicontextual" abridgments underestimated in this instance by Stocking. Regardless, for the record: "I am not now, nor have I ever been" postmodernist. See Boon, *Affinities and Extremes*, xiv–xv; Boon, *Verging on Extra-Vagance*, chaps. 4, 6, 11, 13, pp. 169–175; and Boon, "Accenting Hybridity"; see also note 21 below.

9. James George Frazer, "The Language of Animals," *Archaeological Review* 1 (1898): 81–91, 161–181.

10. *The Encyclopedia of Religion*, 2nd ed., ed. Lindsay Jones (New York: Macmillan), s.v. "Anthropology, Ethnology, and Religion" (by James A. Boon); Ludwig Wittgenstein, *Remarks on Frazer's The Golden Bough*, ed. Rush Rhees, trans. A. C. Miles (Retford, U.K.: Brynmill Press, 1979); and Fraser, *The Making of the Golden Bough*, 206–207.

11. Edmund Leach, "Golden Bough or Gilded Twig?" *Daedalus* 90 (1961): 371–399; and Mary Douglas, "Judgments on James Frazer," *Daedalus* 107 (1978): 151–164. For Jane Harrison, see the new edition of her 1903 *Prolegomena to the Study of Greek Religion*, with an introduction by R. Ackerman (Princeton, N.J.: Princeton University Press, 1991). "Queer theorizing" about this Cambridge school of scholarship is advanced in Jonathan Dollimore, *Sexual Dissidence: Augustine to Wilde, Freud to Foucault* (Oxford: Clarendon Press, 1991) and Richard Dellamora, ed., *Victorian Sexual Dissidence* (Chicago: University of Chicago Press, 1999)—along with Linda Dowling, Yopie Prins, and others. On Pater and Ruskin (and Proust) and Pater and Wilde, and so-called aestheticism, see notes 26 and 51 below.

12. George Steiner, *On Difficulty* (New York: Oxford University Press, 1978); and George Steiner, *After Babel* (New York: Oxford University Press, 1975). Both works stress issues of endlessly translating human languages. See Boon, *Verging on Extra-Vagance*, chap. 6.

13. Neni Panourgiá, *Fragments of Death, Fables of Identity: An Athenian Anthropography* (Madison: University of Wisconsin Press, 1995), 240.

14. On biographical details, see Ackerman, *J. G. Frazer: His Life and Work*.

15. Frazer, as cited in Hyman, *The Tangled Bank*, 203.

16. James George Frazer, ed. and trans., *Pausanias's Description of Greece*, 6 vols. (London: Macmillan, 1898). A nice example of specialists still crediting this study is W. R. Conner, "Seized by the Nymphs: Nympholepsy and Symbolic Expression in Classical Greece," *Classical Antiquity* 7 (1988): 155–189.

17. I allude here to interpretive frames in Kenneth Burke, *Language as Symbolic Action* (Berkeley: University of California Press, 1966); Clifford Geertz, *The Interpretation of Cultures* (New York: Basic Books, 1973); Clifford Geertz, *Local Knowledge* (New York: Basic Books, 1982); and Clifford Geertz, *Available Light* (Princeton, N.J.: Princeton University Press, 2000). One helpful source on philhellenism is Richard Jenkyns, *The Victorians and Ancient Greece* (Cambridge, Mass.: Harvard University Press, 1980); for critical assessments of such enthusiasms, see Stathis Gourgouris, *Does Literature Think? Literature as Theory for an Antimythical Era* (Stanford, Calif.: Stanford University Press, 2003).

18. Joseph Mali, "Benjamin's Homage to Bachofen," *Journal of the History of Ideas* 60 (1990): 180.

19. Cited in Mali, "Benjamin's Homage to Bachofen," 181. See also David Frisby, *Fragments of Modernity: Theories of Modernity in the Work of Simmel, Kracauer, and Benjamin* (Cambridge, Mass.: MIT Press, 1986). Benjamin's piece on Bachofen was written in French; on Bachofen, Basel's institutions, and paradoxes of political literalism and cultural conservatism, see Lionel Gossmann, "Basle and Bachofen," *Journal of the Warburg and Courtauld Institute* 47 (1984): 136–185; and Lionel Gossmann, "Antimodernism in Nineteenth-Century Basle," *Interpretation* 16 (1989): 359–389.

20. Frazer, *Pausanias's Description of Greece*, 2:20. "Being there" is from Clifford Geertz, *Works and Lives: The Anthropologist as Author* (Stanford, Calif.: Stanford University Press, 1987), chap. 1. My essay repeatedly nods toward this notion.

21. Michael André Bernstein, *Five Portraits: Modernism and the Imagination in 20th Century German Writing* (Evanston, Ill.: Northwestern University Press, 2000), 97. Literature on Benjamin's Arcades project is vast; one starting place is Gary Smith, ed., *Benjamin: Philosophy, Aesthetics, History* (Chicago: University of Chicago Press, 1989).

22. Boon, *Verging on Extra-Vagance*, chaps. 1, 3, pp. 269–270; Boon, "Accenting Hybridity"; Boon, *Other Tribes*, chaps. 1, 3.

23. Again, merits of Pausanias's style in Greek remain disputed; more favorably disposed is Peter Levi, introduction to *Guide to Greece*, by Pausanias (London: Penguin, 1971).

24. James George Frazer, *Adonis: Étude de religions orientales comparées*, trans. Lady Frazer, Annales du Musée Guimet, Bibliothèque d'études 29 (Paris: P. Geuthner, 1921), v–vi, 29–30. Compare James George Frazer, *Adonis, Attis, Osiris*, 3rd ed. (New Hyde Park, N.Y.: University Books, 1961).

Instead of my intentionally clumsy, word-for-word rendering, Benjamin may have preferred an interlinear translation: nonstop interruption *in media res*. I sympathize with that "theory" (or task) of translation as well. See Boon, *Other Tribes*, 153, 213–214, 220–221, 230; Boon, *Verging on Extra-Vagance*, chaps. 4, 6; Boon, "Accenting Hybridity"; Walter Benjamin, *Illuminations*, ed. Hannah Arendt (New York, Harcourt, Brace, Jovanovich, 1968); Walter Benjamin, *Das Passagen-Werk*, vol. 1 (Frankfurt am Main: Suhrkamp Verlag, 1983); and Walter Benjamin, *Selected Writings*, ed. Marcus Bullock and Michael W. Jennings, 4 vols. (Cambridge, Mass.: Harvard University Press, 1996–2003).

25. Arthur Schopenhauer, *Essays and Aphorisms*, trans. R. J. Hollingdale (London: Penguin Books, 1970). *Parerga* are a paradoxical organizing device of fluid sequences and simultaneities throughout Panourgiá, *Fragments of Death*; my essay emulates her textual practices.

26. Richard Macksey, "Proust on the Margins of Ruskin," in *The Ruskin Polygon: Essays on the Imagination of John Ruskin*, ed. John Dixon Hunt and Faith M. Holland (Manchester, U.K.: Manchester University Press, 1982), 172–197; see Boon, *Verging on Extra-Vagance*, 118, 298, 135, 299; and Marcel Proust, *A la recherche du temps perdu*, 3 vols. (Paris: Gallimard, 1954); see also Paul L. Sawyer, *Ruskin's Poetic Argument* (Ithaca, N.Y.: Cornell University Press, 1985).

27. On "chronotopes," see Mikhail Bakhtin, *The Dialogic Imagination*, ed. Michael Holquist, trans. Caryl Emerson and Michael Holquist (Austin: University of Texas Press, 1981); using works by Michael Holquist, Caryl Emerson, Jan Kott, Michael Bernstein, and others, I amplify this concept anthropologically in Boon, *Affinities and Extremes*, 67–69; and Boon, *Verging on Extra-Vagance*, chap. 6. Ironically, the date of the latest link (mine) in chronotopes attested in this essay nearly coincided (jived) with 14 *juillet*; may the shade of Lady Lilly forgive my neglecting her national holy day when revisiting her husband's interruptions "of and for" Pausanias.

28. Hitchcock, literally born "Victorian" (in 1899), has been figuratively classed as such for ostensible repressions. See Donald Spoto, *The Dark Side of Genius: The Life of Alfred Hitchcock* (Boston, Little Brown, 1983); and Robin Wood, *Hitchcock's Films Revisited* (New York: Columbia University Press, 1989). Other work suggests that this is a naive view not only of Hitchcock but, since the studies of Stephen Marcus, of Victorians!

29. Dozens of books on Hitchcock (a passion of so many, including me) define "MacGuffin"—for example, Francois Truffaut, *Hitchcock* (New York: Simon & Schuster, 1967); and Thomas Leitch, *The Encyclopedia of Alfred Hitchcock* (New York: Checkmark Books, 2002). This gimmicky notion of a hybrid-arts gimmick became nearly as familiar as Hitch's logo-profile (composed of eight swift strokes). I tend to liken such devices in studio-era movies to analogous tricks in "scenic ethnology" both prior to them and overlapping with

them. For studies of similar interrelations, see Leo Charney and Vanessa Schwartz, eds., *Cinema and the Invention of Modern Life* (Berkeley: University of California Press, 1995).

30. My sense of Greece over the years has been shaped by many anthropologists: John K. Campbell, Ernestine Friedl, Michael Herzfeld, Loring Danforth, Jane Cowan, and above all (including retroactively) Neni Panourgiá. See also Eleana Yalouri, *The Acropolis: Global Fame, Local Claim* (Oxford: Berg, 2001).

31. Stocking, introduction to *The Golden Bough* (1926 abridgment); Fraser, introduction to *The Golden Bough* (new abridgment), xxi.

32. What one might designate *"plus qu'encore plus que parerga"* I have called "cosmomes." Boon, *Verging on Extra-Vagance*, chap. 4. Cosmomes are intersecting places of cultural translation where the emptily cosmopolitan becomes indistinguishable from the utterly local—episodes I also call "Coca-colocalization" (distinct from "Coca-colonization"). Boon, *Verging on Extra-Vagance*, chap. 13, p. 304. To my tastes, a burgeoning critical literature on "cosmopolitanism" remains Enlightenment-tinged: too abstracted from ambiguities in everydayness.

33. Fraser, *The Making of the Golden Bough*, 9.

34. Ibid., 39, 8–11.

35. Frazer, *Pausanias's Description of Greece*, 1:xx–xxii.

36. Hyman, *The Tangled Bank*, 202–203; see Boon, *Other Tribes*, 16–21.

37. On places like Radio City and world expositions (and Burke), see Boon, *Verging on Extra-Vagance*; and Boon, "Showbiz as a Cross-Cultural System." K. Burke's ironic attentiveness to commodity-life, including commercialized culture industry (or something like it), has been neglected by critical anthropologists; so has related attentiveness in Henry Adams, Max Weber, and others. See Boon, *Affinities and Extremes*, xv–xvi; Boon, *Verging on Extra-Vagance*, chap. 5; and Boon, "Also 100 Years Since Weber."

38. Frazer, *The New Golden Bough*, 431–432, 434.

39. Boon, *Verging on Extra-Vagance*, chap. 4; and Boon, "Showbiz as a Cross-Cultural System."

40. Ackerman, *Frazer: His Life and Work*, 58, 64–65.

41. On "panoplies," rereading toward them, and doing so "ultra-objectively," see Boon, *Verging on Extra-Vagance*, chap. 1.

42. Ackerman, *Frazer: His Life and Work*, 117. I'm afraid that I write situated in Scottish-Irish "positionality," personally beset with a little knowledge (in this case no more dangerous than a lot!) of Lacan—for example, Slavoj Zizek, *Looking Awry: An Introduction to Jacques Lacan through Popular Culture* (Cambridge, Mass.: MIT Press, 1991). We all of us have our foibles.

43. Elaborate scholarship on Malinowski and Westermarck cannot be discussed here. I note only that the more we consider what they read (as well as

observed), the less restricted to narrow "method" our sense of their lifeworks becomes. This is the spirit in which my studies have revisited Boasians, Geertz, Weber, Lévi-Strauss, Mauss, Balinese ethnography, and Indonesian ethnology—including the colonialist era and supposedly "since."

44. James George Frazer, "A Suggestion as to the Origins of Gender in Language," *Fortnightly Review*, January 1, 1900, 90.

45. "Book voyages" and "reading navigations" are conceits of Jacobean scholar Samuel Purchas—who forms, I have hinted, a historical parentheses of comparative scholarship with Frazer. See Boon, *Other Tribes*, p. 18, chap. 5.

46. Guy Davenport, *Every Force Evolves a Form* (San Francisco: North Point Press, 1987). Davenport resonates Goethe with various "geographies" and "aesthetics" that also pertain to Lévi-Strauss. See James A. Boon, "Panofsky and Lévi-Strauss (and Iconographers and *Mythologiques*) Re-regarded," in *Meaning in the Visual Arts: Views from Outside*, ed. Irving Lavin (Princeton, N.J.: Princeton University Press, 1995), 33–48.

47. On Frazer's elegiac style, see John B. Vickery, *The Literary Impact of The Golden Bough* (Princeton, N.J.: Princeton University Press, 1973); John B. Vickery, "Frazer and the Elegiac: The Modernist Connection" in *Modernist Anthropology: From Fieldwork to Text*, ed. Marc Manganaro (Princeton, N.J.: Princeton University Press, 1990), 51–68; Marty Roth, "Sir James Frazer's *The Golden Bough*: A Reading Lesson," in Manganaro, *Modernist Anthropology*, 69–79. "Thick" alludes to description in Geertz, *The Interpretation of Cultures*, chap. 1.

48. Ackerman, *Frazer: His Life and Work*, 66.

49. Fraser, introduction to *The Golden Bough* (new abridgment), xxxiii, xxxii.

50. Boon, *From Symbolism to Structuralism*; and Boon, *Other Tribes*, chaps. 1, 4. For parallel approaches to novelists (e.g., Henry James), explorers (e.g., Antonio Pigafetta), scientists (e.g., Alfred Russel Wallace), and hybrids (e.g., A. E. Crawley), see Boon, *Affinities and Extremes*; Boon, *Verging on Extra-Vagance*; and James A. Boon, "The Cross-Cultural Kiss: Edwardian and Earlier, Postmodern and Beyond," in *Four-Field Anthropology for the 21st Century*, ed. Eduardo Brondizio (Bloomington: Indiana University Press, 2007).

51. Walter Pater, *Marius the Epicurean* (London: Penguin Books, 1985); and Walter Pater, *Imaginary Portraits*, ed. Bill Beckley (New York: Allworth Press, 1987). See Dennis Donoghue, *Walter Pater: Lover of Strange Souls* (New York: Knopf, 1995). Pater and Frazer are also broached in Fraser, introduction to *The Golden Bough* (new abridgment), xxxii. In 1989, I taught "Anthropology and Aesthetic Decadence," focused on 1890, the year of both Frazer's *Golden Bough* (with its Turner frontispiece) and Oscar Wilde's *The Picture of Dorian Gray*. Why, the seminar asked, had Frazerian and Wildean discourses intersected so little?

52. Frazer, *Pausanias's Description of Greece*, 2:14.
53. Ibid., 15.
54. Ibid., 17–18.
55. Ibid., 20.
56. Ibid. (emphasis added).
57. Ibid., 21.
58. Ibid., 23.

59. On "thick description" and (hood)winking, see Geertz, *The Interpretation of Cultures*, chap. 1; this winking approach is reprised and seconded in Boon, "Showbiz as a Cross-Cultural System"; and Boon, "Geertz's Style." On reflexivity in everyday Greek life, see Pavlos Kavouras, "Where the Community Reveals Itself: Reflexivity and Moral Judgment in Karpathos, Greece," in *Social Experience and Anthropological Knowledge*, ed. Kirsten Hastrup and Peter Hervik (London: Routledge. 1994), 139–166.

60. "Thinner paper," as requested by Frazer, is mentioned in Ackerman, *J. G. Frazer: His Life and Work*. See James A. Boon, "Among the Golden Boughs," *New York Times Book Review*, March 6, 1988.

61. Pater, *Imaginary Portraits*. I have room only to mention this appealing possibility.

62. Ovid, *Ovid's Fasti*, trans. James George Frazer, Loeb Classical Library (Cambridge, Mass.: Harvard University Press, 1931), 403.

63. Ibid., 376.
64. Ibid., 377–379.

65. James George Frazer, *Aftermath: A Supplement to* The Golden Bough (London: Macmillan, 1937), vi.

66. James George Frazer, *The Golden Bough: A Study in Magic and Religion*, 3rd ed., vol. 5 (London: Macmillan, 1911) (hereafter cited as *The Golden Bough* [3rd edition]). To trace Frazer's sense of Attis and Osiris, see *The Golden Bough* (new abridgment), 817–827.

67. On Purchas and these reading-metaphors, see Boon, *Other Tribes*, chap. 5.

68. Frazer, *The Golden Bough* (3rd edition), 5:253.
69. Ibid., 256.
70. Ibid., 257.
71. Ibid., 259.
72. Ibid., 263.
73. Ibid., 264.
74. Ibid.
75. Frazer, *The New Golden Bough*, 604.
76. On van Eck and this genre, see Boon, *The Anthropological Romance of Bali*, 30–34.

77. For "extravagant" aspects of Bali, such as cremation and noncircumcision (both ethnographically and historically), see Boon, The *Anthropological Romance of Bali*; Boon, *Other Tribes*, chap. 5; Boon, *Affinities and Extremes*; and Boon, *Verging on Extra-Vagance*, chap. 2.

78. So-called functionalism—in practice and historically—is more surprising than routinely (methodologically) made to appear. See Boon, *Other Tribes*, chap. 1; Boon, *The Anthropological Romance of Bali*, part 1; Boon, *Affinities and Extremes*, chap. 2; and Boon, *Verging on Extra-Vagance*, chaps. 1, 3.

79. Frazer, *The New Golden Bough*, 556.

80. Receptions of Frazer by (partly) Boasian Lowie, by (partly) Durkheimian Mauss, or by (partly) Durkheimian-Boasian Lévi-Strauss differ from mine, but only partly. Divergences and compatibilities of such receptions deserve sustained scrutiny. Notable in this regard is Hocart (mentioned as a "Frazer-Boas" hybrid in Stocking, *After Tylor*, 220–228). For more on Hocart and scholars praising him (e.g., Marshall Sahlins, Lévi-Strauss), see Boon, *Affinities and Extremes*, 125–129.

81. One of K. Burke's signature themes is "perspectives in incongruity." See Boon, *Verging on Extra-Vagance*, 3–8; and Boon, *The Anthropological Romance of Bali*, 9.

82. Boon, *Other Tribes*, 23.

83. Panourgiá, *Fragments of Death*, 218 (emphasis added). The late Jean Pouillon once wrote: "*C'est l'incroyant qui croit que le croyant croit* [It's the unbeliever who believes that the believer believes]." See James A. Boon, introduction to *Between Belief and Transgression*, ed. Michael Izard and Pierre Smith (Chicago: University of Chicago Press, 1983). Pouillon's near quip strikes me as a canny wink at "belief"—a category not unrelated to death (as in "belief in immortality"). Such astute, aphoristic insight—worthy of Michel de Montaigne, say (or of Geertz)—converts, if nothing else, inadequate dichotomies (e.g., belief/unbelief) into circumstantial ambiguities, cross-culturally!

84. Fraser, *The Making of the Golden Bough*, 209.

85. Frazer, *The New Golden Bough*, 311–312.

86. I slate for future parerga "translations" across *Phaedra* (the movie), the history of its myth, and museum-going in contemporary Greece (and earlier). Here are just a few token dates and details (cross-cultural, multigenre, high/low). 1931: Frazer's *Fasti* (Ovid) relates Phaedra, via Hippolytus, to Nemi. 1961: Release of (Brooklyn-born) Jules Dassin's movie *Phaedra*—starring Melina Mercouri, his wife, and Anthony Perkins of *Psycho* fame (Hitchcock); Dassin's movie, which *seems* strangely unfaithful to Euripides, conceivably memorializes Phaedra's imagined acts with Hippolytus—much like the monument to her in Athens (described in Pausanias!). 1962: The present author (age sixteen) sees Dassin's *Phaedra*, purchases its soundtrack (LP), and commences (in perplexity) reading Jean Racine's version, the only one I can locate.

1975: George Steiner dismissively alludes to Dassin's movie (in *After Babel*, a book I am asked to review when beginning teaching). 1999: My wife and I encounter a fragment of *Phaedra*—its title sequence (set in a museum), screened incessantly at the Melina Mercouri Foundation, the primary institution promoting Athens (or re-museumizing it). We had stumbled into "Phaedra's" premises via the partially "sub-way" from Piraeus, having traveled Greece-ward to attend a conference in Syros.

Further pursued, chronotopes of coincidence (here barely begun) between Frazer's *Golden Bough*-cum-*Pausanias* and *Phaedra*-then-and-now could suggest interpretive "Anthropolyhippolytuses." See Boon, *Verging on Extra-Vagance*, chap. 6 and preface titles. Regardless, related connections are attested in Pavlos Kavouras, "The Medea of Euripides: An Anthropological Perspective," *Dialectical Anthropology* 13 (1989): 123–142.

87. As last note and would-be tidy "aftermath," I add that Frazer's skepticism, even about skepticism, may explain dismissive responses to his sometimes spellbinding work. This is a hunch that this essay is too discreet to blurt out in the text.

ANAMNESES OF A PESTILENT INFANT:
THE ENIGMA OF MONSTROSITY, OR BEYOND OEDIPUS
Athena Athanasiou

NOTE: I would like to thank Neni Panourgiá, to whose friendship and intellectual stimulation I owe the incentive to write this essay. I began working on this paper during my postdoctoral year at the Pembroke Center for Teaching and Research on Women; I am grateful to Mary Ann Doane, Elizabeth Weed, and all the other participants of the 2001–2002 Pembroke Seminar for offering inspiring conversations. I also thank Elena Tzelepis for her brave questions and responses.

1. Sigmund Freud and Josef Breuer, *Studies on Hysteria*, vol. 2 of *The Standard Edition of the Complete Psychological Works of Sigmund Freud*, trans. and ed. James Strachey (London: Hogarth Press and the Institute of Psycho-Analysis, 1953–1974), 280 (hereafter cited as *The Standard Edition*).

2. Shoshana Felman, "Beyond Oedipus: The Specimen Story of Psychoanalysis," in *Jacques Lacan and the Adventure of Insight: Psychoanalysis in Contemporary Culture* (Cambridge, Mass.: Harvard University Press, 1987), 99–159.

3. See Maurice Blanchot, "La parole analytique," trans. M. Borsh-Jacobsen, in *L' Entretien infini* (Paris: Gallimard, 1969), 343.

4. See Christopher Fynsk, *Infant Figures: The Death of the "Infans" and Other Scenes of Origin* (Stanford, Calif.: Stanford University Press, 2000).

5. Frederic W. H. Myers, "Multiplex Personality," *Proceedings of the Society for Psychical Research* 4 (1889): 502.

6. According to Michel Foucault's theory of biopolitics, *zoē* occupies a central place in the polis (*zoē* is *bios* anyway). In the political writings of Aristotle, Giorgio Agamben finds the first fracture between two semantically distinct terms in ancient Greek for *life*: *zoē* and *bios*: *zoē* (as the thingness of life, the biological concept of life) and *bios* (political life, the manner of living peculiar to a single individual or group). See Giorgio Agamben, *Homo Sacer: Sovereign Power and Bare Life*, trans. Daniel Heller-Roazen (Stanford, Calif.: Stanford University Press, 1998).

7. Jacques Lacan, *Le séminaire*, vol. 1, *Les Écrits techniques de Freud* (Paris: Seuil, 1975), 250.

8. Sigmund Freud, "Remembering, Repeating and Working-Through: Further Recommendations on the Technique of Psycho-Analysis," in *The Case of Schreber, Papers on Technique and Other Works*, vol. 12 of *The Standard Edition*, 145–156.

9. Sigmund Freud, *Moses and Monotheism*, vol. 23 of *The Standard Edition*, 80.

10. Cathy Caruth, *Unclaimed Experience: Trauma, Narrative, and History* (Baltimore: Johns Hopkins University Press, 1996), 17.

11. One is reminded of Freud's usage of the word *Führer* when he talks about the unifying bonds of trust, love, and identification between the leader and his people. See Freud's notion of *Bindung* in "Group Psychology and the Analysis of the Ego," in *Beyond the Pleasure Principle, Group Psychology and Other Works*, vol. 18 of *The Standard Edition*, 97. For a very interesting discussion, see Mikkel Borch-Jacobsen, *The Emotional Tie: Psychoanalysis, Mimesis, and Affect*, trans. Douglas Brick and others (Stanford, Calif.: Stanford University Press, 1993).

12. This particular genealogy of life and death as a misreading of a discourse is central to the history of psychoanalytic discourse itself; in a reading of *Beyond the Pleasure Principle*, Jacques Derrida understands the "survival" of psychoanalysis itself through the survival of the father past his children. See Jacques Derrida, *La carte postale: De Socrate à Freud et au-delà* (Paris: Flammarion, 1980).

13. Lacan writes: "Women in the real order serve, if they'll forgive me saying so, as objects for the exchange required by the elementary structures of kinship and which are sometimes perpetuated in the imaginary order, while what is transmitted in a parallel way in the symbolic order is the phallus." Jacques Lacan, *Écrits: A Selection*, trans. Bruce Fink (W. W. Norton and Company, 2002), 207. Claude Lévi-Strauss, in *The Elementary Structures of Kinship*, rev. ed., ed. Rodney Needham, trans. James Harle Bell and John Richard Von Sturmer (Boston: Beacon Press, 1969), exemplified the *essence* of the incest prohibition: this prohibition, he maintains, is preeminent and universal—at

once social and presocial, not exclusively biological nor exclusively cultural. The prohibition of incest, he writes, "is the fundamental step because of which, by which, but above all in which, the transition from nature to culture is accomplished." Ibid., 24. Since the work of Gayle Rubin, "The Traffic in Women: Notes on the 'Political Economy' of Sex," in *Toward an Anthropology of Women*, ed. Rayna R. Reiner (New York: Monthly Review Press, 1975), 157–210, and the work of David Schneider, *A Critique of the Study of Kinship* (Ann Arbor: University of Michigan Press, 1984), there have been several anthropological contributions concerned with analyzing the limitations of kinship paradigms based on the Oedipal scenario. Important works that criticize functionalist and structuralist perspectives on the problem of kinship include Marilyn Strathern, *Reproducing the Future: Essays on Anthropology, Kinship, and the New Reproductive Technologies* (New York: Routledge: 1992); Kath Weston, *Families We Choose: Lesbians, Gays, Kinship* (New York: Columbia University Press, 1991); John Borneman, "Until Death Do Us Part: Marriage/Death in Anthropological Discourse," *American Ethnologist* 23, no. 2 (1996): 215–235; Rayna Rapp, *Testing Women, Testing the Fetus: The Social Impact of Amniocentesis in America* (New York: Routledge, 1999); and Donna Haraway, *Simians, Cyborgs, and Women: The Reinvention of Nature* (New York: Routledge, 1991). Such works question the stability that Lévi-Strauss accords to kinship and show that kinship rules do not uniformly produce conformity. Beyond anthropology, albeit in creative dialogue with it, Judith Butler has offered a reconceptualization of the incest taboo in relation to kinship, in *Antigone's Claim: Kinship Between Life and Death* (New York: Columbia University Press, 2000), where the ambivalent figure of Antigone exposes the limits of the "elementary structures" of kinship intelligibility.

14. Oedipus's father—or his mother in other accounts—pierced his (or her) son's ankles before disposing of him on Mount Cithaeron.

15. Thebes, the antipodes of Athens, became the "stage" for eight of the tragedies that have been saved: Aeschylus's *Seven against Thebes*; Sophocles' *Oedipus the King, Oedipus at Colonus,* and *Antigone*; and Euripides' *Bacchae, Supplicants, Phoenician Women,* and *Heracles.*

16. Sophocles, *Oedipus the King*, line 28.

17. In the wake of Nazism, another "plague," Albert Camus' *The Plague* (1947), inaugurates the Age of Testimony as the age of the ethical and political imperative of bearing witness to the unthinkability of trauma. See Shoshana Felman, "Camus' *The Plague*, or a Monument to Witnessing," in Shoshana Felman and Dori Laub, *Testimony: Crises of Witnessing in Literature, Psychoanalysis, and History* (New York: Routledge, 1992), 93–119.

18. Freud, *Moses and Monotheism*, 67.

19. See Caruth, *Unclaimed Experience*; see also Cathy Caruth, ed., *Trauma: Explorations in Memory* (Baltimore: Johns Hopkins University Press, 1995).

20. Walter Benjamin, *Illuminations*, trans. Harry Zohn (New York: Schocken Books, 1989), 257.

21. Giorgio Agamben, *Means Without End*, trans. Vincenzo Binetti and Cesare Casarino (Minneapolis: University of Minnesota Press, 2000), 5–6.

22. From Egypt the idea of the Sphinx spread to the Syrians and the Phoenicians and finally to the Greeks. In Egypt the Sphinx is male, whereas in Greece the Sphinx becomes female: she is the offspring of Typhon and Echidna, and she represents a deadly threat against human culture and Greek society in particular. This beast had the face of a woman; the breast, feet and tail of a lion; and the wings of a bird. According to Greek mythology, during the rule of Creon, a calamity befell Thebes: the Sphinx appeared on Mount Phicium, declaring that she would not depart unless someone interpreted the riddle that she proposed and that, in the meantime, she would devour whoever failed to give the correct answer. The riddle was "What is the creature that walks on four legs in the morning, two legs at noon, and three in the evening?" Creon proclaimed that he would give the kingdom of Thebes along with his sister Jocasta in marriage to the man who solved the riddle of the Sphinx. The hero Oedipus—the one with the mutilated feet—advanced to the trial and gave the answer, "Man, who in childhood creeps on hands and knees, in manhood walks erect, and in old age with the aid of a staff," thus causing the Sphinx's death. The gratitude of the people for their deliverance was so great that they appointed Oedipus their king, giving him in marriage their queen Jocasta, Laius's widow. Ignorant of his biological parentage, Oedipus had already become the slayer of his father Laius when he confronted an old stranger in a narrow road near Delphi; in marrying the queen he became the husband of his mother. These horrors remained concealed until the polis of Thebes was afflicted with pestilence and, after the oracle was consulted, the double crime of Oedipus came to light.

23. Rosi Braidotti, "Signs of Wonder and Traces of Doubt: On Teratology and Embodied Difference," in *Between Monsters, Goddesses, and Cyborgs: Feminist Confrontations with Science*, ed. Nina Lykke and Rosi Braidotti (London: Zed, 1996), 150.

24. Marie Delcourt, *Œdipe ou la légende du conquérant* (Paris: Les Belles Lettres, 1981) (first published 1944).

25. Elizabeth Grosz, "Animal Sex: Libido as Desire and Death," in Elizabeth Grosz and Elspeth Probyn, eds., *Sexy Bodies: The Strange Carnalities of Feminism* (New York: Routledge, 1995), 278–299. For a suggestive meditation on becoming-insect, see Rosi Braidotti, *Metamorphoses: Towards a Materialist Theory of Becoming* (Cambridge, U.K.: Polity Press, 2002), especially the chapter "Met(r)amorphoses: Becoming Woman/Animal/Insect," where she considers the "queer" quality of *insexts*.

26. Indeed, we may understand the Sphinx's plunge also in terms of Paul de Man's association of theory with falling. Cathy Caruth has offered an insightful analysis of the connection of problems of theory with literary and philosophical scenes of falling in Paul de Man's work. See Cathy Caruth, "The Falling Body and the Impact of Reference (de Man, Kant, Kleist)," in *Unclaimed Experience*, 73–90.

27. Friedrich Nietzsche, *The Gay Science*, trans. Walter Kaufmann (New York: Vintage Books, 1974).

28. Diana Fuss, *Identification Papers* (New York: Routledge, 1995), 77.

29. Mary Ann Doane, *Femmes Fatales: Feminism, Film Theory, Psychoanalysis* (New York: Routledge, 1991), 47.

30. Agamben, *Means Without End*, 90.

31. Indeed, decapitation has been interpreted as symbolic castration in psychoanalytic literature. See Sigmund Freud, "Medusa's Head," in *Beyond the Pleasure Principle, Group Psychology and Other Works*, vol. 18 of *The Standard Edition*, 273–274; and Sándor Ferenczi, "On the Symbolism of the Head of Medusa," in *Further Contributions to the Theory and Technique of Psycho-Analysis*, ed. John Rickman, trans. Jane Isabel Suttie (London: Hogarth Press, 1926), 360. For a critique, see Hélène Cixous, "Castration or Decapitation?" trans. Annette Kuhn, *Signs* 7, no. 1 (1981): 41–55.

32. Gilles Deleuze, *Difference and Repetition* (London: Continuum International Publishing, 1994), 29.

33. See Hortense Spillers, "Mama's Baby, Papa's Maybe: An American Grammar Book," *Diacritics* 17, no. 2 (1987): 65–81.

34. Cixous, "Castration or Decapitation?" 49.

35. Lacan, *Écrits: A Selection*, 291.

36. Sigmund Freud, *Three Essays on the Theory of Sexuality*, trans. James Strachey (London: Basic Books, 2000).

37. Sigmund Freud, "Leonardo da Vinci and a Memory of His Childhood," in *Five Lectures on Psycho-Analysis, Leonardo da Vinci and Other Works*, vol. 11 of *The Standard Edition*, 80.

38. Georg Wilhelm Friedrich Hegel, *The Philosophy of History*, trans. J. Sibree (New York: Dover, 1956), 220.

39. See Ewa Plonowska Ziarek, "The Abstract Soul of the Commodity and the Monstrous Body of the Sphinx: Commodification, Aesthetics, and the Impasses of Social Construction," *differences* 16, no. 2 (2005): 88–115. In this excellent essay, Ziarek discusses the ways in which the aporetic figure of the Sphinx poses "an enigma of sexual difference and black flesh." Ibid., 108.

40. Philippe Lacoue-Labarthe, "Oedipus as Figure," *Radical Philosophy* 118 (March/April 2003): 8.

41. See Jean-Joseph Goux, *Oedipus, Philosopher*, trans. Catherine Porter (Stanford, Calif.: Stanford University Press, 1993). Goux offers an interpretation of the Oedipus myth as a tragedy of failed masculine initiation. He takes

Oedipus's will to conquer the maternal monster as emblematic of the emergence of a new *homo philosophicus*: one founded on the repudiation of the monstrous alterity and the triumph of reason. He writes: "'Monstricide' is the great unthought element of Freudian doctrine." Ibid., 25.

42. Cixous, "Castration or Decapitation?" 46.

43. Sigmund Freud, "The Uncanny," in *An Infantile Neurosis and Other Works*, vol. 17 of *The Standard Edition*, 248.

44. Jacques Lacan, *Le Séminaire*, vol. 2, *Le Moi dans la théorie de Freud et dans la technique psychanalytique* (Paris: Seuil, 1978), 250. Felman reads, and extends, Lacan's selection of Colonus as the truly psychoanalytic place thus: "For if Colonus—and Colonus only—marks 'the end of Oedipus' psychoanalysis,' it is to the extent that Oedipus' tale of desire ends only through its own dramatic, narrative discovery that the tale has, in effect, no end: the end of Oedipus' analysis, in other words, is the discovery that analysis, and in particular didactic self-analysis, is interminable." Felman, "Beyond Oedipus," 146.

45. I suggest this term (certainly a neologism of my own) to underline the splicing of the monstrous (*teras*) onto the anthropomorphic.

46. Derrida has treated "the question of the question" in *Of Spirit: Heidegger and the Question*, trans. Geoffrey Bennington and Rachel Bowlby (Chicago, University of Chicago Press, 1989), an attempt to reflect on the entanglement of Heidegger's thought with Nazism, and his *blindness* to the death camps. Derrida appends to his text an eight-page footnote on the privilege that Heidegger accords to the question. In a later text, Derrida writes that every footnote is Oedipal—"a symptomatic swelling, the swollen foot of a text hindered in its step-by-step advance." "Typewriter Ribbon: Limited Ink (2) ('within such limits')," in *Material Events: Paul de Man and the Afterlife of Theory*, edited by Tom Cohen and others (Minneapolis: University of Minnesota Press, 2001), 296.

47. Freud, *Three Essays on the Theory of Sexuality*, 61.

48. Sigmund Freud, "Femininity," in *New Introductory Lectures on Psycho-Analysis and Other Works*, vol. 22 of *The Standard Edition*, 113.

49. Felman, "Beyond Oedipus," 103. Although Lacan's work is nowhere preoccupied with any systematic analysis of the Oedipus myth, Oedipus often emerges in Lacan's writings as a literary figure. Lacan is also fully aware of the selective nature of the Freudian appropriation of the myth. He writes: "When we study mythology . . . we see that the Oedipus complex is but a tiny detail in an immense myth. The myth enables us to collate a series of relations between subjects, in comparison with whose complexity and wealth the Oedipus appears to be such an abridged edition that, in the final analysis, it is not always utilizable." Lacan, *Le Séminaire*, vol. 1, 101. For an insightful exploration of the way in which the Oedipus story holds the key to Lacan's insight

into the theoretical teachings of Freud's work, see Felman, "Beyond Oedipus." In Lacan's rendering, the Oedipus complex emerges as a site where the triple relation between clinical event, theory, and literature plays out. As Felman puts it: "For Lacan, in much the same way as for Freud, the Oedipus embodies an unprecedented, revolutionary moment of coincidence between narration and theoretization.... But if for Freud the Oedipus embodies the insightful moment of discovery at which the psychoanalytic narration—in passing through the analytic practice and in turning back upon itself—becomes theory, it could be said that for Lacan the Oedipus embodies the insightful moment of discovery at which the psychoanalytic theory—in passing through the analytic practice and in turning back upon itself—becomes narration: unfinished analytic dialogue, or an ongoing story of the discourse of the Other." "Beyond Oedipus," 127–128.

50. Felman, "Beyond Oedipus," 119.
51. Lacan, *Le Séminaire*, vol. 2, 59.
52. Felman, "Beyond Oedipus," 129.
53. Sophocles, *Oedipus at Colonus*, trans. David Grene, in *Complete Greek Tragedies*, vol. 1, ed. David Grene and Richmond Lattimore (Chicago: University of Chicago Press, 1954), scene 8, line 147.
54. Lacan, *Le Séminaire*, vol. 2, 245.
55. Ibid., 134.
56. Jacques Derrida, *The Gift of Death*, trans. David Wills (Chicago: University of Chicago Press, 1995), 41.
57. Emmanuel Levinas, "La mort et le temps," *L' Herne* 60 (1991): 42 (cited in Derrida, *The Gift of Death*, 42).
58. Emmanuel Levinas, "Bad Conscience and the Inexorable," in *Face to Face with Levinas*, ed. Richard A. Cohen (Albany: State University of New York Press, 1986), 38.
59. Samuel Weber, "In the Name of the Law," in *Deconstruction and the Possibility of Justice*, ed. Drucilla Cornell, Michel Rosenfeld, and David Gray Carlson (New York: Routledge, 1992), 252.
60. Sophocles, *Oedipus at Colonus*, scene 1, line 85.
61. See Agamben, *Homo Sacer*.
62. Muriel Rukeyser, "Myth," in *Breaking Open* (New York: Random House, 1973). I am grateful to Ioulia Pentazou for drawing my attention to this poem.

FRAGMENTS OF OEDIPUS:
ANTHROPOLOGY AT THE EDGES OF HISTORY
Neni Panourgiá

NOTE: I would like to thank the many friends, colleagues, and students who have patiently indulged me in my insistence on *Oedipus* over the years. From the first nebulous idea of *Oedipus* as something more than what Freud and Claude Lévi-Strauss have given us, to the understanding of the deeply political nature of *Oedipus*, my thought has benefited immensely from discussions with Athena Athanasiou, James A. Boon, Vincent Crapanzano, Stathis Gourgouris, Martin Harries, George E. Marcus, Susan McKinnon, Sherry Ortner, Andrew C. Parker, Joel Whitebook, and Michael Wood. Students in my seminar "The Culture of Oedipus" questioned my assumptions and helped me toward a more refined understanding of *Oedipus*. My two guides through *Oedipus* have been Jean-Joseph Goux and Charles Segal.

1. Cf. Theodor W. Adorno, *Negative Dialectics* (New York: Seabury Press, 1973).

2. On the imagined meeting of mother and daughter, Chimera and the Sphinx, see Gustav Flaubert's *The Temptation of Saint Anthony*, where the two monsters attempt first to obliterate each other verbally and then to leave together, failing in both, parting ways at the end. For a reading of the Chimera and the Sphinx as a means to rethink upon theory as it bears on architectural practice, see Mark Jarzombek "Ready-Made Traces in the Sand: The Sphinx, the Chimera, and Other Discontents in the Practice of Theory," *Assemblage*, no 19 (December 1992): 72–95. On the issue of female homosexuality as the danger posed by *Oedipus*, especially as it pertains to the problem of the Sphinx, see Athena Athanasiou's essay in this volume.

3. I have argued elsewhere (Neni Panourgiá, *Fragments of Death, Fables of Identity: An Athenian Anthropography* [Madison: University of Wisconsin Press, 1995]) for the possibilities that *parerga* afford the author. *Parerga* are not simply notes, but they should be thought of as the extremities of a body: necessary but not detectable from close up, without which the text becomes and remains truncated. These are notes to the text that make the text show its complexities.

4. It is nowhere mentioned but it would be safe to assume that only men passed by the Sphinx's corner; women never ventured outside the city walls unaccompanied.

5. Lowell Edmunds states that this version of the riddle by Athenaeus is the most complete one, and it is, of course, the one that brings up the issue of voice and the issue of animality that have systematically been excluded from the analyses of *Oedipus* and that are, nevertheless, constitutive of the questions posed by *Oedipus*. See Lowell Edmunds, *Oedipus: The Ancient Legend and Its Later Analogues* (Baltimore: Johns Hopkins University Press, 1985), 12.

6. Pausanias 9.5.6.

7. Frederick Ahl, in *Sophocles' Oedipus: Evidence and Self-Conviction* (Ithaca, N.Y.: Cornell University Press, 1991), has proposed that Oedipus was not the murderer of Laius but that Oedipus accepts it as the truth, convinced by the argumentation put forth by Creon, Teiresias, and the rest, despite the fact that

there is nothing that ties him to the murder itself. Over and above the many problems that are associated with Ahl's reading (which are uniquely exposed by Charles Segal in his review of Ahl's book in *Classical World* 86 [1992]: 155), the main problem of Ahl's position is that he takes Oedipus as a real person, not as part of myth, so there is no real Oedipus who might have or might not have killed his father.

8. Nicole Loraux, *The Experiences of Tiresias: The Feminine and the Greek Man*, trans. Paula Wissing (Princeton, N.J.: Princeton University Press, 1995).

9. Ibid., 10.

10. Freud claimed in 1908, at two meetings of the Vienna Psychoanalytic Society, that he had not read anything published on the Oedipus myth so that his judgment would not be occluded. As a matter of fact, Freud, not only then but repeatedly, disavowed that he had read any of the commentaries on Oedipus by anyone, including Nietzsche. Referring to Nietzsche in particular, Freud mentioned that his occasional attempts at reading Nietzsche's work in general "were smothered by an excess of interest." Sigmund Freud, *Minutes of the Vienna Psychoanalytic Society*, 2:31, 1:359, quoted in Peter L. Rudnytsky, *Freud and Oedipus* (New York: Columbia University Press, 1987). The evidence, however, that Freud knew Nietzsche's pieces on the Oedipus myth (primarily presented by Rudnytsky, at pages 198–223) is not only convincing but also overwhelming. While studying under Brentano, Freud joined the Reading Group of Viennese German Students, which was primarily concerned with the work of Schopenhauer, Nietzsche, and Wagner. Rudnytsky notes the correspondence between Freud and his friend Eduard Silberstein, where it is mentioned that during his first year at the university in 1873, Freud had read Nietzsche's published work. By 1873 *The Birth of Tragedy* and the first two *Untimely Meditations* had been published, and it is in *The Birth of Tragedy* that Nietzsche's piece on Oedipus appeared.

11. James A. Boon, *Other Tribes, Other Scribes: Symbolic Anthropology in the Comparative Study of Cultures, Histories, Religions, and Texts* (Cambridge, U.K.: Cambridge University Press, 1982), 8. On the muddled beginnings of fieldwork, see especially "Introduction: The Exaggeration of Cultures."

12. Ibid., 9.

13. This is a proposition that is just and justly as problematic as the proposition that attributes the paternity of history to Herodotus—it is just as fictional.

14. In 1968, Terrence Turner proposed a look at the myth of Oedipus as a narrative that spans large segments of time, although he still stayed with the Lévi-Straussian analysis of *Oedipus* as a symbolic rather than as a metaphorical

text. Lévi-Strauss's analysis eschews the narrative in favor of the diagnosed mythemes, something that is also prevalent in the folkloristic analyses of *Oedipus*, such as those presented by Vladimir Propp in his "Edipo alla Luce del Folklore," in *Edipo alla Luce del Folklore*, ed. Clara Strada Janovic (Turin, Italy: Einaudi, 1975), 85–137, as well as in the important collaborative work by the classicist Lowell Edmunds and Alan Dundes, *Oedipus: A Folklore Casebook* (Madison: University of Wisconsin Press, 1983), and in Edmunds's numerous articles on the appearance of Oedipean mythemes throughout the world.

15. Suzette Heald, "Every Man a Hero: Oedipal Themes in Gisu Circumcision," in *Anthropology and Psychoanalysis. An Encounter through Culture*, ed. Suzette Heald and Ariane Deluz (New York: Routledge, 1994), 184–209.

16. Melford Spiro, *Oedipus in the Trobriands* (Chicago: University of Chicago Press, 1982), 1.

17. Allen W. Johnson and Douglass Price-Williams, *Oedipus Ubiquitous: The Family Complex in World Folk Literature* (Stanford, Calif.: Stanford University Press, 1996).

18. Jean-Pierre Vernant and Pierre Vidal-Naquet, *Myth and Tragedy in Ancient Greece*, trans. Janet Lloyd (New York: Zone Books, 1994). See especially the article by Vernant, "Oedipus without the Complex," at pages 85–113.

19. This is juxtaposed to other disciplinary approaches to the theme of *Oedipus*. In classics and philosophy (from Hegel's Antigone and Oedipus to Jean-Joseph Goux's *Oedipus, Philosopher*) the entirety of the myth, including Antigone, the legend of the Seven against Thebes, and Ismene are considered. See Edmunds, *Oedipus: The Ancient Legend* on the encounter of different disciplines with *Oedipus*. For a rare exception in the treatment of the myth in its entirety within psychoanalysis, see John M. Ross, *What Men Want: Mothers, Fathers and Manhood* (Cambridge, Mass.: Harvard University Press, 1994), especially chapter 5, "Oedipus Revisited," 94–128.

20. Pietro Pucci has ingeniously retermed the crime of Oedipus *parincest*, combining thus the horror of regicide with that of incest. As ingenious as this formulation is, however, it further underscores the lack of willingness to engage with Oedipus outside the context that Freud has produced, namely, the shorthand version of the myth as "the person who killed his father and married his mother." Pucci, however, does bring up a question that is quintessentially anthropological, namely, how are the mother and the father conceptualized as categories of existence that become categories of kinship?

21. Ross, *What Men Want*, 100 (emphasis in original).

22. Ibid.

23. Ibid., 105.

24. Jonathan Lear, 1998. "Crossroads" (address at the 452nd Convocation of the University of Chicago, 1998), *University of Chicago Record* 33, no. 1

(October 29, 1998). See also Jonathan Lear, *Open Minded: Working Out the Logic of the Soul* (Cambridge, Mass.: Harvard University Press, 1998).

25. Lear, *Open Minded*, 34.

26. This formulation that underlines the very idiosyncratic relationship between the citizen and the *polis* in Athens is Dennis Slattery's, from *The Wounded Body: Remembering the Markings of the Flesh* (Albany: State University of New York Press, 2000), 52. The particularity of this relationship has been pointed out in different formulations by Jean-Pierre Vernant and Pierre Vidal-Naquet, and by Nicole Loraux in her *The Invention of Athens: The Funeral Oration in the Classical City* (Cambridge, Mass.: Harvard University Press, 1986).

27. What follows is an inevitably elliptical account of this most convoluted and contorted period of modern Greece. For a detailed analysis of the period, the history of the Left in Greece, and the experience of "the islands," see Neni Panourgiá, *Dangerous Citizens: The Flesh of Dissidence and the Terror of the State (Greece 1929–2004)* (Fordham University Press, forthcoming). The end of the Second World War came for Greece in October 1944, when the German occupying forces left the country. The exhilaration of liberation did not last long. On December 3 and 4, 1944, a peaceful demonstration held by unarmed members of EAM (the political branch of the main resistance force against the German occupiers) and ELAS (which comprised mainly the Left and the Communist Party) was met with the armed police forces aided by the British army, which had arrived in Greece as part of an effort to prevent the forces of the Left from seizing power. Winston Churchill advised General Scobie (the chief of military operations in Greece) to act as if in an occupied country. And so Scobie did. Throughout December 1944, the ELAS fought with the British forces and the Greek police in what came to be known as the *Dekembrianá* (the December events). Throughout the month and into the beginning of January 1945, the British forces, aided by the Greek police, identified and arrested as members of the EAM/ELAS resistance more than eight thousand men and boys from ten years old to sixty years old, whom they first interned at the military barracks at Goudi (in Athens) and then sent to the concentration camp of el-Daba'a in Egypt. They were released in waves by June 1945. During the period of White Terror that lasted from the spring of 1945 to the spring of 1946 and was carried out by the members of the paramilitary forces (mainly collaborators of the Germans during the occupation) against the Left, many of those who had been sent to el-Daba'a were arrested and imprisoned or murdered on the spot. The civil war that broke out in Greece in 1946 between the ELAS and its new army, the Democratic Army, and the government forces (this time supported psychologically, militarily, and financially by the United States, after Britain pulled its support in March 1947) lasted until 1949. On the islands themselves, see Polymeris Voglis,

Becoming a Subject: Political Prisoners during the Greek Civil War (New York: Berghahn Books, 2002).

28. Bastinado is the technique of beating the soles of the feet of the prisoner using a bamboo stick or the staff of a rifle or a metal pipe, until the feet swell and spill out of their bounds, mangled flesh with caked blood and dirt on them.

29. Gilles Deleuze, in his reading of *Desert Islands*, engages in the radical deconstruction of the notion of the "desert" island by invoking the lack of recognition by the European traveler/settler of the already existing there humanity. He is primarily thinking of and discussing the European travel literature of the Enlightenment. Deleuze is most emphatically *not* referring to actual *desert* islands, places where only the most tenuous of life can be sustained on the edges of life—life that can be sustained with the scant rainfall of a couple of months a year; places that have no aquifer or only have aquifer that holds contaminated or nonpotable water. Deleuze is speaking of the construction of the desert as part of a discourse that has sustained colonialism. I am speaking of actual desert (not deserted, even metaphorically) islands that for a limited time carried only human life on them in an inversion of this humanity into animality. See Gilles Deleuze, *Desert Islands and Other Texts, 1953–1974* (Los Angeles: Semiotext(e), 2004). Michael Taussig has actually captured not only the horror of the islands as colonies of the undesirables (Nicos Poulantzas's "anti-nationals") but also the complicity between the management of undesirable life with capitalist ventures, especially in the way in which he erects the problem of offshore operations not as simply an economic but a political one. See Michael Taussig, *My Cocaine Museum* (Chicago: University of Chicago Press, 2004); and Nicos Poulantzas, *State, Power, Socialism*, new ed. with an introduction by Stuart Hall (London: Verso Classics, 2000) (first published 1978).

30. Yiorgos D. Yiannopoulos, *Makronissos. Martyries Enos Foititi 1947–1950* [Testimonials of a university student 1947–1950] (Athens, Greece: Vivliorama, 2001).

31. For a critical reading of Agamben's notion of *bios* and *zoē* in reference to the Greek islands, see Neni Panourgiá, "Desert Islands: Ransom of Humanity," *Public Culture* 20:2.

32. The play *Ho Dolophónos tou Laiou kai ta Korákia* [Laius's murderer and the crows] was produced by the Theater Stoa and performed at the ancient theater at Delphi in July 2004. Pontikas uses the gendered term *ándras* (man), not the unmarked term *ánthropos* (human), as his concern is with man and woman, not with Oedipus as a paradigmatic human. I use it here because of the connection that Pontikas draws between the myth of Oedipus and the (still) lived realities of the civil war.

CARNAL HERMENEUTICS:
FROM "CONCEPTS" AND "CIRCLES" TO
"DISPOSITIONS" AND "SUSPENSE"
Eleni Papagaroufali

1. Clifford Geertz, *The Interpretation of Cultures* (New York: Basic Books, 1973).
2. Ibid., 28–29.
3. Ibid., 452 (emphasis added).
4. Ibid., 29.
5. Ibid., 30.
6. Clifford Geertz, "From the Native's Point of View: On the Nature of Anthropological Understanding," in *Local Knowledge: Further Essays in Interpretive Anthropology* (New York: Basic Books, 1983), 69.
7. Ibid., 59 (emphasis added).
8. Ibid., 58 (emphasis added).
9. I have borrowed the term "carnal hermeneutics" from Hwa Yol Jung's excellent work on phenomenology and body politics, "Phenomenology and Body Politics," *Body & Society* 2 (1996): 1–22. Although I consider his theoretical approach similar to mine, I am the only one responsible for what is written here, under this apt metaphor.
10. According to Moore, "The [embodied] intersubjectivity of experience is not confined, of course, to physical appearances, to actual dialogue and to the concrete nature of sociological circumstance. Intersubjectivity is also about identifications and recognitions. It is about desire and the projection and introjection of images of self and others." Henrietta L. Moore, *A Passion for Difference: Essays in Anthropology and Gender* (Cambridge, U.K.: Polity Press 1994).
11. Jung, "Phenomenology and Body Politics," 16 (emphasis added).
12. Geertz, "From the Native's Point of View," 57–58.
13. Pierre Bourdieu, *Outline of a Theory of Practice* (Cambridge, U.K.: Cambridge University Press, 1977), 93.
14. Ibid., 79. Throughout his work, Bourdieu gives many definitions of *habitus* and *dispositions*. Central to all of them is the notion of the "socially informed body," ibid., 124, perceived as the locus of all social practice. On many occasions, however, he speaks of "mental"—as opposed to "bodily"— dispositions, which he identifies with "schemes of thought." Ibid., 15. As it will be shown, this implicit distinction between body and mind pervades his wider separation of the unconscious, practical, nonverbal *habitus* from the conscious, symbolic, verbal mastery of classificatory schemes. Ibid., 88.
15. George E. Marcus and Michael M. J. Fischer, *Anthropology as Cultural Critique: An Experimental Moment in the Human Sciences* (Chicago: University of Chicago Press, 1986), 64.

16. Robert Schrauf, "Costalero Quiero Ser! Autobiographical Memory and the Oral Life Story of a Holy Week Brother in Southern Spain," *Ethos* 25 (1997): 443.

17. Eleni Papagaroufali, "Xenotransplantation and Transgenesis: (Im-)Moral Stories about Human-Animal Relations in the West," in *Nature and Society: Anthropological Perspectives*, ed. Philippe Descola and Gisli Palsson (London and New York: Routledge, 1996), 240–255; Eleni Papagaroufali, "Human- and Animal-Gene Transfers: Images of (Non)-Integrity in Greece," in *Gene Technology and the Public: An Interdisciplinary Perspective*, ed. Susanne Lundin and Malin Ideland (Lund, Sweden: Nordic Academic Press, 1997), 35–47; Eleni Papagaroufali, "Donation of Human Organs or Bodies After Death: A Cultural Phenomenology of 'Flesh' in the Greek Context," *Ethos* 27 (1999): 284–315; Eleni Papagaroufali, "Playing with One's Own Death While Being Alive: The Case of Registered Body-Organ Donors in Greece," *Anthropology and Humanism* 31 (2006): 111–123.

18. In Greece, to obtain a donor card, one must go to a donors' association, a hospital's social services department, or some other official body to declare his or her willingness to become a prospective donor. This decision requires a level of preparation that is probably more complicated than the one expected of, for example, Americans, who can register as donors when they obtain or renew their driver's licenses.

19. Thomas Csordas, in an attempt to elaborate on "embodiment as a paradigm for anthropology"—"Embodiment as a Paradigm for Anthropology," *Ethos* 18 (1990): 5–45—as complementary to textuality and representation, has introduced the construct of "somatic modes of attention" seen as "culturally elaborated ways of attending to and with one's [always already socially informed] body in surroundings that include the embodied presence of others." "Somatic Modes of Attention," *Cultural Anthropology* 8 (1993): 138. Through this intersubjective approach, experiences perceived as individual or personal, and thus "psychological" or "mental" (e.g., intuition, imagination), prove to be socially informed embodied knowledge or dispositions shared by historically concrete people, but felt "as no more than an indeterminate horizon" as long as they remain "unattended." Ibid.

20. George E. Marcus, ed., *Critical Anthropology Now: Unexpected Contexts, Shifting Constituencies, Changing Agendas* (Santa Fe, N.M.: School of American Research Press, 1999), 16.

21. Marcus and Fischer, *Anthropology as Cultural Critique*, 91.

22. Marcus, *Critical Anthropology Now*, 17 (emphasis added).

23. Ibid., 19.

24. Jung, "Phenomenology and Body Politics," 11.

25. Veena Das, "*Wittgenstein* and Anthropology," *Annual Review of Anthropology* 27 (1998): 183–184.

26. Neni Panourgiá, *Fragments of Death, Fables of Identity: An Athenian Anthropography* (Madison: University of Wisconsin Press, 1995), 153 (emphasis added). Nadia Seremetakis has also shown that among Orthodox Greeks "the concern about the destination of flesh overwhelms any concern about the final destination of the soul." *The Last Word: Women, Death and Divination in Inner Mani* (Chicago: University of Chicago Press, 1991), 185. On the fleshly nature of Christian dogma, see also Jonathan Parry, "The End of the Body," in *Fragments for a History of the Human Body*, ed. Michel Feher (New York: Zone, 1989), 513.

27. The view that death is not instantaneous and that there is "a liminal period during which a person is *neither fully alive nor fully dead*" is common in cultures where secondary burial or exhumation are practiced. Loring Danforth, *The Death Rituals of Rural Greece* (Princeton, N.J.: Princeton University Press, 1982), 37 (emphasis added); see also Richard Huntington and Peter Metcalf, *Celebrations of Death: The Anthropology of Mortuary Ritual* (Cambridge, U.K.: Cambridge University Press, 1979), 81–92.

28. Geertz, "From the Native's Point of View," 56.

29. Carnal hermeneutics can also lead to such fears or hopes once the *materiality* of *carne* itself is taken as naturally given, rather than culturally constructed. For example, in supporting his carnal hermeneutic approach, Hwa Yol Jung speaks of "the body-as-flesh" as if "flesh," as well as "body," were panhuman realities. Jung, "Phenomenology and Body Politics," 1–22. For a different approach, see Papagaroufali, "Donation of Human Organs or Bodies After Death."

30. Csordas, "Somatic Modes of Attention," 145.

31. Geertz, *The Interpretation of Cultures*, 15.

32. Geertz, "From the Native's Point of View," 69 (emphasis added).

33. Bourdieu, *Outline of a Theory of Practice*, 120.

34. See, e.g., Maurice Bloch, "Language, Anthropology and Cognitive Science," *Man* (N.S.) 26 (1990): 183; Bourdieu, *Outline of a Theory of Practice*, 117; Jean Jackson, "Chronic Pain and the Tension Between the Body as Subject and Object," in *Embodiment and Experience: The Existential Ground of Culture and Self*, ed. Thomas Csordas (Cambridge, U.K.: Cambridge University Press, 1994), 220; and Judith Okely, "Vicarious and Sensory Knowledge of Chronology and Change: Ageing in Rural France," in *Social Experience and Anthropological Knowledge*, ed. Kirsten Hastrup and Peter Hervik (London and New York: Routledge, 1994), 62. Nevertheless, Bourdieu considers "the language of the body," which he identifies with *habitus*, "incomparably more ambiguous and more overdetermined than the most overdetermined uses of ordinary language." Bourdieu, *Outline of a Theory of Practice*, 120.

35. Angel Diaz de Rada and Francisco Cruces, "The Mysteries of Incarnation," in *Social Experience and Anthropological Knowledge*, ed. Kirsten Hastrup

and Peter Hervick (London and New York: Routledge, 1994), 109. In this dilemma, anthropologists' language is always a priori and one-sidedly conceived as observational, propositional, conscious, inevitably inert, because "representational," whereas "natives'" language is always perceived as experiential, presentational, unconscious, inevitably moving, because "really lived." See, e.g., ibid., 106–109. In fact, according to Geertz, "By definition, only a 'native' makes first order [interpretations]: it's *his* culture." *The Interpretation of Cultures*, 15. However, in a footnote, he also accepts that "informants [like anthropologists] frequently, even habitually, make second order interpretations—what have come to be known as 'native models.'" Ibid. The latter become "intricate matters," especially in "literate cultures, where 'native' interpretations can proceed to higher levels." Ibid. It seems that, whereas natives resemble anthropologists in terms of producing "experience-far concepts," ethnographers do not resemble natives in using "experience-near concepts"!

36. Csordas, "Embodiment as a Paradigm for Anthropology," 25; Das, "*Wittgenstein* and Anthropology," 185.

37. Bourdieu identifies *habitus* with the "practical mastery" of, for example, a poem—that is, with its learning "by hearing" only and unconsciously, "without the learner's having any sense of learning"—and distinguishes it from the poem's "*symbolic* mastery—i.e., [its] *conscious* recognition and *verbal* expression." *Outline of a Theory of Practice*, 88 (emphasis added). In other words, contrary to what will be suggested here, Bourdieu argues that *habitus* may be verbal but only unconsciously, or that conscious, symbolic, verbal expressions are not habitus.

38. Laurence Kirmayer, "The Body's Insistence on Meaning: Metaphor as Presentation and Representation in Illness Experience," *Medical Anthropology Quarterly* 6 (1992): 332.

39. This problem is particularly acute for the "translator-anthropologist" (both in the field and in his or her own society) because "the anthropologist's translation is not merely a matter of matching sentences in the abstract, but of *learning to live another form of life*." Talal Asad, "The Concept of Cultural Translation in British Social Anthropology," in *Writing Culture: The Poetics and Politics of Ethnography*, ed. James Clifford and George Marcus (Berkeley: University of California Press, 1986), 149. For example, when Michele Koven studied the linguistic experience of the "self" among women of Portuguese origin who lived for many years in France and spoke both Portuguese and French, she preferred to use native bilingual interviewers, although she herself knew both languages. Apparently, she felt that her competence in grammar and syntax was not sufficient to capture language-as-"form of life"—or *habitus*. Michele Koven, "Two Languages in the Self / The Self in Two Languages," *Ethos* 26 (1998): 410–455.

40. Bourdieu, *Outline of a Theory of Practice*, 79.
41. Ibid., 81.
42. Janis Jenkins and Martha Valiente, "Bodily Transactions of the Passions: *El Calor* among Salvadoran Women Refugees," in *Embodiment and Experience: The Existential Ground of Culture and Self*, ed. Thomas Csordas (Cambridge, U.K.: Cambridge University Press, 1994), 170.
43. Diaz de Rada and Cruces, "The Mysteries of Incarnation," 101–120.
44. Thomas Csordas, "Genre, Motive, and Metaphor: Conditions for Creativity in Ritual Language," *Cultural Anthropology* 2 (1987): 445–469.
45. Jenkins and Valiente, "Bodily Transactions of the Passions," 172.
46. Michael M. J. Fischer, "Ethnicity as Text and Model" in *Anthropology as Cultural Critique*, 173. According to the linguist John Lyons, the nonlinear, and thus indeterminate, nature of language per se is best exemplified by the fact that the meanings of grammatical categories of time (traditionally defined as "past," "present," and "future" tense) are only deceptively accurate because of their always already contextual character. John Lyons, *Language and Linguistics* (Cambridge, U.K.: Cambridge University Press, 1981). This is why, for example, past tense does not necessarily refer to the past, and present tense has a much wider use than the one denoted by the term. (Also, for the nonlinear character of narrated "stories" and "life-stories," see, e.g., Renato Rosaldo, "Ilongot Hunting as Story and Experience," in *The Anthropology of Experience*, ed. Victor Turner and E. Bruner [Urbana: University of Illinois Press, 1986], 97–139, and Schrauf, "Costalero Quiero Ser!" respectively.)
47. Vincent Crapanzano, "Hermes' Dilemma: The Masking of Subversion in Ethnographic Description," in *Writing Culture: The Poetics and Politics of Ethnography*, ed. James Clifford and George E. Marcus (Berkeley: University of California Press, 1986), 52.
48. Geertz, *The Interpretation of Cultures*, 9.

"REAL ANTHROPOLOGY" AND OTHER NOSTALGIAS
Kath Weston

1. Clifford Geertz, *The Interpretation of Cultures* (New York: Basic Books, 1973).
2. With regard to the literary quality of Geertz's writing—which exerted a transformative effect on thousands of opening paragraphs, if not as much effect on the body of monographs as one might wish—it could also be argued that anthropology experienced not so much an unprecedented turn but rather a re-turn to the value placed on expository writing in nineteenth-century social theory.
3. Renato Rosaldo, "A Note on Geertz as a Cultural Essayist," in *The Fate of "Culture": Geertz and Beyond*, ed. Sherry B. Ortner (Berkeley: University of California Press, 1999), 30–34.

4. Kath Weston, *Long Slow Burn: Sexuality and Social Science* (New York: Routledge, 1998).

5. See Richard G. Fox, ed., *Recapturing Anthropology: Working in the Present* (Santa Fe, N.M.: School of American Research Press, 1991); and Akhil Gupta and James Ferguson, eds., *Anthropological Locations: Boundaries and Grounds of a Field Science* (Berkeley: University of California Press, 1997).

6. Quoted in Virginia Dominguez, "The Marketing of Heritage," *American Ethnologist* 13 (1986): 548.

7. Marc Augé, *An Anthropology for Contemporaneous Worlds*, trans. Amy Jacobs (Stanford, Calif.: Stanford University Press, 1999), x.

8. Talal Asad, ed., *Anthropology and the Colonial Encounter* (New York: Humanities Press, 1973).

9. This observation holds equally well for attempts, however intriguing, to reconceptualize culture as anthropology's proper object. See, for example, Karen Fog Olwig and Kirsten Hastrup's bid to move away from a place-focused understanding of culture by distinguishing between place and space in *Siting Culture: The Shifting Anthropological Object* (New York: Routledge, 1997). On the sometimes fraught relationship between anthropology and cultural studies, see Richard Handler, "Raymond Williams, George Stocking, and Fin-de-Siècle U.S. Anthropology," *Cultural Anthropology* 13, no. 4 (1998): 447–463.

10. Kath Weston, "Kinship, Controversy, and the Sharing of Substance: The Race/Class Politics of Blood Transfusion," in *Relative Values: Reconfiguring Kinship Studies*, ed. Sarah Franklin and Susan McKinnon (Durham, N.C.: Duke University Press, 2002), 147–174.

11. Gilles Deleuze, *Difference and Repetition*, trans. Paul Patton (New York: Continuum International, 2005).

12. Thus it is that Sherry Ortner can characterize Geertz's work as "an alternative to the then-ascendant scientism of the social sciences," while recognizing his commitment to "some form of recognizably 'scientific' endeavor" in his attention to the rich detail of a resolutely material world. Sherry Ortner, *The Fate of "Culture": Geertz and Beyond* (Berkeley: University of California Press, 1999), 1, 3. On the shift away from a search for legalistic rules of social conduct, see John L. Comaroff and Simon Roberts, *Rules and Processes: The Cultural Logic of Dispute in an African Context* (Chicago: University of Chicago Press, 1981).

13. Kath Weston, *Gender in Real Time: Power and Transience in a Visual Age* (New York: Routledge, 2002).

14. See, e.g., Richard P. Feynman, *The Pleasure of Finding Things Out* (Reading, Mass.: Perseus Books, 1999); Richard P. Feynman, *"Surely You're Joking, Mr. Feynman!": Adventures of a Curious Character* (New York: W. W.

Norton and Company, 1985); Max F. Perutz, *I Wish I'd Made You Angry Earlier: Essays on Science, Scientists, and Humanity* (Plainview, N.Y.: Cold Spring Harbor Laboratory Press, 1998); and Ian Stewart, *Nature's Numbers: The Unreal Reality of Mathematics* (New York: Basic Books, 1995). All three scholars draw out qualitative aspects of work and work processes in their respective fields. In addition, there are many fine secondary accounts that place developments in math and science in historical context. See, e.g., Robert P. Crease and Charles C. Mann, *The Second Creation: Makers of the Revolution in Twentieth-Century Physics* (New Brunswick, N.J.: Rutgers University Press, 1996).

15. David Scott, *Refashioning Futures: Criticism after Postcoloniality* (Princeton, N.J.: Princeton University Press, 1999).

16. See Arjun Appadurai, *Modernity at Large: Cultural Dimensions of Globalization* (Minneapolis: University of Minnesota Press, 1996); James Clifford and George E. Marcus, eds., *Writing Culture: The Poetics and Politics of Ethnography* (Berkeley: University of California Press, 1986); Johannes Fabian, *Time and the Other: How Anthropology Makes Its Object* (New York: Columbia University Press, 1983); and George E. Marcus and Michael M. J. Fischer, *Anthropology as Cultural Critique: An Experimental Moment in the Human Sciences* (Chicago: University of Chicago Press, 1986).

17. Weston, *Gender in Real Time*; see also Gananath Obeyesekere, *The Apotheosis of Captain Cook: European Mythmaking in the Pacific* (Princeton, N.J.: Princeton University Press, 1992). In *Of Revelation and Revolution*, Jean Comaroff and John Comaroff conceive their project ("an anthropology of the colonial encounter") in relation to disciplinary doubts about whether, given the anticolonial critique, it is possible to do ethnographic research that is not itself productive of inequality. *Of Revelation and Revolution: Christianity, Colonialism, and Consciousness in South Africa*, vol. 1 (Chicago: University of Chicago Press, 1991), xiii.

18. Scott, *Refashioning Futures*, 16.

19. Melbourne Tapper, *In the Blood: Sickle Cell Anemia and the Politics of Race* (Philadelphia: University of Pennsylvania Press, 1999).

20. George E. Marcus, "Ethnography in/of the World System: The Emergence of Multi-Sited Ethnography," *Annual Review of Anthropology* 24 (1995): 95–117.

21. Roger Rouse, "Mexican Migration and the Social Space of Postmodernity," *Diaspora* 1 (1991): 8–23; Brenda Jo Bright, "'Heart Like a Car': Hispano/Chicano Culture in Northern New Mexico," *American Ethnologist* 25, no. 4 (1998): 583–609; and Brenda Jo Bright, "Nightmares in a New Metropolis: The Cinematic Poetics of Lowriders," *Journal of Latin American Popular Culture* 16 (1997): 13–29.

22. Stewart, *Nature's Numbers*.

CANONICAL AND ANTICANONICAL HISTORIES
Antonis Liakos

1. Marshal Sahlins, *Islands of History* (Chicago: University of Chicago Press, 1987), 58–59.

2. China and Japan: Stefan Tanaka, *Japan's Orient: Rendering Pasts into History* (Berkeley: University of California Press, 1993); W. G. Beasley and E. G. Pulleyblank, eds., *Historians of China and Japan* (London: Oxford University Press, 1961); Chun-Chieh Huang and Erik Zurcher, eds., *Time and Space in Chinese Culture* (Leiden, Netherlands: E. J. Brill, 1995); and Bodo Wiethoff, *Introduction to Chinese History: From Ancient Times to 1912* (London: Thames and Hudson, 1975). India and South Asia: C. H. Philips, ed., *Historians of India, Pakistan and Ceylon* (London: Oxford University Press, 1961). Arab world: Stephen R. Humphreys, *Islamic History: A Framework for Inquiry* (Princeton, N.J.: Princeton University Press, 1991); and Franz Rosenthal, *A History of Muslim Historiography* (Leiden, Netherlands: E. J. Brill, 1968). Jewish tradition: Yosef Hayim Yerushalmi, *Zakhor: Jewish History and Jewish Memory* (Seattle: University of Washington Press, 1982).

3. Karl Keuck, *Historia: Geschichte des Wortes und seiner Bedeutungen in der Antike und in den romanischen Sprachen* (Emsdetten, Germany: J. Lechte, 1934).

4. Arnaldo Momigliano, *Tra storia e storicismo* (Pisa, Italy: Nistri-Lischi, 1985); Arnaldo Momigliano, *Studies in Historiography* (London: Weidenfeld and Nicolson, 1969); and Carlo Ginzburg, "Aristotele, la storia, la prova," *Quaderni Storici* 85 (1994): 5–17.

5. Giovanni Manetti, "Indizi e prove nella cultura greca. Forza epistemica e criteri di validità dell'inferenza semiotica," *Quaderni Storici* 85 (1994): 19–42.

6. Francois Chatelet, *La naissance de l' Histoire* (Paris: Minuit, 1962).

7. Paul Veyne, *Did the Greeks Believe in Their Myths?* (Chicago: University of Chicago Press, 1988).

8. Dionysios of Fourna, *Manuel d'iconographie chretienne*, ed. A. Papadopoulo-Kerameus (St. Petersburg: B. Kirschbaum, 1909). (Denys, or Dionysios, was a Christian Orthodox monk and a painter in the seventeenth century.)

9. Reinhart Kosellek, *On the Semantics of Historical Time* (Cambridge, Mass.: MIT Press, 1985), 21–38.

10. Cited by George Huppert, "The Renaissance Background of Historicism," in *History and Theory* 51 (1966): 48.

11. Masayuki Sato, "Historiographical Encounters: The Chinese and Western Tradition in Turn-of the-Century Japan," *Storia della Storiografia* 19 (1991): 13–21.

12. For an early typology of the historical approaches of the newborn postcolonial states, see David Gordon, *Self-Determination and History in the Third World* (Princeton, N.J.: Princeton University Press, 1971).

13. Robert Young, *White Mythologies* (London: Routledge, 1990).

14. Franco Moretti, "Conjectures on World Literature" *New Left Review* 1 (January/February 2000): 54–68.

15. Pheng Cheah and Jonathan Culler, eds., *Grounds of Comparison: Around the Work of Benedict Anderson* (London: Routledge, 2003), 12.

16. Debora Cohen and Maura O' Connor, *Comparison and History: Europe in Cross-National Perspective* (New York: Routledge, 2004).

17. Jules Michelet, in *The People* (London: Longman, Brown, Green, and Longmans, 1846), 240, wrote of "the grand human movement from India to Greece and to Rome, and from Rome to us [the French]."

18. Gerard Delanty, *Modernity and Postmodernity: Knowledge, Power, the Self* (London: Sage, 2000).

19. Robert van Hallberg, ed., "Canons" special issue, *Critical Inquiry* 10, no. 1 (September 1983).

20. Dick Geary, *The Myth of Nations: The Medieval Origins of Europe* (Princeton, N.J.: Princeton University Press, 2002).

21. Klaus Müller, "Perspectives in Historical Anthropology," in *Western Historical Thinking: An Intercultural Debate*, ed. Jörn Rüsen (New York: Berghahn Books, 2002), 33–52.

22. Müller, "Perspectives in Historical Anthropology," 41.

23. Hugh Trevor-Roper, *The Rise of Christian Europe* (Norwich, U.K.: Thames and Hudson, 1965), 9.

24. Richard Evans, *In Defense of History* (London, Granta Books, 2000), 178.

25. Young, *White Mythologies*, 2.

26. Dipesh Chakrabarty, "Postcoloniality and the Artifice of History: Who Speaks for 'Indian' Pasts?" *Representations* 37 (1992): 5.

27. Roxani Argyropoulos, *Les intellectuals grecs a la recherche de Byzance (1860–1912)* (Athens, Greece: Fondation Nationale de la Recherche, 2001).

28. Spyridon Zambelios, *Dimotika asmata* (Corfu, 1852; reprint, Athens, Greece: Karavias, 1986), 7 (my translation).

29. Yvonne Yazbeck Haddad, *Contemporary Islam and the Challenge of History* (Albany: State University of New York Press, 1982), 166.

30. Partha Chatterjee, *The Nation and Its Fragments: Colonial and Postcolonial Histories* (Princeton, N.J.: Princeton University Press, 1993), 76.

31. Gordon, *Self-Determination and History*, 133.

32. According to this theory, the language was invented by the Turks of Central Asia, who, looking at the sun, utter the first word: "ag" = sun.

33. Cited by Dietrich Jung and Wolfang Piccoli, *Turkey at the Crossroads: Ottoman Legacies and a Greater Middle East* (London, Zed Books, 2001), 60.

34. Halil Berktay, "The Search for the Peasant in Western and Turkish History/Historiography," in *New Approaches to State and Peasant in Ottoman*

History, ed. Halil Berktay and Suraiya Faroqhi (London: Frank Cass, 1992), 156.

35. Often, these classical periods were forgotten inside the country, and knowledge of these periods was reintroduced by the European scholarship.

36. The case of Iran has become more complicated since the 1979 Islamic Revolution, which introduced the Islamic past as a rival to the Persian past. As a consequence, there are two pasts: the secular, based on the history and the genealogy of language, and the religious, based on the history of Islam. Shahrokh Meskoob, *Iranian Nationality and the Persian Language* (Washington, D.C.: Mage Publishers, 1992).

37. "Invention-ism" is a constant feature of national ideologies and a counterweight to the eschatological conception of history in the course of the initial stages of the secularization of historical thought.

38. B. M. Kies, introduction to *The Contribution of the Non-European Peoples to World Civilization*, ed. Maurice W. Hommel (Braamfontin, South Africa: Scotaville, 1989), 1–47.

39. Chatterjee, *The Nation and Its Fragments*, 102.

40. The historian Liang Qichao was the first to introduce to China the writing of history on the principles of Enlightenment historiography in 1902. Prasenjit Duara, *Rescuing History from the Nation: Questioning Narratives of Modern China* (Chicago: University of Chicago Press, 1995), 35. For Japan, see Tanaka, *Japan's Orient*.

41. Chatterjee, *The Nation and Its Fragments*, 102.

42. Ibid., 30.

43. Maria Todorova, *Imagining the Balkans* (New York: Oxford University Press, 1997).

44. I have developed this idea previously in Antonis Liakos, "Modern Greek Historiography (1974–2000): The Era of Tradition from Dictatorship to Democracy," in *(Re)Writing History: Historiography in Southeast Europe after Socialism*, ed. Ulf Brunbauer (Münster, Germany: LIT Verlag, 2004), 351–378.

45. Attila Pok, "Eastern European Historiography in the Twentieth Century," in *An Assessment of Twentieth-Century Historiography*, ed. Rolf Torstendahl (Stockholm, Sweden: Royal Academy, 2000), 115–128.

46. Léopold Sédar Senghor, "Negritude: A Humanism of the Twentieth Century" in *Colonial Discourse and Post-Colonial Theory*, ed. Patrick Williams and Laura Chrisman (New York: Columbia University Press, 1994), 30.

47. Jalal Al-e Ahmad, *Plagued by the West*, trans. Paul Sprachman (Delmor, N.Y.: Center for Iranian Studies, Columbia University, 1982). See Mehrzad Boroujerdi, *Iranian Intellectuals and the West* (Syracuse, N.Y.: Syracuse University Press, 1996).

48. Anthony Gorman, *Historians, State and Politics in Twentieth Century Egypt* (London, Routledge, 2003), 101.

49. Gorman, *Historians, State and Politics*, 103.

50. Gordon, *Self-Determination and History*, 136.

51. Hayden White, *Metahistory* (Baltimore: John Hopkins University Press, 1973), 31.

52. Rossi Paolo, *The Dark Abyss of Time: The History of the Earth and the History of Nations from Hooke to Vico* (Chicago: University of Chicago Press, 1984), 123–187.

53. Cited by Wiethoff, *Introduction to Chinese History*, 13–14.

54. Prasenjit Duara, *Rescuing History from the Nation: Questioning Narratives of Modern China* (Chicago: University of Chicago Press, 1995).

55. Tanaka, *Japan's Orient*, 274.

56. Benedict Anderson, *The Spectre of Comparison* (London: Verso, 1998), 2.

ANTHROPOLOGY AT THE FRENCH NATIONAL ASSEMBLY:
THE SEMIOTIC ASPECTS OF A POLITICAL INSTITUTION
Marc Abélès

1. Clifford Geertz, *Negara: The Theatre State in Nineteenth-Century Bali* (Princeton, N.J.: Princeton University Press, 1980), 120.

2. Ibid., 123.

3. Marc Abélès, *Un ethnologue à l'Assemblée* (Paris: Odile Jacob, 2000).

4. Marc Abélès, *Quiet Days in Burgundy: A Study of Local Politics*, Cambridge Studies in Social and Cultural Anthropology (Cambridge, U.K.: Cambridge University Press, 1991).

5. Guy Debord, *La société du spectacle* (Paris: Gallimard, 2004); and Jean Baudrillard, *A l'ombre des majorités silencieuses ou la fin du social* (Paris: Utopie, 1978).

6. Jürgen Habermas, *Die Einbeziehung des Anderen: Studien zur politischen Theorie* (Frankfurt am Main: Suhrkamp Verlag, 1996).

"LIFE IS DEAD HERE":
SENSING THE POLITICAL IN "NO MAN'S LAND"
Yael Navaro-Yashin

NOTE: I would like to thank Mehmet Yashin, Begona Aretxaga, Neni Panourgiá, James Boon, Stathis Gourgouris, Caroline Humphrey, Jane Cowan, Sarah Green, and Murat Arsel for their comments on earlier versions or presentations of this paper. I would also like to thank participants in senior seminars at the University College London, Cambridge, and Manchester for their reflections. Earlier versions and sections of this paper were also presented at the "Anthropology, Now!" conference organized under the auspices of the Center for Neohellenic Research, of the National Research Center in Athens, at the Hermoupolis seminars, and in an American Anthropological Association panel in 1999, "Memory, Transformations, Death," both organized by Neni Panourgiá and George E. Marcus. The article was published previously in a slightly different form in *Anthropological Theory* 3, no. 1 (2003), 107–125.

1. Tzvetan Todorov, *Facing the Extreme: Moral Life in the Concentration Camps* (New York: Henry Holt, 1996).

2. Yiannis Papadakis has studied the political chasms between Turkish-Cypriots and Greek-Cypriots in reference to the actual "dead zone" that lies between the partitioned north and south of the island. "Perceptions of History and Collective Identity: A Study of Contemporary Greek Cypriot and Turkish Cypriot Nationalism" (Ph.D. diss., University of Cambridge). But the project in this paper is different, studying the subjective experience of living in Northern Cyprus which, as I study it, has been transformed into "no man's land."

3. James Ferguson, working on what he calls "globalization and abjection," refers to the creation of such "abjected spaces" in Africa under neoliberal projects and processes. James Ferguson, *Expectations of Modernity: Myths and Meanings of Urban Life on the Zambian Copperbelt* (Berkeley: University of California Press, 1999).

4. There is an actual "no man's land" between Northern and Southern Cyprus controlled by the United Nations and the city of Varosha (in Turkish, *Maras*); evacuated of its inhabitants and in the hands of the Turkish military, it is a ghost city.

5. Giorgio Agamben, *Homo Sacer: Sovereign Power and Bare Life* (Stanford, Calif.: Stanford University Press, 1998), 119.

6. See, e.g., Arjun Appadurai, *Modernity at Large: Cultural Dimensions of Globalization* (Minneapolis: University of Minnesota Press, 1996).

7. For such dialectical thinking, see Theodor Adorno and Max Horkheimer, *Dialectic of Enlightenment* (New York: Continuum, 1994).

8. See, e.g., Aihwa Ong, *Flexible Citizenship: The Cultural Logics of Transnationality* (Durham, N.C.: Duke University Press, 1999).

9. Talal Asad, "Anthropology and the Analysis of Ideology," *Man* 14 (1979): 607–627.

10. Clifford Geertz, "'From the Native's Point of View': On the Nature of Anthropological Understanding," in *Local Knowledge: Further Essays in Interpretive Anthropology* (New York: Basic Books, 1983), 55–70.

11. Walter Benjamin, "Theses on the Philosophy of History," in *Illuminations*, ed. Hannah Arendt (London: Fontana Press, 1992), 246.

12. Ibid.

13. Juan Rulfo, *Pedro Páramo* (London: Serpent's Tail, 1994).

14. Ibid., 7.

15. Ibid., 50–51.

16. Turkey-fication is different from Turkification. Not only Greek Cypriot village names were changed through this project. Even village names that were formerly Turkish, in the Turkish Cypriot dialect, were changed to names more akin to places and connotations of Turkey.

17. Benedict Anderson, *Imagined Communities: Reflections on the Origin and Spread of Nationalism* (London: Verso, 1983).

18. In certain formerly Ottoman territories like the Sudan, the word *Turk* is still used to refer to a "statesman" or "state official," where *Turquia* is another word for *devlet* or "the state." Charles Jedrej, personal communication.

19. Under Ottoman sovereignty, subjection was based on religion, not ethnicity. Subjects of the empire belonged to distinct religious communities (*millets*) with different rights under the imperial legal system. If subjects of the empire considered themselves "Muslim" or "Greek Orthodox," the concepts "Turkish Cypriot" and "Greek Cypriot" are postcolonial (in reference, here, to British colonialism) and therefore more recent. For a study of the "Turkification" of Muslim Cypriots, see Huseyin Mehmet Atesin, *Kibrisli Müslümanlarin Türklesme ve laiklesme serüveni, 1925–1975* (Istanbul, Turkey: Marifet Yayinlari, 1999).

20. See *North Cyprus Almanack* (London: K. Rustem & Brother, 1987); Hasan Fehmi, *Kuzey Kibris Turk Cumhuriyeti'nin El Kitabi* (Nicosia, Cyprus: Gelisim Off-Set, 1987); Hasmet Gürkan, *Bir zamanlar Kibris'ta* (Nicosia, Cyprus: CYREP Yayinlari, 1986), 134–157; Michael A. Attalides, ed., *Cyprus Reviewed* (Nicosia, Cyprus: Jus Cypri Association, 1977), 78–86; and Vangelis Calotychos, ed., *Cyprus and Its People: Nation, Identity, and Experience in an Unimaginable Community* (Boulder, Colo.: Westview Press, 1998), 6–9.

21. Even Turkey does not properly recognize the "TRNC" as a state, refraining from inviting Turkish Cypriot administrators to international conventions held in Turkey.

22. Calotychos, *Cyprus and Its People*.

23. On the issue of recognition in Cyprus, see Costas M. Constantinou and Yiannis Papadakis, "The Cypriot State(s) In Situ: Cross-Ethnic Contact and the Discourse of Recognition," *Global Society* 15, no. 2 (2001): 125–148.

24. Akhil Gupta, "Blurred Boundaries: The Discourse of Corruption, the Culture of Politics, and the Imagined State," *American Ethnologist* 22, no. 2 (1995): 375–402.

25. Philip Abrams, "Notes on the Difficulty of Studying the State," *Journal of Historical Sociology* 1, no. 1 (1988): 58–89; Timothy Mitchell, "The Limits of the State: Beyond Statist Approaches and their Critics," *American Political Science Review* 85, no. 1 (1991): 77–96; and Michael Taussig, "Maleficium: State Fetishism," in *The Nervous System* (London: Routledge, 1992), 111–140.

26. Yael Navaro-Yashin, *Faces of the State: Secularism and Public Life in Turkey* (Princeton, N.J.: Princeton University Press, 2002).

27. Abrams, "Notes on the Difficulty of Studying the State."

28. Aziz Nesin is one of Turkey's best-known authors. The title of this novel is *Yasar ne yasar ne yasamaz* [Yashar neither lives nor doesn't] (Istanbul: Adam Yayinlari, 1995).

29. Kathleen Stewart, *A Place on the Side of the Road: Cultural Poetics in an "Other" America* (Princeton, N.J.: Princeton University Press, 1996).

30. Anna Lowenhaupt Tsing, *In the Realm of the Diamond Queen: Marginality in an Out-of-the-Way Place* (Princeton, N.J.: Princeton University Press, 1993).

31. Slavoj Zizek, *The Sublime Object of Ideology* (London and New York: Verso, 1989).

32. Taussig, "Maleficium: State Fetishism."

33. Navaro-Yashin, *Faces of the State*.

34. Lisa Malkki, "Citizens of Humanity: Internationalism and the Imagined Community of Nations," *Diaspora* 3, no. 1 (1994): 41–68.

35. See Yael Navaro-Yashin, "Legal/Illegal Counterpoints: Subjecthood and Subjectivity in an Unrecognized State," in *Human Rights in Global Perspective*, ed. Richard Ashby Wilson and Jon P. Mitchell (London and New York: Routledge, 2003), 71–92.

36. For another commentary on temporality in Northern Cyprus, see Moira Killoran, "Time, Space, and National Identities in Cyprus," in *Step-Mothertongue: From Nationalism to Multiculturalism the Literatures of Cyprus, Greece, and Turkey*, ed. Mehmet Yashin (London: Middlesex University Press, 2000).

37. Maronites living within the domain of the "TRNC" do not have the "right" to leave property to their children after they die if the children are not living in the "TRNC."

38. See, e.g., Vassos Argyrou, *Tradition and Modernity in the Mediterranean: The Wedding as Symbolic Struggle* (Cambridge, U.K.: Cambridge University Press, 1996).

39. Peter Loizos, *The Heart Grown Bitter: A Chronicle of Cypriot War Refugees* (Cambridge, U.K.: Cambridge University Press, 1981).

40. Vassos Argyrou has studied rubbish in South Cyprus. However, he has studied the issue solely as a problem of (class) distinction and identity. The history of war in Cyprus is absent from his analysis, where South Cyprus is ethnographically compared with Greece and other Mediterranean contexts. Rubbish figures in Argyrou's study as a site of conflict between middle-class environmentalists from Nicosia and working villagers from Paphos. "'Keep Cyprus Clean': Littering, Pollution, and Otherness," *Cultural Anthropology* 12

(1997): 159–178. The project in this paper is different: I argue that there is no space in the political context of Cyprus, north or south, where living in ruins, as I study it, can be solely interpreted in sociocultural terms, whether in reference to class or identity. The analysis demands a contextualization in the history of war on the island, with impacts on the use of space not only in the north, but also in the south. I would invite Argyrou to consider whether rubbish in Paphos has nothing to do with the structure of feeling of the conflict in Cyprus. I would argue that there must be a "no man's land" quality, as I name it, to existence in South Cyprus, as well.

41. Johannes Fabian, *Time and the Other: How Anthropology Makes Its Object* (New York: Columbia University Press, 1983).

42. For anthropological work that brings out this unarticulated and excessive (psychic) domain of subjective experience, see Begona Aretxaga, *Shattering Silence: Women, Nationalism, and Political Subjectivity in Northern Ireland* (Princeton, N.J.: Princeton University Press, 1997) and Begona Aretxaga, "A Fictional Reality: Paramilitary Death Squads and the Construction of State Terror in Spain," in *Death Squad: The Anthropology of State Terror*, ed. Jeffrey A. Sluka (Philadelphia: University of Pennsylvania Press, 2000), 46–70.

43. *Enosis* means "union" and it implies "union with Greece," and it was the ideal of Greek Cypriot nationalists led by the EOKA group.

44. See, e.g., *Cumhuriyet* (Turkey), July 21, 1998 (front page).

45. Benjamin, "Theses on the Philosophy of History," 247.

46. Ibid., 248.

47. Ibid., 249.

48. Orin Starn, "Missing the Revolution: Anthropologists and the War in Peru," *Cultural Anthropology* 6, no. 1 (1991): 63–91.

49. See, e.g., Appadurai, *Modernity at Large*.

50. Nadia Seremetakis, *The Senses Still: Perception and Memory as Material Culture in Modernity* (Chicago: University of Chicago Press, 1996).

51. Lila Abu-Lughod and Catherine Lutz, eds., *Language and the Politics of Emotion* (Cambridge, U.K.: Cambridge University Press, 1990).

52. See, e.g., Smadar Lavie, *The Poetics of Military Occupation: Mzeina Allegories of Bedouin Identity under Israeli and Egyptian Rule* (Berkeley: University of California Press, 1990).

53. See Gay Becker, *Disrupted Lives: How People Create Meaning in a Chaotic World* (Berkeley: University of California Press, 1997).

54. Maurice Bloch and Jonathan Parry, *Death and the Regeneration of Life* (Cambridge, U.K.: Cambridge University Press, 1982); and Loring M. Danforth, *The Death Rituals of Rural Greece* (Princeton, N.J.: Princeton University Press, 1982).

TEXT AND TRANSNATIONAL SUBJECTIFICATION:
MEDIA'S CHALLENGE TO ANTHROPOLOGY
Louisa Schein

1. Throughout this essay, my emphasis is on visual and usually narrative media such as film, video, CDs, DVDs, and television.

2. E. Valentine Daniel and Jeffrey M. Peck, "Culture/Contexture: An Introduction" in *Culture/Contexture: Explorations in Anthropology and Literary Studies*, ed. E. Valentine Daniel and Jeffrey M. Peck (Berkeley: University of California Press, 1996), 11.

3. Louisa Schein, "Diaspora Politics, Homeland Erotics, and the Materializing of Memory," *Positions* 7, no. 3 (1999): 697–729.

4. See, e.g., Richard Handler, "Raymond Williams, George Stocking, and Fin-de-Siècle U.S. Anthropology," *Cultural Anthropology* 13, no. 4 (1998): 447–463; Stephen Nugent and Cris Shore, eds., *Anthropology and Cultural Studies* (London: Pluto Press, 1997); Renato Rosaldo, "Whose Cultural Studies?" *American Anthropologist* 96 (1994): 524–529; and Paul Willis, "TIES: Theoretically Informed Ethnographic Study," in Nugent and Shore, *Anthropology and Cultural Studies*, 182–192. On disciplining cultural studies in the U.S. academy, see also Sunaina Marr Maira, *Desis in the House: Indian American Youth Culture in New York City* (Philadelphia: Temple University Press, 2002), 200–203; and Ellen Rooney, "Discipline and Vanish: Feminism, the Resistance to Theory, and the Politics of Cultural Studies," in *What Is Cultural Studies?* ed. J. Storey (London: Arnold, 1996), 208–220.

5. Stuart Hall, "Cultural Studies and Its Theoretical Legacies" in *Cultural Studies*, ed. Lawrence Grossberg, Gary Nelson, and Paula Treichler (New York: Routledge, 1992), 286.

6. Ibid., 285.

7. Paul Willis, *Learning to Labor: How Working Class Kids Get Working Class Jobs* (New York: Columbia University Press, 1977).

8. Paul Gilroy, *The Black Atlantic: Modernity and Double Consciousness.* (Cambridge, Mass.: Harvard University Press, 1993).

9. Rosaldo, "Whose Cultural Studies?" 529.

10. Lila Abu-Lughod, "The Interpretation of Culture(s) after Television," *Representations* 59 (Summer 1997): 110.

11. Clifford Geertz, "Deep Play: Notes on the Balinese Cockfight," in *The Interpretation of Cultures* (New York: Basic Books, 1973), 451.

12. Faye Ginsburg, "Culture/Media: A (Mild) Polemic," *Anthropology Today* 10, no. 2 (1994): 6.

13. Janice Radway, "Reception Study: Ethnography and the Problems of Dispersed Audiences and Nomadic Subjects," *Cultural Studies* 2, no. 3 (1998): 366.

14. Tania Modleski, "Some Functions of Feminist Criticism, or, the Scandal of the Mute Body," in *Feminism without Women* (New York: Routledge, 1991), 35–58.

15. Arjun Appadurai, *Modernity at Large: Cultural Dimensions of Globalization* (Minneapolis: University of Minnesota Press, 1996), 53–54.

16. Purnima Mankekar. "National Texts and Gendered Lives: An Ethnography of Television Viewers in a North Indian City," *American Ethnologist* 20, no. 3 (1993): 557.

17. Bronislaw Malinowski, *Argonauts of the Western Pacific* (London: E. P. Dutton, 1960) (first published in 1922).

18. Louisa Schein, "Homeland Beauty: Transnational Longing and Hmong American Video" *Journal of Asian Studies* 63, no. 2 (2004): 433–463.

19. Daniel and Peck, "Culture/Contexture," 5.

20. For some useful discussions of "representation," see W. J. T. Mitchell, "Representation," in *Critical Terms in Literary Study*, ed. Frank Lentricchia and Thomas McLaughlin (Chicago: University of Chicago Press, 1990), 11–22; Timothy Mitchell, *Colonising Egypt* (Cambridge, U.K.: Cambridge University Press, 1988); and Judith Farquhar, Tomoko Masuzawa, and Carol Mavor, "A Note from the Editors," *Cultural Studies* 12, no. 1 (1998): 1–2.

21. Akhil Gupta and James Ferguson, "Discipline and Practice: 'The Field' as Site, Method, and Location in Anthropology," in *Anthropological Locations: Boundaries and Grounds of a Field Science*, ed. Akhil Gupta and James Ferguson (Berkeley: University of California Press, 1997), 38.

22. Sherry B. Ortner, "Generation X: Anthropology in a Media-Saturated World," *Cultural Anthropology* 13, no. 3 (1998): 415.

23. See Aihwa Ong and Donald Nonini, *Ungrounded Empires: The Cultural Politics of Modern Chinese Transnationalism* (New York: Routledge, 1997); and Aihwa Ong, *Flexible Citizenship: The Cultural Logics of Transnationality* (Durham, N.C.: Duke University Press, 1999) for groundbreaking studies on transnational Asian identities and practices, especially for the notions of "flexible citizenship" and "greater China."

24. Louisa Schein, *Minority Rules: The Miao and the Feminine in China's Cultural Politics* (Durham, N.C.: Duke University Press, 2000).

25. This essay represents part of a larger ongoing study of transnationality among Hmong Americans and their co-ethnics in Asia. Louisa Schein, "Rewind to Home: Hmong Media and Gendered Diaspora" (book manuscript in preparation). Field research, ongoing in the United States intermittently since 1978, also included seven trips to urban and rural China in 1982, 1985, 1986, 1988, 1993, 1999, and 2000 and one trip to Thailand in 1982. For research support during those years, I would like to thank the Committee on Scholarly Communications with the People's Republic of China, the Fulbright-Hays

Doctoral Dissertation Research Abroad Program, the Samuel T. Arnold Fellowship Program of Brown University, the University of California at Berkeley, and the Rutgers Research Council, as well as numerous institutions and individuals in the United States, Thailand, and China who sponsored or otherwise facilitated my work. I am grateful to Nouzong Ly, Ly Chong Thong Jalao, and Long Yang for assistance with translations.

26. Estimates of Hmong populations in the diaspora as of 1992 were 120,000 in the United States, 13,000 in France (including 1,500 in French Guiana), 650 in Canada, and 650 in Australia. See Yang Dao, *Hmong at the Turning Point* (Minneapolis, Minn.: WorldBridge Associates, 1993).

27. There is a small but growing literature on uses of media by peoples in diaspora. See monographs by Casey Man Kong Lum, *In Search of a Voice: Karaoke and the Construction of Identity in Chinese America* (Mahwah, N.J.: Lawrence Erlbaum, 1996); Hamid Naficy, *The Making of Exile Cultures: Iranian Television in Los Angeles* (Minneapolis: University of Minnesota Press, 1993); and Adelaida Reyes, *Songs of the Caged, Songs of the Free: Music and the Vietnamese Refugee Experience* (Philadelphia: Temple University Press, 1999); see also Michael M. J. Fischer, "Starting Over: How, What, and for Whom Does One Write about Refugees? The Poetics and Politics of Refugee Film as Ethnographic Access in a Media-Saturated World," in *Mistrusting Refugees*, ed. E. Valentine Daniel and John Chr. Knudsen (Berkeley: University of California Press, 1995), 126–150; Joyce D. Hammond, "Visualizing Themselves: Tongan Videography in Utah," *Visual Anthropology* 1 (1988): 379–400; Dona Kolar-Panov, *Video, War, and the Diasporic Imagination* (London: Routledge, 1997); Dona Kolar-Panov, "Video and the Diasporic Imagination of Selfhood: A Case Study of the Creations in Australia," *Cultural Studies* 10, no. 2 (1996): 288–314; and Jo Ann Koltyk, *New Pioneers in the Heartland: Hmong Life in Wisconsin* (Boston: Allyn & Bacon, 1998), 119–131 (discussing Hmong uses of video in Wisconsin).

28. Music, over the last two decades, has been the largest industry in Hmong media. Local bands are ubiquitous, and some gain national and international fame, touring by invitation to large Hmong functions in parks and auditoriums. Vocalists sing Hmong or Lao lyrics that they have written themselves, sometimes to music borrowed from existing melodies in pop and Asian pop music. Recording is a major part of the business, and those who produce tapes, CDs, or music videos, usually by renting studio time, are the ones who stand to gain widespread acclaim and to make considerable profits. Many of the Hmong in video that I have interviewed got their start in the music scene.

29. Azade Seyhan, "Ethnic Selves / Ethnic Signs: Invention of Self, Space, and Genealogy in Immigrant Writing," in *Culture/Contexture: Explorations in Anthropology and Literary Studies*, ed. E. Valentine Daniel and Jeffrey M. Peck (Berkeley: University of California Press, 1996), 184.

30. George E. Marcus, *Ethnography through Thick and Thin* (Princeton, N.J.: Princeton University Press, 1998).

31. Doreen Massey. "Power-Geometry and a Progressive Sense of Place," in *Mapping the Futures: Local Cultures. Global Change*, ed. Jon Bird and others (London: Routledge, 1993), 61.

32. Koltyk, *New Pioneers in the Heartland*, 119–120.

33. At present writing the series is in part 8.

34. Incest discomfort was not an issue in these relatives acting as lovers for the purpose of the video. By Hmong custom they were not reckoned as kin since the girl had a surname different from that of Ga Moua. In the Hmong patrilineal, clan-exogamous kin system, no matter how close the relationship, if a person's surname denotes a different clan, they may qualify for courtship and marriage. Ga Moua's calling her "niece" was likely out of deference to the American bilateral reckoning he imputed to me.

35. Hamid Naficy, "Phobic Spaces and Liminal Panics: Independent Transnational Film Genre," in *Global/Local: Cultural Production and the Transnational Imaginary*, ed. Rob Wilson and Wimal Dissanayake (Durham, N.C.: Duke University Press, 1996), 121.

36. I write with acute awareness of the controversiality of attempting to treat sexuality as a domain apart from gendered structures. For two foundational pieces that make the case most cogently for a conceptual separation at analytical and political levels, respectively, see Eve Kosofsky Sedgwick, "Axiomatic," in *Epistemology of the Closet* (Berkeley: University of California Press, 1990), 1–63; and Gayle Rubin, "Thinking Sex: Notes for a Radical Theory of the Politics of Sexuality," in *Pleasure and Danger: Exploring Female Sexuality*, ed. Carole S. Vance (New York: Routledge, 1984), 267–319. For an interesting counterargument in critique of Michel Foucault's *History of Sexuality*, vol. 1 (New York: Vintage, 1978), see Judith Butler, "Revisiting Bodies and Pleasures," in *Performativity and Belonging*, ed. Vicki Bell (London: Sage, 1999), 11–20.

37. Purnima Mankekar, *Screening Culture, Viewing Politics: An Ethnography of Television, Womanhood, and Nation in Postcolonial India* (Durham, N.C.: Duke University Press, 1999), 17.

38. Anne-Marie Fortier, "Re-Membering Places and the Performance of Belonging(s)," in *Performativity and Belonging*, ed. Vicki Bell (London: Sage, 1999), 46.

39. The title denotes Ban Vinai, the largest refugee camp of Hmong settlement in Thailand, in Hmong orthography.

40. Ara Wilson, "American Catalogues of Asian Brides," in *Anthropology for the Nineties*, ed. Johnnetta B. Cole (New York: Free Press, 1988), 119.

41. Marriage or sex before the age of eighteen as well as the practice of abducting young women as brides, both of which were practiced routinely

among Hmong in Southeast Asia, have been subject to juridical scrutiny as rape or statutory rape in legal cases in the United States. In some instances, defendants' cases have been pled using a "cultural defense" argument that these practices were within the cultural systems of the perpetrators. See Malek-Mithra Shebanyi, "Cultural Defense: One Person's Culture is Another's Crime," *Loyola of Los Angeles International and Comparative Law Journal* 9, no. 3 (1987): 751–783 for a legal discussion and Kristin Koptiuch, "'Cultural Defense' and Criminological Displacements: Gender, Race, and (Trans)Nation in the Legal Surveillance of U.S. Diaspora Asians," in *Displacement, Diaspora, and Geographies of Identity*, ed. Smadar Lavie and Ted Swedenburg (Durham, N.C.: Duke University Press, 1996), 215–233 for a critical discussion of the disciplinary ramifications of the cultural defense. See also Leti Volpp, "(Mis)Identifying Culture: Asian Women and 'The Cultural Defense,'" *Harvard Women's Law Journal* 17 (Spring 1994): 57–80.

42. Elizabeth Traube, "Secrets of Success in Postmodern Society," *Cultural Anthropology* 4, no. 3 (1989): 273–300.

43. Michael Moffatt, "Do We Really Need 'Postmodernism' to Understand *Ferris Bueller's Day Off*? A Comment on Traube," *Cultural Anthropology* 5, no. 4 (1990): 367–373.

44. Ibid., 371–372.

45. Elizabeth Traube, "Reply to Moffatt," *Cultural Anthropology* 5, no. 4 (1990): 378.

46. Abu-Lughod, "The Interpretation of Culture(s)," 114.

47. Lisa Lowe, *Immigrant Acts: On Asian American Cultural Politics* (Durham, N.C.: Duke University Press, 1996), 32–33.

48. See, e.g., Lila Abu-Lughod, "The Objects of Soap Opera: Egyptian Television and the Cultural Politics of Modernity through the Prism of the Local," in *Worlds Apart: Modernity Through the Prism of the Local*, ed. Daniel Miller (London: Routledge, 1995), 190–210; Mankekar, *Screening Culture*; and Lisa Rofel, "*Yearnings*: Televisual Love and Melodramatic Politics in Contemporary China," *American Ethnologist* 2, no. 4 (1994): 700–722.

49. Appadurai, *Modernity at Large*; Daniel Miller, "The Young and the Restless in Trinidad: A Case of the Local and the Global in Mass Consumption," in *Consuming Technologies: Media Information in Domestic Spaces*, ed. Roger Silverstone and Eric Hirsch (London: Routledge, 1992), 163–182; Louisa Schein, "Of Cargo and Satellites: Imagined Cosmopolitanism," *Postcolonial Studies* 2, no. 3 (1999): 345–375; and Mayfair Mei-hui Yang, "Mass Media and Transnational Subjectivity in Shanghai: Notes on (Re)Cosmopolitanism in a Chinese Metropolis," in *Ungrounded Empires: The Cultural Politics of Modern Chinese Transnationalism*, ed. Aihwa Ong and Donald Nonini (New York: Routledge, 1997), 287–319.

50. Benedict Anderson, *The Spectre of Comparisons: Nationalism, Southeast Asia and the World* (London: Verso, 1998), 73.

51. Mitsuhiro Yoshimoto, "Real Virtuality," in *Global/Local: Cultural Production and the Transnational Imaginary*, eds. Rob Wilson and Wimal Dissanayake (Durham, N.C.: Duke University Press, 1996), 109.

52. Elizabeth A. Povinelli and George Chauncey, "Thinking Sexuality Transnationally: An Introduction." *GLQ: A Journal of Lesbian and Gay Studies* 5, no. 4 (1999): 443.

AFTERWORD
THE ETHNOGRAPHER'S "GAZE":
SOME NOTES ON VISUALITY AND ITS RELATION TO THE REFLEXIVE
METALANGUAGE OF ANTHROPOLOGY
Maria Kakavoulia

1. Michel Foucault, *The Birth of the Clinic: An Archaeology of Medical Perception* (New York: Vintage Books, 1978).

2. Hannah Arendt, *The Life of the Mind* (New York: Harcourt Brace Jovanovich, 1978), 111.

3. Marshall McLuhan, *Understanding Media: The Extensions of Man* (New York: McGraw-Hill, 1964); and Walter J. Ong, *The Presence of the Word: Some Prolegomena for Cultural and Religious History* (New Haven, Conn.: Yale University Press, 1967).

4. Nicholas Mirzoeff, "What is Visual Culture?" in *The Visual Culture Reader*, ed. Nicholas Mirzoeff (London: Routledge, 1998), 53.

5. David Michael Levin, ed., *Sites of Vision: The Discursive Construction of Sight in the History of Philosophy* (Cambridge, Mass.: MIT Press, 1999).

6. Michel Foucault, *The Order of Things: An Archaeology of the Human Sciences* (New York: Random House, 1970), 319.

7. Michel Foucault, *Discipline and Punish: The Birth of the Prison* (New York: Vintage Books, 1979).

8. Jürgen Habermas, *The Philosophical Discourse of Modernity* (Cambridge, Mass.: MIT Press, 1987), 128–129.

9. Irit Rogoff, "Studying Visual Culture," in *The Visual Culture Reader*, ed. Nicholas Mirzoeff (London: Routledge, 1998), 22.

10. David Michael Levin, ed., *Modernity and the Hegemony of Vision* (Berkeley: University of California Press, 1993).

11. Constance Classen, *Worlds of Sense: Exploring the Senses in History across Cultures* (London: Routledge, 1993).

12. Ibid., 54.

13. David Howes, *The Varieties of Sensory Experience: A Sourcebook in the Anthropology of Senses* (Toronto: University of Toronto Press, 1991).

14. Classen, *Worlds of Sense*. See also Gillian Bendelow and Williams Simon, "Pain and the Mind-Body Dualism: A Sociological Approach," *Body and Society* 12 (1995): 83–113; C. Nadia Seremetakis, *The Senses Still* (Chicago: University of Chicago Press, 1994); and Paul Stoller, *Sensuous Scholarship*, Contemporary Ethnography (Philadelphia: University of Pennsylvania Press, 1997). For the growing interest in the "anthropology of the senses," see Sarah Pink, *The Future of Visual Anthropology: Engaging the Senses* (New York: Routledge, 2006).

15. Tim Ingold, *The Perception of the Environment: Essays in Livelihood, Dwelling and Skill* (London: Routledge, 2000).

16. Thomas J. Csordas, *The Sacred Self: A Cultural Phenomenology of Charismatic Healing* (Berkeley: University of California Press, 1994), 79. As an exception, see Margaret Wilson, "A Different Drummer: Vision and the Anthropological Text," *Anthropology and Humanism* 20, no. 2 (1995): 117–123.

17. Gilles Deleuze, *Francis Bacon: Logique de la sensation* (Paris: Éditions de la différence, 1984).

18. Neni Panourgiá, *Fragments of Death, Fables of Identity: An Athenian Anthropography* (Madison: University of Wisconsin Press, 1995).

19. Kenneth Burke, *Permanence and Change* (New York: New Republic, 1935), 49.

20. Donna Haraway, "The Persistence of Vision," in *The Visual Culture Reader*, ed. Nicholas Mirzoeff (London: Routledge, 1998), 191.

21. George E. Marcus, *Ethnography through Thick and Thin* (Princeton, N.J.: Princeton University Press, 1998), 97.

CONTRIBUTORS

Marc Abélès is professor of anthropology at the École des Hautes Études en Sciences Sociales in Paris and director of the Laboratoire d'Anthropologie des Institutions et des Organisations Sociales (EHESS-CNRS). As a political anthropologist, he has conducted fieldwork in such different places as the Gemu highlands of southern Ethiopia, the French province of Burgundy, the French National Assembly, European institutions, and Silicon Valley. Currently he works on globalization and the new transnational forms of governance, focusing his research on a governmental organization, the World Trade Organization (WTO), and a nongovernmental one, Oxfam. He is the author of fifteen books, among them, *Anthropologie de l'Etat* (A. Colin, 1990); *Quiet Days in Burgundy* (Cambridge University Press, 1991); *Un ethnologue à l'Assemblée* (O. Jacob, 2000); *Les Nouveaux riches: Un ethnologue dans la Silicon Valley* (O. Jacob, 2002); and *Politique de la survie* (Flammarion, 2006).

Athena Athanasiou is assistant professor in the Department of Social Anthropology at Panteion University of Social and Political Sciences, in Athens, Greece. She received her Ph.D. at the New School for Social Research, in New York, and was a postdoctoral fellow at the Pembroke Center for Teaching and Research on Women, at Brown University (2001–2002). Her written work on biopolitics, gender theory, sexual politics, and the technologies of the body has been published in various academic journals. She is the author of *On the Fringes of Life: Essays on the Body, Gender, and Biopolitics* (Ekkremes, 2007) and the editor of *Feminist Theory and Cultural Critique* (Nissos, 2006). She is also co-editor (with Elena Tzelepis) of *Re-Writing Difference: Luce Irigaray and "the Greeks"* (State University of New York Press, forthcoming). She is currently working on the politics of affect and mourning.

James A. Boon is professor of anthropology at Princeton University, where he served as department chair in 1998–1999 and 2002–2007. He works in the composite history of anthropology, hybrid arts, and comparative inquiry. He has done fieldwork in Java and Bali, research on colonialist Indonesian studies, and interdisciplinary writing on ritual life, including the poetics of consumption. He attempts fresh readings of cross-cultural discourse in diverse books, most recently, *Verging on Extra-Vagance: Anthropology, History, Religion, Literature, Arts . . . Showbiz* (Princeton University Press, 1999). His next array of essays is tentatively titled *Cultural Comparison, Encore! Novel Returns to Geertz, Weber, Boasians, Frazer, Critical Theory, and Commercial Desire.*

Maria Kakavoulia is assistant professor in rhetoric and narratology in the Department of Communication, Media and Culture at Panteion University of Social and Political Sciences, in Athens, Greece. She previously lectured in Modern Greek at the Ludwig-Maximilian University of Munich, Germany. She has published several articles on Modern Greek literature, discourse analysis, and media language and is the author of *Studies of Narrative Discourse* (Ekdoseis Psychogios, 2003) (in Greek) and *Interior Monologue and Its Discursive Formation in Melpo Axioti's Prosework* "Δύσκολες Νύχτες" (Institut für Byzantinistik und Neugriechische Philologie der Universität, 1992). For her most recent book, *Figures and Words in Eleni Vacalo's Works* (Nephelē, 2004) (in Greek), she was awarded the first Greek state prize for essay and criticism in 2005. Her research interests include the cognitive value of narrative; forms of speech pathology; and the relation of vision, movement, knowledge, and language.

Pavlos Kavouras is professor and chair of the Faculty of Music Studies at the National & Kapodistrian University of Athens. He is a classical guitarist, and holds a bachelor of science degree in naval architecture and marine engineering from the National Technical University of Athens. He also holds an M.A. and a Ph.D. in cultural anthropology from City University of New York and the New School for Social Research, respectively. His doctoral dissertation is focused on the extempore dialogical poetics of Karpathos (Greece), as expressed in the *ghlendi*, a music-cultural ceremony of great symbolic significance for the local population. His ethnographic works include empirical as well as theoretical (i.e., methodological and epistemological) explorations of issues pertaining to the production and consumption of music culture, through the performance and perception of music, examined both as a cultural phenomenon and as a theoretical metaphor for ethnographic reflexivity. His ethnographic publications in English include his doctoral dissertation "Ghlendi & Xenitia: The Poetics of Exile in Rural Greece (Olymbos, Karpathos)"; "Where the Community Reveals Itself: Reflexivity and Moral Judgment in Karpathos, Greece," in *Social Experience and Anthropological Knowledge*, edited by Kirsten Hastrup and Peter Hervik (Routledge, 1994); "The Biography of a Folk Musician: Ethnographic Fieldwork, Interpretation and Fiction," in *Music of Thrace: An Interdisciplinary Approach* (Friends of Music Society, 1999); and "Ethnographies of Dialogical Singing, Dialogical Ethnography," *Music and Anthropology* 10 (2005). He is currently writing a book titled *Trickster and Cain: A Musical Allegory*.

Antonis Liakos is professor of contemporary history and history of historiography at the University of Athens. His main books are *How the Past Becomes History?* (Polis, 2007) (in Greek); *The Nation: How Has It Been Imagined by Those Who Wanted to Change the World?* (Polis, 2006) (in Greek); *L'Unificazione italiana e la Grande Idea (1859–1871)* (Aletheia, 1995); and *Labor and Politics in the Interwar Greece* (Commercial Bank Foundation, 1993) (in Greek). He is a member of the editorial board of the journal *Historein* and of the board of the International Commission of History and Theory of Historiography, and is affiliated with the European Science Foundation Network, National Histories in Europe (NHIST).

George E. Marcus was for twenty-five years chair of the anthropology department at Rice University. During that period, he coedited (with James Clifford) *Writing Culture* (University of California Press, 1986), coauthored (with Michael Fischer) *Anthropology as Cultural Critique* (University of Chicago Press, 1986), inaugurated the journal *Cultural Anthropology*, published *Ethnography through Thick & Thin* (Princeton University Press, 1998), and through the 1990s, created and edited a fin-de-siècle series of annuals, *Late Editions*, eight volumes published by the University of Chicago Press and intended to document the century's end by innovations in representing the ethnographic encounter. His most recent book (with Fernando Mascarenhas) is *Ocasião: The Marquis and the Anthropologist, a Collaboration* (AltaMira Press, 2005). In preparation is a book of conversations with Paul Rabinow entitled *Designs for an Anthropology of the Contemporary*. In 2005, he moved to the University of California, Irvine, as Chancellor's Professor and founded the Center for Ethnography, which is dedicated to examining the vulnerabilities and possibilities of this venerable technology of knowledge making.

Richard P. Martin has been since 2000 the Isabelle and Antony Raubitschek Professor in Classics at Stanford University. Previously he taught for eighteen years at Princeton University. His interests include ancient Greek poetry, especially epic and lyric, of the archaic age; Greek drama; ethnopoetics, oral literature, and performance; and the medieval and modern languages and literatures of Ireland and Greece. He is the author of *Healing, Sacrifice and Battle: Amekhania in Early Greek Poetry* (Innsbruck, 1983); *The Language of Heroes: Speech and Performance in the Iliad* (Cornell, 1989); and *Myths of the Ancient Greeks* (Penguin/NAL, 2003). In addition, he edited Bulfinch's *Mythology* (HarperCollins, 1991) and provided extensive notes (with an introduction) to the new translation of Homer's *Odyssey* by Edward McCrorie (Johns Hopkins, 2004). He is currently at work on mythological representations of performance, and on Greek religion as it interacts with Homeric poetics.

Yael Navaro-Yashin is lecturer in social anthropology at the University of Cambridge and a fellow of Newnham College. She is the author of *Faces of the State: Secularism and Public Life in Turkey* (Princeton, 2002). She has published several articles on spatiality and border practices, documents and administration, and affect and subjectivity, building on her long-term research in Northern Cyprus. She is presently completing a book manuscript based on this research.

Neni Panourgiá is associate professor of anthropology at Columbia University. She is the author of *Fragments of Death, Fables of Identity: An Athenian Anthropography* (University of Wisconsin Press, 1995) and *Dangerous Citizens: The Flesh of Dissidence and the Terror of the State (Greece 1929–2004)* (Fordham University Press, 2008). She has taught at New York University, Princeton University, and Rutgers University, and she was a senior fellow at the American School of Classical Studies (2003–2004). Her articles on neoclassical architecture, the concentration camps in Greece, death and terminal illness, and the myth of Oedipus, and interviews with leading anthropologists have appeared in various journals, among them, *angelaki*, *Public Culture*, *Anthropology and Humanism*, and *Anthropological Theory*. Her new project *Critical Lives* is an interrogation of the concept of life as it is employed in the process of decision making in the context of intensive care units in hospitals in Athens, Greece, and New York City.

Eleni Papagaroufali is associate professor and chair of the Department of Social Anthropology, at Panteion University of Social and Political Sciences, in Athens, Greece. She is the author of articles about biotechnology (in English), and of a book titled *Gifts of Life after Death: Cultural Experiences* (EllinikaGrammata, 2002) (in Greek) on prospective organ and body donors in Greece. Her recent research interests relate to transnational encounters in the European Union and Greece, with an emphasis on town and school twinning.

Louisa Schein teaches anthropology and women's and gender studies at Rutgers University, in New Brunswick. She has conducted research for over two decades on gender and ethnic politics among Hmong/Miao in China and in the United States. She is the author of *Minority Rules: The Miao and the Feminine in China's Cultural Politics* (Duke University Press, 2000) and is currently completing *Rewind to Home: Hmong Media and Gendered Diaspora*. Her articles have been published in various journals, such as *Cultural Anthropology*, *Social Text*, the *Journal of Asian Studies*, *American Quarterly*, *Identities*, *positions*, and others. She has a coedited volume (with Purnima Mankekar), *Media, Erotics and Transnational Asia*, forthcoming from Duke University Press. She is also currently collaborating on two documentary film projects on Hmong immigrants with Va-Megn Thoj and Peter O'Neill.

Kath Weston is professor of anthropology and studies in women and gender at the University of Virginia. She is also a longtime member of the National Writers Union. Her areas of specialization include political economy, political ecology, historical anthropology, kinship, gender and sexuality, surveillance, political theory, history of science in the social sciences, and class relations. She is the author of numerous publications, including *Gender in Real Time: Power and Transience in a Visual Age* (Routledge, 2002); *Families We Choose: Lesbians, Gays, Kinship* (Columbia University Press, 1991); and "Escape from the Andamans: Tracking, Offshore Incarceration, and Ethnology in the Back of Beyond," in *Central Sites, Peripheral Visions*, edited by Richard Handler (University of Wisconsin Press, 2006). Her latest book is *Traveling Light: On the Road with America's Poor* (Beacon Press, 2008).

INDEX

Page numbers in bold indicate the named individual's contributions to the present volume.

Abélès, Marc, 5, **157–67, 258**, 271
Abjection, 5, 83–85, 87–88, 92, 94, 168–69, 259
Abu-Lughod, Lila, 9, 12, 186, 191, 210, 262, 263, 267
Adorno, Theodor W., 2–3, 97, 217, 243, 259
Aesthetics, 29, 33, 36, 41, 44, 152, 218, 219, 230, 233, 240
Affect, 6, 77, 79, 82–83, 92, 95, 207–8, 237, 271, 274
Agamben, Giorgio, 85, 112, 168, 237, 239, 240, 242, 247, 259
Alterity, 6, 23, 77, 83, 85, 87–88, 91, 93–95, 103, 105, 109, 241
Anderson, Benedict, 156, 211, 256, 258, 260, 268
Animal, 54–55, 65, 85–86, 88, 90, 95, 99, 111, 229, 239, 242, 247, 249
Anthropos, 7, 33, 37, 68, 74, 99, 112, 218, 247
Appadurai, Arjun, 169, 193, 254, 259, 262, 264, 267
Asad, Talal, 130, 170, 251, 253, 259
Athanasiou, Athena, 6, **77–96**, 99, **236–42**, 243, 271
Autonomy, 6, 77, 93, 95, 103, 106, 108, 162, 195

Bare life, 84–85, 95, 237, 259
Benjamin, Walter, 7–8, 57–58, 62, 66, 85, 112, 170, 185–86, 230, 231, 239, 259, 262
Biopolitics, 6, 77, 80, 83, 85, 90, 95, 103, 109, 237, 271
Body, 4, 6, 69, 77–89, 99, 101–3, 107–9, 114, 116–19, 121–24, 215–16, 240, 243, 246, 248, 249, 250, 251, 264, 269, 271; body donors, 4, 116–19, 249, 275; embodied knowledge, 5, 83, 88, 115, 120–21, 144, 219, 226
Body politic, 77, 79–82
Boon, James, 7–8, 15, **53–76**, 103, 221, **227–36**, 243, 244, 258, 271
Bourdieu, Pierre, 5, 115, 122, 248, 250, 251, 252
Burke, Kenneth, 56, 61–63, 74–75, 216, 230, 232, 235, 269

Canon, 33, 48, 138, 142–56, 189, 256
China, 9, 10, 19, 67, 118, 138, 154, 189–201, 209, 255, 257, 258, 264, 265, 267, 275
Consciousness, 8, 12, 79, 89, 93, 122, 150, 151, 177, 187, 254, 263; false, 170; historical, 128, 140; negative, 149, 150
Critique, 1, 2, 6, 8, 13–14, 20, 27, 30–32, 37, 38, 40, 42–43, 61; metacritique, 10
Cultural Studies, 9, 54, 130, 188–90, 192, 194–95, 203, 253, 263, 264, 265
Cyprus, 5–6, 47, 167–87, 259–64, 274

Daniel, Valentine E., 9, 263, 265
Death, 46, 55–56, 60, 62–65, 70–72, 74–76, 79–80, 82, 85–88, 90, 93–94, 100, 107–8, 116–20, 123, 139, 154, 168–69, 171, 179–82, 184, 187, 221, 223, 224, 225, 226, 227, 229, 231, 236, 237, 238, 239, 241, 242, 243, 249, 250, 259, 262, 269, 274, 275
Deleuze, Gilles, 77, 86, 88, 98, 132, 240, 247, 253, 269
Derrida, Jacques, 94, 237, 241, 242

Desire, 8–10, 46–48, 72, 80, 82, 87, 89–90, 92–93, 100, 132, 136, 193–94, 200–1, 203–8, 212–14, 225, 239, 241, 248, 272

Difference, 16–17, 22–24, 29, 37, 41, 43, 87–88, 91–93, 95, 132, 140, 142, 147, 149–52, 154, 182, 189–91, 194, 200, 212, 216, 239, 240, 248, 253, 271; cultural difference, 29, 120, 218; sexual difference, 87, 92, 240

Dismemberment, 6, 78–79, 88–89, 109

Douglas, Mary, 20, 21, 54, 229

Enlightenment, 14, 95, 142–43, 145, 151, 214–15, 232, 247, 257

Erotics, 10, 188, 204–6, 212, 263, 275

Ethnography, 1, 9, 27, 29–44, 46, 51–52, 75, 117, 120, 125–26, 130, 135–36, 168–70, 174, 185–90, 192, 194–95, 216, 218, 220, 222, 226, 228, 233, 251, 252, 254, 263, 264, 266, 269, 273

Exile, 4, 79, 91, 93–94, 111, 195, 265, 273

Experience, 1–6, 10–11, 33, 39, 46–47, 58–60, 63, 66, 79–83, 85, 101, 103–5, 108, 114–24, 138–41, 155–56, 168–70, 177–78, 181–82, 185–87, 193, 213, 215–16, 222, 224, 234, 237, 238, 240, 244, 246, 248, 249, 250, 251, 252, 259, 260, 262, 265, 268, 273, 275; co-experience, 120–21; cultural experience, 1, 5

Fabian, Johannes, 35, 181, 219, 254, 262

Femininity, 77, 87–88, 91–92, 206, 241, 244, 264, 275

Feminism, 6, 86, 107, 211, 239, 240, 263, 264, 267, 271

Fieldwork, 4, 8–9, 21–22, 29–44, 46–47, 53, 55–56, 63, 65, 102–3, 114, 119–21, 135–36, 163, 188, 190, 192, 194–95, 197, 216, 218–21, 222, 228, 233, 244, 271, 272, 273

Finitude, 77, 80, 84, 94

Foster, Hal, 37–40, 219

Foucault, Michel, 14, 24–25, 176, 213–14, 218, 229, 237, 266, 268

Frazer, James G., 7–8, 45, 49, 53–76, 104, 106, 107, 221, 227–36, 272

Freud, Sigmund, 6, 17–18, 53, 62, 77–84, 87–90, 92–93, 98, 102–10, 221, 227, 229, 236–38, 240–45

Geertz, Clifford, vii, 3–5, 9, 12, 13, **15–28**, 29, 49, 56, 106, 107, 113, 115, 121, 126, 157, 191, 217, 218, 223, 224, 225, 227, 228, 230, 233, 234, 248, 250, 251, 252, 253, 258, 259, 263, 272

Gender, 9–10, 17, 23, 48, 70, 71, 82, 86, 90, 95, 128, 131, 133, 188, 193, 201–5, 208, 225, 233, 247, 248, 253, 254, 264, 266, 267, 271, 275; in language, 55, 65

Greece (Ancient), 47–49, 51, 56–57, 61, 64, 67, 90, 99, 109, 138, 143, 146, 223–27, 230, 232, 239, 245, 256

Greece (Modern), 2, 6–7, 55, 60, 74, 76, 103, 111–12, 116, 118–19, 146–50, 173–74, 232, 234, 235, 246–47, 249–50, 261–62, 271, 272, 273, 274, 275; travel to, 55–57, 59, 62, 70, 74–75, 236

Habitus, 5, 115, 119, 122–23, 248, 250, 251

Harrison, Jane, 54, 229

Heidegger, Martin, 81, 94, 241

Hellenism, 47, 223; panhellenism, 47, 223; philhellenism, 56, 230

Hermeneutics, 1, 2, 12, 15, 18–19, 114, 223; carnal hermeneutics, 4, 113–25, 248–52

Hesiod, 47, 99

Historiography, 138–56, 255–58, 273

Homer, 8, 46–47, 51, 88, 98, 104, 144, 221–22, 224, 227, 274

Human, 1, 2, 7, 14, 22, 28, 49, 64, 77, 81–96, 97, 99, 102–4, 108, 111–12, 128, 131, 138, 145, 152, 214, 215, 229, 239, 247, 248, 249, 250, 254, 256, 261; humanism, 21, 48, 90, 94, 97, 102, 152, 257; humanities, 4, 16, 97, 216, 254, 268; subhuman, 92

Humphreys, Sally, 8, 45–47, 221, 223, 224, 225

Identification, 8, 9, 87, 90, 143, 159, 175, 193, 200, 216, 221, 237, 247, 248

Imagination, 14, 33, 38, 41, 58, 112, 117, 119, 158, 172, 177, 180, 215, 216, 230, 231, 249, 263, 265

Immediacy, 3–4, 81, 114–15, 120, 122, 143, 147, 213, 220

Interpretive anthropology, 1–4, 7, 12, 14, 15, 17–21, 23–28, 113–14, 126–27, 133, 248, 259

Intersubjectivity, 5, 23–24, 115–16, 121, 194, 217, 248, 249

Index 279

Kakavoulia, Maria, 13–14, **213–16**, **268–69**, 272
Kavouras, Pavlos, **15–28**, **217**, 227, 234, 236, 272
Kinship, 16–17, 21, 36, 80, 82–83, 91, 104–5, 107, 109, 128, 131, 237–38, 245, 253, 275
Knowledge, 3, 5, 11, 13, 14, 26, 31–36, 41–43, 47, 61, 64, 74, 80–81, 86, 89, 92, 95, 96, 102–4, 110–11, 115, 117, 119, 122, 136, 139, 141, 143, 148, 194, 214–15, 218, 230, 232, 234, 248, 249, 250, 256, 257, 259, 272, 273; meta-knowledge, 102; somatic knowledge, 119

Lacan, Jacques, 89, 91, 92–93, 106–7, 232, 236, 237, 240, 241–42
Language, 5, 46, 54–55, 65, 70, 79–82, 84, 88, 92–94, 115, 122, 124, 140–41, 147, 152, 174, 181, 196–98, 200, 214, 226, 229, 230, 233, 250–51, 252, 256, 257, 262, 272, 274; metalanguage, 213, 268; verbal gesture, 5, 122–24
Leach, Edmund, 20, 54, 229
Lear, Jonathan, 109–11, 245–46
Lévi-Strauss, Claude, 13, 20, 65, 98, 106–7, 133, 228, 233, 235, 237–38, 243, 244–45
Liakos, Antonis, 10–12, **137–56**, **255–58**, 273
Liminality, 6, 77, 86, 171, 176–77, 250, 266
Loraux, Nicole, 101–2, 225, 244, 246

Malinowski, Bronislaw, 8, 29–35, 39–42, 44, 53, 65, 74, 98, 102–7, 218, 219, 220–21, 232, 264
Marcus, George, **1–14**, 15, 21, **29–43**, 117, 136, 197, **217–21**, 227, 231, 243, 248, 249, 251, 252, 254, 259, 266, 269, 273
Martin, Richard, 8–9, **44–52**, **221–27**, 273–74
Marx, Karl, 24, 53, 103, 145, 154, 170, 221, 227
Masculinity, 6, 24, 77, 88–89, 91, 193, 240
Media, 9–10, 11, 28, 74, 161–67, 188–204, 210–12, 263–68, 272, 275
Mediation, 3, 28, 42–44, 120, 122, 127, 137, 143, 191, 194, 201, 210, 216, 220, 225

Memory, 51, 62, 64, 78–82, 89, 107, 128, 133, 148, 180, 182, 185, 204–5, 207, 212, 238, 240, 249, 255, 259, 262, 263
Metaphysics, 86–88, 91, 95
Modleski, Tania, 192, 194, 264
Myth, 6, 8–9, 29–30, 38, 44–52, 57, 64, 77, 83, 87, 90–93, 97–98, 99, 101–10, 113, 133, 144, 221, 224, 226, 227, 228, 235, 240, 241, 242, 244–245, 247, 254, 255, 256, 259, 274; anti-myth, 111–12, 230; mythology, 54, 57, 68, 86, 99, 111, 196, 226, 233, 239, 256, 274

Narrative, 3, 14, 61, 78–79, 81–85, 90–95, 101, 104, 106, 132, 137, 140, 145–47, 153, 171, 175, 178, 182, 205, 211, 216, 221, 226, 237, 241, 244–45, 257, 258, 263, 272; meta-narrative, 155; narrativity, 11, 14, 79–80, 93, 216
Nation, 7, 10, 11, 16, 21, 94, 134, 138–56, 157–67, 174, 198, 211, 212, 231, 247, 256, 257, 260, 261, 264, 265, 266, 273; nationalism, 111, 134–35, 142, 148, 149, 155, 172, 173, 175–77, 193, 211, 259, 260, 261, 262, 268
Navaro-Yashin, Yael, vii, 5–6, **168–87**, **258–62**, 274
Nietzsche, Friedrich, 48, 56, 61, 62, 65, 77, 86, 102, 240, 244
Nostalgia, 12–13, 125–37, 162, 201, 204–6, 208–9

Oedipus, 6–7, 18, 49, 77–96, 97–112, 225, 236, 238–47, 274
Orientalism, 141, 145
Ortner, Sherry, 1, 3–4, 195, 217, 243, 252, 253, 264

Panourgiá, Neni, **1–28**, 49, 60, 62, 74–76, **97–112**, 216, **217**, 221, 225, 227, 229, 231, 232, 235, 236, **242–47**, 258, 259, 269, 274
Papagaroufali, Eleni, 4–5, **112–24**, **248–52**, 274–75
Pausanias, 7–8, 53–76, 100, 227–36, 243
Performance, 5, 23, 24, 36, 38, 42, 51–52, 63, 142, 166, 222, 224, 225, 226–27, 266, 272, 274
Phallus, 87, 89, 95, 237
Plato, 46, 48, 55, 222
Poetics, 23–25, 49, 50, 84, 153, 213, 218, 222, 225, 226, 231, 251, 252, 254, 261, 262, 265, 272, 274

Polis, 6, 48, 77, 79–85, 88, 93, 95, 109, 224, 237, 239, 246
Politics, vii, 1–3, 5–7, 9, 11–14, 17–19, 24, 30–31, 34–35, 40–41, 47, 49–51, 77, 85–87, 89, 95–96, 98, 103–11, 117, 123–24, 126, 128–29, 134–35, 142, 145–47, 151, 157–67, 168–87, 189–90, 195, 204, 211–12, 218, 223, 224, 225, 226, 227, 228, 230, 237, 238, 243, 246–47, 248, 249, 250, 251, 252, 253, 254, 258, 259, 260, 262, 263, 264, 265, 266, 267, 271, 273, 275
Postcoloniality, 2, 12, 127, 134–35, 140–41, 149, 213, 228, 254, 255, 256, 260, 266, 267
Psychoanalysis, 1, 7, 78–79, 83, 87–88, 91–93, 97, 103, 106, 110, 236, 237, 238, 240, 241, 245

Rabinow, Paul, 33, 218, 273
Rulfo, Juan, 171, 259

Sahlins, Marshall, 20, 22, 235, 255
Said, Edward, 2, 141, 217
Schein, Louisa, 9–10, **188–212, 263–68**, 275
Secular, 18, 40, 44, 149–50, 153–54, 257, 261, 274
Senses, 5, 13, 115, 186, 188, 215, 262, 268, 269
Sexuality, 54, 80, 82, 86, 87, 89–90, 92, 95, 101–2, 131, 166, 201–2, 204, 206–9, 211–12, 229, 240, 243, 253, 266, 268, 271, 275; homosexuality, 86–87, 89, 109, 165–66, 243; sexual difference, 87, 92, 240
Sophocles, 77, 84, 98, 101, 104, 238, 242, 243
Sovereignty, 6, 14, 77, 79–81, 84–85, 91, 95, 97, 100, 104, 108, 110–11, 148, 174, 214, 237, 259, 260

Spectrality, 79, 83, 90, 95–96
Sphinx, 6, 77, 83–96, 99, 101, 108, 111, 239, 240, 243
Subjectivity, 2, 5–6, 22, 26, 65, 80–87, 90–91, 94, 97–98, 102, 104, 107–8, 152, 154, 168–70, 177, 181–82, 191, 193–94, 197, 200, 206, 211, 218, 219, 241, 250, 259, 261, 262, 267, 274; subjectification, 9–10, 25, 35, 147, 173, 188, 193, 197, 201, 209, 211–12, 263; subjection, 6, 175–78, 210, 260

Temporality, 10, 35, 48, 59–60, 67, 70, 80, 83, 85–86, 115, 117, 120–21, 123–24, 133, 138–39, 166, 172, 187, 261
Theater, 23, 36, 49–50, 163, 166, 220, 224, 247; theatricality, 5, 158, 166
Therapy, 31, 79–80, 85
Tragedy, 49, 77, 79, 82–84, 166, 213, 224, 240, 244, 245
Transnationalism, 6, 9–10, 128, 133, 136, 143, 155, 169, 186, 188–212, 259, 264, 266, 267, 268, 271, 275
Trauma, 37, 78–85, 149, 237, 238
Travel, 7, 30, 53–76, 117–18, 128, 133, 141, 189, 194, 196–97, 201–2, 209–11, 227, 236, 247, 275
Turner, Victor, 2, 20–21, 49, 233, 252

Video, 9, 39, 188–89, 191, 196–206, 207–9, 263–66
Visuality, 13–14, 29, 33, 106, 139, 204–6, 213–16, 233, 253, 263, 265, 267, 268, 269, 275

Weber, Max, 19–20, 145, 157, 228, 232, 233, 272
Weston, Kath, 10, 12–13, **125–37**, 238, **252–54**, 275
Wittgenstein, Ludwig, 19, 54, 229, 249, 251

www.ingramcontent.com/pod-product-compliance
Lightning Source LLC
Chambersburg PA
CBHW031236290426
44109CB00012B/318